Knowledge Engineering and Management

Knowledge Engineering and Management

The CommonKADS Methodology

Guus Schreiber, Hans Akkermans, Anjo Anjewierden, Robert de Hoog, Nigel Shadbolt, Walter Van de Velde, and Bob Wielinga

A Bradford Book
The MIT Press
Cambridge, Massachusetts
London, England

Third printing, 2002

© 2000 Massachusetts Institute of Technology

This book was set in Times Roman by the authors and was printed and bound in the United States of America.

Library of Congress Cataloging-in-Publication Data

Schreiber, August Th.
 Knowledge engineering and management: the CommonKADS methodology /
A. Th. Schreiber, . . . [et al.].
   p.   cm.
 Includes bibliographical references and index.
 ISBN 0-262-19300-0 (hc.: alk. paper)
 1. Expert systems (Computer science). 2. Database management.
I. Schreiber, A. Th.
QA76.76.E95K5773 1999
006.3′32–dc21   99-19680
                                                                          CIP

Contents

Preface

Aim of This Book

This textbook gives a basic but thorough insight into the related disciplines of *knowledge engineering* and *knowledge management*. Knowledge engineering is traditionally concerned with the development of information systems in which knowledge and reasoning play pivotal roles. Knowledge management is a recent area in business administration that deals with how to leverage knowledge as a key asset and resource in modern organizations. These two disciplines have strong ties. Managing knowledge within an organization is nowadays hardly conceivable without exploiting the vast potential of advanced information and knowledge systems. On the other hand, information system developers and knowledge engineers have come to realize that successful technical work is only possible if it is properly situated within the wider organizational context. Knowledge-engineering methods have thus gradually broadened their scope: they are not only used for knowledge-based systems development but have also shown their value in knowledge management, requirements engineering, enterprise modelling, and business process reengineering.

This book presents a comprehensive methodology that covers the complete route from corporate knowledge management to knowledge analysis and engineering, all the way to knowledge-intensive systems design and implementation, in an integrated fashion. This methodology, called "CommonKADS," has been developed by a number of industry-university consortia over the past decade, and CommonKADS is nowadays in use worldwide by companies and educational institutions. The term "knowledge intensive" is intentionally vague, as it is often hard to define a strict borderline between knowledge-rich and knowledge-poor domains. In fact, most complex applications contain components that can be characterized as "knowledge intensive." The applications need not at all be a "classic" knowledge-based system. Beyond information-systems applications, practice has shown that all projects in which knowledge plays an important role significantly benefit from the ideas, concepts, techniques, and experiences that come together in the CommonKADS methodology.

Readership

This book is intended for practitioners and students in information systems engineering as well as in knowledge and information management. We assume that you are willing to consider new ways of managing the increasing complexity of information in applications and organizations. In reading this book, it will be helpful if you have some background in information systems, have some understanding of information analysis or business process modelling, or have experience in the area of information management. The material of this book has proved to be useful for courses, tutorials, and workshops for industrial practitioners, as well as for advanced undergraduate and first-year graduate students in different information-systems related disciplines.

Unique Features of This Textbook

With this book, we aimed to construct several bridges between traditionally different communities within the information-systems and knowledge-management areas:

1. For information analysts and knowledge engineers, we show how knowledge analysis constitutes a valuable and challenging extension of established development approaches, particularly of object-oriented approaches such as the Unified Modelling Language (UML, Booch et al. 1998).
2. For knowledge managers, we show how a seamless transition and integration can be achieved from business analysis to information-technology (IT) systems modelling and design — a feature absent in almost all business process approaches, as well as systems-engineering methodologies.
3. For software engineers, we show how conceptual modelling of information and knowledge naturally provides the necessary baseline structures for reusable software architecture, systems design, and implementation.
4. For IT project managers, we show how one can solve the eternal dilemma of balancing management control vs. flexibility in a structured way that is directly based on quality systems development methodology.

Throughout the book, these points are illustrated by extensive case studies, which have been taken from real-life application projects carried out in different industries we have been working with over the years.

As a guide to readers with different specific interests, the first chapter contains a detailed road map to help you select those parts of the book that are most interesting and relevant to you.

Additional Material

This book contains the consolidated baseline of the CommonKADS methodology. The material in this book is sufficient for readers to start useful work on knowledge-intensive applications. There is a wealth of additional material available, which could not be included in this book. For those who want to learn more about CommonKADS, this material

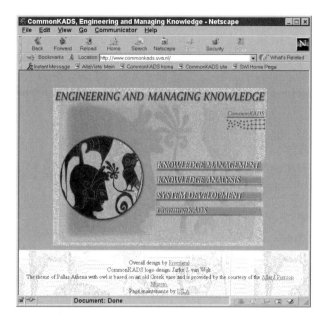

Figure 1
Home page of the CommonKADS website at www.commonkads.uva.nl.

is accessible through the website at `http://www.commonkads.uva.nl` (see Figure 1). This website contains a large repository of additional CommonKADS information, including:

- exercises related to the material discussed in this book;
- case studies of applications;
- access to sample running systems;
- texts about additional modelling techniques, such as a dedicated formal specification language for knowledge systems;
- catalogs of knowledge-model elements developed in previous projects;
- pointers to support tools for CommonKADS, such as diagramming tools, elicitation-support tools, CASE tools, and parsers for the languages used.

Background

CommonKADS is the product of a series of international research and application projects on knowledge engineering dating back as far as 1983. Historically, knowledge systems developed mainly through trial and error. The methodological aspects received little attention, despite a clear need expressed by industry practitioners for guidelines and techniques to structure and control the development process. Accordingly, system developers and managers greatly appreciated the steps made by CommonKADS to fill this gap.

Over the years, the methodology has been gradually extended as a result of feedback from practitioners and scientists. Practical use of CommonKADS showed that many systems projects fail because of a technology-push approach. An organization can implement information and knowledge technology successfully only if both the system's role and its potential impact on the organization are made explicit, and are agreed upon before and during system development. Thus, the introduction of knowledge-oriented methods and techniques for organizational analysis represents a major advance. Organizational analysis aims at creating an application-pull situation. Such an approach provides assurance to users, clients, and stakeholders that a new system will actually solve a real problem or take advantage of a real opportunity within the organization. Other useful additions to the methodology deal with the modelling of complex user-system interaction; with the introduction of new specification techniques; and with the definition of a flexible, risk-driven, and configurable life-cycle management approach that replaces the waterfall model for information-systems projects, as classic as it is overly rigid.

Experiences

Early on, companies began using the knowledge technology products provided by CommonKADS. This contributed greatly to the products' success. As early as 1986, the Dutch company Bolesian Systems, now part of the large European software firm Cap Gemini, exploited the first version of CommonKADS and refined it into their in-house method for knowledge-systems development. They have built a very large number of commercial systems, mostly in the financial sector. More recently, the Everest company is making use of CommonKADS in a similar manner. Many banks and insurance companies in the Netherlands have systems developed with CommonKADS in daily use for assessing loan and mortgage applications. In Japan, several big companies, including IBM, are using CommonKADS in their in-house development; for example, to increase software-architecture reusability. A well-known application in the UK is the credit card-fraud detection program developed by Touche Ross Management Consultants for Barclay Card. All the "Big Six" worldwide accounting and consultancy firms have integrated smaller or larger parts of CommonKADS into their proprietary in-house development methods.

CommonKADS also frequently serves as a baseline for system development and research projects, such as the European IT programme and national government projects. Furthermore, the CommonKADS methods are nowadays in use for purposes other than system development, such as knowledge management, requirements capture, and business-process analysis. The US-based Carnegie Group, for example, has applied CommonKADS in this way in a project for US West. Likewise, the Unilever company uses CommonKADS as its standard both for knowledge-intensive systems development and for knowledge management.

The Authors

Because it is difficult to write a textbook with many different authors, we decided early on that it would be best if only two authors actually wrote the text, and that the others contributed to the drafts. Of course, the material contains ideas and is based on the work of *all* the authors. Accordingly, Guus Schreiber has been responsible for the general editing process and for chapters 5-7 and 10-14, whereas Hans Akkermans wrote most of chapters 1-4, 9 and 15. Nigel Shadbolt contributed chapter 8, Robert de Hoog wrote part of chapter 4, and Anjo Anjewierden checked the CommonKADS Conceptual Modelling Language examples and contributed the appendix.

Acknowledgments

Many persons, companies and institutions have contributed to the CommonKADS knowledge methodology in its various stages of development.

The TRACKS workshop participants, who acted as an international industrial review board for the book, are gratefully acknowledged for their extensive reviews of the material. Their suggestions have led to many improvements in the book. We are particularly grateful to Unilever Research Laboratories in Vlaardingen (The Netherlands), also for their financial support. This book has profited from the input and extensive feedback from many colleagues at Unilever. The CUPIDO platform, a group of companies and institutions in the Netherlands and Belgium, provided many forms of support for this book. Members of CUPIDO are Bolesian, CIBIT, Everest, Platinum, Unilever, and the Royal Dutch Navy. The Aion implementation described in Chapter 12 was developed by Leo Hermans and Rob Proper of Everest. The diagnosis model in Chapter 6 is based on input from Richard Benjamins. The scheduling model in Chapter 6 was kindly provided by Masahiro Hori of IBM-Japan. Brice LePape of the ESPRIT office of the European Commission has supported the development of CommonKADS from the beginning. In the final stages we received funds from the Commission through the TRACKS project (ESPRIT P25087) in order to organize a number of workshops to get feedback on the draft book. This project also supported the construction of the website with additional material. Rob Martil, then at Lloyd's Register, now at ISL, contributed to the development of the CommonKADS model suite and to the ideas about project management. Many ideas about knowledge management (Chapter 4) were developed in cooperation with Rob van der Spek of CIBIT, while teaching CommonKADS to many students with a conventional systems development background at CIBIT helped in clearly focusing ideas about the worldview behind CommonKADS.

Joost Breuker was one of the founding fathers of KADS and developed, together with Paul de Greef and Ton de Jong, the typology for transfer functions (Chapter 5). Peter Terpstra contributed to foundations of the work on knowledge system design and implementation (Chapter 11). The work of Klas Orsvarn (SICS) and Steve Wells (Lloyd's Register) is acknowledged as an inspiration for the description of the knowledge-modelling process (Chapter 7). Kieron O'Hara provided valuable comments and input for Chapter 8. The work of Frank van Harmelen and Dieter Fensel on formal languages for knowledge-model specification were an important source of information. We are grateful for discussions with Ameen Abu-Hanna, Gertjan van Heijst, Wilfried Post, and Annette ten Teije during their Ph.D. and post-doctoral work at SWI. Wouter Jansweijer and other people working on the KACTUS project contributed to the ideas underlying the material on advanced knowledge modelling (Chapter 13). Marc Linster The first author, Guus Schreiber, is grateful for the feedback given by his course students in "Data and Knowledge Modelling," who had to study from draft material, and whose experiences have proved valuable in increasing the quality of the book. The second author, Hans Akkermans, would like to thank Rune Gustavsson (University of Karlskrona-Ronneby, Sweden) for his support and feedback on courses and workshops given in Sweden based on the draft textbook, and to Fredrik Ygge, Alex Ratcliffe, Robert Scheltens, Pim Borst, Tim Smithers, Amaia Bernaras, Hans Ottosson, Ioa Gavrila, Alex Kalos, Jan Top, Chris Touw, Carolien Metselaar, Jos Schreinemakers, and Sjaak Kaandorp for providing case study material and/or giving their feedback on Chapter 1, Chapter 3, Chapter 4, Chapter 9 and Chapter 15. Jacobijn Sandberg provided feedback based on the use she made of CommonKADS in other projects. Machiel Jansen helped to develop the classification model in Chapter 6. Xavier Nicaise and Axel Wegner of ARTTIC played an important role in organizing the support actions for this book. Saskia van Loo and Lenie Zandvliet provided many forms of organizational support. Most figures in this book were drawn with Jan Wielemaker's MODELDRAW program. The CommonKADS logo (elements of which are used in the book cover) was designed by Jarke J. van Wijk.

The research on methodology described in this book has been supported by a number of projects partially funded by the ESPRIT Programme of the Commission of the European Communities, notably projects P12, P314, P1098 (KADS), P5248 (KADS-II), P8145 (KACTUS), and P25087 (TRACKS). The partners in the KADS project were STC Technology Ltd. (UK), SD-Scicon plc. (UK), Polytechnic of the South Bank, (UK), Touche Ross MC (UK), SCS GmbH (Germany), NTE NeuTech (Germany), Cap Gemini Innovation (France), and the University of Amsterdam (the Netherlands). The partners in the KADS-II project were Cap Gemini Innovation (France), Cap Gemini Logic (Sweden), Netherlands Energy Research Foundation ECN (the Netherlands), ENTEL SA (Spain), IBM France (France), Lloyd's Register (UK), the Swedish Institute of Computer Science (Sweden), Siemens AG (Germany), Touche Ross MC (UK), the University of Amsterdam (the Netherlands), and the Free University of Brussels (Belgium). The partners in the KACTUS project were Cap Gemini Innovation (France), LABEIN (Spain), Lloyd's Register (United Kingdom), STATOIL (Norway), Cap Programmator (Sweden), University of Amsterdam (the Netherlands), University of Karlsruhe (Germany), IBERDROLA (Spain), DELOS (Italy), FINCANTIERI (Italy), and SINTEF (Norway). The partners in the TRACKS project were Intelligent Systems Lab Amsterdam (the Netherlands), AKMC Knowledge Management BV (the Netherlands), Riverland Next Generation (Belgium), and ARTTIC (Germany). This book reflects the opinions of the authors and not necessarily those of the consortia mentioned.

Knowledge Engineering and Management

1

Prologue: The Value of Knowledge

Key points of this chapter:

- Knowledge is a valuable asset.
- Knowledge engineering as a discipline lies at the heart of development, distribution and maintenance of knowledge assets.
- This book provides a methodological approach to engineering and managing knowledge.
- The chapter includes a reader's guide for the knowledge analyst, the knowledge system developer, the knowledge manager, and the project manager.

1.1 The Information Society Is Knowledge-Driven

Our economic and social life is becoming more and more knowledge-driven. It has by now become a truism to say that we live in an information society. But we have only just begun to explore and understand the very real and everyday consequences. One of these consequences is the growing importance of knowledge.

A quick scan through the recent literature on the information society illustrates this point with considerable force. Nowadays, one speaks of smart products, knowledge-based services, intelligent systems, expert and knowledge systems, intelligent enterprise, smart homes, knowledge workers, knowledge-intensive and learning organizations, the knowledge economy.

These are not just slogans. The knowledge content of products, services, and social activities in general is steadily growing. Tom Stewart of *Fortune* magazine puts it vividly:

> The quintessential raw materials of the Industrial Revolution were oil and
> steel. Well, more than 50% of the cost of extracting petroleum from the earth

is now information gathering and information processing. As for steel ... big producers used to need three or four man-hours of labor to make a ton of steel. Now steelmaking, using sophisticated computers, requires only 45 man-minutes of labor per ton. The intellectual component has grown and the physical component shrunk.

If steel was the quintessential product of industrialism, the talismanic product of the Information Age is the microchip. The value of all the chips produced today exceeds the value of the steel produced. What makes them valuable? Certainly not their physical component. Chips are made mainly from silicon, that is, from sand, and not much of it. The value is mainly in the design of the chip, and in the design of the complex machines that make it. Its chief ingredient is knowledge.

Add all this up and you come to a simple conclusion: more and more of what we buy and sell is knowledge. Knowledge is the principal raw material.

Knowledge has thus come to be recognized and handled as a valuable entity in itself. It has been called "the ultimate intangible." Surveys consistently show that top executives consider know-how to be the single most important factor in organizational success. Yet, when they are asked how much of the knowledge in their companies is used, the typical answer is about 20%. So, as an observer from a Swiss think tank said, "Imagine the implications for a company if it could get that number up just to 30%!" This book offers some concepts and instruments to help you achieve that.

The value of knowledge can even be expressed in hard figures. James Brian Quinn has made an extensive study of the key role of knowledge in modern organizations in his book *Intelligent Enterprise* (1992). Even in manufacturing industries, knowledge-based service capabilities have been calculated to be responsible for 65% to 75% of the total added value of the products from these industries. More generally, writers on management estimate that intellectual capital now constitutes typically 75% to 80% of the total balance sheet of companies. *Today, knowledge is a key enterprise resource.* Managing knowledge has therefore become a crucial everyday activity in modern organizations.

These developments have fundamentally changed the importance and role of knowledge in our society. As Peter Drucker, in his book *Post-Capitalist Society* (1993), says:

> The change in the meaning of knowledge that began 250 years ago has transformed society and economy. Formal knowledge is seen as both the key personal resource and the key economic resource. *Knowledge is the only meaningful resource today.* The traditional "factors of production" — land (i.e., natural resources), labor and capital — have not disappeared. But they have become secondary. They can be obtained, and obtained easily, provided there is knowledge. And knowledge in this new meaning is knowledge as a utility, knowledge as the means to obtain social and economic results. These devel-

opments, whether desirable or not, are responses to an irreversible change: *knowledge is now being applied to knowledge.*

The Industrial Revolution revolutionized manual labor. In the process, it brought about new disciplines, such as mechanical, chemical, and electrical engineering, that laid the scientific foundation for this revolution. Likewise, the Information Society is currently revolutionizing intellectual labor. More and more people are becoming knowledge workers, while at the same time this work is undergoing a major transformation. New disciplines are emerging that provide the scientific underpinnings for this process. One of these new disciplines is *knowledge engineering*. Just as mechanical and electrical engineering offer theories, methods, and techniques for building cars, knowledge engineering equips you with the scientific methodology to analyze and engineer knowledge. This book teaches you how to do that.

1.2   Knowledge in Context

What *is* knowledge? This is a question frequently asked of people in the fields of knowledge engineering and management. The same question has been at the roots of philosophical investigation for over two millennia. More millennia await us. So it is not likely that we are going to give you a definitive answer. Fortunately, we don't need to — in order to get knowledge to work for us.

Data, *information*, and *knowledge* are three often-encountered words that belong closely together, seem to have slightly different meanings, yet are often used interchangeably as synonyms, and thus lead to continuing confusion. It is customary to talk about knowledge engineering, information technology, databases, and electronic data processing. But it would be equally reasonable, although uncommon, to speak of, for example, electronic knowledge processing, information bases or data technology. Hence, a frequently asked question is what are the differences are between data, information and knowledge? We will give two completely different answers, so that you can make the choice that suits you best.

The first answer, often given by authors who want to give a rigorous definition, provides a demarcation about which there is consensus in the literature.

Data   Data are the uninterpreted *signals* that reach our senses every minute by the zillions. A red, green, or yellow light at an intersection is one example. Computers are full of data: signals consisting of strings of numbers, characters, and other symbols that are blindly and mechanically handled in large quantities.

Information   Information is data equipped with *meaning*. For a human car driver, a red traffic light is not just a signal of some colored object, rather, it is interpreted as an indication to stop. In contrast, an alien being who had just landed on Earth from outer space, and happened to find itself on a discovery tour in his earth shuttle near the Paris périphérique

	characteristic	*example*
Data	uninterpreted raw	...---...
Information	meaning attached to data	S O S
Knowledge	* attach purpose and competence to information * potential to generate action	emergency alert -> start rescue operation

Figure 1.1
Distinctions between data, information, and knowledge.

during the Friday evening rush hour, will probably not attach the same meaning to a red light. The data are the same, but the information is not.

Knowledge   Knowledge is the whole body of data and information that people bring to bear to practical *use in action*, in order to carry out tasks and create new information. Knowledge adds two distinct aspects: first, a sense of *purpose*, since knowledge is the "intellectual machinery" used to achieve a goal; second, a *generative capability*, because one of the major functions of knowledge is to produce new information. It is not accidental, therefore, that knowledge is proclaimed to be a new "factor of production."

Figure 1.1 summarizes the distinctions usually made between data, information, and knowledge. However, there is a second and very different answer to the question of what constitutes a suitable definition of knowledge, namely, *Why bother?* In our everyday practical work, most of us recognize quite well who the knowledgeable people are and what knowledge is when we see it in action. And this is usually good enough for our purposes. The alien traveling on the crowded highways surrounding Paris and ignoring traffic signs will not strike many of us as being very knowledgeable. We don't really need any formal definitions for that.

There are good reasons for such an answer, even beyond pragmatics. In many acknowledged scientific disciplines, the practitioners often have a hard time answering analogous questions. We might ask (probably in vain) various categories of scientists to give a precise and formal definition of the central object of their science, say, of life, civilization, art, intelligence, evolution, organizational culture, the economic value of intangible assets. . . Engineers and physicists, we bet, will often give inadequate or incomplete answers to the question, what exactly is energy (not to mention entropy)? This does not prevent them, however, to build reliable bridges, cars, computers or heating installations. Seen in this light, there is nothing special or mystical about knowledge.

An important reason that the question, What is knowledge? is difficult to answer resides in the fact that knowledge very much depends on *context*. One of the authors of this book, for example, is a first-rate bridge player. To some of the others, all his knowledge does not really make much sense, because they know little more about bridge than that it is a game involving four players and 52 cards. Other authors happen to have a background in quantum physics, so they could explain (if you *really* wanted to know) about excited nuclear states and the Heisenberg uncertainty relations. To others, this is just data, or perhaps more accurately, just uncertainty. For all authors, all this is utterly irrelevant in the context of writing this book. Thus, *one person's knowledge is another person's data*. The borderlines between data, information, and knowledge are not sharp, because they are relative with respect to the context of use.

This observation concerning the context dependence of knowledge is found, in different terminology, across different study fields of knowledge. In knowledge engineering, it has become standard to point out that knowledge is to a large extent *task- and domain-specific*. This book offers a range of practical but general methods to get a grip on the structure of human knowledge, as well as on the wider organizational context in which it is used. Only through such a nontechnology-driven approach can we build advanced information systems that adequately support people in carrying out their knowledge work.

1.3   Knowledge Engineering and Knowledge Systems

We mentioned knowledge engineering as one of the newly emerging disciplines sparked by the Information Age, similar to how the Industrial Revolution gave rise to mechanical and electrical engineering. Let us quote Peter Drucker once again:

> The knowledge we *now* consider knowledge proves itself in *action*. What we now mean by knowledge is information effective in action, information focused on results. Results are *outside* the person, in society and economy, or in the advancement of knowledge itself. To accomplish anything this knowledge has to be highly specialized... It could neither be learned nor taught. Nor did it imply any general principle whatever. It was experience rather than learning, training rather than schooling. But today we do not speak of these specialized knowledges as "crafts." We speak of "disciplines." This is as great a change in intellectual history as any ever recorded. A discipline converts a "craft" into a methodology — such as engineering, the scientific method, the quantitative method or the physician's differential diagnosis. Each of these methodologies converts *ad hoc* experience into system. Each converts anecdote into information. Each converts skill into something that can be taught and learned.

Drucker refers here to disciplines like mechanical engineering, physics, and chemistry that developed out of the craft of, say, building steam engines.

We see that the same is happening in our time in relation to information and knowledge. From the craft of building computers, software programs, databases and other systems, we see new scientific disciplines slowly and gradually evolve such as telematics, algorithmics, information systems management, and knowledge engineering and management.

Knowledge engineering has evolved from the late 1970s onward, from the art of building expert systems, knowledge-based systems, and knowledge-intensive information systems. We use these terms interchangeably, and call them knowledge systems for short. Knowledge systems are the single most important industrial and commercial offspring of the discipline called artificial intelligence. They are now in everyday use all around the world. They are used to aid in human problem-solving ranging from, just to name a few of the CommonKADS applications, detecting credit card fraud, speeding up ship design, aiding medical diagnosis, making scientific software more intelligent, delivering front-office financial services, assessing and advising on product quality, and supporting electrical network service recovery.

What are the benefits of knowledge systems? This is a valid question to ask, since over the years there have been high hopes, heavily publicized success stories, as well as clear-cut disappointments. Therefore, we will cite the results of a recent empirical study, carried out by Martin et al. (1996). Two questions were addressed: (1) What are benefits expected from the use of knowledge systems? and (2) Are expected benefits from an investment in knowledge systems actually realized? To answer these questions, survey data were collected from persons in industry and business, and on this basis the variables linked to knowledge system benefits were explored from the viewpoint of those working with them.

A summary of the empirical data is given in Table 1.1. The numbers represent frequencies, i.e., the number of times an item was mentioned by the respondents in the survey. The top three benefits are:

1. faster decision-making;
2. increased productivity;
3. increased quality of decision-making.

Generally, anticipated benefits are indeed realized. The authors of the survey point out, however, that this occurs in varying degrees (percentages quoted range from 57% to 70%). Faster decision-making is more often felt to be a result of knowledge system utilization than an increase either in decision quality or in productivity. Thus, knowledge systems indeed appear to enhance organizational effectiveness. Although they are employed for a range of purposes, they seem to contribute particularly to the timeliness of knowledge delivery, enabling shorter time-to-market and faster customer response times. The authors further caution both managers and developers to carefully examine the organizational environment in which knowledge systems are to be developed and used. This is a significant issue brought forward by many authors. Indeed, the CommonKADS methodology provides special techniques for investigating this aspect.

Category	Benefit	Anticipated benefit	Perceived as actual benefit
Productivity	Faster decision-making Increased productivity Enhanced problem-solving Solve complex problems Reliability Equipment operation Reduced downtime	75	68
Knowledge preservation	Capture scarce expertise Use in remote locations	10	14
Quality improvement	Increased quality of decisions Dealing with uncertainty	29	18
Training	Educational benefits	15	13
Job enrichment	Flexibility Integrating knowledge of several experts	10	15

Table 1.1
Survey data on anticipated and realized benefits from knowledge systems. Numbers indicate frequency of mentioning the indicated category of benefits by the survey respondents.

In the Information Society, knowledge systems have their place as an important mainstream technology. That is why there is a strong need to convert the art and craft of knowledge systems building into a real scientific discipline. Modern knowledge engineering, as laid down in this book, *is* this discipline. As we will show in detail, it brings several benefits:

- Knowledge engineering enables one to spot the opportunities and bottlenecks in how organizations develop, distribute and apply their knowledge resources, and so gives *tools for corporate knowledge management.*
- Knowledge engineering provides the methods to obtain a thorough understanding of the structures and processes used by knowledge workers — even where much of their knowledge is tacit — leading to a better integration of information technology in *support of knowledge work.*
- Knowledge engineering helps, as a result, to *build better knowledge systems*: systems that are easier to use, have a well-structured architecture, and are simpler to maintain.

1.4   Book Overview

This book explains in detail how to carry out structured knowledge management, knowledge analysis, and associated knowledge-intensive system development. It is comprehensive. The book covers all relevant aspects ranging from the study of organizational benefits to software coding. Along the road, the methods are illustrated by practical examples and case studies. The sum constitutes the CommonKADS standard for knowledge analysis and knowledge-system development. Below we briefly discuss the contents of each chapter. In the next section you will find a road map for reading this book, depending on the type of reader (knowledge manager, knowledge analyst, knowledge implementor, project manager).

Chapter 2 describes the baseline and rationale of CommonKADS, in particular its model-driven approach. This chapter contains some basic terminology used in this field. In Chapter 3 we pay attention to the first part of the analysis process: the modelling of the context or "environment" of a knowledge-intensive task we are interested in. We have learned that one cannot emphasize the need for context modelling enough, because the success of your application depends on it. The knowledge analysis at this level is still coarse-grained and is typically at the level of knowledge management. For this reason the next chapter deals with the issues related to knowledge management. This chapter contains an activity model for knowledge management. Together, Chapters 2, 3, and 4 provide a good introduction for readers interested primarily in knowledge management and coarse-grained knowledge analysis.

In Chapter 5 you will find an introduction to the major topic of this book: the methods for fine-grained knowledge modelling. Through a simple intuitive example you will learn the main ingredients needed. In Chapter 6 you will learn that a nice thing about knowledge analysis is that you do not have to build everything from scratch. For most knowledge-intensive tasks there are a number of reusable knowledge structures that give you a head start. There is a parallel here with design patterns in object-oriented analysis, but you will find the knowledge patterns to be more powerful and precise, in particular because they are grounded on a decade of research and practical experience.

The next two chapters are concerned with the knowledge-modelling process. Chapter 7 provides you with practical how-to-do-it guidelines and activities for knowledge modelling. In Chapter 8 we present a number of elicitation techniques that have proved to be useful in the context of knowledge analysis. This chapter contains practical guidelines for conducting interviews, as well as many other techniques.

In Chapter 9 we turn our attention to communications aspects. Knowledge systems communicate with humans and with other systems. More and more, our systems act as software agents in close interaction with other agents. This chapter provides you with the tools for modelling this interactive perspective. Together, Chapters 3 through 9 contain the baseline of the CommonKADS analysis methods. Chapter 10 illustrates the use of these methods through a case study of a small and easy-to-understand sample application concerned with assigning rental houses to applicants.

In the two subsequent chapters the focus is on system design and implementation. You learn how the analysis results can be turned relatively easily into a working software system. In Chapter 11 specialized CommonKADS system designs are discussed, using a popular object-oriented architecture as the baseline. In Chapter 12 you will see two examples of system implementations for the housing case study described in Chapter 10.

Chapter 13 tackles some more advanced knowledge analysis issues that extend the baseline methods presented earlier. The extensions include advanced domain modelling notations such as multiple subtype hierarchies as well as more complicated ways of modelling the reasoning process. CommonKADS uses UML as a baseline set of notations. In Chapter 14 we give an overview of the UML notations used in this book. This chapter can be used as a reference whenever a UML notation is encountered.

Last but not least, in Chapter 15 we turn our attention to project management. Our approach adopts Boehm's spiral approach, but it is specialized to suit the need of knowledge projects.

1.5   A Road Map for the Reader

We have made an effort to make this book interesting for readers with different backgrounds and goals. Not every part of this book will be of interest to every reader. In this section we sketch four typical routes for navigating this book. This road map is shown graphically in Figure 1.2.

Readers who are mainly into the **analysis for knowledge-system development** will find that the major part of the book is of direct interest. They should read at least Chapters 2, 3, 5, 6, 7, 8, and 10. Chapter 9 on communication modelling is strongly recommended. Chapter 13 tackles the more advanced analysis topics. Chapters 11 and 12 provide the support information that is needed for quickly building a validation prototype.

Readers primarily interested in **knowledge management** should read Chapters 2, 3, and 4 as the core text. Chapters 5 and 6 are strongly recommended. These chapters provide details on knowledge analysis and knowledge-intensive task patterns, and thus provide important background information for coarse-grained knowledge analysis. Also, we recommend the case study in Chapter 10. Many readers will find the material in Chapter 8 on elicitation techniques and in Chapter 15 on project management useful as well. Some of the topics of Chapter 13, in particular those with respect to advanced domain-knowledge modelling, will be relevant support material for knowledge management.

People that are mainly interested in **knowledge-system implementation** should read at least Chapters 2 and 5 as a kind of minimal background information on CommonKADS-based systems analysis. It is also useful to take a look at a few of the task templates in Chapter 6 and at the case study in Chapter 10. Chapters 11 and 12 contain the core material on design and implementation.

Finally, readers interested in **management of knowledge-system development projects** will want to start with Chapters 2, 3, and 15. Chapters 5, 9, 10, and 11 give the necessary information about the content of the system-development work. Chapter 4 is likely to be of interest as well, because knowledge-system development takes place more and more in the context of a knowledge-management strategy of businesses.

		Knowledge analyst	Knowledge manager	Knowledge-system developer	Project manager
Knowledge Engineering Basics	Ch. 2	X	X	X	X
The Task and its Organizational Context	Ch. 3	X	X	•	X
Knowledge Management	Ch. 4	•	X		•
Knowledge Model Components	Ch. 5	X	•	X	•
Template Knowledge Models	Ch. 6	X	•	•	○
Knowledge Model Construction	Ch. 7	X	○	○	○
Knowledge Elicitation Techniques	Ch. 8	X	○		○
Modelling Communication Aspects	Ch. 9	•	○	•	•
Case Study The Housing Application	Ch. 10	X	•	•	•
Designing Knowledge Systems	Ch. 11	○		X	•
Knowledge System Implementation	Ch. 12	○		X	○
Advanced Knowledge Modelling	Ch. 13	•	○		
UML Notations used in CommonKADS	Ch. 14	•	○	○	○
Project Management	Ch. 15	○	•	○	X

Figure 1.2
Road map for reading this book. Legend: cross = core text; bullet = recommended; circle = support material.

1.6   Bibliographical Notes and Further Reading

For the growing value of knowledge in our economy and society, see for example the book entitled *Intellectual Capital* (1997) by *Fortune* magazine journalist Tom Stewart. The quotes from Peter Drucker are from his book *Post-Capitalist Society* (1993). Drucker is often credited with having coined terms such as "knowledge workers" and the "knowledge economy." The study by James Brian Quinn called *Intelligent Enterprise* (1992) contains many data and insights on the growing role of the service sector of the economy, services that are usually information- and knowledge-intensive. There is an overwhelming literature on questions such as What is knowledge? that we cannot even start citing. Many books on knowledge management discuss this question in more or less depth, see the reading notes to Chapter 4. For a detailed perspective on the nature of competence as seen from organizational psychology and human resource management, see Spencer and Spencer (1993). The same question has of course been also extensively reflected upon in the fields of knowledge engineering, artificial intelligence and cognitive science. An interesting collection called *Expertise in Context* (Feltovich et al. 1997) contains a range of state-of-the-art contributions by authors from these different fields. On the benefits of knowledge systems in industrial and business practice, empirical studies have been carried out, for example, by Wong et al. (1994) and Martin (1996). The table on knowledge-system benefits in this chapter has been adapted from the latter study.

Knowledge-Engineering Basics

Key points of this chapter:

- The need for a knowledge-engineering methodology.
- The main principles underlying CommonKADS.
- The CommonKADS suite of models, which acts as both a repository and a checklist for the knowledge-engineering process.
- Roles in knowledge-engineering projects.
- Definitions of frequently used terms.

2.1 Historical Perspective

The CommonKADS enterprise originates from the need to build industry-quality knowledge systems on a large scale, in a structured, controllable, and repeatable way. When the CommonKADS work started back in 1983, there was little interest in such methodological issues. At that time, the prevailing paradigm for knowledge systems was rapid prototyping of one-shot applications, using special-purpose hardware and software such as LISP machines, expert system shells, and so on. Also, it was thought that the structure of knowledge and knowledge systems was rather simple, as in the famous rule-based expert systems (see Figure 2.1).

In Figure 2.2 we see a short history of knowledge systems since around 1965. Over the past 15 years, many developers and managers have started to realize that a structured approach to analysis, design, and management is just as necessary for knowledge systems as it is for other information systems. In addition, the architecture of knowledge has turned out to be much more complex and context-dependent than was realized in the first generation of expert systems. Nowadays, these insights are commonplace. Still, the point is *how* to do it. That is what this book is all about.

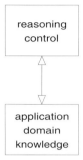

Figure 2.1
The basic architecture of the first generation of expert systems: application knowledge as a big bag of domain facts and rules, controlled by a simple reasoning or inference engine.

general-purpose search engines (GPS)	first-generation rule-based systems (MYCIN, XCON)	emergence of structured methods (early KADS)	mature methodologies (CommonKADS)
1965	1975	1985	1995

=> from art to discipline =>

Figure 2.2
A short history of knowledge systems.

2.2   The Methodological Pyramid

A methodology such as CommonKADS or any other software-development approach consists of a number of elements. These elements can be depicted graphically in the form of a *pyramid* (see Figure 2.3). The methodological pyramid has five layers, where each consecutive layer is built on top of the previous one. In this chapter we mainly talk about the lowest layer: the "worldview" of the methodology. These are in fact the advertising slogans of an approach. These slogans need to be grounded in theory, methods tools and practical case studies which constitute the other four layers. This rest of this book treats these methodology components extensively.

   The slogans of CommonKADS can be formulated as a number of principles that form the baseline and rationale of the approach. The principles are based on the lessons learned about knowledge-system development in the past. We discuss them in some depth in the next section.

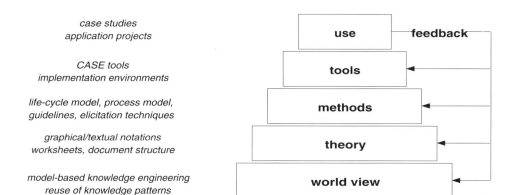

case studies
application projects

CASE tools
implementation environments

life-cycle model, process model,
guidelines, elicitation techniques

graphical/textual notations
worksheets, document structure

model-based knowledge engineering
reuse of knowledge patterns

Figure 2.3
The building blocks of a methodology: the worldview or "slogans," the theoretical concepts, the methods for using the methodology, the tools for applying methods, and the experiences through use of the methodology. Feedback flows down along the pyramid. Once a world view changes, the fundament falls away under an approach, and the time is ripe for a paradigm shift.

2.3 Principles

The CommonKADS methodology offers a structured approach. It is based on a few basic thoughts or principles that have grown out of experience over the years. We briefly sketch the fundamental principles underlying modern knowledge engineering.

Knowledge engineering is not some kind of "mining from the expert's head," but consists of constructing different aspect models of human knowledge.

Traditionally, knowledge engineering was viewed as a process of "extracting" or "mining from the expert's head" and transporting it in computational form to a machine (Figure 2.4). This has turned out to be a crude and rather naive view. Today, knowledge engineering is approached as a modelling activity. *A model is a purposeful abstraction of some part of reality.* Modelling is constructing a good description (that is, good enough for your purpose) of only a few aspects of knowledge and leaving out the rest. Models in this sense are useful because all details of expert knowledge are neither sufficiently accessible to get a complete grip on, nor necessary for the knowledge goals of most projects. A model makes it possible to focus on certain aspects and ignore others. In the CommonKADS view, a knowledge project entails the construction of a set of aspect models which together are an important part of the products delivered by the project. The CommonKADS model suite is a convenient instrument to break down and structure the knowledge-engineering process.

Figure 2.4
The old "mining" view of knowledge engineering.

The knowledge-level principle: in knowledge modelling, first concentrate on the conceptual structure of knowledge, and leave the programming details for later.

Many software developers have an understandable tendency to take the computer system as the dominant reference point in their analysis and design activities. But there are *two* important reference points: the computational artefact to be built, but most importantly, there is the human side: the real-world situation that knowledge engineering addresses by studying experts, users, and their behavior at the workplace, embedded in the broader organizational context of problem-solving. In the CommonKADS approach, the latter is the foremost viewpoint. The knowledge-level principle, first put forward by Alan Newell (1982), states that *knowledge is to be modelled at a conceptual level*, in a way independent of specific computational constructs and software implementations. The concepts used in the modelling of knowledge refer to and reflect (that is, *model*) the real-world domain and are expressed in a vocabulary understandable to the people involved. In the CommonKADS view, the artefact design of a knowledge system is called *structure-preserving design*, since it follows and preserves the analyzed conceptual structure of knowledge.

Knowledge has a stable internal structure that is analyzable by distinguishing specific knowledge types and roles.

It goes without saying that knowledge, reasoning, and problem-solving are extremely rich phenomena. Knowledge may be complex, but it is not chaotic: knowledge appears to have a rather stable internal structure, in which we see similar patterns over and over again. Although the architecture of knowledge is clearly more complicated than depicted in the rule-based systems of Figure 2.1, knowledge does have an understandable structure, and this is the practical hook for doing successful knowledge analysis. Conceptually, knowledge-level models help us understand the universe of human problem-solving by elaborate *knowledge typing*. An important result of modern knowledge engineering is that human expertise can be sensibly analyzed in terms of stable and generic categories, patterns, and structures of knowledge. Thus, we model knowledge as a well-structured functional whole, the parts of which play different, restricted, and specialized *roles* in human problem solving. We will encounter this concept of limited roles of knowledge types and components in many different forms throughout this book. If you want the answer to what knowledge is, this is the way you'll find it in this book, at the level of and in terms of an engineering science.

A knowledge project must be managed by learning from your experiences in a controlled "spiral" way.

The development of simple or very well-known types of information systems usually proceeds along a fixed management route. This is especially clear in the so-called waterfall model of systems development. This consists of a number of predefined stages in a predefined sequence: prepare and plan the project; find out about the customer requirements; specify and design the system; program, test, and deliver it — and in this order only. Knowledge is too rich and too difficult to understand to fit into such a rigid approach. Rapid prototyping has therefore been very popular in knowledge systems because it enables learning on the spot and changing course whenever necessary. The drawback to rapid prototyping is its ad-hoc nature, difficult to predict and manage. CommonKADS therefore favors a configurable and balanced project management approach, more flexible than the waterfall model and more controlled than rapid prototyping. Knowledge project management follows a *spiral approach that enables structured learning*, whereby intermediate results or "states" of the CommonKADS models act as signposts to what steps to take next. In determining these steps, the notions of objectives and risks play a crucial role.

2.4   Model Suite

Figure 2.5 presents the CommonKADS model suite that is the practical expression of the above principles underlying knowledge analysis. It constitutes the core of the CommonKADS knowledge-engineering methodology.

The figure shows three groups of models, because there are essentially three types of questions that must be answered:

1. **Why?**   Why is a knowledge system a potential help or solution? For which problems? Which benefits, costs, and organizational impacts does it have? Understanding the organizational context and environment is the most important issue here.
2. **What?**   What is the nature and structure of the knowledge involved? What is the nature and structure of the corresponding communication? The conceptual description of the knowledge applied in a task is the main issue here.

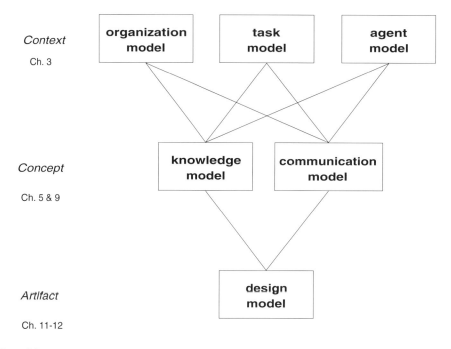

Context

Ch. 3

Concept

Ch. 5 & 9

Artifact

Ch. 11-12

Figure 2.5
The CommonKADS model suite.

3. **How?** How must the knowledge be implemented in a computer system? How do the software architecture and the computational mechanisms look? The technical aspects of the computer realization are the main focus here.

All these questions are answered by developing (pieces of) aspect models. CommonKADS has a predefined set of models, each of them focusing on a limited aspect, but together providing a comprehensive view:

- **Organization model** The organization model supports the analysis of the major features of an organization, in order to discover problems and opportunities for knowledge systems, establish their feasibility, and assess the impacts on the organization of intended knowledge actions.
- **Task model** Tasks are the relevant subparts of a business process. The task model analyzes the global task layout, its inputs and outputs, preconditions and performance criteria, as well as needed resources and competences.
- **Agent model** Agents are executors of a task. An agent can be human, an information system, or any other entity capable of carrying out a task. The agent model describes

the characteristics of agents, in particular their competences, authority to act, and constraints in this respect. Furthermore, it lists the communication links between agents in carrying out a task.

- **Knowledge model**   The purpose of the knowledge model is to explicate in detail the types and structures of the knowledge used in performing a task. It provides an implementation-independent description of the role that different knowledge components play in problem-solving, in a way that is understandable for humans. This makes the knowledge model an important vehicle for communication with experts and users about the problem-solving aspects of a knowledge system, during both development and system execution.

- **Communication model**   Since several agents may be involved in a task, it is important to model the communicative transactions between the agents involved. This is done by the communication model, in a conceptual and implementation-independent way, just as with the knowledge model.

- **Design model**   The above CommonKADS models together can be seen as constituting the requirements specification for the knowledge system, broken down in different aspects. Based on these requirements, the design model gives the technical system specification in terms of architecture, implementation platform, software modules, representational constructs, and computational mechanisms needed to implement the functions laid down in the knowledge and communication models.

Together, the organization, task, and agent models analyze the organizational environment and the corresponding critical success factors for a knowledge system. The knowledge and communication models yield the conceptual description of problem-solving functions and data that are to be handled and delivered by a knowledge system. The design model converts this into a technical specification that is the basis for software system implementation. This process is depicted in Figure 2.5. We note, however, that not always do all models have to be constructed. This depends on the goals of the project as well as the experiences gained in running the project. Thus, a judicious choice is to be made by the project management. Accordingly, a CommonKADS knowledge project produces three types of products or deliverables:

1. CommonKADS model documents;
2. project management information;
3. knowledge system software.

As a final note, we want to emphasize that knowledge systems and their engineering are not life forms totally unrelated to other species of information systems and management. In what follows, we will see that CommonKADS has been influenced by other methodologies, including structured systems analysis and design, object orientation, organization theory, process reengineering, and quality management. For example, the selling point of object orientation is often said to be the fact that objects in information systems model real-world entities in a natural fashion. This has clear similarities to the knowledge-level principle discussed above. (And the consequences of the limited-role concept, introduced later on, will show that there is more to information systems than objects alone!) Thus, there is a gradual transition. CommonKADS has integrated elements of other existing methodologies, and also makes it possible to switch to other methods at certain points. This is in line with the modern view of knowledge systems as enhancements embedded in already existing information infrastructures, instead of stand-alone expert systems. Hence, CommonKADS-style knowledge engineering is to be seen as an extension of existing methods: it is useful when tasks, processes, domains, or applications become knowledge intensive.

2.5   Process Roles

It is important to identify a number of roles that humans play in the knowledge management and engineering processes. We distinguish six different roles, which we briefly discuss below. Note that a certain individual can play several roles, in particular in smaller projects. Figure 2.6 gives a graphical overview of the six process roles.

Knowledge provider/specialist   An important role in the process is played by the human "owner" of knowledge. This is traditionally an "expert" in the application domain, but could also be other people in the organization that do not have the "expert" status. One important problem for a knowledge engineer is to find the "real" experts. Bogus experts are harmful to a project. In Chapter 8 some types of knowledge providers are discussed, as well as techniques for eliciting data about knowledge-intensive tasks from domain specialists.

Knowledge engineer/analyst   Although strictly speaking the term "knowledge engineer" points to workers in all phases of the development process, the term is usually reserved for system-analysis work. Therefore, "knowledge analyst" could in fact be a better term. In this book we use these two terms interchangeably. This book is primarily targeted at the work of the knowledge engineer, as can be deduced from the road map in the previous chapter. Knowledge analysis has from the beginning been perceived as the major bottleneck in knowledge-system development. CommonKADS offers the knowledge engineer a range of methods and tools that make the analysis of a standard knowledge-intensive task (such as assessment) relatively straightforward.

Knowledge-system developer   In a small project, system implementation was often done by the person who did the analysis. As systems are now produced routinely, this is not true anymore. The role of knowledge-system developer has its special characteristics. The knowledge-system developer is responsible for design and implementation. The developer needs to have a basic background in the analysis methods, so she can understand the requirements formulated by the knowledge analyst.

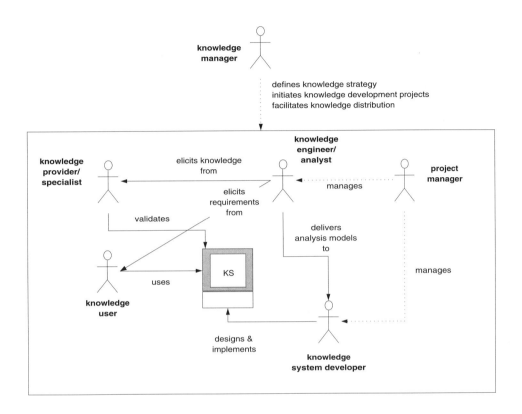

Figure 2.6
Graphical view of the six process roles in knowledge engineering and management.

In practice, it often turns out that in knowledge-system development the main knowledge-related problems have already been solved by the knowledge analyst. Therefore, a knowledge-system developer needs the same skills as "normal" software designers. It is also worth bearing in mind that the more knowledge intensive the task to be automated, the greater need there is for complex interface facilities. An example of an interface facility typically found in a knowledge system is an explanation facility.

Knowledge user   A knowledge user makes use directly or indirectly of a knowledge system. Involving knowledge users from the beginning is even more important than in regular software engineering projects. Automation of knowledge-intensive tasks invariably affects the work of the people involved. For design and implementation it is important to ensure that they interact with the system with their own interface representations. The knowledge engineer also needs to be able to present the analysis results to the potential knowledge users. This requires special attention. One of the reasons for the success of CommonKADS has always been that the knowledge analysis is understandable to knowledge users with some background in the domain.

Project manager   The knowledge-project manager is in charge of running of a knowledge-system development project. The typical project is small to medium-sized with four to six people working on it. The project manager is likely to benefit from a structured approach such as CommonKADS. The model suite gives a powerful and flexible instrument for project planning and control, as we will see in Chapter 15. The main risk the project manager runs is the elusive nature of knowledge-related problems. Therefore, requirements monitoring is of prime importance during the lifetime of the project. The context models of Chapter 3 play a key role in that.

Knowledge manager   The knowledge manager is not directly involved in knowledge-development projects. The knowledge manager formulates a knowledge strategy at the business level. The knowledge manager initiates knowledge development and knowledge distribution activities. These projects can include only knowledge analysis (e.g., for knowledge development), but also working knowledge systems (a vehicle for knowledge distribution). The link between knowledge engineering and knowledge management is made at the level of the CommonKADS context models, as we will see in Chapter 4.

2.6   Some Terminology

Like any other relatively young research discipline, knowledge engineering suffers from an overdose of jargon. The exact meaning of some terms varies among approaches. In the previous chapter we gave a definition of the terms "data," "information," and "knowledge." Here, we have included some additional terminological definitions that we found useful in practice.

Domain   A domain is some *area of interest*. Example domains are internal medicine and chemical processes. Domains can be hierarchically structured. For example, internal medicine can be split into a number of subdomains such a hematology, nephrology, cardiology, etc.

Task   A task is a *piece of work that needs to be done by an agent*. In this book we are primarily interested in "knowledge-intensive" tasks: tasks in which knowledge plays a key role. Example tasks are diagnosing malfunctions in internal organs such as a kidney, or monitoring a chemical process such as oil production.

Agent   An agent is any *human or software system able to execute a task* in a certain domain. For example, a physician can carry out the task of diagnosing complaints uttered by patients. A knowledge system might be able to execute the task of monitoring an oil production process on an oil rig.

Application   An application is the *context provided by the combination of a domain and a task carried out by one or more agents*.

Application domain/task   These two terms are used to refer to the domain and/or task involved in a certain application.

Knowledge(-based) system   The term "knowledge-based system" (KBS) has been used for a long time and stems from the first-generation architecture discussed in the previous chapter, in which the two main components are a reasoning engine and a knowledge base. In recent years the term has been replaced by the more neutral term "knowledge system." It is worthwhile pointing out that there is no fixed borderline between knowledge systems and "normal" software systems. Every system contains knowledge to some extent. This is increasingly true in modern software applications. The main distinction is that in a knowledge system one assumes there is some explicit representation of the knowledge included in the system. This raises the need for special modelling techniques.

Expert system   One can define an expert system as a knowledge system that is able to execute a task that, if carried out by humans, requires expertise. In practice the term is often used as a synonym for knowledge(-based) system. We do not use this term anymore.

2.7   Bibliographical Notes and Further Reading

CommonKADS is not the only knowledge-engineering methodology developed over the last decade. CommonKADS itself has grown out of KADS (Wielinga et al. 1992) and Components of Expertise (Steels 1990). CommonKADS was also influenced by approaches in the United States such as Generic Tasks (Chandrasekaran and Johnson 1993), PROTÉGÉ(Tu et al. 1995) and Role-Limiting Methods (Marcus 1988). The publications about the so-called Sisyphus studies give a good overview of the contemporary knowledge-engineering methods (Linster 1994, Schreiber and Birmingham 1996). Studer et al. (1998) provide a survey of recent developments in knowledge engineering.

The Task and Its Organizational Context

Key points of this chapter:

- Understanding and properly dealing with the wider organizational context is the critical success factor for knowledge systems and other knowledge-management measures.
- How to identify knowledge bottlenecks and opportunities within the organization.
- How to assess the economic, technical, and project feasibility of considered solutions such as knowledge systems.
- How to understand and decide about organizational impacts and needed changes when new knowledge-system solutions are introduced.
- How to integrate knowledge-oriented organization, workplace, and task analysis into information analysis.

3.1 Why Organizational Aspects Are So Important

A knowledge system is useful because and when it performs a demanding task for us, or helps us in carrying out such tasks ourselves, as a kind of intelligent assistant. However, tasks do not take place in an organizational vacuum. Any knowledge or information system can function satisfactorily only if it is properly integrated in the organization-at-large in which it is operational. A knowledge system acts as one agent cooperating with many others, human and nonhuman, and it carries out just a fraction of the many tasks that are performed in the organization. knowledge systems, like information systems in general, must thus be viewed as supporting components within the business processes of the organization — no less and no more.

Generally, knowledge systems fit well into business process improvement approaches. Process improvement is a much more appropriate perspective than the traditional idea of automating expert tasks. "Automation" is misleading for two reasons. First, knowledge-intensive tasks are often so complex that full automation is simply an ill-directed ambition, bound to lead to wrong expectations and ultimately to disappointment. At the same time, knowledge systems can provide active rather than passive help, in contrast to most current automated systems, precisely because they store knowledge and are able to reason about it. On this basis, they can much more actively act and interact with the user. Therefore, the appropriate positioning of knowledge systems is not that of automating expert tasks. Automation is a misleading concept. Zuboff (1987) therefore speaks of "informating" rather than "automating" work. Indeed, knowledge systems are better seen as agents that actively help their user as a kind of intelligent support tool or personal assistant. In this way, they have their partial but valuable role in improving the overall business process in collaboration with their users.

Therefore it is essential to keep track of the organizational environment in which a knowledge system has to operate. Already at an early stage the knowledge engineer has to take measures to ensure that a knowledge system will be properly embedded in the organization. Traditionally, much of the effort of information and knowledge engineers was directed at getting the technical aspects under control. Now that knowledge and information technology have achieved a good degree of maturity and diffusion, this is no longer the main focus. Many factors other than technology determine success or failure of a knowledge system in an organization. They must perform their task well according to set standards, but they must also be acceptable and friendly to the end user, interoperate with other information systems, and fit seamlessly into the structures, processes, and quality systems of the organization as a whole.

It is fair to say that practical experience has shown that often the critical success factor for knowledge systems is how well the relevant organizational issues have been dealt with. Many failures in automation have resulted, not from problems with the technology but from the lack of concern for social and organizational factors. Yet, many system-development methodologies focus on the technical aspects and do not support the analysis of the organizational elements that determine success or failure. CommonKADS offers the tools to cater to this need. These tools for organization and task analysis achieve several important goals:

1. *Identify problems and opportunities:* Find promising areas where knowledge systems or other knowledge management solutions can provide added value to the organization.
2. *Decide about solutions and their feasibility:* Find out whether a further project is worthwhile in terms of expected costs and benefits, technological feasibility, and needed resources and commitments within the organization.
3. *Improve tasks and task-related knowledge:* Analyze the nature of the tasks involved in a selected business process, with an eye on what knowledge is used by the responsible agents in order to carry them out successfully, and what improvements may be achieved in this respect.

4. *Plan for needed organizational changes:* Investigate what impacts a proposed knowledge system has on the various aspects of the organization, and prepare an action plan for associated organizational measures.

The CommonKADS task and organization analysis have a very tight fit to these four goals. Although their aim is a very critical one — uncovering the key success factors of knowledge systems and preparing the needed organizational measures — the methods themselves are easy to understand and simple to use, as we show below.

3.2 The Main Steps in Task and Organization Analysis

The steps in task and organization analysis that the knowledge analyst has to undertake are the following.

1. Carry out a scoping and feasibility study, consisting of two parts:

   a. Identifying problem/opportunity areas and potential solutions, and putting them into a wider organizational perspective.
   b. Deciding about economic, technical, and project feasibility, in order to select the most promising focus area and target solution.

2. Carry out an impact and improvements study for the selected target solution, again consisting of two parts:

   a. Gathering insights into the interrelationships between the task, agents involved, and use of knowledge for successful performance, and what improvements may be achieved here.
   b. Deciding about organizational measures and task changes, in order to ensure organizational acceptance and integration of a knowledge-system solution.

Along the above lines, a comprehensive picture of the organizational situation in which a knowledge system must operate is built up. For the first study, on scope and feasibility, CommonKADS offers the organization model for the description and analysis of the broader organizational environment.

For the second study, on impacts and improvements, CommonKADS offers the task and agent models. This study is more focused and detailed. It zooms in on the relevant part of the organization. The task model focuses on those tasks and task-related knowledge assets that are directly related to the problem that needs to be solved through the knowledge system. These tasks are allocated to agents characterized through the agent model.

For both studies, their first part (1a and 2a) is oriented toward modelling and analysis, whereas the concluding parts (1b and 2b) integrate the model results for the express purpose of managerial decision-making.

Below we discuss how to carry out these studies through the CommonKADS organization, task and agent models. All steps in developing these models can be taken by employing a set of practical and easy-to-use worksheets and checklists.

3.3   The Feasibility Study: Organization Modelling

There exists an overwhelming amount of literature on organization analysis, management theory, business process improvement, and reengineering that yields valuable and relevant insights. The word "overwhelming" is even an euphemism. Generally speaking, it is quite impossible to construct a complete description of an organization. Fortunately, for our purpose of value-adding knowledge-system applications and other knowledge-management solutions, this is not really necessary. The reason is that we look at the organization from a specific viewpoint, namely, that of *knowledge orientation*.

So, the idea underlying the CommonKADS organization model is to take the relevant elements and experiences from various sources — including organization theory, business process analysis, information management — and to integrate them into a coherent and comprehensive package targeted at knowledge orientation in the organization.

The organization model describes the organization in a structured, systems-like fashion. Different aspects, such as organization structure, processes, staff, and resources, come into play and interact when one wants to introduce new knowledge solutions. Therefore, these different aspects of the organization are represented as components in the model. The idea is that in the model these components have to be filled in both for the current and the future situation. By comparing these descriptions, one gets a very good feel for the value, feasibility, and acceptance of new knowledge-oriented solutions. In addition, one can come up with a well-founded action plan for organizational measures and improvements beyond mere systems development.

A corresponding overview of the organization model, and how it relates to the task and agent models, is depicted in Figure 3.1. The construction of these models is done by means of worksheets, as we will now discuss.

3.3.1   Organizational Context, Problems, and Solutions Portfolio

The first part of the organization model focuses on problems and opportunities, as seen in the wider organizational context. The latter contains broad categories such as the organization's mission, goals, strategy, value chain, and external influencing factors. This context is assumed to be relatively invariant (for the present purpose, that is). Nevertheless, opportunities, problems, and knowledge-oriented solutions must always be ultimately judged within such a broader business perspective, so it is important to get a real and explicit understanding of this context. To this end, Table 3.1 gives a worksheet (numbered OM-1) which explains the various aspects to consider, and helps in specifying this part of

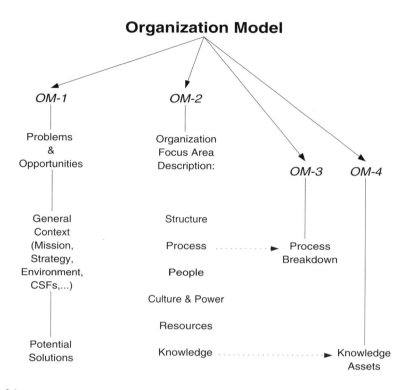

Figure 3.1
Overview of the components of the CommonKADS organization model.

Organization Model	Problems and Opportunities Worksheet OM-1
PROBLEMS AND OPPORTUNITIES	Make a shortlist of perceived problems and opportunities, based on interviews, brainstorm and visioning meetings, discussions with managers, etc.
ORGANIZATIONAL CONTEXT	Indicate in a concise manner key features of the wider organizational context, so as to put the listed opportunities and problems into proper perspective. Important features to consider are: 1. Mission, vision, goals of the organization 2. Important external factors the organization has to deal with 3. Strategy of the organization 4. Its value chain and the major value drivers
SOLUTIONS	List possible solutions for the perceived problems and opportunities, as suggested by the interviews and discussions held, and the above features of the organizational context.

Table 3.1
Worksheet OM-1: Identifying knowledge-oriented problems and opportunities in the organization.

the organization model. One may see this activity as covering the visioning part of the organization study. The problem-opportunity portfolio and potential knowledge solutions can be created by interviews with key staff members (but perhaps also customers!), brainstorming and visioning meetings, discussions with managers, and so on. For a successful knowledge project, it is important to identify at the start the various *stakeholders* that have an interest

- *Knowledge providers:* The specialists or experts in whom the knowledge of a certain area resides.
- *Knowledge users:* The people that need to use this knowledge to carry out their work successfully.
- *Knowledge decision-makers:* The managers that have the position to make decisions that affect the work of either the knowledge providers or the knowledge users.

Identifying these people and their roles at an early stage helps to quickly focus on the appropriate business processes, problems, and opportunities. Usually, knowledge providers, users, and decision-makers are very different persons with very different interests. Interviewing them helps you to understand what is at stake for them in relation to your knowledge project. Divergent views and conflicts of interests are common in organizations, but it takes effort to understand them. Without such an understanding, however, a good knowledge solution is not even possible.

3.3.2   Description of Focus Area in the Organization

The second part of the organization model concentrates upon the more specific, so-called variant, aspects of the organization. Here, we cover aspects such as how the business process is structured, what staff is involved, what resources are used, and so on. These components of the organization model may change (hence "variant") as a result of the introduction of knowledge systems. As an aid to the analysis, Table 3.2 gives a worksheet (numbered OM-2). It explains what important components of the organization to consider. We note that this analysis relates to a single problem-opportunity area, selected out of the list produced previously (in worksheet OM-1). It might be the case that this step has to be repeated for other areas as well.

The process component in OM-2 plays a central role within the CommonKADS organization-analysis process, as we will also see in the next worksheet. A good guideline is construct an UML activity diagram of the business process, and use this diagram as a filler of the slot in worksheet OM-2. Figure 3.2 shows a simplified business process of a company designing and selling elevators, described with the use of an activity diagram, A nice feature of activity diagrams is that we can locate the process in parts of the organization, and can include both process flow as well as information objects involved. Readers not familiar with the notation can read Section 14.2, which provides a short description of the main ingredients of this notation.

Organization Model	Variant Aspects Worksheet OM-2
STRUCTURE	Give an organization chart of the considered (part of the) organization in terms of its departments, groups, units, sections, ...
PROCESS	Sketch the layout (e.g., with the help of a UML activity diagram) of the business process at hand. A process is the relevant part of the value chain that is focused upon. A process is decomposed into tasks, which are detailed in worksheet OM-3.
PEOPLE	Indicate which staff members are involved, as actors or stakeholders, including decision makers, providers, users or beneficiaries ("customers") of knowledge. These people do not need to be actual people, but can be functional roles played by people in the organization (e.g., director, consultant)
RESOURCES	Describe the resources that are utilized for the business process. These may cover different types, such as: 1. Information systems and other computing resources 2. Equipment and materials 3. Technology, patents, rights
KNOWLEDGE	Knowledge represents a special resource exploited in a business process. Because of its key importance in the present context, it is set apart here. The description of this component of the organization model is given separately, in worksheet OM-4 on knowledge assets.
CULTURE & POWER	Pay attention to the unwritten rules of the game, including styles of working and communicating ("the way we do things around here"), related social and interpersonal (nonknowledge) skills, and formal as well as informal relationships and networks.

Table 3.2
Worksheet OM-2: Description of organizational aspects that have an impact on and/or are affected by chosen knowledge solutions.

3.3.3   Breakdown of the Business Process

The process is also specified in more detail with the help of a separate worksheet. The business process is broken down into smaller tasks, because an envisaged knowledge system always carries out a specific task — and this has to fit properly into the process as a whole. Often, some process adaptations are needed by changing tasks, or combining or connecting them differently. To investigate this aspect better, Table 3.3 presents a worksheet (numbered OM-3) to specify details of the task breakdown of the business process. A rough indication is given how knowledge-intensive these tasks are and what knowledge is used. You might find it difficult to establish the knowledge-intensiveness of a task at this point, but after reading more about knowledge-intensive task types in Chapter 6 you will have background knowledge to help you in this respect.

Also, an indication is given of the *significance* of each task, e.g., on an ordinal scale of 1-5. There are no hard rules for assessing task significance and it can be tricky, but it is typically a combination of effort required, resources required, task criticality, and task complexity.

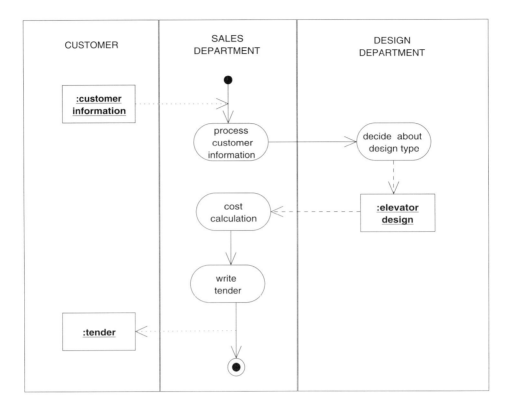

Figure 3.2
Business process of a company designing and selling elevators, specified through a UML activity diagram.

The business process is modelled down to the level of detail that enables us to make decisions about a task, e.g., construct a knowledge model to automate or explicate that task.

3.3.4   Knowledge Assets

Let's turn now to the "knowledge" element in worksheet OM-2. Evidently, knowledge is the single most important aspect of the organization to analyze here in detail. Accordingly, Table 3.4 provides a worksheet (numbered OM-4) to describe knowledge assets. This worksheet provides the specification of the knowledge component of the CommonKADS organization model. Later on, this specification will be further refined, first in the task

Organization Model	Process Breakdown Worksheet OM-3					
NO.	TASK	PER-FORMED BY	WHERE?	KNOWL-EDGE ASSET	INTEN-SIVE?	SIGNIFI-CANCE
task identi-fier	task name (some part of the process in OM-2)	a certain agent, either a human (see 'People" in OM-2) or a software system (see "Resource" in OM-2))	some location in the organization structure (see OM-2)	list of knowledge resources used by this task	boolean indicating whether the task is considered knowledge-intensive?	indication of how significant the task is considered to be (e.g., on a five-point scale in terms of frequency, costs, resources or mission criticality)

Table 3.3
Worksheet OM-3: Description of the process in terms of the tasks of which it is composed.

Organization Model	Knowledge Assets Worksheet OM-4					
KNOWL-EDGE ASSET	POS-SESSED BY	USED IN	RIGHT FORM?	RIGHT PLACE?	RIGHT TIME?	RIGHT QUALITY?
Name (cf. worksheet OM-3)	Agent (cf. worksheet OM-3)	Task (cf. worksheet OM-3)	(Yes or no; comments)	(Yes or no; comments)	(Yes or no; comments)	(Yes or no; comments)

Table 3.4
Worksheet OM-4: Description of the knowledge component of the organization model.

Organization Model	Checklist for Feasibility Decision Document: Worksheet OM-5
BUSINESS FEASIBILITY	For a given problem/opportunity area and a suggested solution, the following questions have to be answered: 1. What are the expected benefits for the organization from the considered solution? Both tangible economic and intangible business benefits should be identified here. 2. How large is this expected added value? 3. What are the expected costs for the considered solution? 4. How does this compare to possible alternative solutions? 5. Are organizational changes required? 6. To what extent are economic and business risks and uncertainties involved regarding the considered solution direction?
TECHNICAL FEASIBILITY	For a given problem/opportunity area and a suggested solution, the following questions have to be answered: 1. How complex, in terms of knowledge stored and reasoning processes to be carried out, is the task to be performed by the considered knowledge-system solution? Are state-of-the-art methods and techniques available and adequate? 2. Are there critical aspects involved, relating to time, quality, needed resources, or otherwise? If so, how to go about them? 3. Is it clear what the success measures are and how to test for validity, quality, and satisfactory performance? 4. How complex is the required interaction with end users (user interfaces)? Are state-of-the-art methods and techniques available and adequate? 5. How complex is the interaction with other information systems and possible other resources (interoperablity, systems integration)? Are state-of-the-art methods and techniques available and adequate? 6. Are there further technological risks and uncertainties?

Table 3.5
Worksheet OM-5: Checklist for the feasibility decision document (Part I).

model and very extensively (of course) in the knowledge model. This piecemeal approach gives more opportunities for flexibility in knowledge project management.

Thus, the knowledge asset worksheet (OM-4) is meant as a first-cut analysis. The perspective we take here is that those pieces of knowledge are significant as an asset, that are in active use by workers within the organization for the purpose of a specific task or process. An important issue in this part of the study is to single out dimensions in which knowledge assets may be improved, in form, accessibility in time or space, or in quality. This analysis is not only important in knowledge-systems engineering, but perhaps even more so in knowledge management actions in general.

3.3.5   Feasibility Decision-Making

Now, after carrying out the steps represented in the worksheets of Tables 3.1–3.4, we have all the information ready related to the CommonKADS organization model of Figure 3.1.

Organization Model	Checklist for Feasibility Decision Document: Worksheet OM-5 (continued)
PROJECT FEASIBILITY	For a given problem/opportunity area and a suggested solution, the following questions have to be answered: 1. Is there adequate *commitment* from the actors and stakeholders (managers, experts, users, customers, project team members) for further project steps? 2. Can the needed *resources* in terms of time, budget, equipment, staffing be made available? 3. Are the required *knowledge* and other *competences* available? 4. Are the *expectations* regarding the project and its results realistic? 5. Are the *project organization* and its internal as well as external *communication* adequate? 6. Are there further project risks and uncertainties?
PROPOSED ACTIONS	This is the part of the feasibility decision document that is directly subject to managerial commitment and decision making. It weights and integrates the previous analysis results into recommended concrete steps for action: 1. *Focus:* What is the recommended focus in the identified problem-opportunity areas? 2. *Target solution:* What is the recommended solution direction for this focus area? 3. What are the expected *results, costs, and benefits*? 4. What *project actions* are required to get there? 5. *Risks:* If circumstances inside or outside the organization change, under what *conditions* is it wise to reconsider the proposed decisions?

Table 3.6
Worksheet OM-5: Checklist for the feasibility decision document (Part II).

The final step is to wrap up the key implications of this information in a document, on the basis of which commitments and decisions by management are made. At this stage of a knowledge system project, decision-making will focus on:

- What is the most promising opportunity area for applications, and what is the best solution direction?
- What are the benefits versus the costs (business feasibility)?
- Are the needed technologies for this solution available and within reach (technical feasibility)?
- What further project actions can successfully be undertaken (project feasibility)?

Tables 3.5 and 3.6 present an extensive and self-contained checklist for producing the feasibility decision document (worksheet OM-5). This completes the CommonKADS organizational analysis. The further stages focus more on the features of specific tasks, pieces of knowledge, and individuals involved. But before going into these topics, we will first further illuminate the above organization analysis by an illustrative case example.

3.4   Case: Social Security Services

In this section we illustrate the above organizational model study by a real-life case study.

3.4.1   Problem-Opportunity Context

In the Netherlands, the administration of a range of social security benefits is carried out by municipalities. The most important ones are general assistance benefits. The latter category is an end-of-the-line type of benefit, in the sense that if no other regulations apply, a person may ultimately apply for this type of benefit. At the time of the project, in the municipality of Amsterdam, approximately 60,000 people were supported by these general assistance benefits. In order to qualify for this financial assistance, each applicant is screened in great detail. The rules for this are codified in in or can be derived from several volumes of laws and regulations.

In Amsterdam, a considerable backlog in dealing with (the growing numbers of) clients had accumulated over the years. This led to long queues in the offices, as well as long elapse times between initial client intake and final decision. At the level of the directorate of the responsible municipal service, this backlog created concerns over the efficiency of the work being done. Moreover, the clients themselves started to complain about the delays, and these complaints found their way into the local media. In this context, the secretary of the directorate suggested the use of knowledge systems to help reduce the backlog. It is highly important to stress the initial hypothesis because it shows how crucial modelling organizational features is. Briefly, the initial problem/opportunity formulation was:

> Because the applicable laws and regulations are so complex, it takes a long time for the staff involved to reach a decision. If we can assist these people with a knowledge system that stores the needed legal decision-making knowledge, the decision process can be speeded up, so that more clients can be served in the same time and the application backlog will be significantly reduced.

Thus, at the beginning a very clear idea existed about the problem area, the direction of the solution, and the benefits for the organization at large. Although we give this part of the case study in a narrative form, it is obvious how the above information constitutes fillers for the invariant components of the organization model, according to the problems and opportunities worksheet (Table 3.1, worksheet OM-1).

3.4.2   Organization Model: Variant Components

The next step in the study is to consider the various aspects of the organization model, as indicated in Figure 3.1 and particularly in the variant component worksheet (Table 3.2, worksheet OM-2). For the social security service case, we briefly discuss the main elements and results below.

Structure   The formal organizational structure of the social security service is given in the form of an organization chart, as presented in Figure 3.3. The service consists of a central office and a branch office in each of the sixteen boroughs of the municipality of Amsterdam. The structure of each of these branch offices is the same. The central office has a mixture of line and staff departments. In addition, the chart includes the computer center of the municipality of Amsterdam, although it is strictly speaking not a part of the service organization (hence the dotted lines). However, it is important to include the connection, since the computer center performed a sizable amount of work for the social security service, and (at that time) every municipal institution was formally required to use this center for all its computer work.

People   In a complex organization, there are many different people playing many different organizational roles, requiring very different levels of expertise. Given the brief for the project (see the problem-opportunity component of the organization model), only a very limited area has been taken into account, mostly staff members that are directly involved in some way in the decision-making process.

The major roles played by people in the organization in our case can be found in Figure 3.3.

Culture and power   Power relations among the main people in the organization are shown in Figure 3.4. This figure shows not only formal relationships of authority between people but also informal influencing relationships.

To get a grip on these aspects is often not easy, because informal relationships between disparate actors may be difficult to detect. Three types of power relationships are shown in Figure 3.4. Strong official lines of formal authority are indicated by solid lines. These relations are formally laid down in the organization and its hierarchy. For example, the branch director is the boss of a branch office, and as such has formal authority over chiefs and testers in this office. Rather strong informal power relations are shown in the figure by means of dashed lines. These relations have often slowly grown over time, and have come to be viewed as more or less regular. For example, the regulations expert from the central office can convene meetings at which all testers of the branch offices are present. Moreover, he can use these meetings to launch certain quality-control campaigns. This can be done almost without interference from the branch director, in spite of his formal authority over the tester in the branch office. Finally, weak informal relations of influence are the hardest to uncover, because they reflect occasional but sometimes very important links between persons in the organization (see dotted lines in Figure 3.4). This influence is mainly exercised through informal meetings and telephone calls.

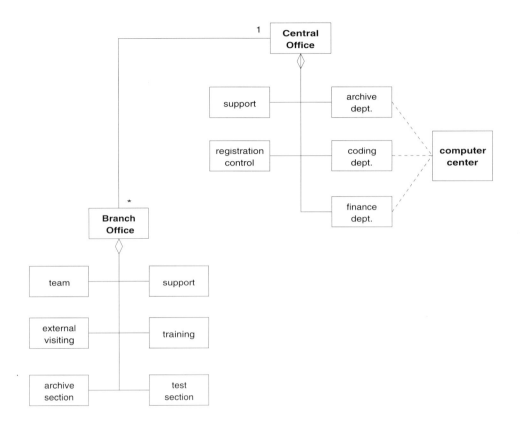

Figure 3.3
The structure component in the social security service case.

Resources   For the present project, the following resources were deemed to be most relevant:

- *Computers*: In the service as a whole, at the time of the project, only a limited number of computers were available. All computing was done by the central computer Center (see Figure 3.3). In each of the branch offices there were a few terminals connected to the central computer. In some branch offices, local experiments with personal computers had started to take over routine work, such as producing letters of notification.
- *Office space*: Some branch offices were inadequately housed, leading to insufficient facilities for doing the client intake work.

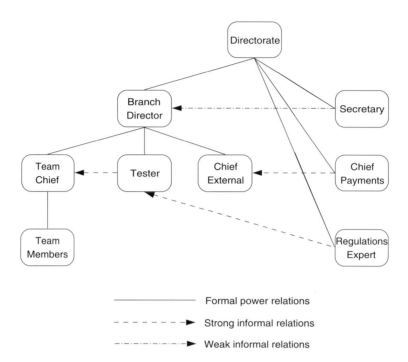

Figure 3.4
Various power relationships in the social security service case.

Process, knowledge   As follows from the brief for the project, the main focus was the knowledge for the decision-making process about benefits by the social security service. These aspects are treated separately in the next subsection.

Generally, we note that a flexible use of the organization model and its representation techniques gives the best results. It is neither always helpful nor necessary to fill in all slots of all organization model components and worksheets. This should only be done if the information bears relevance to conclusions and has implications for action. However, this selectivity must be a conscious decision on the part of the knowledge engineer, whereby the given worksheets provide guidance as comprehensive checklists. In addition, the form of representing the collected information will generally vary. Short pieces of text, e.g., filling in slots of worksheets, are useful, but as we have seen sometimes simple diagrams, charts, or pictures are much more clear and effective. Thus, the knowledge engineer should feel free to pick the most appropriate form. The criterion here is what means will be the most effective in communicating with the persons for whom the study is carried out.

3.4.3   Process Breakdown and Knowledge Assets

The process and knowledge components of the organization model are modelled with the help of separate worksheets (Table 3.3, worksheet OM-3, and Table 3.4, worksheet OM-4, respectively). Now, we will give the most important results, in various forms, for the process breakdown in tasks and the associated knowledge assets in the social security service case.

Process breakdown in tasks   On the basis of interviews with key personnel, among others the secretary of the directorate, the following main parts (tasks) of the overall process were identified.

- *Intake*: This task refers to obtaining all relevant information about a client, for example, age, address, additional sources of income, various aspects of the personal situation of the client. Direct person-to-person contact is commonly involved in the intake work.
- *Archiving*: Keeping and maintaining files and documents for all clients throughout the life cycle of their being clients of the social security service.
- *Decision-making*: Taking the decision, based on the data concerning the personal situation of the client (as obtained from the intake work) and the applicable laws and rules, whether the client qualifies for a benefit, as well as deciding about the amount of money he or she is entitled to.
- *Notifying*: Informing the client about the decisions made. Without a written notification a decision has no legal status.
- *Reporting*: Writing an internal report about the client. This report serves, for example, as input for paying.
- *Paying*: Making the actual payment to the client.
- *Quality control*: Controlling whether the decisions made are correct in view of the applicable laws and regulations. This control task is carried out "after the fact." It is based on sampled cases from the decision-making task, as laid down in the reporting task.

An overall view of what the process looks like, in terms of the tasks it is composed of and their mutual dependencies, is shown in Figure 3.5. Some tasks, such as archiving, occur at several points within the process. There is a distinction between the primary process and the supporting tasks (see the two "compartments" in Figure 3.5).

The start focus of the project was on the decision-making task, but now it has become clear that it is directly linked to the intake and notifying tasks, and that in addition there is likely to be some interaction with the archiving task.

Knowledge assets and task significance   From the study it became clear that only some of the tasks were knowledge intensive, namely intake, decision-making, and quality control. In intake, other competences are also important, particularly interpersonal and communication skills. As the project's focus was on speeding up decision-making, it was a

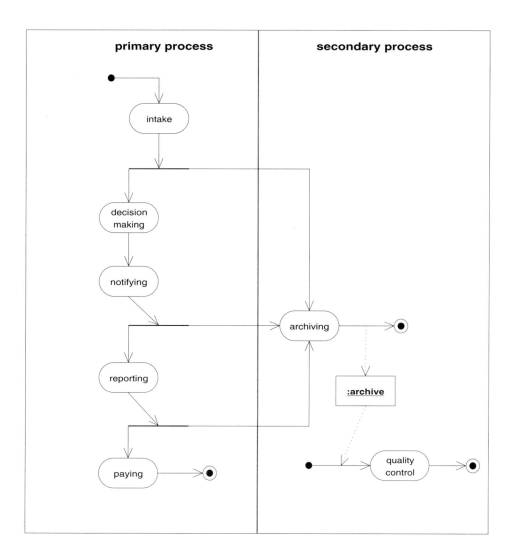

Figure 3.5
Activity diagram of the tasks in the business process of the social security service.

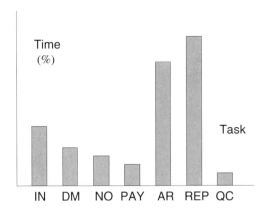

Figure 3.6
Task significance: Workload in the social security service case, expressed in percentage of total time spent.

straightforward step to investigate in more detail the knowledge underlying the decision-making task. Given the above process results, it was also natural to look at the intake and notifying tasks, since there are direct input-output dependencies with decision-making.

After some initial knowledge acquisition it became clear that there are at least two aspects of decision-making that were insufficiently understood, and therefore might compromise the construction or functioning of the envisaged knowledge system. First, clients sometimes cheat about their data in order to qualify for a benefit. Detecting this is a highly sensitive process that relies strongly upon all kinds of nonverbal cues. Personnel doing the intake were very good at interpreting these cues. A knowledge system, however, will of course have a very hard time in distinguishing between such true and (slightly) false client data.

Second, civil servants do have the (understandable) tendency to sometimes adjust the client data somewhat when they feel a client is justified in getting the benefit but the official rules do not cover the special case. Again, a knowledge system would entirely miss this point of fudging client data. It would produce advice that is, strictly speaking, correct, but that does not take into account special circumstances. This would make at least some of the proposed decisions hard to accept for the responsible decision-makers. Both the cheat and fudge factors represents a delicate gray area in decision-making. It lies outside the competence of a knowledge system, consequently restricting its scope and usability.

Finally, as a check on the initial project hypothesis that the problem source was related to the decision-making task, a field study was undertaken to estimate the actual workload for the various tasks within the process. During two weeks the work of the people in a number of sampled branch offices was followed closely. During this investigation it was captured how often decision-making problems occurred as a result of the complexities of the regulations, and how this was reflected in the average workload. The results are shown in Figure 3.6.

A striking result of this analysis is that the major workload is not due to the complexity of decision-making. Over 60% of the time is spent in archiving and reporting. This was the result of the paper-based archives in use at that time in the social security service. Much time had to be spent in finding lost client files, and overcoming or bypassing all kinds of bureaucratic hurdles and procedures.

In order to assess the relative task significance (cf. Table 3.3, worksheet OM-3) these observations are of prime importance. It yields one clear quantitative measure of the relative significance of tasks in the process. If we take time spent as an indicator of process cost (which is probably quite adequate in this case), it is evident that the cost and inefficiency drivers are in archiving and reporting, rather than in decision-making. Even if decision-making could be fully automated (which is judged to be highly unrealistic given the nature of the knowledge assets), the maximum gain would be about 10% (as seen from Figure 3.6) relative to the total process. Much more modest improvements (more realistic and easy to achieve, say on the order of 10% only) within archiving and reporting would already result in similar gains relative to the overall process. Thus, focusing on these tasks is much more likely to result in speeding up the total process and reducing backlogs.

3.4.4   Scope and Feasibility Decision-making

Given the above results of the organization model study, ample material is now available for well-founded decision-making on feasibility and scope. Very briefly, following the format given for this in worksheet OM-5 the main proposed conclusions and decisions are as follows.

Business feasibility   From the study it is clear that building a knowledge system for decision-making will not, in itself, solve the problem. Higher benefits in speeding up the overall process can be expected by focusing on improvements in archiving and reporting instead. Quantitative indicators have been given above. The knowledge-system solution would be limited with respect to needed changes in the organization. It would require a more decentralized PC-based computer infrastructure, and associated changes with respect to the individual offices. Also, the position of the testers would clearly change, while people at the intake might lose some of their discretionary power in making "gray area" decisions. If archiving and reporting is chosen as the target area, the impact on the organization is likely to be much more important. As can be seen by comparing the structure and process/task components of the organization model, several different departments play a role, and moreover these tasks reoccur at different places in the overall process. Even the external computer center, largely outside the control of the organization, would have to be involved.

Technical feasibility The main technical risk associated with the knowledge system according to the above analysis is how to deal with (or perhaps better, how to leave it to humans) the gray aspects (improper cheat or fudge data) of decision-making. These provide very good examples of tacit knowledge in the organization, hard to explicate and formalize in a computational fashion. The alternative solution, focusing on improving archiving and reporting, did not appear to pose technical risks, at least at the first stage (we mention in passing that it did later on).

Project feasibility For the knowledge-system solution, the technical risk combined with the limited benefits expected in terms of time saved gives rise to wonder whether it is wise to continue now in the initially suggested direction. On the other hand, a project targeted at archiving and reporting would need, as a first step, to ensure participation and commitment from the various actors, or need to downscale desired procedural changes to a more restricted and local level to start with.

Proposed actions Based on the organization model results, the best proposal obviously is to redirect the project from a knowledge system for decision-making, to simplifying the workflow and procedures related to archiving and reporting. Therefore, it was proposed to refrain from building a knowledge system for decision support, and to start working on the bottlenecks in archiving, which were now perceived — due to the organization model study — as the most crucial ones in dealing with the application backlog.

This case study shows how important it is to pay attention to organizational factors at an early stage, and it shows the capability of the CommonKADS methodology to clarify these factors in a step-by-step manner. This is even more pressing when the results are different from what one expects at the beginning, as was the case here. However, the experience described in the case study is not at all uncommon in practice. It points to an important lesson ensuing from knowledge management. As knowledge in an organization is often tacit, one should not be surprised when it turns out to be quite different from what you initially expect.

3.5 Impact and Improvement Analysis: Task and Agent Modelling

We now imagine that a feasibility study has been concluded positively, and that the knowledge project has got the green light to continue. So, it's time to take the next step, and to zoom in on the features of the relevant tasks, the agents that carry them out, and on the knowledge items used by the agents in performing tasks. All these aspects refine the results from the organization model. For their description CommonKADS offers the task and agent models. The outcome of this study is detailed insight into the impact of a knowledge system, and especially what improvement actions are possible or necessary in the organization in conjunction with the introduction of a knowledge system.

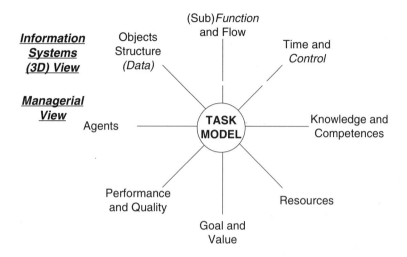

Figure 3.7
Overview of the CommonKADS task model.

The notion of task, although important, has different connotations. As a commonsense concept, it is a human activity to achieve some purpose. In the above organizational study it has been viewed in the (not incompatible) sense of a well-defined subpart of a business process. The notion of task has also emerged as a crucial one in the theory and methodology of knowledge systems and of knowledge sharing and reuse. Later we will see that it is a core technical concept in the modelling of expertise.

Thus, we need a link between the notion of task in the human and organizational sense of the word, and the more information systems-oriented concept we will employ later on. The CommonKADS task model serves as this linking pin between the organizational aspect and the knowledge-system aspect of a task.

In this perspective, the following definition is suitable. A task is a subpart of a business process that:

- represents a goal-oriented activity adding value to the organization;
- handles inputs and delivers desired outputs in a structured and controlled way;
- consumes resources;

- requires (and provides) knowledge and other competences;
- is carried out according to given quality and performance criteria;
- is performed by responsible and accountable agents.

A corresponding impression of the CommonKADS task model is depicted in Figure 3.7.

3.5.1   Task Analysis

Following this definition (and Figure 3.7) of what a task is, the information covered in the task model is specified with the help of worksheet TM-1, given in Table 3.7. It can be viewed as a refinement of the data from worksheet OM-3 (Table 3.3).

A few points are worth noting here. Some of the items in the task model, such as value, quality, and performance, refer directly to organizational considerations. They predominantly have a management and business administration flavor. Here, CommonKADS provides the opportunity to integrate information from, e.g., quality assurance systems existing in the organization.

Other items in the task model, notably dependency/flow, objects handled, and time/control, have a natural link with state-of-the-art approaches to information-systems modelling, such as structured analysis and design, information engineering, and object-oriented methodology. In all these approaches, we find what we may call a three-dimensional view on information modelling. Such a *3D information model* consists of the following dimensions:

Functional view   A decomposition into subtasks, their inputs and outputs, and the I/O flow connecting these subtasks into an overall information flow network. Traditional data-flow diagrams are a widely used technique here. If you want to use a UML notation the best candidate is (again) an activity diagram (see the object-flow notations in Section 14.2).

Static information structure   A description of the information content and structure of objects that are handled in the task, such as its input and output objects, in terms of entities and their relationships (or objects and associations). The UML class diagram is the notation of choice for modelling the information structure. This simplifies the link with subsequent detailed knowledge modelling. The main ingredients of the UML class-diagram notations can be found in Section 14.4.

Control or dynamic view   A description of the temporal order of and control over the subtasks, providing a picture of the triggering events, decision-making points, and other knowledge about time aspects. Depending on the type of control, this aspect is commonly represented by means of either state diagrams (in case control is dominated by external events or is strongly asynchronous) or by means of activity diagrams (in case of (mostly) synchronous internal control). A quick introduction to state diagrams can be found in Section 14.3.

Task Model	Task Analysis Worksheet TM-1
TASK	Task identifier and task name
ORGANIZATION	Indicate the business process this task is a part of, and where in the organization (structure, people) it is carried out
GOAL AND VALUE	Describe the goal of the task and the value that its execution adds to the process this task is a part of
DEPENDENCY AND FLOW	*Input tasks*: tasks delivering inputs to this task *Output tasks*: tasks that use (some of) the outputs of this task You can use a data-flow diagram or an activity diagram here to describe this.
OBJECTS HANDLED	*Input objects*: The objects, including information and knowledge items, that are input to the task *Output objects*: The objects, including information and knowledge items, that are delivered by the task as outputs *Internal objects* Important objects (if any), including information and knowledge items, that are used internally within the task but are not input or output to other tasks You may want to include a class diagram here to describe the information objects handled by the task.
TIMING AND CONTROL	Describe frequency and duration of the task. Describe the control relation with other tasks. For this you may want to use a state diagram or a activity diagram. Describe control constraints: (i) *preconditions* that must hold before the task can be executed; (ii) *postconditions* that must hold as result of execution of the task.
AGENTS	The staff members and/or the information systems (cf. OM-2 and OM-3) that are responsible for carrying out the task
KNOWLEDGE AND COMPETENCE	Competences needed for successful task performance. For the knowledge items involved, there is a separate worksheet TM-2. List other relevant skills and competences here. Indicate which elements of the task are knowledge intensive. Note that tasks can also *deliver* competences to the organization, and it may be worthwhile to indicate that here.
RESOURCES	Describe and preferably quantify the various resources consumed by the task (staff time, systems and equipment, materials, financial budgets. The description is typically a refinement of the resource descriptions in OM-2
QUALITY AND PERFORMANCE	List the quality and performance measures that are used by the organization to determine successful task execution

Table 3.7
Worksheet TM-1: Refined description of the tasks within the target process.

Note that most of the time these descriptions already exist, at least partially. We also want to point out that the knowledge model exploits a similar multidimensional view of knowledge modelling. These three dimensions are clearly reflected in the items in the task model indicated as dependency/flow, objects handled, and time/control. Hence, the task model provides an integrative link with accepted standard methodology for information modelling and analysis.

3.5.2   Knowledge Bottleneck Analysis

Next, the item of knowledge and competence is a key item in our task model, and for this reason it is again modelled by means of a separate worksheet TM-2, presented in Table 3.8. It constitutes a refinement of the data from worksheet OM-4 (Table 3.4) on knowledge assets. As with the other worksheets, it is rather self-explanatory. It has a highly important function, since it concentrates in detail on bottlenecks and improvements relating to specific areas of knowledge. Hence, this analysis is not only worthwhile for knowledge systems but is a useful step in knowledge management in general, to achieve superior use of knowledge by the organization.

Much of this information can be obtained by simple and direct questions to the people involved. Examples are: How often do you carry out this task? How much time does it take? Who depends on your results? Whom do you talk to in carrying out this task? What do you need in order to start with it? What happens to the organization if it goes wrong? What may go wrong, and what do you do then? How do you know that the task is successfully concluded? Such questions are best asked with the help of concrete task examples. With the answers you can write down a task *scenario*. Scenario techniques are very helpful in getting a practical understanding, and later on they are useful in validating the information and setting up a system test plan.

3.5.3   Agent Descriptions

The above steps in the impact and improvement study were dominated by the viewpoint of tasks to be carried out. It is also useful to consider the information from the rather different perspective of individual agents (staff workers; sometimes also information systems can be viewed as agents). This is done in the CommonKADS agent model, displayed in Table 3.9 by means of a rather straightforward worksheet AM-1. The purpose of the agent model is to understand the roles and competences that the various actors in the organization bring with them to perform a shared task. The information contained in the agent specification is for a large part a rearrangement of information already existing in previous worksheets. However, the present arrangement may be useful to better judge impacts and organizational changes from the viewpoint of the various agents. It also yields input information for other CommonKADS models, especially the communication model.

To show graphically how agents participate in (new) tasks carried out by a (new) system, it is useful to construct a UML use-case diagram. This diagram shows what services are provided by a "system" to agents involved. Use-case diagrams are helpful when presenting potential solutions to stakeholders. A brief introduction into use-case diagrams can be found in Section 14.5.

Task Model	Knowledge Item Worksheet TM-2	
NAME	Knowledge item	
POSSESSED BY	Agent	
USED IN	Task identifier and name.	
DOMAIN	Wider domain the knowledge is embedded in (specialist field, discipline, branch of science or engineering, professional community)	
Nature of the knowledge		**Bottleneck / to be improved?**
Formal, rigorous		
Empirical, quantitative		
Heuristic, rules of thumb		
Highly specialized, domain-specific		
Experience-based		
Action-based		
Incomplete		
Uncertain, may be incorrect		
Quickly changing		
Hard to verify		
Tacit, hard to transfer		
Form of the knowledge		
Mind		
Paper		
Electronic		
Action skill		
Other		
Availability of knowledge		
Limitations in time		
Limitations in space		
Limitations in access		
Limitations in quality		
Limitations in form		

Table 3.8
Worksheet TM-2: Specification of the knowledge employed for a task, and possible bottlenecks and areas for improvement.

3.5.4   Recommendations and Actions

Finally, with the worksheets TM-1, TM-2, and AM-1 we have collected all information related to the task and agent models (see also Figure 3.7). The remaining step is to integrate this information into a document for managerial decision-making about changes and improvements in the organization. For this purpose, Table 3.10 presents a complete checklist (constituting worksheet OTA-1).

Proposed actions for improvement are accompanying measures, but are not part of the knowledge-systems work itself. However, they are highly important for ensuring com-

Agent Model	Agent Worksheet AM-1
NAME	*Name of the agent*
ORGANIZATION	Indicate how the agent is positioned in the organization, as inherited from the organization-model worksheet descriptions, including the type (human, information system), position in the organization structure, ...
INVOLVED IN	List of tasks (cf. TM-1)
COMMUNICATES WITH	List of agent names
KNOWLEDGE	List of knowledge items possessed by the agent (cf. TM-2)
OTHER COMPETENCES	List of other required or present competences of the agent
RESPONSIBILITIES AND CONSTRAINTS	List of responsibilities the agent has in task execution, and of restrictions in this respect. Constraints may refer to limitations in authority, but also to inside or outside legal or professional norms, or the like.

Table 3.9
Worksheet AM-1: Agent specification according to the CommonKADS agent model.

mitment and support from the relevant players in the organization. The major issues for decision-making here are:

- Are organizational changes recommended and if so, which ones?
- What measures have to be implemented regarding specific tasks and workers involved? In particular, what improvements are possible regarding use and availability of knowledge?
- Have these changes sufficient support from the people involved? Are further facilitating actions called for?
- What will be the further direction of the knowledge system project?

This completes the organization-task-agent analysis. Even without building knowledge systems, it is likely that this analysis brings to the surface many measures and improvements that lead to better use of knowledge by the organization.

3.6   Case: Ice-Cream Product Development

Did it ever occur to you that ice cream is a very knowledge-intensive product? Ice cream, as simple as it may seem, actually involves deep knowledge about an amalgam of delicate product structures and properties, about sophisticated production processes, and last but not least, about consumer preferences that are often local and change over time. In a successful ice-cream business, these very different knowledge areas have to be strongly intertwined. Catering to ever-changing consumer interests in addition requires a steady stream of new ice-cream products that appear on the market in a timely fashion.

Ice cream thus represents a tough knowledge management challenge. At the Unilever company this challenge has been taken up. As a case study, we discuss the PARIS project

Organization, Task, Agent Models	Worksheet OTA-1: Checklist for Impact and Improvement Decision Document
IMPACTS AND CHANGES IN ORGANIZATION	Describe which impacts and changes the considered knowledge system solution brings with respect to the organization, by comparing the differences between the organization model (worksheet OM-2) in the current situation, and how it will look in the future. This has to be done for all (variant) components in a global fashion (specific aspects for individual tasks or staff members are dealt with below). 1. Structure 2. Process 3. Resources 4. People 5. Knowledge 6. Culture & power
TASK/AGENT-SPECIFIC IMPACTS AND CHANGES	Describe which impacts and changes the considered knowledge system solution brings with respect to individual tasks and agents, by comparing the differences between the task and agent models (worksheets TA-1/2 and AM-1) in the current situation, and what they will look like in the future. It is important to look not only at the staff members directly involved in a task but also other actors and stakeholders (decision-makers, users, clients). 1. Changes in task layout (flow, dependencies, objects handled, timing, control) 2. Changes in needed resources 3. Performance and quality criteria 4. Changes in staffing, involved agents 5. Changes in individual positions, responsibilities, authority, constraints in task execution 6. Changes required in knowledge and competences 7. Changes in communication
ATTITUDES AND COMMITMENTS	Consider how the individual actors and stakeholders involved will react to the suggested changes, and whether there will be a sufficient basis to successfully carry through these changes
PROPOSED ACTIONS	This is the part of the impacts and improvements decision document that is directly subject to managerial commitment and decision-making. It weights and integrates the previous analysis results into recommended concrete steps for action: 1. *Improvements:* What are the recommended changes, with respect to the organization, as well as individual tasks, staff members, and systems? 2. *Accompanying measures:* What supporting measures are to be taken to facilitate these changes (e.g., training, facilities) 3. What further *project action* is recommended with respect to the undertaken knowledge system solution? 4. *Expected results, costs, benefits*: reconsider items from the earlier feasibility decision document 5. If circumstances inside or outside the organization change, under what *conditions* is it wise to reconsider the proposed decisions?

Table 3.10
Worksheet OTA-1: Checklist for the impacts and improvements decision document.

Organization Model	Problems and Opportunities Worksheet OM-1
PROBLEMS AND OPPORTUNITIES	* Speed-up time to market of new ice-cream products * Leverage-associated knowledge across functions and sites
ORGANIZATIONAL CONTEXT	Vision and strategy: * Achieve a situation as depicted in Figure 3.8 External factors: * Local and changing consumer preferences * Variety in relevant national legislation * Branding issues * Strong international competition Major value drivers: * Fast-moving alignment with local consumer markets by new product introductions
SOLUTIONS	Solution 1: Upgrade current IT systems for product development Solution 2: Develop new functionalities through knowledge systems (e.g., assessment, processing support) Solution 3: Let specific solution direction be the result of a stakeholder-driven process, as depicted in Figure 3.9

Table 3.11
Worksheet OM-1: Problems, organizational context and possible solutions for the PARIS ice-cream project.

which comprised a feasibility study on ways to improve knowledge management and knowledge-systems support for the ice-cream business at Unilever. In this and similar projects, the CommonKADS approach is being used as the standard methodology by the responsible unit for knowledge management and engineering. The PARIS study clearly exemplifies, first, how important organizational analyses are in IT systems strategy and development, and second, how standard knowledge methodology supports knowledge management and engineering applications that go way beyond building knowledge systems.

3.6.1   Ice-Cream Organization Model

In the preparatory phase of the PARIS study, a variety of potential application ideas were listed by the project team, including different types of knowledge systems (design, assessment, manufacturing), ways to prevent loss of skills due to retirement, and new functionalities of existing conventional IT support systems. As a fundamental principle, any knowledge project must have active and direct support from the (in this case, ice-cream) business itself. Therefore, initial and open interviews were held with various business executives in order to establish the main directions of the PARIS project and the business support for them.

OM-1: Organizational context, problems, solutions portfolio   Outcomes of this initial analysis are shown in Table 3.11 presenting the first worksheet OM-1. Important problem/opportunity areas were identified: (1) reducing the time to market of new ice-cream products, and (2) leveraging associated knowledge across different functions and sites (in

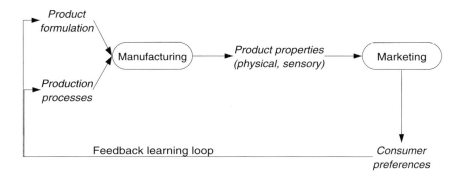

Figure 3.8
A vision for ice-cream knowledge management, seen as an organizational learning feedback loop.

view of the fact that Unilever has a range of ice-cream factories in many different countries spanning several continents). Interestingly, from the early business interviews a vision picture emerged that is presented in Figure 3.8. It shows how the different knowledge areas — product and development knowledge, manufacturing processes expertise, market knowledge — should ideally be integrated into what was described as an organizational learning cycle. Information systems support is important if it functions within this cycle, but it also became clear that such support is only one component within a broader cross-function and cross-site ice-cream knowledge management.

As seen from worksheet OM-1, different solution directions are possible. At this stage, the PARIS project team chose not to preselect a specific system solution, but to drive this through a strongly stakeholder-oriented knowledge-pull project approach (thus, the process-oriented solution No. 3 was chosen). From the stakeholder interviews it appeared that the strongest knowledge pull from the ice-cream business was to be expected in the area of product formulation and development, for which there already was a conventional but limited IT support tool. The approach selected, where stakeholders in the business act as the project sponsors, is shown in Figure 3.9.

OM-2: Description of focus area in the organization   After the initial phase of stakeholder interviewing, studies were done by surveying several ice-cream factories in different countries of Europe, as well as in the United States. The selected focus area, new product development, appears to be a key business process for continued market success. The second worksheet OM-2 in Table 3.12 describes some results of this part of the study. A general picture of the organizational structure of an ice-cream factory is given in Figure 3.10. Product development is the focal business process, and it has a number of major sequential stages running from product idea generation to product postlaunch review. However, it

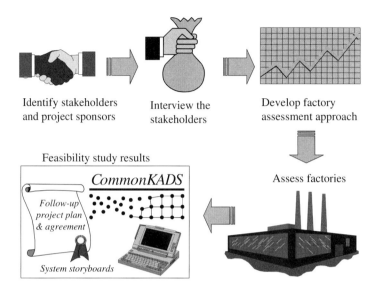

Figure 3.9
The PARIS stakeholder-driven project approach.

is clear from the *people* slot that many different functional areas are involved in product development, even including legal staff. These strong cross-functional aspects are very relevant to devising knowledge management actions.

OM-3: Breakdown of the product development business process   This worksheet OM-3, Table 3.13, describes the main tasks giving a breakdown of the "process" slot in the previous worksheet OM-2. Each task listed is concluded by a go/no-go decision before the next product development task may commence. For any new product introduction on the market (many dozens every year), all tasks must have been concluded successfully, in the indicated sequential order. All tasks are in their own way knowledge intensive, especially the feasibility phase and to a lesser extent the planning phase. This is because the subtasks in these phases necessitate a more experimental approach and therefore tend to be iterative; the more knowledge is applied in the first cycle, the less iterations are needed. We note that here only the top-level task breakdown of the product development process has been presented. Every task mentioned in worksheet OM-3 is in its turn decomposed into a dozen or so subtasks. In the PARIS project they were specified in similar worksheets, but in this case study we can only consider a small fragment of them.

OM-4: Example knowledge assets in the ice-cream domain   The fourth worksheet, OM-4, gives a description of the main knowledge assets in the part of the organization we

Organization Model	Variant Aspects Worksheet OM-2
STRUCTURE	See Figure 3.10
PROCESS	Product development process: involves five major phases. See high-level breakdown in worksheet OM-3 (Table 3.13)
PEOPLE	Wide range of functional areas is involved in product development: e.g., marketing, sales, logistics, quality management, operations planning, manufacturing, and the legal department
RESOURCES	* *Information systems*: existing system for storage of ice-cream formulations, capable of making certain predictive calculations of product properties, used as a tool for product development managers * ...
KNOWLEDGE	Linked to the different functional areas listed above, evidently wider than product development *sec*
CULTURE & POWER	* Focus on features of own market * Local cross-functional interplay between marketing, process technology and operations people

Table 3.12
Worksheet OM-2: Description of variant organization aspects of an ice-cream factory.

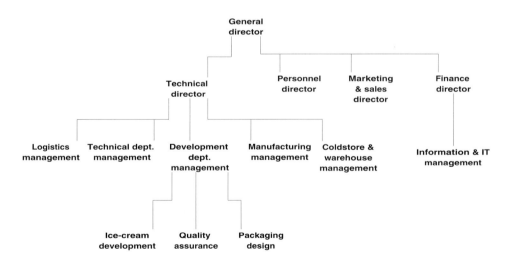

Figure 3.10
A typical organization structure of an ice-cream company.

Organization Model	Process Breakdown Worksheet OM-3					
NO.	TASK	PER-FORMED BY	WHERE?	KNOWL-EDGE ASSET	KNOWLEDGE INTENSIVE?	SIGNIFI-CANCE
1	Product idea genera-tion	Marketing, develop-ment (mainly)	–	New product-market combina-tions	Yes	Any new product must subsequently pass all listed tasks successfully
2	Feasibil-ity phase	Develop-ment core team formed from several departments	–	Concept de-velopment, experimen-tation, and testing	Very high	See above
3	Produc-tion and sales planning	Packaging, manufactur-ing (and others)	–	Capabilities evaluation, experimen-tation, and planning	High	See above
4	Imple-menta-tion and rollout	Manufactur-ing, packaging, quality, training, marketing	–	Operations expertise for the various functional areas	Yes	See above
5	Post-launch review	Various	–	Evaluation, standards confor-mance	Medium	See above

Table 3.13
Worksheet OM-3: Top-level task breakdown for the ice-cream product development process.

are focusing on. In Table 3.14 a small fragment is shown of the knowledge asset analysis related to the feasibility task within the product development process. The task typically requires knowledge from a number of different areas, and moreover it is performed by staff from different departments. Thus, communication and sharing of knowledge is highly im-portant, the more so because ice-cream products are becoming increasingly complex. This is why ice-cream processing knowledge (mixing, freezing, extrusion, etc.) is sometimes at the wrong place — available at one department, but needed at another one. Furthermore, ice-cream processing knowledge is often heuristic, experiential, and incomplete, so that its quality is an issue. In contrast, finished product specifications can be clearly nailed down, but a more appropriate and faster form (more electronic, less paper-based) would facilitate knowledge sharing.

Organization Model		Knowledge Assets Worksheet OM-4					
KNOWL-EDGE ASSET	POS-SESSED BY	USED IN	RIGHT FORM?	RIGHT PLACE?	RIGHT TIME?	RIGHT QUALITY?
Concept develop-ment and testing: ice-cream processing	Manufac-turing	2. Feasibility phase	Yes	No (needed at Devel-opment)	Yes	No (in-complete, heuristic)
...	...	...	...	...	...	...
Concept develop-ment and testing: finished product specifica-tion	Develop-ment core team	2. Feasibility phase	No: paper form too limited	Yes	Yes	Yes

Table 3.14
Worksheet OM-4: An excerpt from the knowledge assets analysis.

OM-5: First decision document: Knowledge-improvement scenarios   The final work-sheet of the organization model, OM-5, intends to indicate the feasibility of potential so-lutions to perceived organizational problems. In the present case, the stakeholder-oriented process approach combined with the ice-cream organization model led, first, to a clear identification of the main knowledge bottlenecks and, second, to a number of *different* op-portunities for knowledge improvement. It was concluded that especially the feasibility phase of ice-cream product development was highly knowledge-intensive, with knowledge bottlenecks related to properties (e.g., sensory, physical) of raw materials and of products, and related to ice-cream processing and associated equipment. The most important goals for knowledge management and IT/knowledge system development were defined to be the speedup of the time to market of new products, and (consequently) the quick dissemination of knowledge across different functional departments involved in product development.

To this end, the PARIS project group came up with different knowledge-improvement opportunities, called scenarios. These scenarios refer to different aspects of ice-cream product development, and carry corresponding names. Among them there was a process-ing scenario (make explicit the effects of processing on product properties), an optimization scenario (provide procedures to optimize one or more parameters in the whole product for-mulation), a supply chain scenario (design a system to follow one ice-cream brand through the whole process chain from raw materials sourcing to final product storage and distribu-tion), knowledge transfer scenario (create methods for quicker dissemination of research knowledge to the business units), and so on.

Organization Model	Checklist for Feasibility Decision Document: Worksheet OM-5
BUSINESS FEASIBILITY	Based on the organization-model analysis, the most important knowledge bottlenecks in product development have been clarified. In addition, a number of different scenarios for knowledge improvement opportunities have been identified for product development, e.g., a processing scenario, optimization scenario, supply chain scenario, internal knowledge transfer scenario. Each scenario represents a promising, feasible (to varying degrees), but different solution direction.
TECHNICAL FEASIBILITY	An important requirement is that any new system, including knowledge-based modules, has to fit into the overall IT strategy and must be interoperable with currently used tools. This is a reason to consider an upgrade of the existing product formulation and development tool. As any new IT system will make key business knowledge more explicit and available in a rather centralized way, very sound security measures are crucial.
PROJECT FEASIBILITY	Due to the stakeholder-driven approach, there is good basis for further work. To maintain support, it is advisable to develop and demonstrate a first knowledge module that demonstrates limited but visible results at an early stage.
PROPOSED ACTIONS	* Further rank and prioritize the knowledge improvement scenarios, by detailed task/agent/knowledge item analysis, leading to both short-term and mid-term recommendations and actions. * Consider how the current IT architecture can be gradually extended to a broader and more knowledge-intensive support environment. * Select a first system module with a high potential impact that can be developed relatively quickly.

Table 3.15
Worksheet OM-5: First decision document, comprising various feasible knowledge-improvement scenarios for product development.

As an outcome of this part of the study, a decision was taken to further refine, assess, and prioritize the suggested knowledge-improvement scenarios, and to select a first knowledge module for rapid development and demonstration. This further detailing and decision-making was done on the basis of task/agent modelling.

3.6.2 Ice-Cream Task/Agent Modelling

From the ice-cream organization model study it became clear that all tasks in product development are knowledge-rich, but this conclusion turned out to be particularly strong for the feasibility phase task within the product development process. Therefore, we consider the task model for this feasibility task in greater detail. The task model has two associated worksheets. The first, TM-1, gives a refined task decomposition and analysis. The second worksheet, TM-2, takes a closer look at the knowledge items involved in the task. Both worksheets are similar to, but more detailed than, the corresponding worksheets OM-3 and OM-4 of the organization model.

Task Model	Task Analysis Worksheet TM-1
TASK	2. Feasibility phase task
ORGANIZATION	Part of the ice-cream product development process; different departments involved (see Table 3.12, Table 3.13, and Figure 3.10)
GOAL AND VALUE	This task aims to establish the feasibility (in terms of both product properties, processing requirements, packaging, and marketing needs) of a new product idea, by turning this into an finished and agreed-upon product specification. This task is a necessary (but not sufficient) precondition for new product introduction to the market.
DEPENDENCY AND FLOW	*Input tasks*: Product idea generation *Output tasks*: Production and sales planning For task decomposition and flow: see Figure 3.11
OBJECTS HANDLED	*Input objects*: Marketing brief *Output objects*: Finished product specifications *Internal objects*: See Figure 3.11
TIMING AND CONTROL	*Frequency*: In the order of dozens of times per year, but variable *Duration:* Several months, but variable *Control*: See Figure 3.11; for each new product this task *must* be carried out. *Constraints*: National legal requirements must be satisfied, including environmental and safety regulations
AGENTS	From various functional areas; cf. OM-2 and OM-3 for examples
KNOWLEDGE AND COMPETENCE	Variety of domains; cf. OM-4 and TM-2 for examples
RESOURCES	Time is a resource of prime importance here, particularly because trials for product and production testing are by their nature highly iterative and time-consuming
QUALITY AND PERFORMANCE	ISO 9000 standards (e.g., development, production); environmental life-cycle analysis (LCA) indicators (e.g., packaging)

Table 3.16
Worksheet TM-1: Analysis of the "feasibility phase" task within the ice-cream product development business process.

TM-1: Business task decomposition and analysis   Worksheet TM-1 in Table 3.16 *zooms in* on the feasibility task, numbered 2 in the product development process breakdown of worksheet OM-3 (Table 3.13). The task structure of the feasibility phase is depicted in Figure 3.11, which again brings out the cross-functional nature of ice-cream product development.

TM-2: Detailed knowledge bottleneck analysis   In the task model we also take a closer look at the knowledge assets involved in the task. Worksheet TM-2 is used for this purpose (it speaks of knowledge items, which are just further detailed knowledge assets of smaller grain size; there is no principal difference). In this worksheet we characterize the nature of a knowledge item in terms of attributes related to nature, form, and availability of the knowledge. In the feasibility phase task, many different knowledge items are involved. We already saw a few examples in worksheet OM-4 (Table 3.14). For every knowledge item

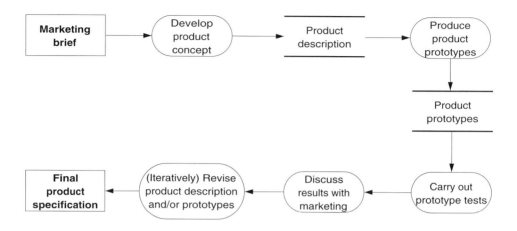

Figure 3.11
Flow diagram for the subtasks of the feasibility phase task within ice-cream product development.

in a task, a separate worksheet TM-2 is needed. In Table 3.17 we show one instance of this worksheet for the knowledge item "consumer desires."

As remarked previously in this chapter, the agent model rearranges organization and task information from the perspective of the implications for a specific agent or actor. For space reasons, we do not discuss the ice-cream agent model here. Instead, based on the TM-1 and TM-2 task model results it was possible to rank and prioritize the different knowledge-improvement scenarios listed in worksheet OM-5 (Table 3.15). The results of the scenario comparison are given in Table 3.18.

OTA-1: Decision summary of recommendations and actions   We complete the CommonKADS context analysis for ice-cream product development with worksheet OTA-1. It summarizes the proposed organizational recommendations, improvements, and actions. The worksheet for the ice-cream case is shown in Table 3.19. From the comparison of knowledge-improvement scenarios in Table 3.18, it appears that the processing and optimization scenarios are the most promising ones. Hence, the short-term recommendations (A and B in Table 3.19) were directed toward this. Also, a number of longer-term recommendations emerged from the study (e.g., C and D in Table 3.19; a number of other recommendations made are not shown here). With the decision-making baseline contained in worksheet OTA-1, underpinned by the organization, task, and agent models, and related support documentation (interviews, data, reports), the CommonKADS context analysis is concluded, and ready for decision-making. In the ice-cream case study, the context analysis documents were complemented by a follow-up draft project charter and contract (see the

Task Model	Knowledge Item Worksheet TM-2
NAME	Consumer desires
POSSESSED BY	Marketing, research
USED IN	2. Feasibility phase
DOMAIN	Ice-cream consumer marketing

Nature of the knowledge		Bottleneck / to be improved?
Formal, rigorous		
Empirical, quantitative	X	
Heuristic, rules of thumb	X	
Highly specialized, domain-specific	X	
Experience-based	X	
Action-based		
Incomplete	X	X
Uncertain, may be incorrect	X	
Quickly changing	X	
Hard to verify	X	X
Tacit, hard to transfer	X	X
Form of the knowledge		
Mind	X	X
Paper		
Electronic		
Action skill		
Other		
Availability of knowledge		
Limitations in time		
Limitations in space	X	X
Limitations in access		
Limitations in quality	X	X
Limitations in form		
Remarks: Consumer desires constitute a difficult area for several reasons: (i) how to find out what the consumer actually wants; (ii) how to identify and interpret consumer desires; (iii) how they relate to properties of the ice-cream product.		

Table 3.17
Worksheet TM-2: Characterization of the "consumer desires" knowledge item.

final part of Figure 3.9). These summarized the impacts of the proposed knowledge system module on the organization from a business perspective, in a form suitable for presentation to and assessment by the project stakeholders.

Some PARIS afterthoughts   After this feasibility and improvement study, the decision was taken to build a knowledge system module as proposed. The focus of this PARIS system was on ice-cream processing knowledge for product developers, and several trials were run with end users. A case study confirmed that the system could lead to a reduction

First module opportunity	Available knowledge	Technical feasibility	Potential benefits	Costs	Risks
Processing scenario	Good	Good	Good	Medium	Low
...	...	...	...	...	...
Optimization scenario	Medium	Medium / poor	Good	High	Medium
...	...	...	...	...	...
Supply chain scenario	Medium / poor	Medium	Poor	Medium	High
Knowledge transfer scenario	Good	Good	Unknown	High	Medium

Table 3.18
Comparison of knowledge-improvement scenarios in the ice-cream case, based on task and knowledge asset analysis.

Organization-Task-Agent Models	Checklist for Impact and Improvement Decision Document: Worksheet OTA-1
IMPACTS AND CHANGES IN ORGANIZATION	For proposals A and B below, meant as short-term recommendations, these are relatively limited. Proposals C and D, intended for the midterm, require the setup of a proper archive maintenance process (C), and the design of new cross-site team meetings and reporting (D).
TASK/AGENT-SPECIFIC IMPACTS AND CHANGES	Product developers may have to take on new knowledge-archiving and maintenance tasks. Members of cross-site teams will have new knowledge-sharing and reporting tasks, which takes time off their earlier, normal duties.
ATTITUDES AND COMMITMENTS	The short-term proposals have been positively received. The midterm recommendations need further investigation in this regard, because they bring with them new duties for various parties.
PROPOSED ACTIONS	A. Develop a first knowledge module for ice-cream processing, so that product developers can consider manufacturing knowledge upfront in concept development. B. Start preparations for the addition of an optimization function to the existing (conventional) product development tool. C. Archive past formulations and the experiences with them in electronic form. D. Develop structured knowledge management approaches to facilitate knowledge sharing in multidisciplinary, cross-site teams.

Table 3.19
Worksheet OTA-1: Summary of organizational recommendations and actions in the ice-cream case.

of needed tests in product development, thus saving time in line with the original goal. A less anticipated result of PARIS was that less experienced developers were quite pleased with the system, as a result of having so much "knowledge at your fingertips." In hindsight, one of the knowledge engineers involved in the PARIS project concluded that the fundamental stakeholder-driven approach was a crucial choice. No system project can do without organization analysis and support if it intends to be successful. One of the conclusions drawn from the PARIS project is that this stakeholder-oriented approach must be proactively continued also during systems design and even after installment and handover. Namely, organizations are dynamic entities, people regularly move to different jobs, and so the organizational support for IT systems activities must be actively maintained all along the way.

3.7 Guidelines for the Context Modelling Process

To summarize, organizational aspects often constitute the critical success factor for the introduction of knowledge systems. Envisaged systems must be well-integrated within the overall business process, and accepted in their task as knowledge provider by the user. In this chapter, we have shown how task and organization analysis is applied for this purpose. This has been illustrated by some real-life case studies. Also Chapter 10 contains a full-fledged case study.

For this analysis, the CommonKADS methodology offers three models: the organization, task, and agent models. These models provide a solid basis for decision-making, first, concerning opportunities offered by and the feasibility of envisaged knowledge-system solutions, and second, concerning specific impacts on and measures to be taken by the organization to improve the use of knowledge.

The process of building these models proceeds in a number of small steps. First, a scoping and feasibility study is carried out:

a. identifying problem/opportunity areas and potential solutions, and putting them into a wider organizational perspective;
b. deciding about economic, technical, and project feasibility, in order to select the most promising focus area and target solution.

The CommonKADS organization model provides the tool for this scoping and feasibility analysis. Subsequently, an impact and improvement study, for the selected target area and solution is undertaken:

a. gathering insights into the interrelationships between the task, agents involved, and use of knowledge for successful performance, and what improvements may be achieved here;
b. deciding about organizational measures and task changes, to ensure organizational acceptance and integration of a knowledge-system solution.

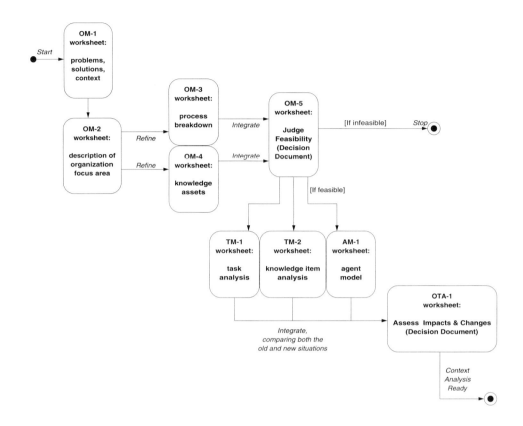

Figure 3.12
A road map for carrying out knowledge-oriented organization and task analysis.

As tools for this part of the analysis, CommonKADS offers the task and agent models. Building all of these models is done by following a series of small steps supported by practical and easy-to-use worksheets and checklists. In this way, a comprehensive picture of how an organization uses its knowledge is built up. Constructing in this way a *knowledge atlas* of the organization starts with an understanding of the broader organizational context. Then, we progressively zoom in on the promising knowledge-intensive organizational processes, guided by previous modelling results all along the line. This enables, as well as requires flexible knowledge project management.

A pictorial overview of the process of organizational context modelling is given in Figure 3.12. Accordingly, organization and task analysis constitutes in our opinion a key professional competence of knowledge engineers. From practical experience there are some good guidelines for the *process* of carrying out an organization and task study:

- Identify the stakeholders (knowledge providers, users, decision-makers) of your project at an early stage. Interview them, also separately. Learn to understand their perspectives and interests, to the extent that you can explain them to others.
- Consider the support that exists in the organization for proposed knowledge solutions. Clearly differentiate the interests from different stakeholder groups. You may do this by making an evaluation matrix, with the list of stakeholder groups as one dimension, and the list of possible knowledge solutions as the other. Explicate for yourself the different criteria that each stakeholder group will use to judge, support, or resist proposed changes and solutions. Be sensitive to the fact that some of this may be tacit: the unwritten rules of the game in the organization.
- Ask concrete, factual questions in interviews to clarify how tasks are carried out and what they require. Ask for and use concrete examples. You really understand a business process or task if you are able to write a script or scenario for it.
- Business process analysis is an important activity in knowledge projects, because here often lies the key to improvements. Process models can be understandably expressed by means of various types of flow diagrams or charts, such as IDEF diagrams or UML activity diagrams. Distinguish between the primary process leading to the main product or service of an organization, and secondary processes that have a support role.
- It is very helpful to indicate in process models what subprocess is carried out by what part of the organization. This can be achieved by making a matrix where the subprocesses are put along the horizontal axis, and the organization subparts along the vertical axis. Subsequently adding the flow connections between subprocesses then shows very clearly the working relationships between the subparts of the organization in the overall process.
- A similar matrix technique is helpful in evaluating how big or small the support within the organization is for alternative knowledge solutions. Put the organization subparts or stakeholders on the horizontal axis, and the evaluation criteria (as proposed by different stakeholders) on the vertical axis. Then put in the matrix cells the associated score, e.g., on a five-point scale (1 = very much against, 3 = neutral, 5 = strongly in favor). Such an evaluation matrix explicates very well the different views on alternative solutions and simplifies their ranking. An example of this technique is presented in a case study (Post et al. 1997). Include the existing situation as it is the main yardstick for comparison for most people.
- Focus on the added value of what you are doing. Always ask yourself the question: What difference would it make if we did this and this? Prioritize the things that give the most value with the least effort. Be on the lookout for small but visible results.
- Keep it simple. Organization and task analysis is a vast area. The CommonKADS steps and methods give a good framework, but you should not do everything. Pick out the

steps and pieces that are most useful to you in your project. Use the rest of the Com-monKADS methodology as a checklist so that you don't miss important things. This selective approach is a cornerstone of CommonKADS project management discussed later on in Chapter 15.

The results of the analysis as described in this chapter provide important inputs to other CommonKADS models, namely, the communication model (especially the agent information) and the knowledge model (in particular the task structure). In addition, the techniques and results of the present analysis can be imported to activities outside the knowledge-systems area. We have indicated the integrative links with quality assurance, process improvement, and conventional information-systems analysis. In the last case, for example, the task model provides a top-level information model (covering information object structure, function, and control), as we find it in information engineering and object-oriented methodologies.

Finally, the analysis in this chapter is extremely worthwhile in itself. Far beyond knowledge systems, it offers many practical insights into knowledge management in gen-eral, to achieve higher value and leverage from the knowledge in the organization.

3.8   Bibliographical Notes and Further Reading

The CommonKADS model for knowledge-oriented organizational analysis was first de-veloped by de Hoog et al. (1996). A full-blown and instructive case study not discussed in this book is provided by Post et al. (1997). The practical and useful worksheet techniques we present in this book are based directly on the further developments by the knowledge management unit of Unilever.

The CommonKADS approach intentionally combines and integrates ideas coming from various areas in organizational analysis and business administration. It has, for ex-ample, been influenced by soft systems methodology (Checkland and Scholes 1990), espe-cially in its thinking on how to come to a clear and agreed picture of what the real problems and opportunities in an organization are. In this regard, it is also useful to consult litera-ture on organizational learning, such as Argyris (1993). A good reader on many aspects of organizational strategy is Mintzberg & Quinn (1992). A standard text on organizational culture is Schein (1992). Interesting reading for knowledge engineers and managers is Scott-Morgan (1994), showing that not only is knowledge often tacit, but also that there are many social rules for decision-making and management within organizations.

CommonKADS aims to integrate organization process analysis and information anal-ysis. In many knowledge projects they are very hard to separate anyway. Practical ap-proaches to business process modelling and reengineering are proposed, e.g., in Johansson et al. (1993) and Watson (1994). The latter makes a clear link between thinking on business process reengineering and improvement, and total quality management which is reviewed concisely in Peratec (1994). Currently, most information systems methodologies are very limited in their consideration of wider organizational feasibility and benefits aspects. This still even holds for the very recent object-oriented approaches (Eriksson and Penker 1998). One of the very few exceptions is James Martin's Information Engineering approach (Martin 1990).

In job, task, and workplace analysis, there is, of course, also much existing work relevant to knowledge engineering and management, from the areas of organizational behavior (Harrison 1994), human resource management (Fletcher 1997), and ergonomics (Kirwan and Ainsworth 1992). Ideas and techniques from these areas you will find reflected in the CommonKADS task and agent modelling. All in all, CommonKADS contains a state-of-the-art organization and workplace analysis method, with a special emphasis on the knowledge aspects and on its integration with modern information modelling.

4

Knowledge Management

Key points of this chapter:

- How knowledge management and knowledge engineering can be seamlessly linked by using parts of the CommonKADS model suite.
- Some do's and don'ts for carrying out the three main knowledge management activities.
- What knowledge engineering can contribute to knowledge management, and vice versa.

4.1 Introduction

Organization and task analysis are knowledge-engineering activities that directly hook up with business administration and managerial aspects. A recent field that has emerged in business administration is knowledge management. It takes knowledge as a central subject for organizational decision-making in its own right, and attempts to deal with the management control issues regarding leveraging knowledge. In this chapter, we give a brief sketch of some central concepts in knowledge management and indicate how they are related to features of the CommonKADS methodology. To understand the basics is important for knowledge engineers and system builders, because knowledge engineering and knowledge management touch or even overlap each other at several points.

4.2 Explicit and Tacit Knowledge

In the area of knowledge management, it has been pointed out — based upon old work in philosophy, by the way — that a large part of knowledge is not explicit but *tacit*. That is,

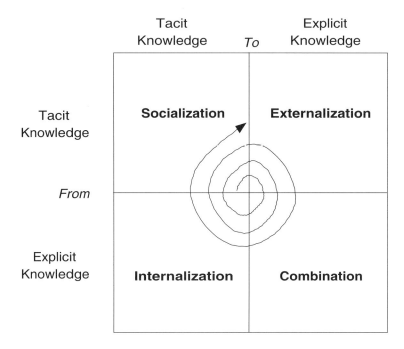

Figure 4.1
Nonaka's model of the dynamics of knowledge creation, built upon the distinction between explicit and tacit knowledge.

knowledge is often not explicitly describable by the people who possess it, nor is it easy to explain and to formalize in books or manuals. Instead, it is a "background" capability, partly unconscious and stemming from experience, that is used in problem-solving and other human tasks. Knowledge is knowledge in action. As Hugh Cottam, a researcher in knowledge acquisition, phrased it: "You may know more than you think!"

In their book *The Knowledge-Creating Company*, Nonaka and Takeuchi (1995) have built a whole theory about knowledge and its creation, on the basis of this distinction between tacit and explicit knowledge. As shown in Figure 4.1, four modes of knowledge production are identified:

1. from tacit to tacit knowledge (= socialization): we can teach each other by showing rather than speaking about the subject matter;

2. from tacit to explicit knowledge (= externalization): knowledge-intensive practices are clarified by putting them down on paper, formulate them in formal procedures, and the like;

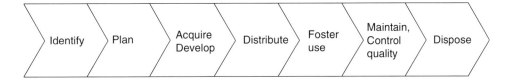

Figure 4.2
Activities in knowledge management and the associated knowledge-value chain.

3. from explicit to explicit knowledge (= combination): creating knowledge through the integration of different pieces of explicit knowledge;
4. from explicit to tacit knowledge (= internalization): performing a task frequently leads to a personal state where we can carry out a task successfully without thinking about it.

According to these authors, organizational knowledge creation continuously needs all four types of knowledge production. The aim of knowledge management is to properly facilitate and stimulate these knowledge processes, so that an upward, dynamic spiral of knowledge emerges. In such a view, knowledge engineering as discussed in this book is a methodology especially useful in "externalization," that is, converting tacit into explicit knowledge. This is a unique feature of knowledge engineering, because there is hardly any other mature scientific methodology capable of externalizing tacit knowledge. Also, the combination of knowledge is well supported in knowledge engineering, e.g., through libraries of reusable task and domain models. The importance of tacit knowledge is nowadays widely acknowledged in knowledge engineering and management.

4.3   The Knowledge Management Cycle

Today, there are many frameworks for knowledge management around. They all have in common their intention to cover the complete *life cycle of knowledge* within the organization. Typically, the following activities with respect to knowledge and its management are distinguished by many authors (see Figure 4.2).

*   *Identify* internally and externally existing knowledge.
*   *Plan* what knowledge will be needed in the future.
*   *Acquire* and/or *develop* the needed knowledge.
*   *Distribute* the knowledge to where it is needed.
*   *Foster the application* of knowledge in the business processes of the organization.

- *Control* the quality of knowledge and *maintain* it.
- *Dispose* of knowledge when it is no longer needed.

Thus, a simple, but very practical definition of knowledge management is: a framework and tool set for *improving the organization's knowledge infrastructure, aimed at getting the right knowledge to the right people in the right form at the right time*. Although this book is not on knowledge management per se, the CommonKADS knowledge engineering methodology does offer a number of practical instruments in this direction, particularly the techniques for knowledge-oriented organization and task analysis, and the methods to enhance knowledge sharing and reuse.

Obviously, knowledge management is not a one-shot activity. Authors see knowledge management as embedded in a cyclic model of the *learning organization*. This is based, for example, on Argyris' model of "double-loop" organizational learning — the first loop is direct learning about an application, product, or activity; the second loop runs on top of that and is learning about knowledge and learning itself — whereby the mission, goals, and strategy of the organization act as the driving force. Knowledge management helps the organization to obtain feedback and continuously learn from its own experiences, on the basis of which it improves its knowledge infrastructure for the future.

Accordingly, the listed knowledge-process activities form the elements of a coherent whole, called the *knowledge-value chain*, and depicted in Figure 4.2. This is in analogy to the famous value chain, proposed by Michael Porter (1985). Here, an organization is considered as consisting of a collection of activities jointly aimed at the creation of value, which is embodied in products and services that are appreciated by its customers. In this value-chain concept, knowledge management is a support activity focusing on facilitating and improving the application of organizational knowledge.

4.4   Knowledge Management Has a Value and Process Focus

Figure 4.3 sketches the wider context of knowledge and its management within the organization. As outlined previously, knowledge is a prime enabler to successfully carry out the business processes within the organization, which in turn create value for the recipients of its products and services. The formulation of a knowledge-management strategy follows the opposite, *outside-in* direction. It starts by considering the value-creation goals of the organization, and how this value is delivered by the organization's business processes. Knowledge assets are those bodies of knowledge that the organization employs in its processes to deliver value. The knowledge management question then is what actions are useful for increasing the leverage of the knowledge underlying these processes. Knowledge engineering as discussed in this book is one of the instruments available for this purpose.

A very wide range of managerial actions to enhance the flow and leverage of knowledge are conceivable. Many case studies, such as those done in industries in Japan, show

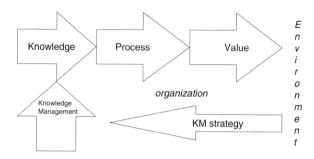

Figure 4.3
Knowledge management in relation to the business processes and value creation by the organization.

the importance of creating multifunctional and cross-disciplinary teams to build a richer knowledge base for innovative product design. In some cases, knowledge is concentrated within special expertise centers in order to achieve a sufficient critical mass, e.g., in emerging advanced technology areas.

In other cases, knowledge is spread out, by reallocating specialist knowledge from headquarters to small local offices by means of decision support systems: this has been done, for example, by banking and insurance companies in Europe, in order to better and more quickly serve the local customer with financial services such as loans and mortgages. Research organizations rethink and redesign their "knowledge logistics," seeking new ways of transferring their knowledge to target groups and taking advantage of the new opportunities for attractive visualization of information on the Internet and its World Wide Web. Here, information gathering is supported by intelligent software agents that assist us as a kind of knowledge broker. US-based internationally operating enterprises have installed knowledge repositories, for example, in the form of a distributed database of projects carried out and lessons learned, in order to strengthen worldwide management consulting.

Other forms of organizational memory enhancing knowledge sharing exist in libraries of reusable model fragments, information, and software components, to facilitate assembly of new information systems (this book devotes a special chapter to this topic), speed up engineering design studies, and reduce time to market. Automotive companies have created new knowledge feedback loops by organizing special regular meetings with their car dealers and customers, the results of which are then used in car redesign. Yet other organizations experiment with network-oriented, so-called virtual organizations speeding up the flow of knowledge, for example, in faster creation of new customer services and strengthening its competitive position in a deregulating energy utility market. Knowledge systems based on top-level specialist expertise act as task assistants at different geographical locations of food-processing plants, to disseminate best practices, and achieve top-quality standardization. And so on.

When we look at this great, perhaps even bewildering, variety, it is clear that there is no silver bullet in knowledge management. But although this is a young field, there are several clear lessons to be learned from the experience of organizations at the forefront of knowledge-based thinking. Here are a number of them.

- **The new truism: Knowledge is a key asset, but it is often tacit and private.** The knowledge manager's challenge is to deal with the fact that knowledge is an *organizational* asset, and at the same time mostly resides in *individual* people. Moreover, in contrast to assets like plants and buildings, human knowledge assets are mobile and may easily walk away at 5 o'clock (to their home or to the nearest competitor). Knowledge management and engineering actions should therefore not have a mechanistic or bureaucratic nature. Instead, they have to be people-oriented.
- **Knowledge is not what you *know* but it is what you *do*!** The notion of asset can be a bit deceiving, as it has a passive "just-sitting-there" connotation like a plant. Instead, we repeatedly stress the nature of knowledge as a potential for *action*. Knowledge can realize its value only when it is used. What knowledge is depends on the context of use.
- **Creating knowledge pull instead of information push: Knowledge management has an outside-in, value, and process focus.** The information society and its new technological capabilities have a tendency to overload us with information. The information society may well begin to develop the signs of a new disease: information infarction. Knowledge management needs to counteract this danger by introducing selectivity and enhancing focus, a point already discussed (cf. Figure 4.3). Basic communication of information is not sufficient, and may even lead to overload, if it is not supplemented with goal-oriented sharing of experience and expertise. Knowledge management often has a bottom-up orientation in order to become practically successful, creating and sustaining pull derived from ongoing application project needs.
- **Knowledge transfer is not just handing over something: There is no such thing as a knowledge-burger.** Knowledge has traditionally been viewed as an attribute of competent people, rather than as an entity in itself. The latter view (that we also adhere to in this book) is quite recent, linked as it is to reflections about the impact of the Information Age. It is a step forward, but the knowledge-as-a-substance view also has its limitations and dangers. Knowledge is not like a hamburger you can just produce at one place and hand over at another. Many failed knowledge and technology transfer projects are witness to the fact that you cannot treat knowledge as a thing you throw over the wall.
- **The knowledge exchange mechanism: Knowledge sharing = communication + knowledge *re*creation.** Much more appropriate than a simplistic transport or sender-receiver view on knowledge transfer, is the idea of knowledge sharing. Transfer is bet-

ter thought of in terms of coproduction or comakership of knowledge. This is reason to stress the importance of multifunctional and multidisciplinary teamwork in knowledge-intensive organizations. Similar experiences are reported by so-called virtual organizations, where different companies at different locations form a network to achieve a joint goal. In knowledge engineering, experience has led to discarding the old idea that knowledge can be "mined" as jewels out of the expert's head. Rather, knowledge engineering is a constructive and collaborative activity in which modelling of knowledge is central.

- **Knowledge management is about facilitating knowledge sharing by** *people*. **It is about increasing their connectivity.** This is what you will hear many experienced knowledge managers say. Simple bottom-up measures will often do the job. Most see knowledge management as a *lightweight* activity that balances soft and hard aspects. It has a facilitatory role, helping to create knowledge pull, instead of installing rigid structures ultimately giving rise to information overload.

Although this only sketches a high-level picture, it does give the general flavor of what knowledge management is.

4.5   Knowledge Management with CommonKADS

As has been said in the introduction and elsewhere, knowledge management can be seamlessly linked to knowledge engineering. Substantial parts of the CommonKADS models will be instantiated as a result of knowledge-management actions, thus reducing the need to develop them again in a knowledge-intensive system project. This also works the other way: in a knowledge-system project, building CommonKADS models will produce information that can be useful for knowledge-management purposes. The goal of this section is to elaborate on this link.

4.5.1   Basic Approach

Our basic approach to knowledge management is visualized in Figure 4.4. It distinguishes a *management* level and a knowledge *object* level. This is very similar to the distinction made between management-level activities and development work in knowledge projects (see Chapter 15).

The upper part, the knowledge-management level, comprises management tasks. When we see knowledge as a resource, then this level has to manage this resource, just as any other resource. Basically, this means that the resource has to be made available:

- at the right time;
- at the right place;
- in the right shape;

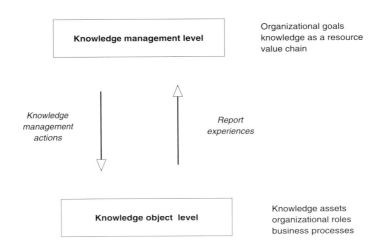

Figure 4.4
Knowledge management, like other management tasks, can be seen as a metalevel activity that acts on an object level.

- with the needed quality;
- against the lowest possible costs.

Knowledge as a resource has certain properties which make this management task rather different from managing physical, tangible resources (see Wiig et al. (1997b) for an enumeration of these properties). This justifies the existence of a separate discipline of knowledge management and knowledge engineering. Knowledge management initiates and executes knowledge-management actions which operate on the knowledge object level, consisting of knowledge assets, organizational roles, and business processes. It monitors the achievements through reports and observations.

To make knowledge management a viable enterprise, more flesh must be added to the skeletal model in Figure 4.4. This means describing a *process model* for the management level and an "object model" for the object level. Note that this is very similar to what CommonKADS does for knowledge engineering. The project management approach in Chapter 15 is the specification of the management level, while the models elaborated in Chapters 3, 5, 9, and 11 specify the project work level. For specifying the object level in knowledge management, large parts of the CommonKADS model suite can be reused.

Let us first present a model for the knowledge-management level. As depicted in Figure 4.5, knowledge management is a cyclic process, consisting of three different type of management activities: conceptualize, reflect, and act. Note that this is different from the model of Figure 4.2, not only in the activities it contains but also in its cyclic nature. We discuss the three main activities in some detail later on.

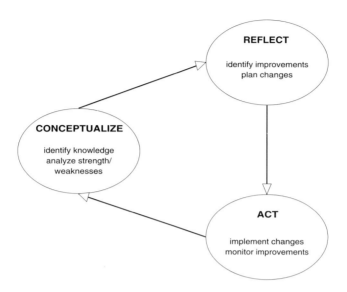

Figure 4.5
Knowledge management consists of a cyclic execution of three main activities: conceptualize, reflect, and act.

The knowledge object level is defined in Figure 4.6. The three main components making up the knowledge object level — agents, business processes, and knowledge assets — are shown. The knowledge-management actions indicated in Figure 4.4 will effect changes in one or more of these components: in practice most actions will affect all three. These actions will aim at improvements in one or more of the quality criteria for resources mentioned above. If we take the housing application, which will be elaborated in Chapter 10, we can see the building of that knowledge system as a knowledge-management action which will increase, for example, the quality of the knowledge and its availability in terms of time and place. The system will change the agents (some assets move from people to software, new agents are introduced), the business process (the way requests are handled), and features (form, nature) of the knowledge asset (housing allocation knowledge).

A closer look at this simple housing example shows that the components affected by the knowledge-management actions (the object level) to a large extent coincide with what is modelled by the CommonKADS models addressing the *context* of a knowledge system. This is indicated in Figure 4.6 by the notes attached to agents, business process, and knowledge assets. They refer precisely to those elements from the CommonKADS model suite which can be linked to knowledge management. The organization model will show the resulting change in people and (possibly) structure; the agent model will deal with new agents; the organization model and task model will reflect the change in the process and

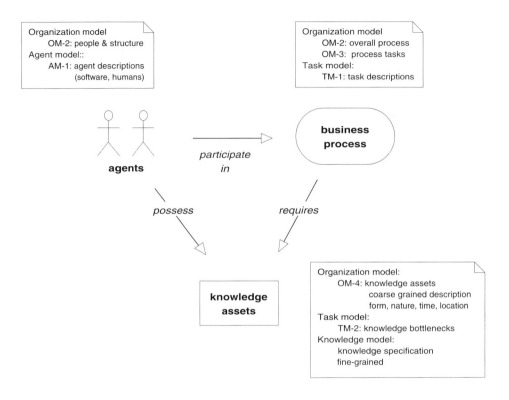

Figure 4.6
Knowledge-management actions are defined in terms of three objects: agents that possess knowledge assets and participate in the business process. The notes indicate which parts of the CommonKADS models describe these objects.

the resolved knowledge bottlenecks. The housing application does not lead to a new fine-grained knowledge specification, but in many cases this will happen. This in turn can be part of Nonaka's model of model creation: the move from tacit to explicit knowledge (see Figure 4.1). This implies, in our terminology, that the knowledge has changed its form.

What has been said here emphasizes the seamless linking of knowledge management and knowledge engineering. However, it should be kept in mind that, although linked, they are still essentially different because they are attached to organizational roles with a different scope, purview, and discretion. Confusing knowledge management and knowledge engineering is not a good idea. Building knowledge systems (whether based on explicit knowledge representation or on machine-learning techniques) is not to be portrayed as coinciding with knowledge management.

Knowledge systems should be viewed as tools for knowledge management. They offer potential solutions to knowledge resource problems detected, analyzed, and prioritized by knowledge management. The resulting action, building a knowledge system, is "delegated" to knowledge engineering. This is visualized in Figure 2.6 where there is a clear distinction between the "knowledge manager" and the "project manager." If you wonder in Chapter 15 where the management reports from the project manager will be sent to, than the answer is the knowledge manager. These are the reports shown in Figure 4.4.

However, a strong point of the CommonKADS methodology is that the models indicated in Figure 4.6 can be *shared* between the knowledge manager and the project manager, and in a wider sense between all agents shown in Figure 2.6. In this way they create a common ground, thus counteracting one of the most destructive tendencies in any human endeavor, not understanding what the other means. In addition it reduces redoing work: filling parts of models can be done either from the knowledge-management side or from the knowledge-engineering side. But as both sides need them for their work, there is no need to redo filling parts of models, when it has already been done by the other side.

Thus, the main link between knowledge management and knowledge engineering is found at the knowledge object level. For the management level the similarities are far less, which is to be expected, since managing knowledge is definitely not the same as managing a knowledge-system development project.

The main model for the management-level activities in knowledge management is the cycle depicted in Figure 4.5. Below we briefly discuss the three main activities in this cycle.

4.5.2   Conceptualize

The main goals of the conceptualize activity are to get a view on the knowledge in the organization and its strong and weak points. The first goal will be served by filling the knowledge object level, while the second can be supported by bottleneck analysis based on a closer inspection of the properties of the knowledge assets involved. In carrying out this activity most of the guidelines from Chapter 3 can be applied. However, from the knowledge-management perspective a few must be added.

Guideline 4-1:   FIND A PROPER SCOPE FOR THE CONCEPTUALIZATION
Rationale: As knowledge management is far less constrained than building knowledge-systems, there is a danger that without a good scoping the activity will go on without clear purpose or end, because only rarely can "everything" be described. Good starting points for scoping are initial bottlenecks, new business opportunities, and human resource problems.

Guideline 4-2:   CHOOSE THE PROPER LEVEL OF DETAIL
Rationale: For knowledge-management purposes it is almost never necessary to go into too much detail. This holds in particular for analyzing the knowledge. Generally speaking the coarse-grained level in worksheet TM-2 will be sufficient

Guideline 4-3:   BE AWARE OF "HIDDEN" KNOWLEDGE
Rationale: There is not a straightforward relation between the visibility of knowledge and its importance. This holds especially for "informal" knowledge that everybody takes for granted.

Guideline 4-4:   NEVER RELY ON A SINGLE SOURCE WHEN TRYING TO LINK KNOWL-EDGE TO AGENTS
Rationale: People don't know always what other people know. A simple technique for dealing with this issue is network analysis: asking people where they turn to when they have a problem they can't solve.

Guideline 4-5:   BEAUTY IS IN THE EYE OF THE BEHOLDER
Rationale: When analyzing strong and weak points there is not a single universally valid point of view to take. Alternate between different viewpoints; this will certainly bring new insights.

Guideline 4-6:   SOME QUANTIFICATION IS BETTER THAN NO QUANTIFICATION AT ALL
Rationale: Though quantification of the value of knowledge is notoriously hard, put some effort into obtaining statements that go beyond gut feeling. Even with simple procedures one can achieve better insights into this area. As a minimum, require and deliver justifications for opinions of the type, "This knowledge is indispensable to the organization."

4.5.3 Reflect

The activity of conceptualization will produce a set of bottlenecks, problems, opportunities, weaknesses, and so on, for which improvements must be identified. When not everything can be realized at the same time, priorities must be set. After the choice has been made, improvement plans should be devised. At this point, knowledge management starts to diverge from knowledge engineering. This is stressed in some of the guidelines below.

Guideline 4-7:   TAKE A MAXIMUM DISTANCE FROM METHODOLOGIES SUCH AS COMMONKADS
Rationale: This sounds strange, but it serves to prevent a bias toward knowledge-system solutions that may be associated with using elements of the CommonKADS methodology during the conceptualize activity.

Guideline 4-8:   AVOID THE TRAPDOORS OF "SOLVING THE WRONG PROBLEM" AND "SELECTING THE WRONG SOLUTION"
Rationale: For some reason there is a tendency to associate knowledge management with information technology, and this pernicious misconception spawns a bias toward solutions relying entirely on information technology. Take a look from the other side; a simpler, more effective, and cheaper solution might be there.

Guideline 4-9:   THERE ARE NO SILVER BULLETS
Rationale: Again, almost a truism, but the necessary companion of the previous one. Life, and in particular organizations and knowledge, are too complex to believe that one single measure will lead you into paradise. Don't believe it when someone tells you that your knowledge-sharing and -exchange problems can be solved by installing program XYZ on your network. It probably will generate more problems than it solves.

Guideline 4-10:   ABIDE BY MURPHY'S LAW
Rationale: The juiciest fruits are hardest to grasp. Only rarely will your improvements also be the ones that are easiest to implement. When planning your improvements be very aware of risks. There may be reasons to reject the preferred improvements because the risks are too high. Keep a keen eye on unexpected side effects.

Guideline 4-11:   SLEEP ON IT
Rationale: There is a wealth of psychological literature on the mistakes people can make when judging and deciding. It is good practice to review your reflect process on the undetected occurrence of these biases.

4.5.4   Act

Acting in the framework presented here means initiating the agreed- upon improvement plans and monitoring their progress. As knowledge management is tangential to many other management concerns in an organization, one should be very conscious of the boundaries of discretion involved. Knowledge management carries the seeds of becoming everything, which of course in the end will reduce it to nothing. Bordering disciplines are human resource management, knowledge engineering, information technology, and organizational consultancy, to name a few.

A simple example can clarify where boundaries can be set. From a knowledge-management perspective it may have been decided that in order to solve a knowledge problem or grasp a knowledge opportunity, some of the personnel have to be trained in a new knowledge area. In our view, organizing this training program (finding training staff, scheduling courses, allocating personnel) is the job of the human resources department (or if there is no such department, the person playing the role of human resources manager), whereas monitoring the progress of the courses and the effects on the knowledge in the organization belongs to the "act"ivity. In the same vein, the relation with knowledge engineering can be described; see again the differentiation in roles as shown in Figure 2.6. For the "act" part of the knowledge-management cycle some guidelines can be formulated.

Guideline 4-12:   GO FOR MEASURABLE OBJECTIVES
Rationale: The intangible nature of knowledge makes it easy to talk in vague terms about results. However, proper monitoring can only be done when there are clear yardsticks against which progress can be measured.

Guideline 4-13:   THINGS DO NOT RUN THEMSELVES
Rationale: Assign clear responsibilities and give clear briefs.   Carry out control on progress quite frequently.   It is a mistake to believe that all is said and done, after an action has been initiated.

4.6   Knowledge Management and Knowledge Engineering

Knowledge engineering and knowledge-systems have to be viewed and embedded in this perspective: knowledge engineering as a methodology to be used as one of the instruments, and knowledge systems as one of the important products to be used in knowledge management. Knowledge engineering as discussed in this book offers many useful concepts and methods for knowledge management. To name a few:

- Knowledge-oriented organization analysis helps to quickly map out fruitful areas for knowledge-management actions. The methods presented are very suitable for quick knowledge scans or audits, or for one-day workshops with responsible managers.
- Task and agent analysis has shown to be very useful for clarifying knowledge bottle necks in specific areas. It is not uncommon that these turn out to be different from the accepted wisdom in the organization. Techniques like these are relevant to business process redesign and improvement where knowledge work is involved. Because CommonKADS provides a gradual transition between business and information analysis, this is also key to a better integration of information technology into the organization.
- Knowledge engineering places strong emphasis on the conceptual modelling of knowledge-intensive activities. The often graphical techniques have proved to be very useful in clarifying the major tacit aspects of knowledge, in a (nontechnical, nonsystems) way enabling and stimulating fruitful communications with a variety of people (managers, specialists, end users, customers) who often do not have a background in information technology.
- The accumulated experience of knowledge engineering shows that there are many recurring structures and mechanisms in knowledge work. This has, for example, led to libraries of task models that are applicable across different domains. This approach offers many useful insights into constructing the reusable information architectures and software components that are increasingly needed in modern IT-based organizations.

Therefore, knowledge engineering has several different applications. The construction of knowledge systems is only one of them, albeit an important one. CommonKADS has also been used in knowledge-management quick scans and workshops, in IT strategy scoping and feasibility projects, and it further gives a sound support in the early stages of requirements elicitation and specification in systems projects. In all applications of knowledge engineering, the conceptual modelling of knowledge at different levels of detail is a central topic. This is the subject to which we now turn.

4.7   Bibliographical Notes and Further Reading

Knowledge management has received enormous attention over the last few years. This has led to "guru" books like Stewart (Stewart 1997) Drucker (1993) (see Chapter 1), books and articles focusing on guidelines and techniques of which there still only a few (Wiig 1996, Sveiby 1997, Edvinsson and Malone 1997, Wiig et al. 1997a, Tissen et al. 1998), books and articles with case studies (too many to mention), and "old wine in new bottles" publications (see, for example, conference proceedings of PAKM '96 (Wolf and Reimer 1996).

The basic approach in this chapter is taken from van der Spek and de Hoog (1994) (see also Wiig et al. (1997b), which was inspired by notions borrowed from CommonKADS). Some of the first theoretical notions can be found in van der Spek and Spijkervet (1994) and van der Spek and de Hoog (1994). The first explicit link between knowledge management and CommonKADS can be found in Benus and de Hoog (1994).

The theory of organizational knowledge processes, built upon the distinction between tacit and explicit knowledge, is discussed extensively in Nonaka and Takeuchi (1995), which also contains several interesting case studies on knowledge creation in industrial innovation processes. Some books out of the wave of recent general writings on knowledge management from the perspective of business administration are Davenport and Prusak (1998) and Tissen et al. (1998); see also the reading notes to Chapter 1. Many works emphasize the value orientation that knowledge management should have. The concept of the business-value chain was developed by Porter (1985). The knowledge-value chain as sketched in this chapter was taken from Weggeman (1996). That study is part of a collection containing a wide range of views from different fields concerning knowledge management, including information technology aspects. For a discussion of the relation between knowledge engineering and knowledge management, see Wielinga et al. (1997).

5

Knowledge Model Components

Key points of this chapter:

- Knowledge is a complex form of information.
- Analyzing and modelling knowledge requires specialized tools.
- The CommonKADS knowledge model is such a specialized tool.
- The knowledge model contains the building blocks for constructing a knowledge model: "task," "inference," "domain schema" and "knowledge base."
- A combined graphical-textual representation is provided for describing the knowledge model.

5.1 The Nature of "Knowledge"

"Knowledge" is a term of which all of us have a good intuitive understanding of what it means, but which is hard to define in any formal way. Many people have tried to come up with satisfactory definitions, but these seem to be at best good approximations.

Knowledge is closely related to "information." We would say that the fact that a patient has a temperature of 39.0°C is a piece of information, and that physicians have knowledge to derive from this fact that the patient has a fever. From a systems-engineering point of view, knowledge is probably best seen as a special type of information, namely "information about information." Knowledge tells us something about certain information items. A simple form of knowledge is incorporated in subclass hierarchies, which have become a common tool in data modelling. A subclass link between two classes provides us with information about two classes. Knowledge thus typically has an "aboutness" character: it tells us about the way to understand some other piece(s) of information.

Knowledge can often be used to *infer* new information. To stay with the previous example, a subclass link can be used to inherit information from the superclass to the subclass. This *generative* property of knowledge has been used by some as the feature distinguishing between knowledge and information, but in practice this is difficult. For example, is a formula for computing the sales tax knowledge? In this book we take the (somewhat simplified) position that there is no hard borderline between knowledge and information. Knowledge is "just" complex information, typically telling us something about other information.

5.2   Challenges in Representing Knowledge

Before diving into the detailed issues related to modelling knowledge, let's take a simple example. Consider a financial application concerned with providing loans to people. Two classes for this domain are shown in Figure 5.1 together with some typical attributes. The figure also illustrates the difference between information and knowledge. Information is typically that a person X has a loan Y. We would model this information with an information **type**, in this case something like a **has-loan** relation between **person** and **loan**. The figure also contains three statements that we intuitively would call knowledge. For example, all persons applying for a loan should be at least 18 years old. Note that the definition of knowledge as "information about information" holds here: the statements tell us something about the information stated above. The knowledge fragments tell us something about persons and loans *in general*, and not just about particular person-loan instances.

If we look a bit closer at the knowledge fragments in Figure 5.1, we can see that there are patterns in there. For example, the two "rules" about the relation between the amount of the loan and the height of the person's income have the same basic structure. One of the challenges for any knowledge-engineering methodology is to find appropriate ways of modelling knowledge in a schematic way. We do not just want to list all the possible pieces of knowledge, just as we do not list the contents of a database.

What we do not want is one large flat knowledge base containing all the rules. Instead, we are striving for a fine-grained structure in which we divide the knowledge base up into small partitions (e.g., rule sets) that share a similar structure (see Figure 5.2). This is a requirement for any form of useful knowledge analysis, validation, and maintenance. In this chapter we will see how this goal of structuring knowledge can be achieved.

5.3   The Knowledge Model

5.3.1   Role of the Knowledge Model

Detailed requirements engineering is split in CommonKADS into two parts. The knowledge model specifies the knowledge and reasoning requirements of the prospective system;

INFORMATION

John has a loan of $1,750
Harry has a loan of $2,500

KNOWLEDGE

A person with a loan should be at least 18 years old
A person with an income up to $10,000 can get a maximum loan of $2,000
A person with an income between $10,000 and $20,000 can get a maximum loan of $3,000

Figure 5.1
Two object classes in the loan domain with some corresponding information and knowledge items.

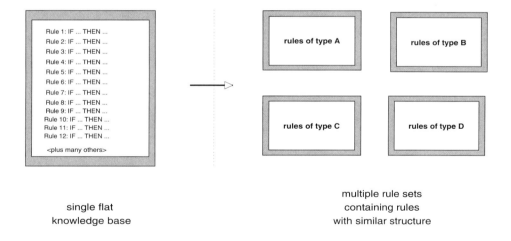

Figure 5.2
CommonKADS moves away from the idea of one large knowledge base. Instead, the purpose is to identify parts of the knowledge base in which the knowledge fragments (e.g., rules) share a similar structure.

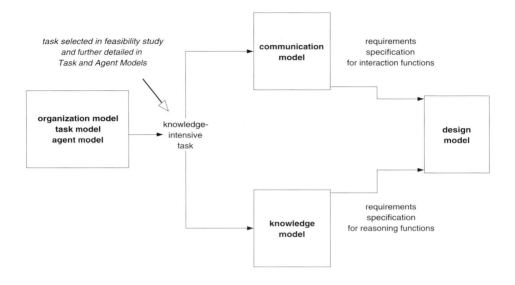

Figure 5.3
Schematic view of the role of the knowledge model in relation to the other models.

the communication model specifies the needs and desires with respect to the interfaces with other agents: i.e., a user interface or an interface with some software system. Together, the knowledge model and the communication model form the input for system design and implementation. Input for the knowledge-modelling process is a certain task identified in the organization model (see worksheet OM-3) and further detailed in the task model (see worksheets TM-1 and TM-2) and the agent model. We assume that the task selected is characterized as being knowledge intensive, and that formalization of the task and its related knowledge is considered a feasible enterprise from both a technical, economical and project perspective. Figure 5.3 gives a schematic view on the role of the knowledge model in relation to the other models.

The knowledge model itself is a tool that helps us clarifying the structure of a knowledge-intensive information-processing task. The knowledge model of an application provides a specification of the data and knowledge structures required for the application. The model is developed as part of the analysis process. It is therefore phrased in the vocabulary of the application, meaning both the domain (e.g., cars, houses, ships) and the reasoning task (e.g., assessment, configuration, diagnosis). The knowledge model does *not* contain any implementation-specific terms. These are left for the design phase. It is seen as essential that during analysis implementation-specific considerations are left out as much as possible. For example, when we talk during analysis about "rules," we mean the rules that the human experts talk about. Whether these natural rules are actually represented in the final system through a "rule" formalism, is purely a design issue, and not considered relevant during analysis. This clear separation frees the analyst from all worries concerning implementation-specific decisions. This requires, of course, that the analyst has a means of knowing that the knowledge models she writes down are "designable." This issue is addressed in more detail in Chapter 11.

The knowledge model has a structure that is in essence similar to traditional analysis models in software engineering. The reasoning task is described through a hierarchical decomposition of functions or "processes." The data and knowledge types that the functions operate on are described through a schema that resembles a data model or object model. The notations are, on purpose, similar to the ones found in other contemporary methods. There are, of course, a number of crucial differences. At the end of this chapter we include a special section discussing in detail the differences between the CommonKADS knowledge model and analysis models in general software engineering. Experienced software engineers might first want to read that section before moving on.

5.3.2 Knowledge Model Overview

A knowledge model has three parts, each capturing a related group of knowledge structures. We call each part a *knowledge category*.

The first category is called the *domain knowledge*. This category specifies the domain-specific knowledge and information types that we want to talk about in an application. For example, the domain knowledge of an application concerning medical diagnosis would contain definitions of relevant diseases, symptoms, and tests, as well as relationships between these types. A domain knowledge description is somewhat comparable to a "data model" or "object model" in software engineering.

The second part of the knowledge model contains the *inference knowledge*. The inference knowledge describes the basic *inference steps* that we want to make using the domain knowledge. Inferences are best seen as the building blocks of the reasoning machine. In software engineering terms the inferences represent the lowest level of functional decomposition. Two sample inferences in a medical diagnosis application could be a "hypothesize" inference that associates symptoms with a possible disease, and a "verify" inference that identifies tests that can be used to ascertain that a certain disease is indeed the factor that causes the observed symptoms.

The third category of knowledge is the *task knowledge*. Task knowledge describes what goal(s) an application pursues, and how these goals can be realized through a decomposition into subtasks and (ultimately) inferences. This "how" aspect includes a description of the dynamic behavior of tasks, i.e., their internal control. For example, a simple medical diagnosis application could have DIAGNOSIS as its top-level task, and define that it can be realized through a repeated sequence of invocations of the "hypothesize" and "verify"

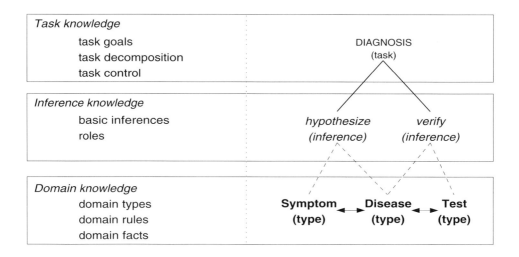

Figure 5.4
Overview of knowledge categories in the knowledge model. At the right some examples are shown of knowledge elements in a medical diagnosis domain.

inferences. Task knowledge is similar to the higher levels of functional decomposition in software engineering, but also includes control over the functions involved.

Figure 5.4 gives a brief overview of the three knowledge categories, as well as some sample knowledge elements in each category. In the following sections, we discuss each of the three categories in more detail.

5.3.3   Knowledge-Model Notations

As we will see in the next section, we model domain knowledge with a notation similar to a UML class diagram. A difference is that in knowledge modelling we do not model functions (i.e., operations, methods) within information objects. Thus, we will see that the notion of "concept" is almost the same as a UML class, but without any operations. This difference is due to the special role that functions (i.e., inferences and tasks) have within knowledge modelling. The reader is referred to the final section of this chapter for a more elaborate discussion of this topic.

Task and inference knowledge have their own special graphical notations, as there is no direct UML equivalent. You will also note that the graphical notation is based on an underlying textual notation. We introduce this textual notation at some places (in particular for task knowledge) in a loose, informal manner. Where possible, we limit the knowledge-model notations to the diagrams. Details of the language can be found in the appendix. Additional detail and examples of knowledge models are available on the CommonKADS website, together with language support tools.

5.4   Domain Knowledge

The *domain knowledge* describes the main static information and knowledge objects in an application domain. A domain-knowledge description typically consists of two types of ingredients: namely one or more *domain schemas* and one or more *knowledge bases*:

Domain schema   A domain schema is a schematic description of the domain-specific knowledge and information through a number of *type definitions*. The schema describes the static information/knowledge structure of the application domain. As we will see in Chapter 13, it may also contain generalizations of the domain structures in several directions. From a general software-engineering point of view the domain schema resembles a *data model* or *object model*.

Knowledge base   A knowledge base contains instances of the types specified in a domain schema. A major difference between a knowledge system and, for example, a database application is that in database applications, one is, during analysis, seldom interested in the actual facts that have to be placed in the database. In a knowledge system, a knowledge base typically contains certain pieces of knowledge such as rules, which are of interest (although also to a limited extent, as we will see later on). In knowledge modelling we typically distinguish multiple knowledge bases containing different types of knowledge (e.g., instances of different rule types).

In the remainder of this section we show how one can specify a domain schema and a knowledge base. As illustrations we use examples derived from a simple application concerning the diagnosis of problems with a car. Figure 5.5 shows in an intuitive fashion some pieces of knowledge that are found in in this domain.

5.4.1   Domain-Schema Specification

The knowledge model provides a set of modelling constructs to specify a domain schema of an application. Most constructs are similar to the ones encountered in modern O-O data models. In particular we follow as much as possible the notations provided by the UML class diagram. A synopsis of the class-diagram notation can be found in Section 14.4. As the UML description is written as a self-contained section, there is some overlap with the descriptions in this chapter.

In addition to the class diagram, constructs are included to cover modelling aspects that are specific to knowledge-intensive systems. In practice, the three main modelling constructs are **CONCEPT**, **RELATION**, and **RULE TYPE**. In addition, several other constructs

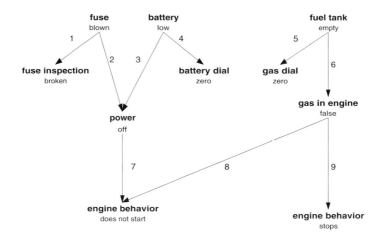

Figure 5.5
Knowledge pieces in the car-diagnosis domain.

are available such as **SUPERTYPE-OF/SUBTYPE-OF** and **AGGREGATE/PART**. A basic set of constructs is introduced in this chapter. Chapter 13 describes some more advanced modelling constructs.

Concept   A **CONCEPT** describes a set of objects or instances which occur in the application domain and which share similar characteristics. The notion of concept is similar to what is called "class" or "object class" in other approaches. A difference with object-oriented approaches is that we **do not** include functions (i.e., operations, methods) in the concept descriptions. Examples of concepts in the car domain could be a **gas tank** and a **battery**. Concepts can be both concrete things in the world, like the examples above, or abstract entities such as a **car design**.

Characteristics of concepts can be described in various ways. The simplest way is to define an **ATTRIBUTE** of a concept. An attribute can hold a **VALUE**: a piece of information that instances of the concept can hold. These pieces of information should be *atomic*, meaning that they are represented as simple values. Thus, a concept cannot have an attribute containing an instance of another concept as its value. Such things have to described using other constructs (typically relations; see further).

For each attribute, a **VALUE TYPE** needs to be defined, specifying the allowable values for the attribute. Standard value types are provided such as boolean, number (real, integer, natural), number ranges, and text strings, as well as the possibility to define sets of symbols (e.g., "normal" and "abnormal"). The value type **UNIVERSAL** allows any value. In the appendix a full listing of standard value types can be found. By default, attributes have

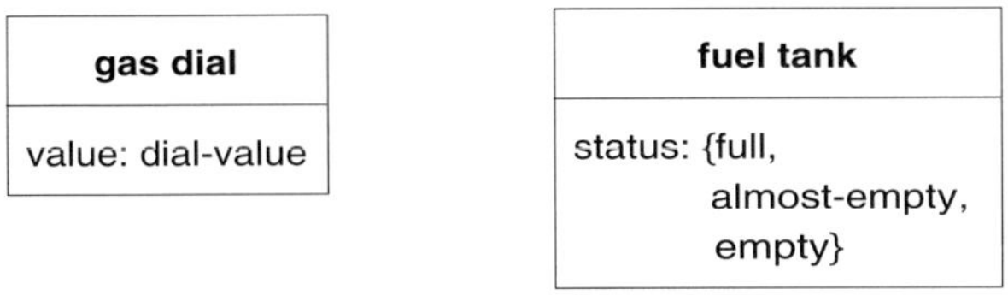

```
        gas dial              |           fuel tank
  ----------------            |  ----------------------------
  value: dial-value           |     status: {full,
                              |             almost-empty,
                              |             empty}
```

CONCEPT gas dial;
    ATTRIBUTES:
        value: dial-value;
    END CONCEPT gas-dial;

CONCEPT fuel-tank;
    ATTRIBUTES
        status: {full, almost-empty, empty};
    END CONCEPT fuel-tank;

VALUE-TYPE dial-value;
    VALUE-LIST: {zero, low, normal};
    TYPE: ORDINAL;
    END VALUE-TYPE dial-value;

Figure 5.6
Graphical and textual specification of concepts and their attributes and corresponding value types. A concept is graphically represented as a box consisting of two parts. The concept name is written in the upper half. Attributes are listed in the lower half, together with the names of their value-types. The textual specification is an explicit value-type definition.

a cardinality of 0–1, meaning that for each instance an attribute can optionally store one value. Other types of cardinality have to be defined explicitly.

Two sample concept definitions with attributes are given in Figure 5.6. As can be seen in this figure, we use both textual and graphical representations for knowledge-model components. The textual representation is the "baseline," and may contain details that are not easy (or not necessary) to represent graphically.

Graphically, concepts are shown as a box consisting of two parts. The concept name is written in bold face in the upper half. Attributes are listed in the lower half, together with the names of their value types. The textual specification shows that the type for the attribute **value** of **gas-dial** is defined explicitly as a separate VALUE TYPE. This is typically useful if one expects more than one concept attribute to use this value type. If concepts occur at more than one place in diagrams, the attribute compartment can be omitted the second time.

Figure 5.7 shows some other concepts, in this case connected to an apple-classification problem. In the right-hand part of this figure a number of instances of **apple-class** are shown. For instances the UML notation for objects is used: the name of the instance plus the name of the concept it belongs to are written in bold and underlined.

Concepts are usually the starting point for domain modelling. One important reason for defining something as a separate concept and not as an attribute of another concept is that it deserves to have its own "existence" independent of other concepts. Identification

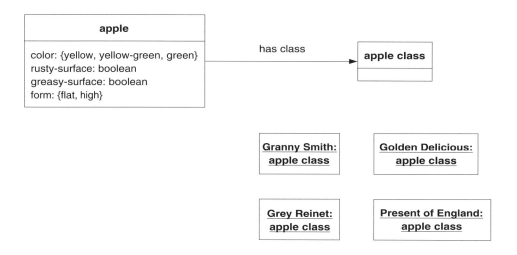

Figure 5.7
The concepts "apple" and "apple-class." In the right-hand part of this figure a number of instances of apple-class are shown. For instances the UML notation for objects is used: the name of the instance plus the name of the concept it belongs to are written in bold and underlined.

of concepts cannot be done in a neutral way: what is considered a concept depends on the context provided by the application domain. This scoping provided by the application (both by the domain itself and by the task) enables keeping the domain-modelling process "do-able." If this context does not exist, inexperienced knowledge engineers either model too much or, alternatively, do not produce anything because they are scared off by the complexity that comes with a widely applicable schema.

Relation   Relations between concepts are defined with the **RELATION** or **BINARY RELA-TION** construct. Relations can be used in the standard entity-relationship (E-R) fashion, but can also be used for more complicated types of modelling. Relations are defined through a specification of **ARGUMENT**s. For each argument the **CARDINALITY** (sometimes called "multiplicity") can be defined. The default cardinality is 1, meaning that the participation in the relation is obligatory. In addition, one can specify a **ROLE** for an argument, iden-tifying the role the argument plays in the relation.   Relations can have any number of arguments. However, the bulk of relations have precisely two arguments. Therefore, a spe-cialized construct **BINARY RELATION** is provided. Relations may also have attributes, just like concepts. Such attributes are values that depend on the relation context, and not just on one of its arguments. The standard example of such an attribute is the **wedding-date** of the **married-to** relation between two people.

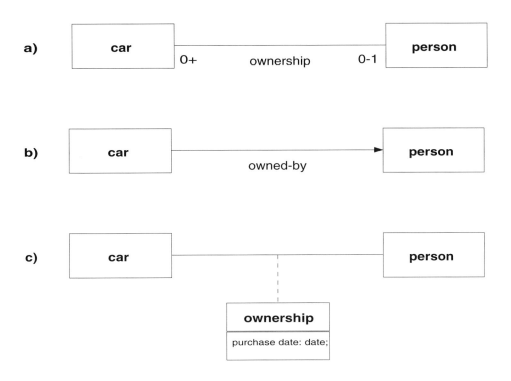

Figure 5.8
Three graphical representations of a binary relation for the car example. Part a) shows the simple nondirectional representation. The name of the relation is written as a label next to the line connecting the relation arguments. The numbers indicate the minimum and maximum cardinality of the relation argument. Part b) shows the same relation, but with a directional name. An arrow is included to reflect the directional nature. Part c) shows a more complex representation, in which the relation becomes an object in its own right. The relation box is attached by a dashed line to the relation line. The relation box may contain attribute definitions. Also, the relation itself may be involved as an argument in other relations.

Binary relations can be shown graphically in a number of ways. The simplest form is just to draw a line between two concepts and label it with the name of the relation. An example of this is shown in Figure 5.8a. The relation **ownership** holds between instances of **car** and instances of **person**. The number close to the concept box indicates the cardinality: a car can be owned by at most one person; a person can own any number of cars. If the name of a binary relation is of a directional nature, an arrow may point to indicate the direction. This is the case in Figure 5.8b. The relation **owned-by** has a direction from the car to the person who owns it. In the case of directional relation names, there may also be a need to introduce an inverse relation (e.g., **owns**). Generally speaking, it is best to choose as much as possible nondirectional relation names. Nondirectional names emphasize the static characteristics of a relationship, and are thus the least likely to change when the functionality of the application changes.

If a relation has attributes of its own, or if the relation itself takes part in other relations, this simple relation representation is not sufficient. In that case we omit the text label and draw the relation in a fashion similar to concepts: namely as a box with attributes connected with a dashed line to the relation line. This graphical representation is shown in Figure 5.8c. This particular representation is also called *reification* of a relation. Mathematically speaking, one treats a relation tuple as a single, complex object. Relation reification is a powerful modelling mechanism that can be used in many knowledge-intensive domains. The textual description follows quite naturally from the graphical one. An example is shown below:

```
BINARY-RELATION owned-by;
    INVERSE: owns;
    ARGUMENT-1: car;
        CARDINALITY: 0-1;
    ARGUMENT-2: person;
        CARDINALITY: ANY;
    ATTRIBUTES:
        purchase-date: DATE;
END BINARY-RELATION owned-by;
```

This sample specification captures a relation type that is a mix of Figure 5.8b+c. This relation is a binary relation and thus has exactly two arguments. The relation name is directional (from **car** to **person**), and thus the **INVERSE** slot is used to indicate the inverse relation name (**owns**, from **person** to **car**). Note that the implied meaning of the cardinality slot of an argument is that it specifies the number of times that one instance of the argument may participate in the relation with one particular related object. In the graphical representation it is common to draw it the other way around: the fact that a car can be owned by at most one person is indicated at the "person" side of the relation (see Figure 5.8). The sample relation also has an attribute **purchase-date**. This is necessary because the attribute value is dependent on both arguments **car** and **person**.

Relations with three or more arguments are shown with a different notation. The relation name is placed in a diamond-shaped box, with arguments linked to the diamond. An example of a four-place relation is shown in Figure 5.9. In this figure we try to model an observation in a medical context. The relation has four arguments: (1) the agent making the observation, (2) the patient for which the observation is made, (3) the location in which the observation is made (hospital ward, outpatient clinic), and (4) the type of observable (e.g., skin color, heart sounds). Again, the relation is represented here as a reified relation. This is necessary because the relation itself has three attributes: namely the observed value and a time stamp (date plus time).

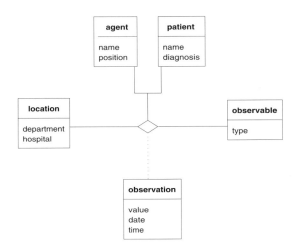

Figure 5.9
A four-place relation modelling an observation about a patient in a hospital setting. In these multiargument relations there should not be a relation argument which completely depends on another argument.

Analysts usually try to reduce relations with three or more arguments to binary relations. This can be done if one of the relation arguments fully depends on another relation argument. This is not the case in the **observation** relation: each argument is necessary to uniquely identify a relation instance. For example, the same observable could be observed at the same location for a certain patient by two different agents (e.g., a doctor and a nurse). In this particular example we could even turn it into a five-place relation by introducing a **time-stamp** as an extra concept (replacing the time and date attributes in the relation itself). Again, such a decision depends on whether one views a time-stamp as being a "first-class" object in its own right *in the context of this application* (see the discussion before on concepts and attributes).

Reified relations provide powerful forms of abstraction. The resulting concept can be treated in a similar way as "normal" concepts. From a formal point of view, reified relations are of the form of second-order relations. Reified relations occur in any domain with a certain degree of complexity (see, e.g., the **application** relation in Chapter 10).

Sub/supertype   The knowledge model supports the specification of generalization/specialization relations. Concepts can be organized in subtype hierarchies through the **SUBTYPE-OF** construct. The subtype definition is placed inside the definition of the subconcept. The examples in Figure 5.10 define two subconcepts of **residence**. Subconcepts inherit the attributes and relations of the supertype, and may add their own, such as the **entrance-floor** of an apartment. Defining subtypes is not limited to concepts. Rela-

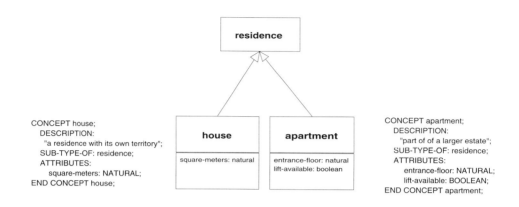

CONCEPT house;
    DESCRIPTION:
        "a residence with its own territory";
    SUB-TYPE-OF: residence;
    ATTRIBUTES:
        square-meters: NATURAL;
END CONCEPT house;

CONCEPT apartment;
    DESCRIPTION:
        "part of of a larger estate";
    SUB-TYPE-OF: residence;
    ATTRIBUTES:
        entrance-floor: NATURAL;
        lift-available: BOOLEAN;
END CONCEPT apartment;

Figure 5.10
Subtype relations are shown graphically through unlabeled lines, with an large open arrowhead pointing to the supertype. In the textual description, the subtype specification should be part of the subconcept.

tions can also have subtypes. For example, a relation **ownership** of a **vehicle** could be specialized into **car-ownership** and **bicycle-ownership**.

Subtypes are shown graphically through unlabeled lines, with a large open arrowhead pointing to the supertype. Figure 5.11 shows subtypes of concepts in the car domain. There are two hierarchies, one for **car-state** and one for **car-observable**. This distinction between observables and states is a distinction made in many diagnostic applications. The states are further divided into states that we can notice in some way (and thus can give rise to a complaint) and states that are completely internal to the system (**invisible-care-state**). This figure in fact represents information about the nodes in Figure 5.5 plus a number of supertypes that give additional meaning to each node.

Note that for most subtypes in Figure 5.11 no new attributes are added. Instead, the value set of an inherited attribute such as **status** is restricted. Typically, three types of specialization can be introduced when creating a subtype:

1. **New feature**   Add a new attribute or a new participation in a relation.
2. **Type restriction**   Restrict the value set of an attribute or the types of related concepts.
3. **Cardinality restriction**   Restrict the number of attribute values or the number of participations in a relation.

Sometimes it is useful to introduce subtypes even without any specialized features. This is done if a term acts as a central concept in an application domain. Such subtypes can be seen as "blown-up attributes," because technically speaking they can always be replaced by introducing an attribute, where the subtypes appear as possible values. These modelling issues are discussed in more detail in Chapter 7.

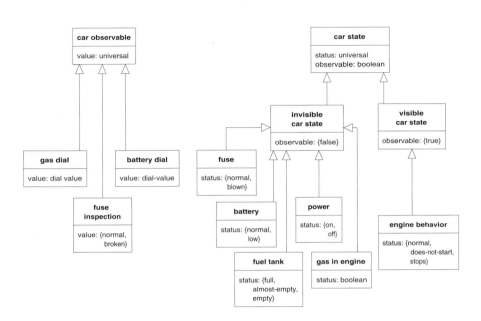

Figure 5.11
Subtype relations between concepts in the car-diagnosis domain.

In Chapter 13 we introduce more sophisticated methods for defining sub- and super-types. In particular, we allow for multiple subtype hierarchies along different dimensions, where each dimension represents a different "viewpoint" on a concept. The need for multiple hierarchies turns up in many real-life applications.

Rule type   So far, the reader may have wondered what the difference is between a domain schema and a traditional data model. However, the situation becomes more complex when we want to model the directed lines in Figure 5.5. These lines represent dependencies between car concepts. If we want to represent these dependencies in a schematic form (without listing all the instances), how can we do this? Take two examples of dependencies between car states that can be derived from this figure (represented in a simple intuitive logical language):

```
FUEL-TANK.status = empty => GAS-IN-ENGINE.status = false
BATTERY.status = low => POWER.status = off
```

These dependencies are a sort of natural rules, indicating a logical relationship between two *logical statements*. The logical statements in such rules are typically *expressions about an attribute value of a concept*. These rules are thus a special type of relation. The relation is not (as usual) between concept instances themselves, but between *expressions* about concepts.

In describing a domain schema for an application there is usually a need to describe such rules in a schematic way. For example, we would like to describe the general structure of the dependencies in Figure 5.5. The same is true for the knowledge rules in the beginning of this chapter in Figure 5.1. To model the *structure* of such rules we provide a **RULE TYPE** construct. The rule type for modelling the two rules listed above would look like this:

```
RULE-TYPE state-dependency;
    ANTECEDENT: invisible-car-state;
        CARDINALITY: 1;
    CONSEQUENT: car-state;
        CARDINALITY: 1;
    CONNECTION-SYMBOL:
        causes;
END RULE-TYPE state-dependency;
```

A rule-type definition looks a bit like a relation, where the **ANTECEDENT** and the **CONSEQUENT** can be seen seen as arguments. But the arguments are of a different nature. Antecedents and consequents of a rule type are not concept instances, but represent expressions *about* those instances. For example, the statement that **invisible-car-state** is the antecedent in this rule type means that the antecedent may contain *any* expression about **invisible-car-state**. Examples of instances of antecedent expressions are `fuel-tank.status = empty` and `battery.status = low`.

The rule type **state-dependency** models six of the arrows in Figure 5.5, namely lines 2–3 and 6–9 (see the numbers in the figure), precisely those between concepts of type **car-state**. The other three dependencies do not follow the structure of the **state-dependency** rule type. The dependencies 1, 4, and 5 connect an invisible car state to an expression about a **car-observable**. These rules represent typical manifestations of these internal states. The rule type below models this rule structure:

```
RULE-TYPE manifestation-rule;
    DESCRIPTION: "Rule stating the relation between an internal state
        and its external behavior in terms of an observable value";
    ANTECEDENT:
        invisible-car-state;
    CONSEQUENT:
        car-observable;
    CONNECTION-SYMBOL:
        has-manifestation;
END RULE-TYPE manifestation-rule;
```

The rule-type construct enables us to realize the requirement posed earlier in this chapter, namely to structure a knowledge base into smaller partitions (e.g., rule sets) which share a similar structure (cf. Figure 5.2). A rule type describes "natural" rules: logical connections that experts tell you about in a domain. The rules need not (and usually are not) strictly logical dependencies such as implications. Often, they indicate some heuristic relationship between domain expressions. For this reason, we specify for each rule type a **CONNECTION SYMBOL** that can be used to connect the antecedent and the consequent, when writing down a rule instance. The examples of dependencies mentioned earlier in this section would look like this as instances of the **state-dependency** rule type:

```
fuel-supply.status = blocked
    CAUSES
gas-in-engine.status = false;

battery.status = low
    CAUSES
power.value = off;
```

Note that the examples of rule types exploit the subtype hierarchy of Figure 5.11 to provide types for the antecedent and the consequent of the causal rules. Figure 5.12 shows the graphical representation of a rule type, using the two rule types of the car domain as examples. A directed line is drawn from the antecedent(s) to the connection symbol, and from the connection symbol to the consequent. The rule-type name is placed in an ellipse and connected with a dashed line to the connection symbol. The dashed-line notation is used because of the similarity between a rule type and a "relation as class": instances of both are complex entities. The numbers connected to the lines indicate the cardinality. The cardinality is used to put restrictions on the minimum and maximum number of expressions in the antecedent and/or consequent. In this case the rules must have precisely one condition and conclusion.

In this way we can build a number of rule types for a domain that capture in a schematic way knowledge types that we find useful to distinguish. In Figure 5.13 you see a rule type for the knowledge rules presented earlier this chapter as a challenge (see Figure 5.1). Below the schema itself the actual rules are listed as "instances" of this rule type. For the moment we assume an intuitive informal representation of these instances. Later (see Chapter 13) we introduce more precise syntax for writing down rule-type instances.

Please note that the notion of "rule" as we use it here is not connected in any way to the implementation-specific rule formalisms. It might be the case that such a formalism turns out to be an adequate coding technique, but there is no guarantee nor a need for this to be true. The rule types are an analysis vehicle and should capture the structural logical dependencies that occur in an application domain, independent of their final representation in a software system.

5.4.2 Knowledge Base

A domain schema describes domain-knowledge *types*, such as concepts, relations, and rule types. A knowledge base contains *instances* of those knowledge types. For example, in the car-diagnosis domain we could have a knowledge base with instances of the rule types

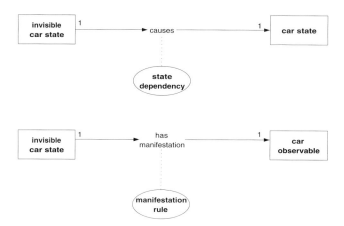

Figure 5.12
Graphical representation of a rule type. A directed line is drawn from the antecedent(s) to the connection symbol, and from the connection symbol to the consequent. The rule-type name is placed in an ellipse and connected by a dashed line to the connection symbol. The numbers indicate the cardinality (the minimum/maximum number of expressions in the antecedent/consequent).

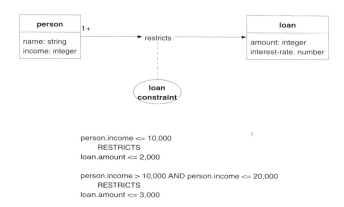

Figure 5.13
Rule type for loan-assessment knowledge.

state-dependency and **manifestation-rule**. Figure 5.14 shows how we can define such a knowledge base. A knowledge-base specification consists of two parts:

1. The **USES** slot defines which types of domain-knowledge instances are stored in the knowledge base. The format is:

$$< type > \text{FROM} < domain\ schema >$$

where the latter part defines in which domain schema the type is defined. In the car example we have only one schema, but we will see in Chapter 13 that in more complex applications there is often a need to introduce multiple domain schemas.

2. The **EXPRESSIONS** slot contains the actual instances. The rule instances can be described in a semiformal way, where the connection symbol is used to separate the antecedent expression from the consequent. Alternatively, a formal language can be used here. It should be noted, however, that knowledge bases may easily change in form and extent during analysis, so it is important to avoid excessive formalization of the rule instances in cases where the knowledge type has not been verified and validated yet.

Figure 5.14 shows a sample knowledge base, containing the causal model of the car application. It **uses** the two rule types defined in Figure 5.12. The instances in Figure 5.14 correspond to the knowledge pieces listed in Figure 5.5.

The fact that a notion like a knowledge base exists is a typical characteristic of knowledge modelling. For a database one would not dream of writing part of the actual data set that will be stored in the database during analysis. In knowledge modelling, these instances are of interest: they contain the actual knowledge on which the reasoning process is based.

This does not mean that our knowledge bases have to be completed during analysis. Often, the knowledge engineer will be satisfied in the early phases of development with a partial set of instances, and complete the knowledge bases once the knowledge model is stable enough.

The separation of "domain schema" and "knowledge base" means that we have to reinterpret the term "knowledge acquisition" as consisting of at least two steps: (1) defining a knowledge type such as a rule type, and (2) eliciting the instances of this type and putting them in a knowledge base. There is often a feedback loop between these two steps, where the type definition can be seen as a hypothesis about the format of certain knowledge structures in a domain, and the knowledge-elicitation process functions as a verification or falsification of this hypothesis by answering the question: can we elicit (a sufficient amount of) knowledge of this form?

The techniques that can be used for knowledge elicitation vary considerably. A wealth of techniques exist to support this, ranging from manual methods (e.g., interview techniques) to automated learning techniques. A discussion of this topic can be found in Chapter 8.

```
KNOWLEDGE-BASE car-network;
  USES:
    state-dependency FROM car-diagnosis-schema,
    manifestation-rule FROM car-diagnosis-schema;
  EXPRESSIONS:
    /* state dependencies */

    fuse.status = blown CAUSES power.status = off;
    battery.status = low  CAUSES power.status = off;
    power.status = off CAUSES
        engine-behavior.status = does-not-start;
    fuel-tank.status = empty CAUSES gas-in-engine.status = false;
    gas-in-engine.status = false CAUSES
        engine-behavior.status = does-not-start;
    gas-in-engine.status = false CAUSES
        engine-behavior.status = stops;


    /* manifestation rules */

    fuse.status = blown HAS-MANIFESTATION
        fuse-inspection.value = broken;
    battery.status = low HAS-MANIFESTATION battery-dial.value = zero;
    fuel-tank.status = empty HAS-MANIFESTATION gas-dial.value = zero;
END KNOWLEDGE-BASE car-network;
```

Figure 5.14
The knowledge base "car-network" contains instances of the rule types state-dependency and manifestation-rule.

5.5   Inference Knowledge

Domain knowledge is described as a static information/knowledge structure of the application domain. In the inference knowledge we describe how these static structures can be used to carry out a reasoning process. The main ingredients of the inference knowledge are the *inferences*, the *knowledge roles*, and the *transfer functions*.

5.5.1   What Are Inferences?

The inference knowledge in the knowledge model describes the lowest level of functional decomposition. These basic information-processing units are called "inferences" in knowledge modelling. An inference carries out a primitive reasoning step. Typically, an inference uses knowledge contained in some knowledge base to derive new information from its dynamic input.

Why do we give primitive functions such a special status? A major reason is that inferences are *indirectly* related to the domain knowledge. This feature is realized through the notion of a *knowledge role*, as we will see further on in this section. This indirect coupling of inference and domain knowledge enables us to reuse inference descriptions, as we will see at length in Chapter 6.

In software engineering it is common to request a *process specification* for every leaf function. The nature of the specification is usually left open: either procedural (algorithm, pseudocode) or declarative (pre- and post-conditions, invariants). In knowledge engineering, we take a more rigorous position:

> A leaf function (i.e., an inference) is fully described through a declarative specification of its input and output. The internal process of the inference is a black box, and is considered not of interest for knowledge modelling.

This approach provides us with a guideline for deciding when to stop functional decomposition, a frequently occurring problem in system analysis. The guideline is in essence very simple: be satisfied with the grain size of your set of leaf functions, if and only if these inferences provide you with an *understandable* reasoning trace. This guideline builds on a property that many knowledge-intensive systems share: these systems need to *explain* their information-processing behavior in order for the results to be acceptable to the user.

5.5.2   Inferences and Knowledge Roles

The main feature that distinguishes an inference from a traditional "process" or "function" is the way in which the data on which the inference operates are described. Inference I/O is described in terms of *functional roles*: abstract names of data objects that indicate their *role* in the reasoning process. We call such a role a *knowledge role*. A typical example of a knowledge role is "hypothesis": a functional name for a domain object that plays the role of a candidate solution.

We distinguish two types of knowledge roles, namely *dynamic* roles and *static* roles. Dynamic roles are the run-time inputs and outputs of inferences. Each invocation of the inference typically has different instantiations of the dynamic roles. Let's take an example inference. Assume we have a cover inference that uses a causal model to find explanations that could explain ("cover") a complaint about the behavior of the car. Such an inference would have have two dynamic knowledge roles: (1) an input role **complaint**, denoting a domain object representing a complaint about the behavior of the system, and (2) an output role **hypothesis**, representing a single candidate solution.

Static roles, on the other hand, are more or less stable over time. Static roles specify the collection of domain knowledge that is used to make the inference. For example, the above-mentioned inference cover could use the state-dependency network described in the previous section to find candidate solutions.

Figure 5.15 shows a sample textual specification of the cover inference and its dynamic and static roles. The first part of the specification shows how the knowledge roles (both the dynamic and static ones) are bound to the domain. Objects of domain type **visible-**

```
INFERENCE cover;
  ROLES:
    INPUT: complaint;
    OUTPUT: hypothesis;
    STATIC: causal-model;
  SPECIFICATION:
    "Each time the inference is invoked, it generates a candidate
     solution that could have caused the complaint. The output
     should be an initial state in the state-dependency network
     which causally 'covers' the input complaint.";
END INFERENCE cover;

KNOWLEDGE-ROLE complaint;
  TYPE: DYNAMIC;
  DOMAIN-MAPPING: visible-state;
END KNOWLEDGE-ROLE complaint;

KNOWLEDGE-ROLE hypothesis;
  TYPE: DYNAMIC;
  DOMAIN-MAPPING: invisible-state;
END KNOWLEDGE-ROLE hypothesis;

KNOWLEDGE-ROLE causal-model;
  TYPE: STATIC;
  DOMAIN-MAPPING: state-dependency FROM car-network;
END KNOWLEDGE-ROLE causal-model;
```

Figure 5.15
The inference "cover" has two dynamic knowledge roles: the input role "complaint" and the output role "hypothesis." The output is supposed to be a causal explanation of the complaint. The static knowledge role "causal model" provides the knowledge needed for making the inference.

state can play the role of complaint. In our miniexample, this means that only instances of **engine-behavior** can be complaints (see Figure 5.11). The role **hypothesis** can be played by all **invisible-states**. The static role <u>causal-model</u> maps to the state dependencies in the knowledge base **car-network**.

Figure 5.16a depicts in a graphical way how an inference is bound to domain-knowledge types via the intermediate route of knowledge roles. The graphical conventions used in this figure are discussed further on. The inference-domain mappings realize in fact a function-data decoupling, a feature we discuss in more detail in the final section of the chapter. As we will see, knowledge modelling differs in this significantly from standard methods, where the name of the domain object types would have been directly associated with the function. Figure 5.16b shows the data-flow diagram (DFD) representation of Figure 5.16a. In this figure the knowledge roles have disappeared and are replaced with domain-specific data types. The DFD representation is much simpler but makes reuse of inference knowledge more difficult. As we will see in Chapter 6, the introduction of knowl-

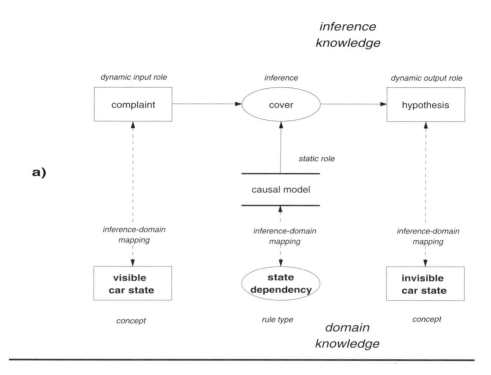

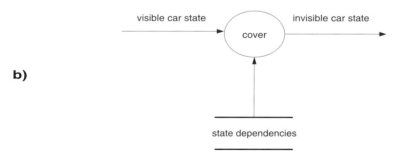

Figure 5.16
Part a): The sample inference "cover" has three knowledge roles, each of which is bound to domain objects that can play this role. Here, knowledge modelling differs significantly from standard methods, where the name of the domain object types would have been directly associated with the function. Part b) shows the data-flow diagram (DFD) representation.

edge roles enables us to construct catalogs of recurring reasoning patterns. The price we have to pay is the increased complexity of the specification of leaf functions.

The notion of "knowledge role" gives us a separate vocabulary for talking about the behavior of domain objects in the reasoning process. Each reasoning task has its own role vocabulary, independent of the domain the task is performed in. For example, in diagnostic tasks we encounter knowledge roles such as **hypothesis**, **complaint**, **differential** (= the active set of hypotheses), **finding**, and **evidence**.

5.5.3   Transfer Functions: Communicating with the External World

In the knowledge model we abstract from the communication with other agents: users, other systems. The emphasis lies on the structure of the reasoning process. However, one cannot completely leave out the interaction with the external world. Some of these interactions play a role in the reasoning process itself, for example, obtaining additional observations in a diagnostic process. For this reason, we introduce the notion of *transfer function*. A transfer function is a function that transfers an information item between the reasoning agent described in the knowledge model and the outside world (another system, some user). Transfer functions are black boxes from the knowledge-model point of view: only their name and I/O are described. Detailed specifications of the transfer functions should be placed in the communication model (see Chapter 9).

Transfer functions have standard names. These names are based on two properties that transfer functions have: who has the initiative and who is in possession of the information item being transferred? Based on these properties we distinguish four types of transfer functions:

1. **Obtain**   The reasoning agent requests a piece of information from an external agent. The reasoning agent has the initiative. The external agent holds the information item.
2. **Receive**   The reasoning agent gets a piece of information from an external agent. The external agent has the initiative and also holds the information item.
3. **Present**   The reasoning agent presents a piece of information to an external agent. The reasoning agent has the initiative and also holds the information item.
4. **Provide**   The system provides an external agent with a piece of information. The external agent has the initiative. The reasoning agent holds the information item.

Figure 5.17 shows this typology of transfer functions based on the dimensions "initiative" and "information holder." The transfer functions obtain and receive are the ones most commonly found in knowledge models. In particular, obtain is frequently used; receive appears in many real-time tasks and is typically associated with asynchronous control. Figure 5.18 shows the specification of the transfer function to obtain a finding in the car-diagnosis example. The transfer function is a black box from the knowledge-model point of view and defines just the input-output roles and the transfer-function type. Other information about the transfer function should be placed in the communication model.

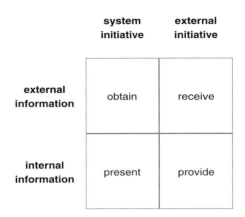

Figure 5.17
Typology of transfer functions based on the "initiative" and "information-holder" dimensions.

```
TRANSFER-FUNCTION obtain;
    TYPE:
        OBTAIN;
    ROLES:
        INPUT: expected-finding;
        OUTPUT: actual-finding;
END TRANSFER-FUNCTION obtain;
```

Figure 5.18
Specification of a transfer function to obtain a finding. The transfer function is a black box from the knowledge-model point of view and defines just the input-output roles and the transfer-function type (obtain, receive, present, or provide).

5.5.4   Depicting Data Dependencies between Inferences

Together, the inferences form the building blocks for a reasoning system. They define the basic inference actions that the system can perform and the roles the domain objects can play. The combined set of inferences specifies the basic inference capability of the target system. The set of inferences can be represented graphically in an *inference structure*. Figure 5.19 shows an example of such an inference structure for the car-diagnosis problem. In an inference structure the following graphical conventions are used:

- Rectangles represent dynamic knowledge roles. The name of the knowledge role is written in the rectangle.
- Ovals represent inferences. Arrows are used to indicate input-output dependencies between roles and inferences.

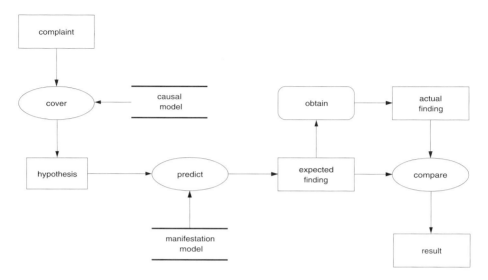

Figure 5.19
Inference structure for a simple diagnosis application.

- A rounded-box notation is used to indicate a transfer function. An example is the obtain function in Figure 5.19.
- A static role name is written between two thick horizontal lines. This representation is purposely similar to data stores in DFDs, as static roles incorporate the same "storage" notion. Static roles are connected via a directed line to the inference in which they are used. Including static roles is traditionally optional in inference structures, where the main emphasis lies on the dynamic data-flow aspects. We usually include static roles in the inference structure during the construction process.
- A knowledge role constitutes a functional name for a set of domain objects that can play this role. Some inferences operate on or produce *one particular* object, others work on a *set* of these objects. This can lead to ambiguities in inference structures, for example, if one inference produces one object and another inference works on a set of these objects, possibly generated by some repeated invocation of the first inference. The graphical notation allows for making this distinction explicit: if a data-dependency line starts with a small solid circle, it indicates that the input or output should be interpreted as a set of objects playing this role. This notation is used in various places in this book, e.g., the inference structure for classification in the next chapter (see Figure 6.3).

Figure 5.19 shows examples of the graphical conventions. It depicts an inference struc-ture for the car-diagnosis example. The cover inference takes as input the dynamic role **complaint** and produces a **hypothesis** as output. The **causal-model** is used as a static role

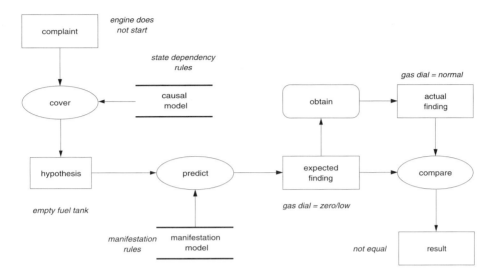

Figure 5.20
Inference structure in which the roles are annotated with domain-specific examples.

by this inference. The predict inference delivers an expected finding for the hypothesis, typically some observation that could act as support evidence for this hypothesis. The inference structure also contains a transfer function obtain (cf. the rounded-box notation) for "getting" the actual finding. The third inference is a simple comparison of the actual finding with the expected finding. The result is some equality value.

An inference structure is an abstract representation of the possible steps in the reasoning process. To make it a bit less abstract one can also construct an annotated inference structure. In this figure all knowledge roles are annotated with domain-specific examples. Figure 5.20 shows an annotated version of the inference structure for the car-diagnosis example. It should be noted that, although there are some similarities between inference structures and DFDs, the differences are also significant. The static roles typically correspond to data stores in DFDs; the dynamic roles would need to be represented as data flows. Control flows are obsolete in inference structures. Actors are not shown in inference structures, as those would be part of the communication model.

The inference structure summarizes the basic inference capabilities of the prospective system. It also defines the vocabulary and dependencies for control, but *not* the control itself. This latter type of knowledge is specified as *task knowledge*.

5.6 Task Knowledge

Reasoning always has a "reason." In other words, an important aspect of knowledge is what we want to do with it. What are the goals we intend to achieve by applying knowledge? We mention some typical goals:

- We want to assess a mortgage application in order to minimize the risk of losing money.
- We want to find the cause of a malfunction in a photocopier in order to restore service as quickly as possible.
- We want to design an elevator for a new building.

Task knowledge is the knowledge category that describes these goals and the strategies that will be employed for realizing goals. Task knowledge is typically described in a hierarchical fashion: top-level tasks such as DESIGN-ELEVATOR are decomposed into smaller tasks, which in turn can be split up into even smaller tasks. At the lowest level of task decomposition, the tasks are linked to inferences and transfer functions.

Two knowledge types play a prominent role in the description of task knowledge: the *task* and the *task method*. A task defines a reasoning goal in terms of an input-output pair. For example, a DIAGNOSIS task typically has as input a complaint, and produces as output a fault category plus the supporting evidence. A task method describes how a task can be realized through a decomposition into subfunctions plus a control regimen over the execution of the subfunctions. The task and the task method can best be understood as respectively the "what" view (what needs to be done) and the "how" view (how is it done) on reasoning tasks.

Figure 5.21 shows a graphical representation of the hierarchical structure of task knowledge. In this case, a top-level task DIAGNOSIS is decomposed by a task method DIAGNOSIS-THROUGH-GENERATE-AND-TEST. This leads to the four subfunctions we already encountered in the previous section: three inferences and one transfer function. In most real-life models, one level of decomposition is insufficient. In that case, a top-level task is decomposed in several new tasks, which again are decomposed through other methods, and so on. At the lowest level of decomposition, the inferences and transfer functions appear. Tasks that are not decomposed further into other tasks are called *primitive* tasks; the other tasks are called *composite* tasks.

5.6.1 Task

A task defines a complex reasoning function. The top-level task typically corresponds to a task identified in the task model (cf. Chapter 3). The specification of a task tells us what the inputs and the outputs of the task are. The main difference with traditional nonleaf function descriptions in DFDs is that the data manipulated by a task are described in a domain-independent way. For example, the output of a medical diagnosis task would not be a "disease," but an abstract name such as "fault category."

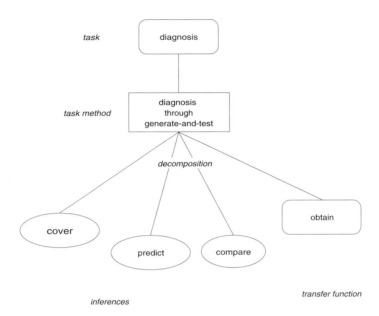

Figure 5.21
Task-decomposition diagram for the car-diagnosis application showing the two main task-knowledge types: "task" and "task method." Only one single level of task-decomposition is present, so diagnosis is defined here as a primitive task, which decomposes directly into leaf functions.

Figure 5.22 shows a simple specification of the DIAGNOSE task. The **GOAL** and **SPECIFICATION** slots give an informal textual description of, respectively, the goal of the task and the relation between task input and output. Note that there is no domain-dependent term to be found in the definition. The specification talks about a "system" about which we have received a "complaint." As we shall see, this type of definition may sometimes be a bit harder to read because of its generic character, but it enables us to employ powerful forms of reuse.

Task I/O is, just like inferences, specified in terms of functional role names. There are, however, two main differences with inferences:

1. We do not include static roles in task specifications. Static roles are only introduced at the level of inferences.
2. We do not specify the mapping of the roles onto domain-specific terms. The mapping is an indirect one: task roles are linked to inference roles through the control structure (see the next subsection). Inference roles each have an associated mapping to domain constructs.

```
TASK car-diagnosis;
  GOAL:
    "Find a likely cause for the complaint of the user";
  ROLES:
    INPUT:
      complaint: "Complaint about the behavior of the car";
    OUTPUT:
      fault-category: "A hypothesis explained by the evidence";
      evidence: "Set of observations obtained during the
                 diagnostic process";
  SPEC:
    "Find an initial state that explains the complaint and is
    consistent with the evidence obtained";
END TASK car-diagnosis;
```

Figure 5.22
Specification of the car-diagnosis task.

Each task should have a corresponding task method that describes how the task is realized in terms of subtasks and/or inferences[1].

5.6.2   Task Method

A task method describes how a task is realized through a decomposition into subfunctions. Such subfunctions can either be another task, an inference defined in the inference knowledge, or a transfer function such as obtain. The core part of a method is formed by the so-called control structure. This control structure describes in what order the subfunctions should be carried out. The control structure typically reads like a small program, in which the subfunctions are the procedures and the roles act as parameters of the procedures. The control structure is intended to capture the reasoning strategy employed in solving a problem.

A task method may define additional task roles, which are used to store temporary reasoning results. A typical example of such an additional task role is a **hypothesis** in which the candidate solution that is currently being pursued is stored. In Figure 5.23 a sample task method for the task DIAGNOSE is given. The method decomposes the task into four subfunctions: three inferences and one transfer function. The control specifies a generate-and-test strategy:

1. At the start of the task the inference cover is invoked to generate a candidate solution (the **hypothesis**) on the basis of the original complaint.

---

[1]Actually, it is allowed to define multiple methods for the same task. In that case, we need additional knowledge to choose dynamically a particular method. This leads to a much more complicated but also more flexible system. We come back to this issue in Chapter 13.

```
TASK-METHOD diagnosis-through-generate-and-test;
  REALIZES: car-diagnosis;
  DECOMPOSITION:
    INFERENCES: cover, predict, compare;
    TRANSFER-FUNCTIONS: obtain;
  ROLES:
    INTERMEDIATE:
      hypothesis: "A candidate solution";
      expected-finding: "The finding predicted,
        in case the hypothesis is true";
      actual-finding: "The finding actually observed";
      result: "The result of the comparison";
  CONTROL-STRUCTURE:

    WHILE NEW-SOLUTION cover(complaint -> hypothesis);
    DO
      predict(hypothesis -> expected-finding);
      obtain(expected-finding -> actual-finding);
      evidence := evidence ADD actual-finding;
      compare(expected-finding + actual-finding -> result);
      IF result == equal;
        THEN "break from loop";
      END IF
    END WHILE

    IF result == equal
      THEN fault-category := hypothesis;
      ELSE "no solution found";
    END IF

  END TASK-METHOD diagnosis-through-generate-and-test;
```

Figure 5.23
Example task method for the car-diagnosis task. This method follows a generate-and-test strategy.

2. Subsequently, the candidate solution is tested to see whether it is consistent with other data. This test consists of specifying an expected finding for the hypothesis (the inference predict), obtaining the actual value of the finding from the user or some other external agent (the transfer function obtain), and finally comparing the actual and the expected finding to see whether these are equal.

3. The observations made by obtain are added to the knowledge role **evidence**, the second output of diagnosis which collects all additional data gathered.

4. If the comparison delivers a difference, the cover inference is invoked again to generate another hypothesis, and the testing process is repeated,

5. The task method for diagnosis terminates if either the inference compare returns an `equal` value (in which case the current hypothesis becomes the solution) or the cover

inference fails to produce a new hypothesis, in which case the task method fails to find a solution.

The strategy sketched is of course just one possibility. In this particular example, the method apparently assumes that there exist observations that can verify the existence of a hypothesis. In Chapter 6 we will see a somewhat more comprehensive diagnostic strategy, in which all candidate solutions are generated in the first step.

In the appendix a full description of the pseudocode language is given. Here, it suffices to say that the imperative pseudocode for control structures typically consists of the following elements:

- A simple "procedure" call, i.e., an invocation of a task, an inference, or a transfer function. Note that we only use the dynamic roles as arguments for inference invocations, because these vary over time.
- Data operations on role values: e.g., assign a value to a role, add a set of values to a role, and so on.
- The usual control primitives for iteration and selection: repeat-until, while-do, if-then-else.
- Conditions used in control statements (e.g., until ....) are typically statements about values of roles (e.g., "result == equal").
- There are two special types of conditions. First, one can ask of an inference whether it is capable of producing a new solution. This is typically used in loop conditions. An example of the use of the **NEW-SOLUTION** predicate can be found at the start of the control structure in Figure 5.23. Second, one can ask whether an inference produces a solution with a particular input. This predicate is called **HAS-SOLUTION**. It is particularly useful for inferences that can fail, such as tests and verifications. The method for assessment (see Figure 6.5) contains an example of the use of **HAS-SOLUTION**. These two special conditions are a direct consequence of the specific way in which the control of inferences should be viewed from a task perspective. We assume that *within the execution of a certain task* an inference has a memory, and that each invocation will produce a new value (in the context of this task). An inference fails if it can produce no more solutions.

An alternative for the pseudocode is to model the method control with the help of an activity diagram. This UML notation is described in Section 14.2. Figure 5.24 shows the method control for the car-diagnosis task. Some people will probably prefer this graphical notation.

During knowledge-model construction the task decomposition often changes a number of times. What was viewed as an inference early on might later be viewed as a task which itself can be decomposed. The main guideline to be followed here is:

> If the internal behavior of a function is important for explaining the behavior of the system as a whole, then one needs to define this function as a task.

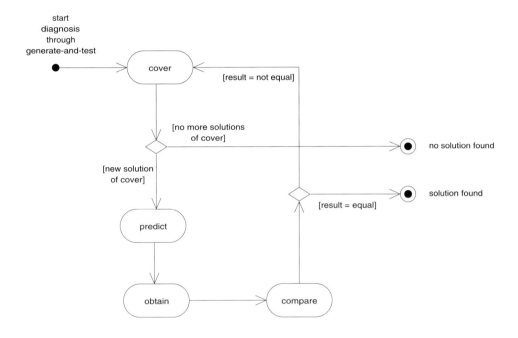

Figure 5.24
Alternative representation of method control using an activity diagram.

This guideline is based on the fact that inferences are treated as black boxes. The behavior of the inference is assumed to be self-explanatory if one looks at the inputs and outputs. Note that the black box view of inferences is only true in the context of the knowledge model. The inference might well be realized in the final system by a complex computational technique. Inferences provide us with a potentially powerful abstraction technique in the analysis stage, which helps us to shift much of the burden to the design phase. We come back to this issue in the chapter on the process of knowledge-model construction (Chapter 7).

5.7   Typographic Conventions

In this book we use typographic conventions to indicate knowledge-model component types such as task, role, inference, and so on. The conventions are listed in Table 5.1.

Construct	Typography		Example
Task	Capital letters		DIAGNOSIS
Method	Small capitals		GENERATE & TEST
Inference, transfer function	Sans serif		abstract, obtain
Role	Bold underlined		**hypothesis**
Domain type	Bold		**car**
Domain instance	Fixed-width		`my-car`
Metatype	Bold capitals		**CONCEPT**

Table 5.1
Typographic conventions used in this book for knowledge-model components. The category "metatype" is used to indicate elements of the language itself.

5.8   Comparison with Other Analysis Approaches

At several places in this chapter we have made remarks about the similarities and differences between knowledge analysis in CommonKADS and general analysis techniques. We summarize the main issues because a good insight may help to understand and appreciate the specific demands and requirements of knowledge-intensive applications.

5.8.1   Four Major Differences

There are four crucial differences between the CommonKADS knowledge model and more general analysis approaches. These differences all arise from the specific nature of knowledge analysis.

Difference 1: "Data model" contains both data and knowledge   The "data model" of a knowledge model contains elements that are usually not found in traditional data models. As we saw in the car example, the representation of even simple pieces of knowledge poses specific problems. This results from the fact that knowledge can be seen as "information about information." It implies that parts of the "data model" describe how we should interpret or use other parts. For example, if we have information types for **observations** and **diseases** of patients, we also want to describe a domain-knowledge type that allows us to infer the latter from the former. This requires specialized modelling tools, in particular the construct **RULE TYPE** discussed in this chapter.

Difference 2: "Functions" are described datamodel-independent   In describing functions, knowledge engineering has transgressed to a more sophisticated level than general software-engineering approaches. This is not a real surprise, because the scope of the application tasks covered is much smaller, namely only knowledge-intensive tasks. In the knowledge-engineering literature, a typology of such tasks has been developed, together with standard functional decompositions that have proved useful for a particular task type. Example knowledge-intensive task types are assessment, planning, and diagnosis.

The availability of a catalog of functional decompositions is a powerful tool for the system analyst, as we will see in Chapter 6. However, this feature of knowledge modelling requires that all functions are described in a domain-independent terminology. This means that the input/output of functions in an knowledge model is not described in terms of data-model elements, but in terms of task-oriented "role" names. These "roles" act as placeholders for data-model elements. Effectively, knowledge roles **decouple** the description of the static information structure on the one hand and the functions on the other hand.

Decoupling of functions and data makes a knowledge model more complex, but it enables exploitation of powerful forms of reuse. The function-data decoupling is the main area in which CommonKADS differs from object-oriented approaches (see Figure 5.25).

Difference 3: The need to represent "internal" control So far we we have mainly looked at the way functions and data are represented. There is also difference with respect to the specification of control.

In approaches such as Modern Structured Analysis and OMT, control is specified through state-transition diagrams. Such diagrams are especially useful for systems in which information processing is mainly driven by external events. In reasoning tasks, however, there is usually a clear need to represent also the internal control of the reasoning process. The way in which the reasoning functions are ordered is an important element of expertise. Experts employ sophisticated reasoning strategies, which we want to capture in our specifications. This means that in knowledge modelling more emphasis is placed on specifying the sequencing of reasoning steps. Thus, the emphasis is on internal control.

Difference 4: Knowledge model abstracts from communication aspects The emphasis on internal control also arises from the fact that knowledge model abstracts from all issues concerning interaction with the outside world. Communication is described only with the help of transfer functions. All details of agent-agent interaction are described in a separate model: the communication model (see Chapter 9).

Keeping these differences in mind, will hopefully enable the reader to understand the rationale underlying the knowledge model, and explain how the elements relate to general software-engineering concepts.

5.8.2 The Data-Function Debate

If we take a somewhat broader view, we can indicate the position CommonKADS takes in what can be called the "data-function" debate. This term refers to the point made by the advocates of object-oriented analysis approaches. They reject the traditional functional decomposition approaches such as Structured Analysis in which the "data" are secondary to the functions. O-O people state that the information structures ("data") are usually much more stable (and thus less likely to change) than the functions of a system. Therefore, in O-O analysis, the data view is the entry point for modelling an application domain.

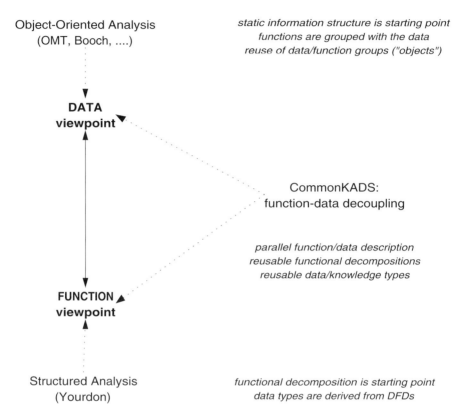

Figure 5.25
Schematic view of the data-function debate. In the Yourdon approach, functional decomposition is the starting point of analysis; in the modern object-oriented approaches the "data" are the initial focus of attention.
CommonKADS takes an intermediate position,assuming both data and function descriptions can be stable and
reusable.

In CommonKADS we take a position between these two approaches. As you will see
in Chapter 6 we claim that functional decompositions can also be stable and potentially
reusable, similar to the static information and knowledge structures. To enable reuse of
both "functions" and "data", CommonKADS employs a data-function decoupling with the
help of knowledge roles. This dual approach can also be found in the guidelines of Chapter 7, where we advise you to do an initial task analysis and a domain conceptualization in
parallel.

Figure 5.25 gives a schematic view of the various positions taken in the data-function
debate.

5.9   Bibliographical Notes and Further Reading

The CommonKADS knowledge model is one of a series of modelling frameworks proposed in the knowledge engineering literature.   Some other well-known approaches are PROTÉGÉ (Tu et al. 1995), Generic Tasks (Chandrasekaran 1988), Role-Limiting Methods (Marcus 1988), Components of Expertise (Steels 1993), DIDS (Runkel et al. 1996), MIKE (Angele et al. 1998), and DESIRE (Brazier et al. 1996). Examples of the use of these approaches using the same data set can be found in two special issues of the International Journal of Human-Computer Studies (Linster 1994, Schreiber and Birmingham 1996).

The literature on analysis models in general software engineering is immense. The book by Yourdon (1989), *Modern Structured Analysis*, is a good description of this almost classic approach (in the positive sense of the word). Two influential object-oriented analysis methods are the OMT approach (Rumbaugh et al. 1991) and the approach advocated by Booch (1994). A unification of these approaches has been proposed in the form of a Unified Modelling Language for object-oriented analysis (Booch et al. 1998).

6

Template Knowledge Models

Key points of this chapter:

- Knowledge models can often partially be reused in new applications.
- The type of task is the main guide for reuse. For most task types *task templates* are available: predefined decompositions into functions (tasks, inferences) plus requirements about the structure of the domain knowledge.
- This chapter contains a small set of task templates for simple problem-solving tasks. These task templates have proved useful in practice.
- In the modern O-O jargon these templates would be called "patterns" of knowledge-intensive tasks.
- More task templates can be found in various repositories, although the quality and consistency vary.

6.1 Reusing Knowledge-Model Elements

6.1.1 The Need for Reuse

There are several ways in which knowledge models can be used to support the knowledge-modelling process. A potentially powerful approach is to *reuse* combinations of model elements. When one models a particular application, it is usually already intuitively clear that large parts of the model are not specific to this application, but re-occur in other domains and/or tasks. CommonKADS (as do most other approaches to knowledge modelling) makes use of this observation by providing a knowledge engineer with a collection of predefined sets of model elements. These catalogs can be of great help to the knowledge engineer. They provide the engineer with ready-made building blocks and prevent her from "reinventing the wheel" each time a new system has to be built. In fact, we believe that these libraries are a *conditio sine qua non* for improving the state of the art in knowledge engineering.

In this chapter we have included a number of simple partial knowledge models of the *task template* type (see further). These models have proved to be useful in developing a range of common straightforward systems. We expect these to be of use when modelling a relatively simple knowledge-intensive task. The full collection of reusable models is much larger, although rather heterogeneous and represented in nonstandard ways. We give references in the text where you can find these; the knowledge engineer tackling more complex problems might find them useful input.

There is a parallel between task templates and the notion of "design patterns" (Gamma et al. 1995) in O-O analysis. Task templates can be viewed design patterns for knowledge-intensive tasks. We are bold enough to claim that you will find these "knowledge" patterns to be more powerful and precise than those in use in O-O analysis, in particular because they are grounded on a decade of research and practical experience.

6.1.2   Task Templates

Task templates form a common type of a reusable combination of model elements. A task template is a partial knowledge model in which inference and task knowledge are specified. A task template supplies the knowledge engineer with inferences and tasks that are typical for solving a problem of a particular type. In addition, a task template specifies a typical domain schema that would be required from the task point of view (see Chapter 13 for a discussion on the task view of domain schemas). Task templates can be used by the knowledge engineer as a template for a new application and thus support top-down knowledge analysis.

6.1.3   Task Types

An advantage of knowledge engineering, when compared with software engineering in general, is that the range of task types is limited. In cognitive psychology literature task typologies for knowledge-intensive (human) reasoning tasks are given. Several authors have adapted and refined these for use in knowledge engineering. We use the task hierarchy shown in Figure 6.1.

We distinguish two groups of task types: *analytic* tasks and *synthetic* tasks. The distinguishing feature between the two groups is the "system" the task operates on. "System" is an abstract term for the object to which the task is applied. For example, in technical diagnosis the system is the artifact or device being diagnosed; in elevator configuration it is the elevator to be designed. In analytic tasks the system preexists although it is typically not completely "known." All analytic tasks take as input some data about the system, and produce some characterization of the system as output. In contrast, for synthetic tasks the system does not yet exist: the purpose of the task is to construct a system description. The

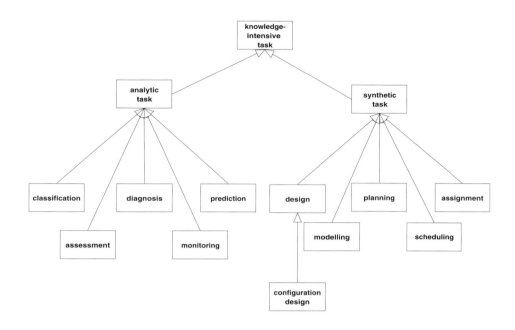

Figure 6.1
Hierarchy of knowledge-intensive task types based on the type of problem being solved.

input of a synthetic task typically consists of requirements that the system to be constructed should satisfy.

Analytic and synthetic tasks are further subdivided into a number of task types, as can be seen in Figure 6.1. This subdivision of tasks is based on the *type of problem* tackled by the task. For example, a "diagnosis" problem is concerned with finding a malfunction that causes deviant system behavior. A diagnosis task is a task that tackles a diagnostic problem. Although in theory, "problem" and "task" are distinct entities, in practice we use these terms interchangeably. We often use a term such as "diagnosis" for a diagnostic problem as well as for the task of solving this problem. Tables 6.1 and 6.2 provide an overview of the main features of, respectively, analytic and synthetic task types.

Analysis tasks   A well-known analytic task type is **classification**. The classification of plants and animals is the prototypical example of this task type. In classification, an object needs to be characterized in terms of the class to which it belongs. The underlying knowledge typically provides for each class constraints on the values of object features. Classification usually involves "natural" (not manmade) objects.

Task type	Input	Output	Knowledge	Features
Analysis	System observations	System characterization	System model	System description is given.
Classification	Object features	Object class	Feature-class associations	Set of classes is predefined.
Diagnosis	Symptoms / complaints	Fault category	Model of system behavior	Form output varies (causal chain, state, component) and depends on use made of it (troubleshooting).
Assessment	Case description	Decision class	Criteria, norms	Assessment is performed at one particular point in time (cf. monitoring).
Monitoring	System data	Discrepancy class	Normal system behavior	System changes over time. Task is carried out repeatedly.
Prediction	System data	System state	Model of system behavior	Output state is a system description at some future point in time.

Table 6.1
Overview of analytic task types.

Diagnosis differs from classification in the sense that the desired output is a malfunction of the system. Diagnosis of faults in an electrical network is an example of this task type. In diagnosis the underlying knowledge typically contains knowledge about system behavior, such as a causal model. The output of diagnosis (the fault category) can take many forms: it can be a faulty component, a faulty state, a causal chain, or even an abstract label without any internal system meaning. Diagnosis tasks are frequently encountered in the area of technical systems.

The task type **assessment** is often found in financial and community service domains. The goal of assessment is to characterize a case in terms of a decision class. For example, in loan assessment the task input is a case of a person applying for a loan, and the output is a decision class such as "yes/no/more info needed" indicating whether a loan should be given or not. The underlying knowledge typically consists of a set of norms or criteria that are used for the assessment. The housing case in Chapter 10 is an example of an assessment task.

In **monitoring**, the system being analyzed is of a dynamic nature, typically an ongoing process. Example monitoring tasks are nuclear plant monitoring and monitoring of a software project. Each monitoring cycle looks a bit like an assessment task. The main difference is that in monitoring the output is simply a discrepancy (is the system behavior normal or not?) instead of a decision class. Also, data from previous cycles are used in each new cycle.

We have placed **prediction** also in the group of analytic tasks, although it also has some synthetic features. In prediction, one analyzes current system behavior to construct

Task type	Input	Output	Knowledge	Features
Synthesis	Require-ments	System structure	Elements, constraints, preferences	System description needs to be generated.
Design	Require-ments	Artifact description	Components, constraints, preferences	May include creative design of components.
Configura-tion design	Require-ments	Artifact description	Components, skeletal designs, constraints, preferences	Subtype of design in which all components are predefined.
Assignment	Two object sets, requirements	Mapping set 1 → set 2	Constraints, preferences	Mapping need not be one-to-one.
Planning	Goals, requirements	Action plan	Actions, constraints, preferences	Actions are (partially) ordered in time.
Scheduling	Job activities, resources, time slots, requirements	Schedule = activities allocated to time slots of resources	Constraints, preferences	Time-oriented character distinguishes it from assignment.
Modelling	Require-ments	Model	Model elements, template models, constraints, preferences	May include creative "synthesis."

Table 6.2
Overview of synthetic task types.

a description of the system state at some future point in time. Weather forecasting is a prediction task. A prediction task is often found in knowledge-intensive modules of teaching systems, e.g., for physics. The inverse of prediction also exists: *retrodiction*. The big-bang theory is a well-known example of retrodiction.

Synthesis tasks   **Design** is a synthetic task in which the system to be constructed is some physical artifact. An example design task is the design of a car. Design tasks in general can include creative design of components, as is usual in car design. Creative design is too hard a nut to crack for current knowledge technology. In order for system construction to be feasible, we generally have to assume that all components of the artifact are predefined. This subtype of design is called **configuration design**. Building a boat from a set of Lego blocks is a well-known example of a configuration-design task. Another example is the configuration of a computer system.

   Assignment is a relatively simple synthetic task, in which we have two sets of objects between which we have to create a (partial) mapping. Examples are the allocation of offices to employees or of airplanes to gates. The assignment has to be consistent with constraints

("Boeing 747 cannot be placed on gates 35–38") as well as conform with preferences ("KLM airplanes should be parked in Terminal 1").

Planning shares many features with design, the main difference being the type of system being constructed. Whereas design is concerned with physical object construction, planning is concerned with activities and their time dependencies. Examples of planning tasks are travel planning and the planning of building activities. Again, automation of planning tasks is usually only feasible if the basic plan elements are predefined. Because of their similarity, design models can sometimes be used for planning and *vice versa*.

Scheduling often follows planning. Planning delivers a sequence of activities; in scheduling, such sequences of activities ("jobs") need to be allocated to resources during a certain time interval. The output is a mapping between activities and time slots, while obeying constraints ("A should be before B") and conforming as much as possible with the preferences ("lectures by C should preferably be on Friday"). Scheduling is therefore closely related to assignment, the major distinction being the time-oriented character of scheduling. Examples of scheduling are the scheduling of lectures at a university department and job-shop scheduling in a process line of a factory.

For completeness, we mention **modelling** as a synthetic task type.   In modelling, we construct an abstract description of a system in order to explain or predict certain system properties or phenomena. Knowledge modelling itself is an example of a modelling task. Another example is the construction of a simulation model of a nuclear accident. Modelling tasks are seldom automated in a system, but are sometimes used in the context of knowledge management. A real-life example we have been involved with is the construction of a knowledge model of the modelling expertise of a retiring expert in nuclear accident simulations.

6.2   A Small Task Template Catalog

In this chapter we have included a small task template catalog of relatively simple knowledge-intensive tasks. The templates were selected because they have proved useful in prior knowledge-engineering projects.

The catalog contains task templates for classification, diagnosis, assessment, monitoring, configuration design, assignment, planning, and scheduling. Each task template description consists of the following parts:

General characterization   Describes typical features of a task: goal, input, output, terminology. Also, some remarks are made about the relation with other task types.

Default method   A method for a task type is described in terms of roles, subfunctions, and a description of the internal control (through a control structure). We show an inference structure for the functions at the lowest level of decomposition. However, the reader should be aware that these inferences are of a provisional nature, as in practice it might well be necessary to decompose one or more inferences and thus to view them as tasks with internal complexity (see also the discussion in Chapter 5 of the distinction between tasks and inferences).

Method variations   Some frequently occurring variations of the default method are described. For example, in the default classification method an abstraction task could be included. We do not show the changed diagrams and specifications for each variation, but these should be straightforward to construct.

Typical domain schema   Each method makes assumptions about the nature of the underlying domain knowledge. For example, the classification method we describe makes assumptions about knowledge linking classes to observed features. We describe these assumptions in a tentative domain schema. Please note that the word "domain" in this latter term should be regarded with some caution: the schema can, by definition, contain no domain-specific types! The schema can best be viewed as requirements on the domain schema that the knowledge engineer has to construct for the application.

The issue of the relation between a method-related domain schema and a domain-specific schema is discussed in more detail in Chapter 13.

The major part of this chapter presents the catalog of templates. At the end we come back to the issue of using these templates in an application.

6.3   Classification

General characterization

Goal	Classification is concerned with establishing the correct class (or category) for an object. The object should be available for inspection. The classification is based on characteristics of the object.
Typical example	Classification of an apple. Classification of the minerals in a rock.
Terminology	**Object**: the object of which one wants to find the class or category, e.g., a certain apple. **Class**: a group of objects that share similar characteristics, e.g., a Granny Smith apple. **Attribute**: a characteristic that can either be observed or inferred, e.g., the color of an apple. **Feature**: an attribute-value pair that holds for a certain object, e.g., "color = green."
Input	The object of which the class needs to be established.
Output	The class(es) found.
Features	Classification is one of the simplest analytic tasks, for which many methods exist. Other analytic tasks can sometimes be reduced to a classification problem. Especially for diagnosis is this

often done. Full diagnosis requires knowledge about causal behavior, but if one can simplify this to direct associations between
symptoms and malfunctions, then it takes the form of a classification problem.

Default method   A first decision one has to make is whether one chooses a data-driven
or a solution-driven method. The data-driven approach starts off with some initial features, which are used to generate a set of candidate solutions. A solution-driven method
starts with the full set of possible solutions and tries to reduce this set on the basis of the
information that comes in.

In most applications the solution-driven approach works best. In the first step we
generate a full set of candidate solutions, e.g., all potential apple classes. Then we prune
this set by gathering information about the object. We specify a characteristic that we are
interested in, and obtain its value. On the basis of this new information, we eliminate
candidate solutions that are inconsistent with this information. We repeat this process until
we have no further means of reducing the candidate set.

The specification of this method is shown in Figure 6.2. The first **while** loop generates
the set of candidate solutions. The second **while** loop prunes this set by obtaining new
information. The method finishes if one of the following three conditions is true (see the
condition of the second **while** loop):

1. A single candidate remains. This class becomes the solution.
2. The candidate set is empty. No solution is found.
3. No more attributes remain for which a value can be obtained. A partial solution is
   found in the form of the remaining set of candidates.

Figure 6.3 shows the corresponding inference structure. Three inferences are used in
this method plus a transfer function for obtaining the attribute value:

- **Generate candidate**   In the simplest case, this step is just a look-up in the knowledge
  base of the potential candidate solutions.
- **Specify attribute**   There are several ways of realizing this inference. The simplest
  way is to just do a random selection. This can work well, especially if the "cost" of
  obtaining information is low. Often however, a more knowledge-intensive attribute
  specification is required. One possibility is to define an explicit attribute ordering as is
  the case in a decision tree. This requires domain knowledge of the form "if attribute a
  has value x then ask about attribute b." Often, experts can provide this type of attribute-
  ordering information. The specification knowledge then takes the form of a decision
  tree. A more comprehensive approach is to compute the attribute that has the highest
  information potential. Several algorithms for this exist. This last approach can be very
  efficient but may lead to system behavior that (although theoretically optimal) is alien
  to users and experts.

```
TASK classification;
  ROLES:
    INPUT: object: "Object that needs to be classified";
    OUTPUT: candidate-classes: "Classes consistent with the object";
END TASK classification;

TASK-METHOD prune-candidate-set;
  REALIZES: classification;
  DECOMPOSITION:
    INFERENCES: generate, specify, match;
    TRANSFER-FUNCTIONS: obtain;
  ROLES:
    INTERMEDIATE:
      class: "object class";
      attribute: "a descriptor for the object";
      new-feature: "a newly obtained attribute-value pair" ;
      current-feature-se: "the collection of features obtained";
      truth-value: "indicates whether the class is consistent with
        object features obtained during the reasoning process";
  CONTROL-STRUCTURE:
    WHILE NEW-SOLUTION generate(object -> class) DO
      candidate-classes := class ADD candidate-classes;
    END WHILE
    WHILE NEW-SOLUTION specify(candidate-classes -> attribute)
        AND SIZE candidate-classes > 1 DO
      obtain(attribute -> new-feature);
      current-feature-set := new-feature ADD current-feature-set;
      FOR-EACH class IN candidate-classes DO
        match(class + current-feature-set -> truth-value);
        IF truth-value == false
        THEN
          candidate-classes := candidate-classes SUBTRACT class;
        END IF
      END FOR-EACH
    END WHILE
END TASK-METHOD prune-candidate-set;
```

Figure 6.2
Pruning method for classification.

- **Obtain feature**   Usually, one should allow the user to enter an "unknown" value. Also, sometimes there is domain knowledge that suggests that certain attributes should always be obtained together.
- **Match**   This inference is executed for every candidate, and produces a truth value indicating whether the candidate class is consistent with the information collected so far. The inference should be able to handle an "unknown" value for certain attributes. The normal approach is that every candidate is consistent with an "unknown" value.

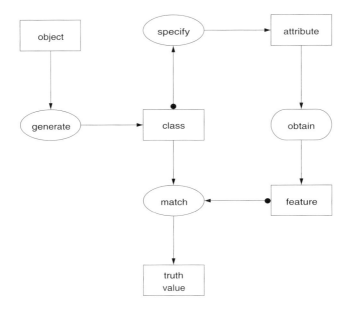

Figure 6.3
Inferences structure for the pruning classification method.

Method variations

- **Limited candidate generation**   If the full set of candidate solutions is too large, one adds a small data-driven element into the method by giving a small set of features as input to the generate step, with the idea that only those candidates are considered that are consistent with these initial data. In most cases the choice of this initial set will be quite straightforward. This set can either contain a fixed set of attributes or be dependent on the context (e.g., the location where the object is found).
- **User control over attribute selection**   In some applications we have seen that users want to control the order in which new information is provided. In this case, the attribute produced by the specify inference can be used as a suggestion to the user, who has the final control over the information to be provided. This can be achieved by changing the control flow slightly. Replace the obtain function in the second **while** loop of the control structure (see Figure 6.2) with the following two transfer-function invocations:

  1. A present function that shows the user the suggested new information item (i.e., a certain attribute).

2. A receive function that "reads in" the new feature. It can be different from the one suggested.

- **Hierarchical search through class structure**   In some domains, natural subtype hierarchies of classes exist. Such a hierarchy can be exploited in two ways:

  1. The hierarchy is used for attribute selection, because the supertypes often suggest attributes that discriminate between disjunct sets of candidates. The supertypes themselves are not used in the candidate set.
  2. The hierarchy is used to guide the pruning process. Supertypes are incorporated in the candidate set. If a supertype is ruled out, all its subtypes are also ruled out.

Typical domain schema   Figure 6.4 shows a sort of minimal domain schema for classification. The **object-type** is the overall category to which the objects to be classified belong, e.g., `apple` or `rock`. The object type is linked to multiple **object-class**es that represent the categories that will act as output of the classification task, e.g., a `James Grieves` apple or a `granite` rock. An object type can be characterized by a number of attributes, such as color, shape, composition, and so on. The main knowledge category used in classification is specified in the **class-constraint** rule type, which allows us to define dependencies between object classes and attribute values, e.g., the object class `James Grieves` restricts the value of the color attribute to `green` or `yellow-green`.

6.4   Assessment

General characterization

Goal	Find a *decision category* for a *case* based on a set of domain-specific *norms*.
Typical example	Decide whether a person gets a loan she applied for.
Terminology	**Case**: the case to be assessed, e.g., data about the lender and the requested loan. **Decision category**: e.g., eligible-for-loan yes or no. **Norms**: domain knowledge that is used in making the decision, e.g., rules relating income to the amount requested.
Input	Data about the case (always), case-specific norms (sometimes).
Output	A decision category.
Features	The structure of assessment can look very much like monitoring. There are two main differences. First, in monitoring there is always a time aspect: assessment is done at one particular point in time, while in monitoring the task is performed at intervals. Second, the output is different. Monitoring delivers a discrepancy and not a decision category. This second difference is rather

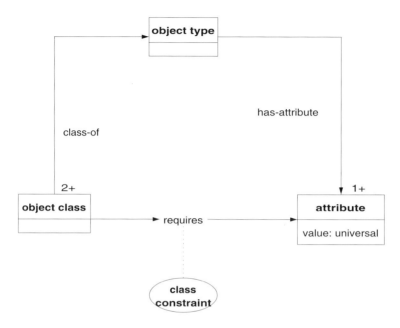

Figure 6.4
Typical domain schema for classification tasks.

subtle and often not so clear. With some effort one could view monitoring as a succession of assessment tasks in which previous results are used again in a new assessment cycle.

Default method   In Chapter 10 we will see an example of an assessment method. It turns out that this assessment model is, with some variations, widely applicable to simple assessment tasks. The method specification is shown in Figure 6.5. It contains the following inferences:

- **Abstract case**   Almost always, some of the case data need to be abstracted. For example, in the housing application (see Chapter 10) the age and household type of the applicant need to be abstracted. The abstractions required are determined by the data used in the norms (see further). Abstraction is modelled here as an inference that is repeated until no more abstractions can be made. The abstracted features are added to the case.
- **Specify norms**   After abstraction, the first step that needs to be taken is to find the norms or criteria that can be used for this case. In most assessment tasks the norms used are at least partially dependent on the case, and the case thus acts as an input role

```
TASK assessment;
  ROLES:
    INPUT: case-description: "The case to be assessed";
    OUTPUT: decision: "the result of assessing the case";
END TASK assessment;

TASK-METHOD assessment-with-abstraction;
  REALIZES: assessment;
  DECOMPOSITION:
    INFERENCES: abstract, specify, select, evaluate, match;
  ROLES:
    INTERMEDIATE:
      abstracted-case: "The raw data plus the abstractions";
      norms: "The full set of assessment norms";
      norm: "A single assessment norm";
      norm-value: "Truth value of a norm for this case";
      evaluation-results: "List of evaluated norms";
  CONTROL-STRUCTURE:
    WHILE
      HAS-SOLUTION abstract(case-description -> abstracted-case)
    DO
      case-description := abstracted-case;
    END WHILE
    specify(abstracted-case -> norms);
    REPEAT
      select(norms -> norm);
      evaluate(abstracted-case + norm -> norm-value);
      evaluation-results := norm-value ADD evaluation-results;
    UNTIL
      HAS-SOLUTION match(evaluation-results -> decision);
    END REPEAT
  END TASK-METHOD assessment-with-abstraction;
```

Figure 6.5
Method for assessment.

for this inference. An example of a norm in a loan assessment application would be "loan amount matches income."

- **Select norm** From the set of norms generated by the previous inference, one norm needs to be selected for evaluation. In the simplest case, this selection is done at random. Often however, there is domain knowledge available that indicates an ordering of norms evaluation. This knowledge can be used to guide the selection. It is not necessary for the selection knowledge to be complete: the system can always fall back on random selection as the default method.

- **Evaluate norm** Evaluate the selected norm with respect to the case data. This function produces a truth value for the norm, e.g., "loan amount matches income is false." This function is usually a quite straightforward computation.

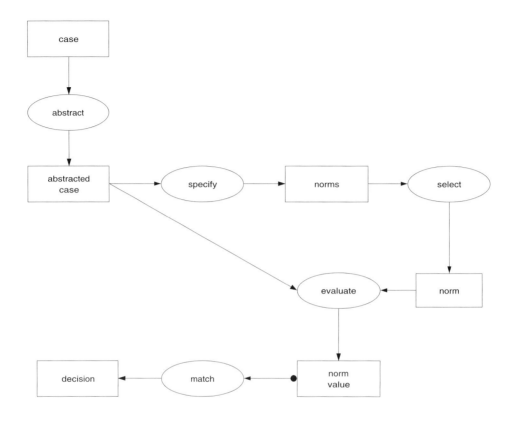

Figure 6.6
Inference structure of the assessment method.

- **Match to see whether a solution can be found**   This inference checks whether the
  results of the evaluation lead to a decision. Sometimes, the truth value of one norm is
  sufficient to arrive at a decision. For example, if in the housing application in Chapter 10 one of the four norms turns out to be false for a certain case, the decision found
  by the match function is "not eligible for this house."

   The inferences described are shown graphically in the inference structure of Figure 6.6.

Method variations   One variation of assessment is demonstrated by the application in
Chapter 10: some norms might be case-specific. For example, in the housing application
(see Chapter 10) some norms were residence-specific, and could therefore not be part of
the knowledge base. The method adaptations are relatively simple: make sure the case-

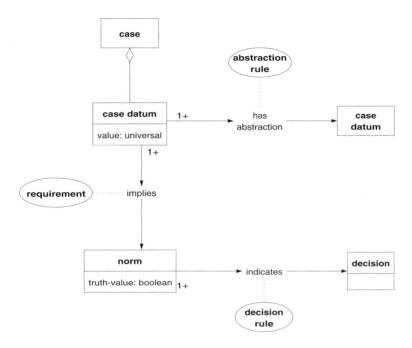

Figure 6.7
Domain schema for the assessment method.

specific norms are introduced as an additional task input, and act as additional input to the specify and/or evaluate functions. This variation is depicted in Figure 10.5.

In some applications case abstraction is not needed, and can therefore be left out. This usually does not mean that there is no abstraction, but that the input data are already provided in an abstracted form!

Another variation already mentioned above is the knowledge-intensiveness of the norm-selection function. This can be done randomly, or be guided by heuristic or statistical knowledge (e.g., "highest predictive value"). A smart selection order can be a key to efficient realization of complex assessment problems. Another issue is that norm-evaluation order is typically dictated by human expertise, and is only acceptable if done in a way understandable to experts.

Typical domain schema   An overview of this assessment domain schema is given in Figure 6.7. There are four main information and knowledge types used in the default method:

1. Specification of *case data*: this is often a combination of features of two domain types, e.g., the applicant and the requested loan (in the loan assessment domain).
2. Case abstraction knowledge: specifies dependencies between case data (see the **has-abstraction** rule type in Figure 6.7).
3. Norm-evaluation knowledge: specifies logical dependencies between case data and norms. As discussed, norm-ordering knowledge can be added as well.
4. Decision knowledge: specifies the decision options that can act as task output, as well as logical dependencies between norm values and a particular decision.

This schema is phrased in domain-neutral terms. For a particular application these types have to mapped onto domain-specific types. For example, the case data have to be linked to domain types that represent the case, e.g., a **loan-applicant** and a **loan**.

6.5   Diagnosis

General characterization

Goal	Find the fault that causes a system to malfunction
Typical example	Diagnosis of a technical device, such as a copier.
Terminology	**Complaint/symptom:** the data that initiate a diagnostic process
	Hypothesis: a potential solution (thus a fault)
	Differential: the set of active hypotheses
	Finding(s)/evidence: additional data about the system being diagnosed
	Fault: the solution found by the diagnostic reasoning process. The nature of the fault representation varies, e.g., an internal system state, a component, a causal chain, or a heuristic label.
Input	Symptoms and/or complaints
Output	Fault(s) plus the evidence gathered for the fault(s)
Features	In principle, a diagnosis task should always have some model of the behavior of the system being diagnosed. Sometimes however, a diagnosis task is reduced to a classification task by replacing the behavioral model with direct associations between symptoms and faults. In the default method we assume that the underlying domain knowledge contains an (albeit quite simple) causal model of system behavior.

Default method   The default method is somewhat different from the method used in the car-diagnosis application of Chapter 5. The method assumes a simple causal model in which symptoms and potential faults are placed in a causal network, and in which internal system states act as intermediate nodes. The network also contains causal links that indicate typical findings for some state (see the domain schema further on).

```
TASK diagnosis;
  ROLES:
    INPUT:
      complaint: "Finding that initiates the diagnostic process";
    OUTPUT:
      faults: "the faults that could have caused the complaint";
      evidence: "the evidence gathered during diagnosis";
END TASK diagnosis;

TASK-METHOD causal-covering;
  REALIZES: diagnosis;
  DECOMPOSITION:
    INFERENCES: cover, select, specify, verify;
    TRANSFER-FUNCTIONS: obtain;
  ROLES:
    INTERMEDIATE:
      differential: "active candidate solutions";
      hypothesis: "candidate solution";
      result: "boolean indicating result of the test";
      expected-finding: "data one would normally expect to find";
      actual-finding: "the data actually observed in practice";
  CONTROL-STRUCTURE:
    WHILE NEW-SOLUTION cover(complaint -> hypothesis) DO
      differential := hypothesis ADD differential;
    END WHILE
    REPEAT
      select(differential -> hypothesis);
      specify(hypothesis -> observable);
      obtain(observable -> finding);
      evidence := finding ADD evidence;
      FOR-EACH hypothesis IN differential DO
        verify(hypothesis + evidence -> result);
        IF result == false
          THEN differential := differential SUBTRACT hypothesis;
        END IF
      END FOR-EACH
    UNTIL
      SIZE differential <= 1 OR "no more observables left";
    END REPEAT
    faults := differential;
END TASK-METHOD causal-covering;
```

Figure 6.8
Default causal-covering method for the diagnosis task.

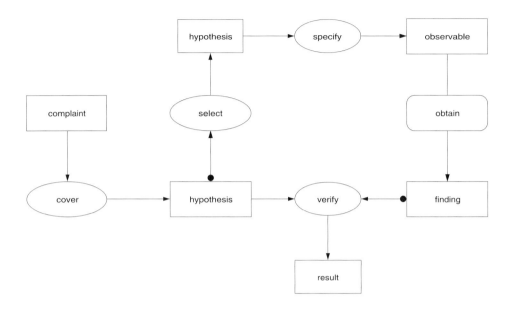

Figure 6.9
Inference structure for the default diagnostic method.

Figure 6.8 shows the method specification. The corresponding inference structure is shown in Figure 6.9. The method follows a generate-and-test strategy. The method decomposes the diagnosis task into five subfunctions: four inferences and one transfer function, which are briefly discussed below.

- **Cover** This inference searches backward through a causal network to find potential causes of the complaint. This inference is executed until no more hypotheses can be found. The set of hypotheses is placed in the differential.
- **Select** The select inference selects one hypothesis from the differential. We assume that a simple form of preference knowledge is used in this selection process, e.g., knowledge about the *a priori* probability of the fault.
- **Specify** This inference specifies some observable entity, the value of which can be used to limit the number of candidate faults. The observable may not only tell us something about the presence of the hypothesis that acts as input for this step but can also be used to rule out other hypotheses.
- **Obtain** This is a simple transfer function to obtain the actual value of the observable used for testing the candidates.
- **Verify** This inference is used to check a candidate fault (a hypothesis). The result is a

boolean, indicating whether the candidate should be kept in the differential. The verify step can be modelled as a single inference in the case of a simple verification method such as the one used in the car-diagnosis application, where the domain knowledge is assumed to contain direct association between hypotheses and expected values of observables. However, in many applications the verify step will need to be modelled in more detail. Some frequently occurring variations are discussed further on.

The last four functions are executed in a loop in which the candidates are tested in the order dictated by the select inference. The loop terminates either when the differential contains at most one hypothesis or when no more observables can be specified. Thus, the method can lead to three situations:

1. The differential is empty: no fault is found. This implies that the evidence is inconsistent with all faults known to the system.
2. Precisely one solution is found. This is usually the ideal outcome.
3. A set of faults remains. The system cannot differentiate between the remaining fault candidates.

Method variations   The method sketched is in fact a simple form of what is called "model-based diagnosis" in the literature. There is a complete research field connected to diagnosis, and knowledge engineers interested in complex diagnostic applications will probably make themselves familiar with this literature. A good starting point is the library of diagnostic methods described by Benjamins (1993). The default method described here is a variation of one of the methods described by Benjamins. Here, we limit the discussion to a few common and relatively simple extensions and variations of the diagnostic method without any claim of completeness.

- **Verification through explanation or consistency**   In the verify step several techniques can be used. For example, one can either require that all findings need to be fully explained by the hypotheses, or alternatively that the hypotheses only need to be consistent with the evidence found. The latter option is the most common one, because we usually do not have complete knowledge to enforce explanation-based diagnosis. Mixed forms are also possible, e.g., by stating that only a subset of the findings needs to be explained. One usually requires that at least the initial complaint is explained.
- **Abstraction of findings**   Often it is useful to add an inference in which one tries to find an abstraction of the findings obtained. Knowledge about faults is often expressed in abstract terminology, which does not relate directly to the findings found.
- **Multiple faults**   The default method assumes that there is only one fault that causes the complaint. If this assumption cannot be made, the method has to be refined. This can be done by inserting an inference after the cover step that transforms the differential into a set of potential fault sets. A common way of realizing this inference is through set covering.

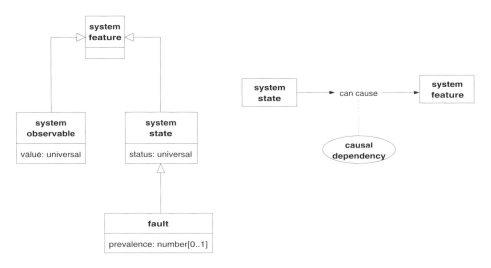

Figure 6.10
Typical domain schema for diagnosis.

- **Fault selection**   A the end of the method we can introduce an inference that, if necessary, selects the most promising ones from the remaining fault candidates. Several preference techniques exist for this. The introduction of this step is particularly useful if the method is extended to cope with multiple faults, because in that case the number of hypotheses usually increases considerably and the verification step may not be able to rule out a sufficient number of candidates.
- **Add simulation methods**   In the verification step one can use simulation methods to derive expected values for findings. This requires two major extensions:
  1. Additional domain knowledge about system behavior, e.g., a model that can be used for quantitative or qualitative prediction of behavior.
  2. A separate prediction step within verification. Note that prediction can be a complex task in its own right.

Typical domain schema   Figure 6.10 shows a typical domain schema for simple diagnosis. It assumes that each system being diagnosed can be characterized in terms of a number of system features. There are two types of system features, namely those that can be observed (e.g., a certain color) and those that represent an internal state of the system (e.g., some disease process). Faults are defined as subtypes of internal states, meaning that not every internal system state may act as a fault. For example, often only the starting points in the causal networks are allowed as faults, as is the case in the car-diagnosis example.

The structure of the causal system model used by the cover and the specify inference (see the static roles in Figure 6.9) is represented as a rule type **causal-dependency**. This rule type describes rules in which the antecedent (some expression about an internal system state) **can-cause** the consequent (some expression about a system feature, which could be either another state or an observable value). The connection symbol **can-cause** is chosen deliberately to make clear that the causal transition is not certain, but depends on unknown other factors.

6.6   Monitoring

General characterization

Goal	Analyze an ongoing process to find out whether it behaves according to expectations.
Typical example	Monitoring progress in a software project. Monitoring an industrial plant.
Terminology	**Parameter**: an entity for which the current value can be relevant to the purpose of detecting abnormal behavior. **Norm**: the expected value or value range of a parameter in the case of normal behavior. **Discrepancy**: this indicates abnormal behavior of the system being monitored; sometimes there is an ordered list of the potential discrepancies, e.g., `small-deviation`, `medium-deviation`, and so on.
Input	Historical data about the system being monitored, usually gathered during prior monitoring cycles.
Output	The discrepancy found (if any).
Features	The crucial distinction between monitoring and diagnosis lies in the nature of the output. Monitoring "just" observes a discrepancy, without any exploration of the cause or fault underlying the deviant system behavior. However, in many domains monitoring and diagnosis are tightly coupled tasks: when monitoring leads to a discrepancy, a diagnosis task is started, using the monitoring information as input. A main feature of monitoring is the dynamic nature of the system being analyzed. This is the main distinguishing feature when compared to assessment.

Default method   Figure 6.11 shows the default method that is applicable to most simple monitoring tasks. The method is event-driven: the method becomes active every time new data come in. This is modelled with the use of the transfer function receive in which an external agent (a human user or another system) has the initiative (see Chapter 5 and

```
TASK monitoring;
  ROLES:
    INPUT:
      historical-data: "data from previous monitoring cycles";
    OUTPUT:
      discrepancy: "indication of deviant system behavior";
END TASK monitoring;

TASK-METHOD data-driven-monitoring;
  REALIZES: monitoring;
  DECOMPOSITION:
    INFERENCES:
      select, specify, compare, classify;
    TRANSFER-FUNCTIONS: receive;
  ROLES:
    INTERMEDIATE:
      finding: "some observed data about the system";
      parameter: "variable to check for deviant behavior";
      norm: "expected normal value of the parameter";
      difference: "an indication of the observed norm deviation";
  CONTROL-STRUCTURE:
    receive(new-finding);
    select(new-finding -> parameter);
    specify(parameter -> norm);
    compare(norm + finding -> difference);
    classify(difference + historical-data -> discrepancy);
    historical-data := finding ADD historical-data;
END TASK-METHOD data-driven-monitoring;
```

Figure 6.11
Method specification for the data-driven method for monitoring. A data-driven method typically starts with a "receive" transfer function, meaning that system control is dependent on the reception of external data. For this reason, the role "new-finding" is not listed as a task input: it is an input during the task.

Chapter 9 for more details on transfer functions). Once a new finding has come in, four inferences are defined for processing the data:

1. **Select**   A system parameter is selected that can tell us something about the new data.
2. **Specify**   A norm value is specified for the parameter. Typically, a monitoring system will have as domain knowledge a system model, consisting of a number of parameters. For each parameter knowledge needs to be provided about the normal parameter values in different system contexts. For example, if we have a system for monitoring intensive care for premature infants, heart rate could be a parameter, and the normal value would typically be a value above 100 beats/minute.
3. **Compare**   A comparison is made of the new finding with the norm, leading to a difference description (e.g., 5 beats/minute below the norm).

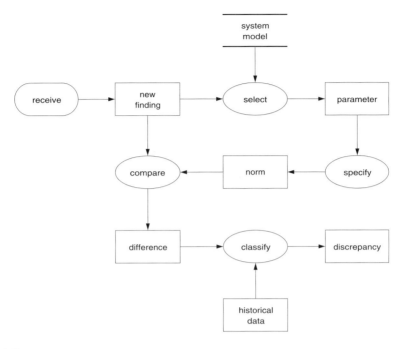

Figure 6.12
Inference structure of the task template for monitoring.

4. **Classify**   A classification is performed of the difference into a discrepancy class, e.g., *minor* or *major* disturbance. Often, data from previous monitoring cycles are used in this inference. For example, a difference of 5 beats/minute in a newborn infant could be classified as a minor disturbance if the value is the same as in previous cycles; a sudden decrease in time would however be characterized as a major disturbance.

Figure 6.12 shows the corresponding inference structure.

Method variations   In some domains the method *model-driven monitoring* is more appropriate. Model-driven monitoring describes a monitoring approach where the system has the initiative. This type of monitoring is typically executed at regular points in time, e.g., each month the progress of a software project is measured. The system actively acquires new data for some selected set of parameters (through an obtain transfer function) and then checks whether the observed values differ from the expected ones.

In some cases classification is quite complex, and is best treated as a subtask with internal structure. The classification method discussed earlier might be of help then.

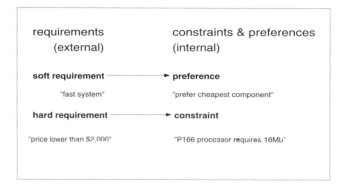

Figure 6.13
Terminology in synthetic tasks. The examples are taken from a PC configuration domain.

6.7   Synthesis

Although "synthesis" is in essence just a common denominator for a group of task types, some of which are described further on, we found it useful to include a general synthesis model, because it turns out that in many synthetic tasks a similar reasoning pattern appears. The model sketched here should be viewed as an "ideal" model, which often cannot be used in precisely this form, or should be extended in various ways. The terminology used is by definition very abstract.

General characterization

Goal	Given a set of requirements construct a system structure that fulfills these requirements
Terminology	**System structure**: the system being synthesized, e.g., a physical artifact, a plan, a schedule, or a set of assignments.
	Constraint, preference, requirement These three terms appear in most synthesis domains. In the literature, different definitions are given of these terms. We propose to use the terminology depicted in Figure 6.13. The main property of requirements in general is that they are external to the system. When the requirements are "operationalized" for use in an application it usually turns out that there are two types of requirements: "hard" requirements and "soft" requirements. Typically, hard requirements have the same role and representation as the "constraints" which dictate inherent limitations in system structure and are part of the domain knowledge. Therefore, hard requirements are sometimes called "exter-

nal constraints," but this terminology easily leads to confusion. For soft requirements and preferences the same story holds: soft requirements and preferences share many features. This type of knowledge also has an associated preference category (indicating the relative importance of the preference), the representation of which differs per application domain.

Input   A set of requirements.

Output   A (list of) system-structure description(s).

Features   This synthesis method can be used in synthetic application tasks in which the amount of possible system structures is limited. For example, in some therapy-planning tasks the design space is limited. This method therefore actually works well for this class of planning tasks. The system structure is in this case equivalent to a plan.

Default method Figure 6.14 shows the specification of this idealized method for synthetic tasks. It consists of four steps:

1. **Operationalize requirements**   This inference analyzes the requirements and transforms these into an operational representation. The output is usually two different sets of requirements: hard and soft requirements (see Figure 6.13).

2. **Generate possible system structures**   In this step all possible system structures are generated, based on the static knowledge the system has about potential system structures. The requirements provide us with the general goal, e.g., "design a car," "configure a mixer," or "plan a therapy for an apple pest." Because design spaces can be very large or even infinite, this step may not be feasible in many design applications. You will see that more specific synthetic methods, such as the method for configuration design, use "smart" methods to limit the number of designs generated. There still remain a number of simple synthetic tasks in which the space of possible designs is limited to a manageable number. Note that this "manageable number" goes up with the increasing power of computer systems.

3. **Select valid system structures**   In this step the constraints and hard requirements are applied to the possible system structures in order to filter out valid system structures. The constraints are usually based on physical laws or empirical design knowledge ("the minimum strength of cable X should be ..."). In some cases a subset of the constraints is included in the generate function, with the goal of reducing the number of candidates.

4. **Sort systems in preference order**   Often, the space of valid designs is still very large. To reduce this set we need to apply preference criteria. Typically, we have two types of preference-related knowledge:

   a. The actual preferences, e.g., that the system should be as cheap as possible. In our society this is often an important, if not the only preference criterion.

```
TASK synthesis;
  ROLES:
    INPUT: requirements: "the requirements that need to be
      fulfilled by the artifact";
    OUTPUT: system-structure-list: "partially ordered list
      of preferred system structures";
END TASK synthesis;

TASK-METHOD idealized-synthesis-method;
  REALIZES:
    synthesis;
  DECOMPOSITION:
    INFERENCES:
      operationalize, generate, select-subset, sort;
    ROLES:
      INTERMEDIATE:
        hard-requirements: "requirements that need to be met";
        soft-requirements: "requirements that act as preferences";
        possible-system-structures: "all possible system structures";
        valid-system-structures: "all system structures that are
          consistent with the constraints";
  CONTROL-STRUCTURE:
    operationalize(requirements
        -> hard-requirements + soft-requirements);
    generate(requirements
        -> possible-system-structures);
    select-subset(possible-system-structures + hard-requirements
        -> valid-system-structures);
    sort(valid-system-structures + soft-requirements
        -> system-structure-list);
END TASK-METHOD idealized-synthesis-method;
```

Figure 6.14
Specification of an idealized method for synthetic tasks.

b. The relative importance of the preferences. Preferences are often rated according to some preference scale.

If there is a strict ordering in the set of preferences, this step is not very difficult. However, preference order is often tangled and no clear preference order exists. In this case, some balancing function needs to be introduced to decide about the ordering.

Figure 6.15 shows the corresponding inference structure. We do not describe this method in more detail. As you will see, the methods described in the rest of this chapter are in fact variations and refinements of this general method.

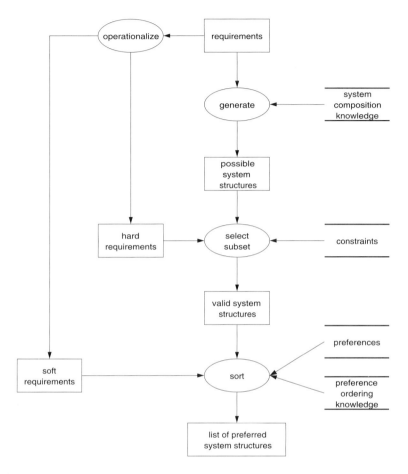

Figure 6.15
Inference structure of the "ideal" method for synthesis tasks.

6.8 Configuration Design

General characterization

Goal   Given a set of predefined components, find an assembly of components that satisfies the requirements and obeys the constraints.

Typical example   Configuration of an elevator. Configuration of a computer system.

Terminology   **Component**: a part of the assembly, e.g., the car of an elevator, the hard disk of a computer.

Parameter: a characteristic of either a component (e.g., the storage capacity of a hard disk) or of an assembly of components (e.g., the total price of a computer system).

Constraint: defines a restriction on the choice of a certain component (e.g., "CPU board x can hold no more than y Mb internal memory") or the value of a certain parameter ("the maximum load of the hoist cable is z").

Preference: allows the choice of a particular design in a space of valid designs. Design problems are usually open-ended and have many "correct" solutions. Preferences are used to indicate the most desired design. For example, minimizing price is an often encountered preference. Preferences can be ordered on an ordinal scale.

Requirement: needs and desires of the future users of the system to be configured, e.g., the total price, the speed. Requirements are typically translated into either constraints ("hard requirements") or preferences ("soft requirements").

Input   A set of requirements.

Output   An assembly consisting of components and instantiated parameter values.

Features   Configuration design is a form of design that is well suited to automation. However, computationally the task is usually much more demanding than analysis tasks.

Default method   A vast bulk of literature exists on configuration-design methods. We have selected a variation of the propose-critique-modify class of methods described by Chandrasekaran (1990). The conceptual method specification is shown in Figure 6.16. The basic structure of the method is:

1. Propose a design extension.
2. Verify the current design; if the extended design is OK, then continue with step 1, else go to step 3.
3. Critique the current design and generate an ordered list of actions to revise the current design.
4. Select an action and modify the design accordingly until the verify function succeeds.
5. Return to step 1. If no further extensions are available, report the configuration found.

We discuss each of the functions mentioned in Figure 6.16 in some detail.

- **Operationalize requirements**   The needs and desires of the user have to be translated into operational constraints and preferences that the method can work on. For example, the "soft" requirement `fast system` is translated into the preference "maximize the

```
TASK configuration-design;
  ROLES:
    INPUT: requirements: "requirements for the design";
    OUTPUT: design: "the resulting design";
END TASK configuration-design;

TASK-METHOD propose-and-revise;
  REALIZES: configuration-design;
  DECOMPOSITION:
    INFERENCES: operationalize, specify, propose, verify, critique,
        select, modify;
  ROLES:
    INTERMEDIATE:
      soft-requirements: "requirements to be used as preferences";
      hard-requirements: "requirements that are hard constraints";
      skeletal-design: "set of design elements";
      extension: "a single new value for a design element";
      violation: "constraint violated by the current design";
      truth-value: "boolean indicating result of the verification";
      action-list: "ordered list of possible repair (fix) actions";
      action: "a single repair action";
  CONTROL-STRUCTURE:
    operationalize(requirements -> hard-requirements
        + soft-requirements);
    specify(requirements -> skeletal-design);
    WHILE NEW-SOLUTION propose(skeletal-design + design
            + soft-requirements -> extension) DO
      design := extension ADD design;
      verify(design + hard-requirements
        -> truth-value + violation);
      IF truth-value == false
      THEN
        critique(violation + design -> action-list);
        REPEAT
          select(action-list -> action);
          modify(design + action -> design);
          verify(design + hard-requirements
              -> truth-value + violation);
        UNTIL truth-value == true;
        END REPEAT
      END IF
    END WHILE
END TASK-METHOD propose-and-revise;
```

Figure 6.16
Propose-and-revise method for configuration design.

parameter "speed" of the component "processor." This operationalization is by no means always trivial, and extensive knowledge elicitation may be required.

- **Specify skeletal design**   A skeletal design is a predefined format for the design: which typical collection of components should the solution contain? In many simple configuration-design problems there is just one fixed basic artifact structure with some optional components. Configuration of a personal computer system is an example of this. In this case, this function is simply a look-up of the default skeletal design. In more complex applications, several skeletal designs exist, one of which needs to be selected.

- **Propose design extension**   This function is typically a task by itself with at least two alternative inferences for proposing a design extension:

  1. Compute a design extension, given the component choices in the current design. Parameter values are usually logically dependent on the selected component type. For example, a certain processor has a certain price and speed. For computed values, it is useful to keep a record of the values this computation depends on. This can be used in the modification function later on.

  2. Prefer a design extension by using preferences in the knowledge base and user preferences to select a component or parameter value in the skeletal design that is not yet instantiated. If an ordinal scale of preferences exists use this in the selection. Again, it is useful to keep a record of the preferences used to select a value for a component.

  The straightforward approach is to try to find a computed extension first, before the preference inference is invoked.

- **Verify current configuration**   Check with the help of the internal constraints and those supplied by the user whether the current configuration is internally consistent. If the verification fails, produce the violated constraint as an additional output.

- **Critique the current design**   A simple but effective form of critiquing is to include domain knowledge that associates a constraint with "fixes": actions that can be undertaken to modify the design such that the violation disappears. For example, a violation of the constraint "minimum storage capacity" can be fixed with the action "upgrade hard disk." Such fixes typically suggest an ordered list of possible actions. In more complex cases, the fix can involve updates of more than one design value. As a general rule, only design elements for which a value has been "preferred" can be subject to fixing.

- **Select an action**   This is usually a simple selection of the first untried element of the action list generated by the critique function.

- **Modify the configuration**   This function actually applies the fix action to the design. The function also removes all components for which the value depended on the changed element, and invokes the inference compute to recompute new values.

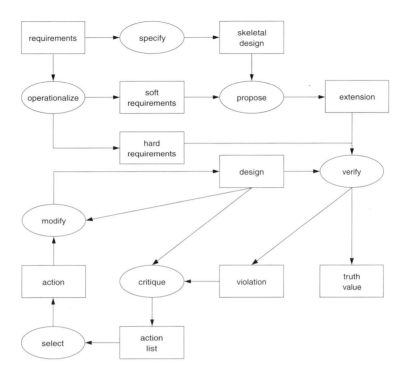

Figure 6.17
Inference structure for the propose-and-revise method.

Figure 6.17 shows the inference structure for the default configuration-design method. Some functions are likely to turn out as complex tasks in an actual application.

Method variations   Two major variations have to be considered:

1. *Perform verification plus revision only when a value has been proposed for all design elements.* This change requires in fact only a simple adjustment of the control structure of the method, but can have a large impact on the competence of the method. Consult Motta et al. (1996) for a detailed discussion of this issue.
2. *Avoid the use of fix knowledge.* Fixes can be viewed as search heuristics to guide the potentially extensive space of alternative designs once a constraint is violated. However, it could turn out that fixes are not or only fragmentary available in the application. In that case, the knowledge engineer will have to fall back on a technique such as chronological backtracking to realize the revision process. This solution is usually computationally much more demanding.

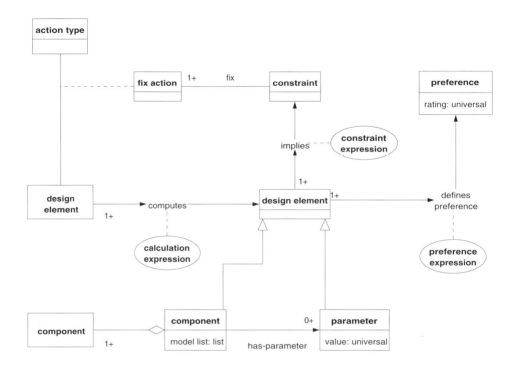

Figure 6.18
Typical domain knowledge types in configuration design through propose-and-revise.

Typical domain schema   Figure 6.18 shows the main domain knowledge types involved
in configuration design using the default method. The central concept is **design element**.
This is a supertype of **component** and **parameter**. Parameters are linked to a certain
component. Components themselves also act as a kind as a kind of parameter: their "value"
is the "model" selected for the component. For example, for a hard-disk component we
can select several models, each with its own parameter values (for capacity, access type,
price, etc.). The propose-and-revise method in fact treats components in a similar manner
to parameters. Components can be organized in an aggregate component structure through
an aggregation relation (see the lower left of Figure 6.18).

The domain schema contains three rule types. The rule type **calculation-expression**
describes knowledge pieces that represent computational dependencies between design
elements. An example is the weight parameter of an aggregate component which can
be derived from the combined weights of it subcomponents. The rule type **constraint-
expression** describes constraints on design elements. The antecedent consists of one or

more logical expressions about design elements. If the antecedent evaluates to true, the construct is assumed to be true. The conclusion of the rule is an expression about some constraint label, e.g., that the constraint "minimum-storage-capacity" has been exceeded. Finally, the rule type **preference-expression** defines a dependency between a design element and a preference. An example would be the preference "Intel inside" which requires as an antecedent that the parameter `maker` of the component `processor` holds the value "Intel." Preferences are associated with a preference rating, indicating the relative importance of the preferences. The exact representation of the preference rating is application-specific.

A fix is modelled in the schema as a complex relation. It links a constraint to a set of **fix-action**s that can be applied to the design in case the constraint is violated. A **fix-action** is a relation class (see Chapter 5) and thus itself also a relation, namely between an action (e.g., `upgrade`, `downgrade`, `increase`) and a design element. An instance of a fix in a computer-configuration domain could look like this:

```
fix( constraint( minimum-required-storage-capacity ) ,
     fix-action( action( upgrade ), design-element( hard-disk )))
```

In words: if the constraint `minimum-required-storage-capacity` is violated, a possible fix is to carry out the fix action `upgrade hard-disk`, where `upgrade` is the action and `hard-disk` the design element to which the action should be applied.

6.9   Assignment

General characterization

Goal	Create a relation between two groups of objects, subjects and resources, that meets the requirements and obeys the constraints.
Typical example	Assignment of offices to employees. Assignment of airplanes to gates.
Terminology	**Subject**: An object (employee, airplane) that needs to get a certain resource.
	Resource: An object (office, gate) that can used for a certain purpose by a subject.
	Subject-group: A group of subject objects, usually constructed for the purpose of joint subject assignment to a resource.
	Allocation: A relation between a subject and a resource.
Input	Two object sets, one set consisting of subjects and the other set consisting of resources available for assignment. Possible additional inputs: existing assignments, component-specific requirements.
Output	A set of allocations of subject-resource allocations.

Features   Assignment is a relatively simple synthetic task. One can see it as a variation of configuration design, the main difference being the underlying system structure which in assignment is not a physical artifact.

Default method   The template defined in this section covers only a simple method for assignment which has proved useful. If this method is not appropriate, e.g., because extensive backtracking is required, it is best to use a configuration design method instead. The method specification is shown in Figure 6.19. The method contains three inferences:

1. **Select subset of subjects**   This inference selects a subset of the subjects to be assigned based on domain-specific priority criteria. For example, in an office-assignment domain the management staff could be assigned first. At Schiphol airport, KLM airplanes may have priority. The knowledge that is used here can range from formal regulations to heuristics used to constrain the search.

2. **Group subjects**   This inference generates a group of subjects that can be assigned jointly to a single resource. In many assignment domains the resources are not all for single-subject use. For example, offices may host more than one employee.

   Grouping typically brings a special kind of domain knowledge into play related to constraints and preferences regarding subject-subject interaction. For example, placing a smoker with a nonsmoking person is nowadays not considered acceptable. If no grouping is needed, this step is best viewed as a no-op, in which a single subject is (randomly) selected and becomes the "subject-group," which in this case would consist of just a single element. This inference may actually require complex reasoning. It may be useful to view grouping as a task and decompose it further to describe the internal process in more detail. An effective method is the following:

   a. First, generate all the possible groupings.
   b. Then apply successive "select-subset" steps in which constraints and preferences are used in a specific order to filter out unwanted or less-preferred groupings.

   This is not a method you will see an expert apply, but a computer can handle it without any problem! The advantage is that you are sure of getting the optimal solution, whereas this remains unsure when you use heuristic expert knowledge for generating groupings. This grouping method is in fact an instantiation of the idealized method for synthetic tasks in general (presented earlier in this chapter).

3. **Assign**   In the assign step a resource is selected that fits best with the constraints and preferences connected to the subjects involved. The current allocations are often an important input, because some assignments may actually depend on where some subject is placed (e.g., a secretary needs to be placed close to the person she works for).

Figure 6.20 shows the corresponding inference structure.

```
TASK assignment;
  ROLES:
    INPUT:
      subjects: "The subjects that need to get a resource";
      resources: "The resources that can be assigned";
    OUTPUT:
      allocations: "Set of subject-resource assignments";
END TASK assignment;

TASK-METHOD assignment-method;
  REALIZES: assignment;
  DECOMPOSITION:
    INFERENCES: select-sub-set, group, assign;
  ROLES:
    INTERMEDIATE:
      subject-set: "Subset of subjects with the same
        assignment priority";
      subject-group: "Set of subjects that can jointly be assigned
        to the same resource. It may consist of a single subject.";
      resource: "A resource that gets assigned";
      current-allocations: "Current subject-resource assignments";
  CONTROL-STRUCTURE:
    WHILE NOT EMPTY subjects DO
      select-subset(subjects -> subject-set);
      WHILE NOT EMPTY subject-set DO
        group(subject-set -> subject-group);
        assign(subject-group + resources
          + current-allocations -> resource);
        current-allocations :=
          < subject-group, resource > ADD current-allocations;
        subject-set := subject-set DELETE subject-group;
        resources := resources DELETE resource;
      END WHILE
      subjects := subjects DELETE subject-set;
    END WHILE
  END TASK-METHOD assignment-method;
```

Figure 6.19
Default method for assignment without backtracking.

Method variations   As we noted earlier, the method sketched above cannot handle backtracking over allocations already made. If this is required for the application task, you should probably use the configuration-design method described in this chapter. The following variations of the assignment method occur relatively frequent:

- **Existing allocations**   In some applications, there may be existing allocations at the point where the task starts (e.g., assignment of airplanes to gates). In that case you may need this as an additional input for all three subfunctions.

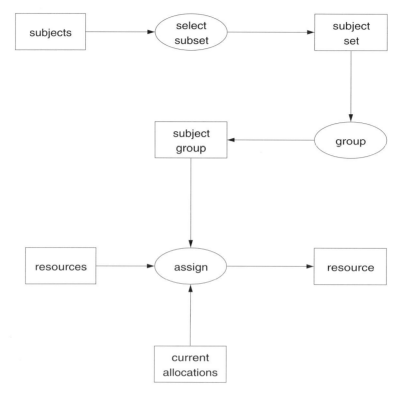

Figure 6.20
Inference structure for the assignment method.

- **Subject-specific constraints and preferences**   The default method specification assumes that the constraints and preferences are all of a static nature and can be specified in advance in the domain knowledge. A constraint in the knowledge base could be that smokers and nonsmokers should not be grouped together. With data about the subjects the system can apply this constraint. However, sometimes a subject has a specific preference at a specific point in time. For example, an airplane wants to have a gate close to another gate because it is late and passengers need to catch a connecting flight. In that case, we need an additional inference that takes in the case-specific requirements and operationalizes these into constraints and preferences (see the configuration-design method for a similar construction).

6.10   Planning

General characterization

Goal	Given some goal description, generate a plan consisting of a (partially) ordered set of actions or activities that meet the goal.
Typical example	Planning of therapeutic actions for treating a disease.
Terminology	**Goal**: the goal that one intends to achieve through carrying out the plan, e.g., cure an acute bacterial infection.
	Action: a basic plan element, e.g., "give antibiotic type A three times per day for a period of one week in a dosage of 500 mg."
	Plan: a partially ordered collection of actions, e.g., the administration of two antibiotics in parallel.
Input	The goal to be achieved by the plan plus additional requirements.
Output	The action plan aimed at achieving the goal.
Features	Be aware that in many domains the term "planning" is used in a different sense. The term "planning" may map to "scheduling" in the terminology of this chapter: allocation of activities to time slots. In other domains the term "planning" has a wider meaning and covers both the task types "planning" and "scheduling." These two types are seen frequently in combination, as scheduling takes the output of planning as input.

Default method   We have not included a separate template for planning. Instead, you can use two previous templates to model a planning task, namely the synthesis template or the configuration-design template. We advise the following modelling strategy:

* If the space of possible plans is not too large, use the synthesis template. The design space is determined by the set of basic plan actions plus the ways in which these elements can be combined. In some therapy-planning domains both the action set and the combinations are limited, so that the synthesis template can be used. The advantage of the synthesis template is that it will always find the "best" plan. For applying the template to planning you have to add a few simple refinements to the template. First, you have to separate the **goal** role from the other requirements, and use it as input for the **generate** step. Also, the role terminology can be made specific for planning. Figure 6.21 shows the inference structure instantiated for the planning task.
* If the space of possible plans is large, we advise you to use the method described for configuration design. This propose-and-revise method requires using several types of additional knowledge to prune the search space. The method is easy to adapt to planning.

Both methods assume, as with configuration design, that the set of basic plan components (the actions) is fixed. If this assumption is not true, automation of the task is likely

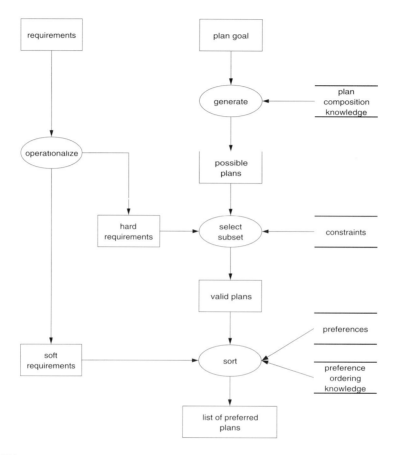

Figure 6.21
Inference structure for planning based on the synthesis template.

to be infeasible with current techniques. Also, if the grain size of the plan action is small, the methods described may work poorly.

6.11   Scheduling

General characterization

Goal   Given a set of predefined jobs, each of which consists of temporally sequenced activities called units, assign all the units to resources, while satisfying constraints.

Typical example	Production scheduling in plant floors.
Terminology	**Job**: a temporal sequence of units.
	Unit: an activity to be performed at a resource.
	Resource: an agent that may satisfy a demand of a unit.
	Constraint: a restrictive condition on the mapping of units on resources.
Input	A set of jobs consisting of units.
Output	Mapping of units on resources, in which all start and end times of units are determined.
Features	Scheduling problems take activities whose temporal sequences are predefined as input, while the creation of such temporal sequences of activities is a goal of planning problems. Furthermore, a resource in scheduling problems provides a time range, in which units can be occupied to satisfy their demands. It is a typical feature of scheduling problems that units are allocated on a time axis of a resource. In assignment problems, two parties of entities are considered to establish mappings between members of each party. However, the assignments are not necessarily established on a time axis as in scheduling problems, but may be done on a spatial region as in a room assignment problem.
Reference	This description of the scheduling template is, with permission, taken from Hori (1998)

Default method   The scheduling method assigns every unit to a resource, fixing the start and end times of each unit. The method specification is given in Figure 6.22. After the creation of an initial schedule, several inferences are called iteratively, in order to select a candidate unit, select a target resource, assign the unit to the resource, evaluate a current schedule, and modify the schedule. The following inferences are included in the method:

- **Specify an initial schedule**   A schedule is a place holder of input entities, and also a skeletal structure of the output. An initial schedule usually does not contain yet any assignments between units and resources.
- **Select a candidate unit to be assigned**   This inference picks up a single unit as a candidate for assignment. A unit can be selected with reference to its temporal relation to other units. For example, it is possible to select a unit with the latest end time in order to complete jobs as closely as possible to due dates, or to select a unit with the earliest start time to release available jobs as early as possible.
- **Select a target resource for the candidate unit**   This inference picks up a target resource for a selected unit. A typical condition to be considered here is a resource type

```
TASK scheduling;
  ROLES:
    INPUT: jobs: "activities that need to be scheduled";
    OUTPUT: schedule: "activities assigned to time slots";
END TASK scheduling;

TASK-METHOD temporal-dispatching;
  REALIZES: scheduling;
  DECOMPOSITION:
    INFERENCES: specify, select, select, assign, modify, verify;
  ROLES:
    INTERMEDIATE:
      candidate-unit: "activity selected for next assignment";
      target-resource: "resource selected for next assignment";
      truth-value: "boolean indicating result of verification";
  CONTROL-STRUCTURE:
    specify(jobs -> schedule);
    WHILE HAS-SOLUTION select(schedule -> candidate-unit) DO
      select(candidate-unit + schedule -> target-resource);
      assign(candidate-unit + target-resource -> schedule);
      verify(schedule -> truth-value);
      IF truth-value == false
        THEN modify(schedule -> schedule);
      END IF
    END WHILE
END TASK-METHOD temporal-dispatching;
```

Figure 6.22
Default method for scheduling.

constraint, which excludes a resource whose type is not equivalent to a resource type designated by the unit. Since a load of each resource can be calculated by accumulating that of all the units assigned to the resource, it is possible to take account of load balance of alternative resources by selecting a resource with minimum load.

- **Assign the unit to the target resource**   This function establishes an assignment of a candidate unit to a target resource. Two types of constraints are considered here: a resource capacity constraint and a unit precedence constraint. The capacity constraint is to prevent a resource from being allocated to more units than it can process at one time. The precedence constraint restricts the process routing to follow a predefined temporal sequence.

- **Verify the current schedule**   This function checks whether the current schedule satisfies the given constraints or evaluation criteria. Typical criteria in scheduling problems are the number of jobs processed within a certain time interval (i.e., throughput), and the fraction of time in which a resource is active (i.e., resource utilization).

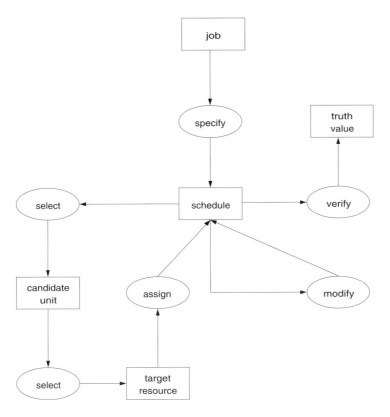

Figure 6.23
Inference structure for the default scheduling method.

- **Modify the current schedule**   This function adjusts the position of a unit. This modification may require further adjustment for either units assigned to the same resource, or units that are temporally sequenced under a job.

Figure 6.23 shows the corresponding inference structure.

Method variations   Two types of scheduling methods are well known in the literature: constructive methods and repair methods (Zweben et al. 1993). Both methods are often employed complementarily in practical situations. The constructive scheduling methods incrementally extend valid, partial schedules until a complete schedule is created or until backtracking is required. The repair methods begin with a complete, but possibly flawed, set of assignments and then iteratively modify the assignments.

In the specification of Figure 6.22, the method primarily realizes a constructive

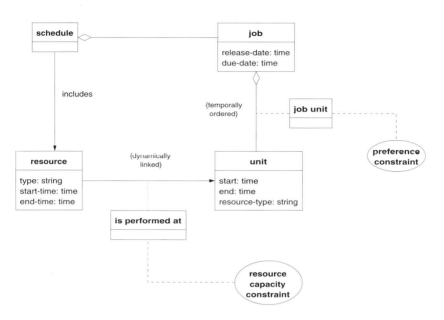

Figure 6.24
Typical domain schema for scheduling problems.

method, and a repair method is interleaved at the end of the main iteration loop. However, it is possible to put the repair method outside the main loop. Scheduling under unreliable environments often requires dynamic repairs in response to variable conditions. In such cases, repair methods play a more important role, and are devoted to local repairs rather than (re)scheduling from scratch.

It must be noted here that the inference structure in Figure 6.23 captures a high-level inference flow regardless of ways of composing the constructive and repair methods. Some other variations in scheduling methods are found in Hori et al. (1995) with examples of components elicited from existing scheduling systems. A broader collection of scheduling problems and methods is included in Zweben and Fox (1994).

Typical domain schema   Figure 6.24 shows a typical domain schema for scheduling problems. An essential feature of scheduling problems lies in one-to-many associations between a resource and units, which is established dynamically by a scheduling method. The resource capacity constraint mentioned earlier is a condition imposed on this relation. A job aggregates several units that are sequenced temporally. This aggregate relation is fixed in advance in a problem specification, and must be maintained as a unit precedence constraint. Resources and jobs are held by a single entity called a schedule. The schedule

Task-type combination	Description
Monitoring + diagnosis	This is a natural task combination, because the output of one can act as input for the other. Many technical systems now have built-in monitoring-diagnosis functionality.
Monitoring + assessment	In applications where there is no possibility for "real" diagnosis (due to unavailability of experts, system data, or adequate causal models), monitoring is typically followed by an assessment in which a decision is taken about the course of action (e.g., ask for help from experts).
Diagnosis + planning	This is also a logical combination. The result of diagnosis can be used as a goal for planning of corrective actions. In technical domains this task combination is often called "troubleshooting."
Planning + scheduling	Planning delivers a partially ordered set of actions/activities. This output can be used by scheduling to generate an allocation of activities to time slots and resources.
Assessment + planning	An example of this combination is "rescue planning," where there is usually first some kind of assessment ("should something be done, and if so what type of action?") followed by planning of the rescue action.
Classification + planning	This combination is frequently seen in a command & control situation, e.g., in military domains. An incoming signal is interpreted and classified (e.g., enemy or friend), potentially followed by planning (taking countermeasures).

Table 6.3
Typical combinations of task types in application tasks.

entity is exploited by inference functions such as select and modify in the default scheduling method.

The schema in Figure 6.24 captures an essential core of domain knowledge for scheduling problems. It is possible for the schema to be further elaborated taking account structural regularities in a concrete application domain. A domain schema given in Hori and Yoshida (1998) can be regarded as an elaboration of this schema to be exploited for scheduling problems in plant floors.

6.12   Task-Type Combinations

In many applications, the application task consists of a combination of knowledge-intensive task types. In fact, there are a number of typical task-type combinations that are seen frequently together. For example, monitoring and diagnosis are often seen in combination. The output of monitoring is used as input for the diagnosis task. Table 6.3 lists a number of typical task-type combinations. Of course, other combinations are possible as well. The table lists the basic combinations. Combinations of combinations are also possible, e.g., monitoring, diagnosis, and planning.

6.13   Relation to Task and Organization Models

Although the task types discussed in this chapter occur in almost any knowledge-intensive application, there is not a simple one-to-one mapping from application task to task type. The application task is what we call a "real-life" task: a task carried out in a real-world setting. The task types are best seen as generalizations of recurring patterns in knowledge-intensive tasks. In addition to the task-type combinations we saw in the previous section, one should also be aware that not all elements of an application task need to be knowledge-intensive.

Thus, the mapping from application task to task types can be quite complex. In knowledge-engineering practice the task types and task combinations act as background knowledge for the task decomposition in the organization and task models. Usually the aim in the latter models is to decompose tasks down to the level of the task types discussed in this chapter. The knowledge model is thus in fact a continuation of the task decomposition in the context models.

6.14   Bibliographical Notes and Further Reading

Some more advanced topics concerning task templates are discussed in Chapter 13, such as the notion of problem-solving methods and the possibility of having multiple methods for a single task.

In recent O-O work on reusable objects some notions have come up that resemble the task templates described in this chapter. In particular, the "strategy pattern" described by Gamma et al. (1995) is based on a similar idea. The main difference is that the task scope for CommonKADS is much smaller, and therefore the templates can be much more specific.

Task typologies for use in knowledge engineering were first proposed by Hayes-Roth *et al.* (1983) and later, in adapted form, by Clancey (1985). Breuker and Van de Velde (1994) use another variation of the task hierarchy and describe a large set of detailed task templates. Puppe (1990) uses a different task-type hierarchy than most others, but the terms he uses can easily be mapped back. His template models are somewhat computationally oriented, but can still prove to be a useful source of ideas. Stefik (1993) limits the typology to classification, configuration design, and diagnosis, but his description is extensive and covers both conceptual (analysis) as well as computational (design) aspects. The book by Benjamins (1993) contains a large and detailed collection of diagnosis models, and proves to be of particular use when constructing more complex diagnosis models. The diagnosis template in this chapter is based on one of the simpler models in his catalog.

Task templates are sometimes called *interpretation models*, because they can guide the interpretation of verbal data obtained from the expert (see the protocol-analysis technique in Chapter 8). The term is used in the first KADS catalog which may be found in a technical report of the first KADS project (Breuker et al. 1987).

Knowledge Model Construction

Key points of this chapter:

- The process of knowledge-model construction can be decomposed into a number of stages in which certain activities need to be carried out. For each activity a number of techniques exist. Guidelines help the knowledge engineer in deciding how to carry out the activities.
- The three main stages are knowledge identification, knowledge specification, and knowledge refinement.
- This chapter prescribes a particular approach with some variations, but the knowledge engineer should be aware of the fact that modelling is a constructive activity, and that there exists no single correct solution nor one optimal path to it.

7.1 Introduction

So far, we have mainly concentrated on the *contents* of the knowledge model. As in any modelling enterprise, inexperienced knowledge modelers also want to know how to undertake the process of model construction. This is a difficult area, because the modelling process itself is a constructive problem-solving activity for which no single "good" solution exists. The best any modelling methodology can do is provide a number of guidelines that have proved to have worked well in practice.

This chapter presents such a set of guidelines for knowledge-model construction. The guidelines are organized in a process model that distinguishes a number of *stages* and prescribes a set of ordered *activities* that need to be carried out. Each activity is carried out with the help of one or more *techniques* and can be supported through a number of guidelines. In describing the process model we have tried to be as prescriptive as possible.

Where appropriate, we indicate sensible alternatives. However, the reader should bear in mind that the modelling process for a particular application may well require deviations from the recipe provided. Our goal is a "90%-90%" approach: it should work in 90% of the applications for 90% of the knowledge-modelling work.

As pointed out in previous chapters, we consider knowledge modelling to be a specialized form of requirements specification. Partly, knowledge modelling requires specialized tools and guidelines, but one should not forget that more general software-engineering principles apply here as well. At obvious points we refer to those, but these references will not be extensive.

This chapter does not cover the elicitation techniques often used in the knowledge analysis and modelling process. An overview of useful elicitation techniques can be found in Chapter 8.

7.2   Stages in Knowledge-Model Construction

We distinguish three stages in the process of knowledge-model construction:

1. Knowledge identification   Information sources that are useful for knowledge modelling are identified. This is really a preparation phase for the actual knowledge model specification. A lexicon or glossary of domain terms is constructed. Existing model components such as task templates and domain schemas are surveyed, and components that could be reused are made available to the project. Typically, the description of knowledge items in the organization model and the characterization of the application task in the task model form the starting point for knowledge identification. In fact, if the organization-model and task-model descriptions are complete and accurate, the identification stage can be done in a short period.

2. Knowledge specification   In the second stage the knowledge engineer constructs a specification of the knowledge model. First, a task template is chosen and an initial domain schema is constructed, using the list of reusable model components identified in the previous stage Then, the knowledge engineer will have to "fill in the holes" in the knowledge model. As we will see, there are two approaches to complete the knowledge-model specification, namely starting with the inference knowledge and then moving to related domain and task knowledge, or starting with domain and task knowledge and linking these through inferences. The choice of approach depends on the quality and detailedness of the chosen task template (if any). In terms of the domain knowledge, the emphasis in this stage is on the domain schema, and not so much on the knowledge base(s). In particular, one should not write down the full set of knowledge instances that belong to a certain knowledge base. This can be left for the next stage.

3. Knowledge refinement   In the final stage, attempts are made to validate the knowledge model as much as possible and to complete the knowledge bases by inserting a more

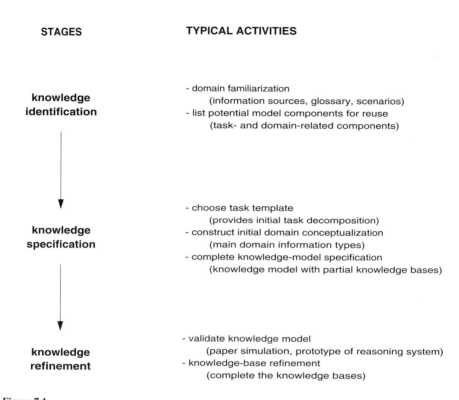

STAGES   **TYPICAL ACTIVITIES**

**knowledge
identification**

- domain familiarization
   (information sources, glossary, scenarios)
- list potential model components for reuse
   (task- and domain-related components)

**knowledge
specification**

- choose task template
   (provides initial task decomposition)
- construct initial domain conceptualization
   (main domain information types)
- complete knowledge-model specification
   (knowledge model with partial knowledge bases)

**knowledge
refinement**

- validate knowledge model
   (paper simulation, prototype of reasoning system)
- knowledge-base refinement
   (complete the knowledge bases)

Figure 7.1
Overview of the three main stages in knowledge-model construction. The arrows indicate typical but not absolute time dependencies. For each stage some activities are listed on the right.

or less complete set of knowledge instances (e.g., instances of rule types). An important technique for validating the initial specification that comes out of the previous stage is to construct a simulation of the scenarios gathered during knowledge identification. Such a simulation can either be paper-based or involve the construction of a small, dedicated prototype. The results of the simulation should give an indication whether the knowledge model can generate the problem-solving behavior required. Only if validation delivers positive results is it useful to spend time on completing the knowledge bases.

These three stages can be intertwined. Sometimes, feedback loops are required. For example, validation may lead to changes in the knowledge-model specification. Also, completion of the knowledge bases may require looking for additional information sources. The general rule is: feedback loops occur less frequently if the application problem is well understood and similar problems have been tackled successfully in prior projects. We now look at the three stages in more detail. For each stage we indicate typical activities, techniques, and guidelines.

7.3 Knowledge Identification

7.3.1 Activity Overview

When we start constructing a knowledge model we assume that a knowledge-intensive task has been selected, and that the main knowledge items involved in this task have been identified. Usually, the application task has also been classified as being of a certain type, e.g., assessment, configuration design (see the task types in Chapter 6).

The goal of knowledge identification is to survey the knowledge items and prepare them in such a way that they can be used for a knowledge-model specification in the second stage. This includes carrying out the following two activities:

- Explore and structure the information sources for the task, as identified in the knowledge item listings. During this process, create a lexicon or glossary of terms for the domain.
- Study the nature of the task in more detail, and check or revise the task type. List all potential reusable knowledge-model components for this application,

7.3.2 Activity 1.1: Domain Familiarization

The starting point for this activity is the list of knowledge items described in worksheet TM-2. One should study this material in some detail. Two factors are of prime importance when surveying the material:

1. **Nature of the sources**   The nature of the information sources determines the type of approach that needs to be taken in knowledge modelling. Domains with well-developed domain theories are usually easier than ill-specified domains with many informal and/or diffuse sources.
2. **Diversity of the sources**   If the information sources are very diverse in nature, with no single information source (e.g., a textbook or manual) playing a central role, knowledge modelling requires more time. Sources are often conflicting, even if they are of the same type. For example, having multiple experts is a considerable risk factor. In the context of this book we cannot go into details about the multiexpert situation, but the references at the end of this chapter include a number of useful texts.

Techniques used in this activity are often of a simple nature: text marking in key information sources such as a manual or a textbook, one or two unstructured interviews to get insight into the application domain. The goal of this activity is to get a good insight, but still at a global level. More detailed explorations may be carried out in less understood areas, because of their potential risks. The main problem the knowledge engineer is confronted with is to find a balance between learning about the domain without becoming a full domain expert. For example, a technical domain in the processing industry concerning the diagnosis of a specific piece of equipment may require a large amount of background knowledge to understand, and therefore the danger exists that the exploration activity will take long. This is in fact the traditional problem with all knowledge-engineering projects. One cannot avoid (nor should one want to) becoming a "layman expert" in the field. The following guidelines may be helpful in deciding upon the amount of detail required for exploring the domain material:

Guideline 7-1: TALK TO PEOPLE IN THE ORGANIZATION WHO HAVE TO TALK TO EXPERTS BUT ARE NOT EXPERTS THEMSELVES
Rationale: These "outsiders" have often undergone the same process you are now undertaking: trying to understand the problem without being able to become a full expert. They can often tell you what the key features of the problem-solving process are on which you have to focus.

Guideline 7-2: AVOID DIVING INTO DETAILED, COMPLICATED THEORIES UNLESS THEIR USEFULNESS IS PROVEN
Rationale: Usually, detailed theories can safely be omitted in the early phases of knowledge modelling. For example, in an elevator configuration domain the expert can tell you about detailed mathematical theories concerning cable traction forces, but the knowledge engineer typically only needs to know that these formulas exist, and that they act as a constraint on the choice of the cable type.

Guideline 7-3: CONSTRUCT A FEW TYPICAL SCENARIOS WHICH YOU UNDERSTAND AT A GLOBAL LEVEL
Rationale: Spend some time with a domain expert to collect or construct scenarios, and ask nonexperts involved whether they agree with the selection. Try to understand the domain knowledge such that you can explain the reasoning of the scenario in superficial terms. Scenarios are useful to construct and/or collect for other reasons as well. For example, validation activities often make use of predefined scenarios.

Never spend too much time on this activity. Two person-weeks should be the maximum, except for some very rare difficult cases. If you are doing more than that, you are probably overdoing it. The results achieved at the end of the activity can only partly be measured. The tangible results should be:

- listing of domain knowledge sources, including a short characterization;
- summaries of selected key texts;
- description of scenarios developed.

However, the main intangible result, namely your own understanding of the domain, stays the most important one.

7.3.3   Activity 1.2: List Potential Model Components

The goal of this activity is to pave the way for reusing model components that have already been developed and used elsewhere. Reuse is an important vehicle for quality assurance. This activity studies potential reuse from two angles:

1. **Task dimension**   A characterization is established of the task type. Typically, such a type has already been tentatively assigned in the task model. The aim here is to check whether this is still valid using the domain information found in the previous step. Based on the selected task type, one starts to build a list of task templates that are appropriate for the task.

2. **Domain dimension**   Establish the type of the domain: is it a technical domain?, Is the knowledge mainly heuristic?, and so on. Then, look for standardized descriptions of this domain or of similar domains. These descriptions can take many forms: field-specific thesauri such as the Art and Architecture Thesaurus (AAT) for art objects or the Medical Subject Headings (MeSH) for medical terminology, "ontology" libraries, reference models (e.g., for hospitals), product model libraries (such as the ones using the ISO STEP standard). Over the last few years there have been an increasing number of research efforts constructing such standardized domain-knowledge descriptions.

Guidelines for task-type selection   Selecting the right task type is important. The guidelines below may help you in making the right choice.

Guideline 7-4:   APPLICATION TASKS ARE OFTEN COMBINATIONS OF TASK TYPES
Rationale: Be aware of the point made in Chapter 6, that there is hardly ever a one-to-one match between application task and a task type. Ideally, these distinctions will already have been disclosed in the task model, but it may happen that you only find out during knowledge modelling.

Guideline 7-5:   NAMES GIVEN TO APPLICATION TASKS DO NOT NECESSARILY MAP TO GENERIC TASK-TYPE NAMES
Rationale: This guideline refers to the frequently occurring situation in which the application task has already a name that also occurs in the task-type list, e.g., "travel planning." These application task labels do not necessarily match with the definition of the task type used in this book. The meaning of a term like "planning" varies and our task-type definitions are in a sense arbitrary decisions about where to put borderlines between tasks. Consult carefully the "features" slot in the general characterization of each task-template description to learn about typical confusions with other task types. For example, "diagnosis" performed by nonexperts (or by experts who have little data available) is often actually a task of the "assessment" type.

7.4 Knowledge Specification

7.4.1 Activity Overview

The goal of this stage is to get a complete specification of the knowledge model, except the *contents* of the knowledge bases: these typically only contain some example knowledge instances. The following activities need to be carried out to build such a specification:

- choose a task template;
- construct an initial domain schema;
- specify the three knowledge categories.

7.4.2 Activity 2.1: Choose Task Template

Chapter 6 contains a small set of task templates for a number of task types such as diagnosis and assessment. The chapter also gives pointers to other repositories where one can find potentially useful task templates. We strongly prefer an approach in which the knowledge model is based on an existing template. This is both efficient and gives some assurance about the model quality, depending of course on the quality of the task template used and the match with the application task at hand.

Several features of the application task can be important in choosing an appropriate task template:

- the nature of the output (the "solution"): e.g., a fault category, a decision category, a plan;
- the nature of the inputs: what kind of data are available for solving the problem?
- the nature of the system the task is analyzing, modifying, or constructing: e.g., a human-engineered artifact such as a photocopier, a biological system such as a human being, or a physical process such as a nuclear power plant;
- constraints posed by the task environment: e.g., the required certainty of the solution, the costs of observations.

The following guidelines can help the selection of a particular template:

Guideline 7-6:   PREFER TEMPLATES THAT HAVE BEEN USED MORE THAN ONCE
Rationale: Empirical evidence is still the best measurement of quality of a task template: a model that has proved its use in practice is a good model.

Guideline 7-7:   IF YOU THINK YOU HAVE FOUND A SUITABLE TEMPLATE, CON- STRUCT AN "ANNOTATED" INFERENCE STRUCTURE
Rationale: In an annotated inference structure one adds domain examples to the generic figure. This is a good to way to get an impression about what the "fit" is between the template and the application domain. An example of an annotated inference structure was shown in Figure 5.20.

Guideline 7-8:   IF NO TEMPLATE SEEMS TO FIT WITH THE APPLICATION TASK, QUESTION THE KNOWLEDGE-INTENSIVE CHARACTER OF THE TASK
Rationale: If no suitable template can be found, it might be the case that the task is not really a "reasoning" task, but a task of another type. An example is the actual assignment task in the housing case study in Chapter 10, which is in essence only the application of a formula. This situation is not necessarily bad; it simply means that CommonKADS does not give you any particular advantages when modelling this task.

Guideline 7-9:   A BAD TEMPLATE IS BETTER THAN NO TEMPLATE
Rationale: Although it is strongly recommended that a good template model be used in the knowledge-modelling process, this may not always be possible. A task may be new or may have exotic characteristics. Experience has shown that it still is useful to select a template even if it does not completely fit the task requirements. Such a "bad" template can serve as a starting point for the construction of a better one.

7.4.3   Activity 2.2: Construct Initial Domain Schema

The goal of this activity is to construct an initial data model of the domain independent of the application problem being solved or the task methods chosen. Typically, the domain schema of a knowledge-intensive application contains at least two parts:

1. **Domain-specific conceptualizations**   These are the domain structures that we recognize directly in a domain, and that are likely to be present in any application independent of the way in which it is being used. Examples of this type of construct in the car-diagnosis domain are **battery** and **fuel-tank**.
2. **Method-specific conceptualizations**   A second set of domain constructs is introduced because these are needed to solve a certain problem in a certain way. Examples in the car-diagnosis domain domain are the rule types for the causal network.

   This activity is aimed at describing a first version of the *domain-specific* conceptualizations. These are a good starting point, because these definitions tend to be reasonably stable over a development period. If there are existing systems in this domain, in particular database systems, use these as points of departure.

Guideline 7-10:   BASE DOMAIN-SPECIFIC CONCEPTUALIZATIONS ON EXISTING DATA MODELS AS MUCH AS POSSIBLE
Rationale: Even if the information needs for your application are much higher (as they often are in knowledge-intensive applications), it is still useful to use at least the same *terminology* and/or a shared set of basic constructs. This will make future cooperation, both in terms of exchange between software systems and information exchange between developers and/or users, easier.

Guideline 7-11:   LIMIT USE OF THE COMMONKADS KNOWLEDGE-MODELLING LANGUAGE TO CONCEPTS, SUBTYPES AND RELATIONS

Rationale: The domain-specific part of the domain schema can usually be handled by the "standard" part of the CommonKADS language. The notions of concepts, subtypes and relations have their counterparts in almost every modern software-engineering approach, small variations permitting. The description often has a more "data-oriented" than "knowledge-oriented" flavor. This activity bears a strong resemblance to building an initial object model (without methods!) in object-oriented analysis.

Constructing the initial domain schema can typically be done in parallel with the choice of the task template. In fact, if there needs to be a sequence between the two activities, it is still best to proceed as if they are carried out in parallel. This is to ensure that the domain-specific part of the domain schema is specified without a particular task method in mind.

7.4.4   Activity 2.3: Complete Specification of the Knowledge Model

There are basically two routes for completing the knowledge model once a task template has been chosen and an initial domain schema has been constructed:

Route 1: Middle-out   Start with the inference knowledge, and complete the task knowledge and the domain knowledge, including the inference-domain role mappings. This approach is the preferred one, but requires that the task template chosen provide a task decomposition that is detailed enough to act as a good approximation of the inference structure.

Route 2: Middle-in   Start in parallel with decomposing the task through consecutive applications of methods, while at the same time refining the domain knowledge to cope with the domain-knowledge assumptions posed by the methods. The two ends (i.e., task and domain knowledge) meet through the inference-domain mappings. This means we have found the inferences (i.e., the lowest level of the functional decomposition). This approach takes more time, but is needed if the task template is still too coarse-grained to act as an inference structure.

Figure 7.2 summarizes the two approaches. The middle-out approach can only be used if the inference structure of the task template is already at the required level of detail. If decomposition is necessary, the process essentially becomes "middle-in." Deciding on the suitability of the inference structure is therefore an important decision criterion. The following guidelines can help in making this decision:

Guideline 7-12:   THE INFERENCE STRUCTURE IS DETAILED ENOUGH IF AND ONLY IF THE EXPLANATION IT PROVIDES US OF THE REASONING PROCESS IS SUFFICIENTLY DETAILED
Rationale: A key point underlying the inference structure is that it provides us with an abstraction mechanism over the details of the reasoning process. An inference is a black

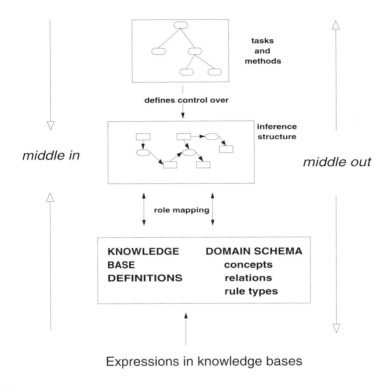

Figure 7.2
Middle-in and middle-out approaches to knowledge-model specification. The middle-out approach is preferred, but can only be used if the inference structure of the task template is already at the required level of detail. If decomposition is necessary, the process essentially becomes "middle-in".

box, as far as the specification in the knowledge model is concerned. The idea is that one should be able to understand and predict the results of inference execution by just looking at its inputs (both dynamic and static) and outputs.

Guideline 7-13: THE INFERENCE STRUCTURE IS DETAILED ENOUGH IF IT IS EASY TO FIND FOR EACH INFERENCE A SINGLE TYPE OF DOMAIN KNOWLEDGE THAT CAN ACT AS A STATIC ROLE FOR THIS INFERENCE
Rationale: This is not a hard rule, but it often works in practice. The underlying rationale is simple: if there are more than two static roles (types of static domain knowledge in the knowledge base) involved, then it is often required to specify control over the reasoning process. By definition, no internal control can be represented for an inference; we need to consider this function as a task that needs to be decomposed.

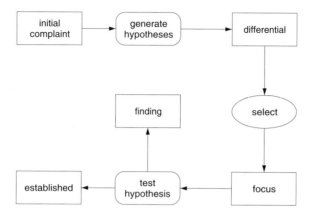

Figure 7.3
Example of a provisional inference structure. "Generate" and "test" are functions. These functions will ultimately either be viewed as tasks (and thus be decomposed through a task method) or be turned into direct inferences in the domain knowledge. The knowledge engineer still has to make this decision.

Although in the final model we "know" what are tasks and what are inferences, this is not true at every stage of the specification process. We use the term "function" to denote anything that can turn out to be either a task or an inference. We can sketch what we call "provisional inference structures" in which functions appear that could turn out to be either tasks or inferences. In such provisional figures we use a rounded-box notation to indicate functions. Figure 7.3 shows an example of a provisional inference structure. In this figure GENERATE and TEST are functions. These functions will ultimately either be viewed as tasks (and thus be decomposed through a task method) or be turned into direct inferences in the domain knowledge.

An important technique at this stage is protocol analysis. This technique, which is discussed in more detail in the next chapter, usually gives excellent data about the structure of the reasoning process: tasks, task control, and inferences. The adequateness of a task template can be assessed by using it as an "overlay" of the transcript of an expert protocol. The idea is that one should be able to interpret all the reasoning steps made by the expert in the protocol in terms of a task or an inference in the template. Because of this usage, task templates have also been called "interpretation models."

If the task template is too coarse-grained and requires further decomposition, a self-report protocol (in which an expert tries to explain his own reasoning, see the next chapter) usually gives clues as to what kind of decompositions are appropriate. Because we require of the knowledge model that it can explain its reasoning in expert terms, the self-report protocol is the prime technique for deciding whether the inference structure is detailed enough. Also, such protocols can provide you with scenarios for testing the model (see the knowledge refinement activities further on).

Guidelines for specifying task knowledge   The following guidelines apply to the specification of tasks and task methods:

Guideline 7-14:   WHEN STARTING TO SPECIFY A TASK METHOD, BEGIN WITH THE CONTROL STRUCTURE
Rationale: The control structure is the "heart" of the method: it contains both the decomposition (in terms of the tasks, inferences, and/or transfer functions mentioned in it), as well as the execution control over the decomposition. Once you have the control structure right, the rest can more or less be derived from it.

Guideline 7-15:   WHEN WRITING DOWN THE CONTROL STRUCTURE, DO NOT CONCERN YOURSELF TOO MUCH WITH DETAILS OF WORKING MEMORY REPRESENTATION
Rationale: The main point of writing down control structures is to characterize the reasoning strategy at a fairly high level: e.g., "first this task, then this task" or "do this inference until it produces no more solutions." Details of the control representation can safely be left to the design phase. If one spends much time on the control details in this stage, it might well happen that the work turns out to be useless when a decision is made to change the method for a task.

Guideline 7-16:   CHOOSE ROLE NAMES THAT CLEARLY INDICATE HOW THIS DATA ITEM IS USED WITHIN THE TASK
Rationale: Knowledge modelling (as in modelling in general) is very much about introducing an adequate vocabulary for describing the application problem, such that future users and/or maintainers of the system understand the way you perceived the system, The task roles are an important part of this naming process, as they appear in all simulations or actual traces of system behavior. It makes sense to choose these names with care.

Guideline 7-17:   DO NOT INCLUDE STATIC KNOWLEDGE ROLES AS PART OF TASK INPUT/OUTPUT
Rationale: The static knowledge roles only appear when we describe inferences. The idea is to free the task specification from the burden of thinking about the required underlying knowledge structures. Of course, methods have their assumptions about the required underlying domain knowledge, but there is no point in already fixing the exact underlying domain-knowledge type.

Guideline 7-18:   FOR REAL-TIME APPLICATIONS, CONSIDER USING A DIFFERENT REPRESENTATION THAN PSEUDOCODE FOR THE CONTROL STRUCTURE OF A TASK METHOD

Rationale: Real-time systems require an asynchronous type of control. The transfer function "receive" can be useful for emulating this in pseudocode, but in many cases a state-transition type of representation is more natural, and thus worth using.

Guidelines for specifying inference knowledge   The following guidelines may help you in developing a specification of inferences and their corresponding knowledge roles:

Guideline 7-19: START WITH DEVELOPING THE GRAPHICAL REPRESENTATION OF THE INFERENCE STRUCTURE
Rationale: Although the inference structure diagram contains less information than the textual specification, it is much more transparent.

Guideline 7-20: USE A STANDARD SET OF INFERENCES AS MUCH AS POSSIBLE
Rationale: Earlier versions of KADS prescribed a fixed set of inference types, many of which are also used in this book. Experience has taught that prescribing a fixed set of inference types is too rigid an approach. Nevertheless, we recommend adherence to a standard, well-documented set as much as possible. This enhances understandability, reusability, and maintenance. In Chapter 13 we have included a catalog of inferences used in this book, each with a number of typical characteristics. Aben (1995) and Benjamins (1993) give descriptions of sets of inference types that have been widely used and are well documented. It is also useful to maintain your own catalog of inferences.

Guideline 7-21: BE CLEAR ABOUT SINGLE OBJECT ROLES OR SETS
Rationale: A well-known confusion in inference structures is caused by the lack of clarity whether a role represents one single object or a set. For example, a select inference takes a set as input. In an inference structure a special notation can be used to indicate sets of objects (see the glossary of graphical notations).

Guideline 7-22: INFERENCES THAT HAVE NO INPUT OR THAT HAVE MANY OUTPUTS ARE SUSPECT
Rationale: Although CommonKADS has no strict rules about the cardinality of the input and output roles of inferences, inferences without an input are considered unusual and inferences with many outputs (more than two) are also unusual in most models. Often these phenomena are indications of incomplete models or of overloading inferences (in the case of many outputs).

Guideline 7-23: CHOOSE DOMAIN-INDEPENDENT ROLE NAMES
Rationale: It is tempting to use role names that have a domain-specific flavor. However, it is recommended to use domain-independent role names as much as possible. This enhances reusability. Anyway, you can still add the domain-specific terms as annotations to the roles.

Guideline 7-24:   STANDARDIZE ON LAYOUT
Rationale: Like data-flow diagrams, inference diagrams are often read from left to right. Structure the layout in such a way that it is easy to detect what the order of the reasoning steps is. The well-known "horseshoe" form of heuristic classification (Clancey 1985) is a good example of a layout that has become standardized.

Guideline 7-25:   DO NOT BOTHER TOO MUCH ABOUT THE DYNAMICS OF ROLE OB-
JECTS IN THE INFERENCE STRUCTURE
Rationale: Inference structures are essentially static representations of a reasoning pro- cess. They are not very well suited to represent dynamic aspects, such as a knowledge role that is continuously updated during reasoning. A typical example is a "differential," an ordered list of hypotheses under consideration. During every reasoning step the cur- rent differential is considered and hypotheses are removed, added, or reordered. In the inference structure this would result in an inference that has the differential as input and as output. Some creative solutions have been proposed (e.g., double arrows with labels), but no satisfactory solution currently exists. We recommend being flexible and not bothering too much about this problem.

Guideline 7-26:   USE THE SPECIFICATION SLOT FOR A CLEAR SPECIFICATION OF
WHAT THE INFERENCE IS SUPPOSED TO DO, AND POSSIBLY WHAT METHODS CAN BE
CONSIDERED IN THE DESIGN PHASE
Rationale: Although an inference is considered to be a black box in the knowledge model, it is important input to the design phase to specify the conception that the knowledge engineer has in mind. Optionally, a number of possible methods to realize the inference can be enumerated.

Guidelines for specifying domain knowledge   Specifying domain knowledge is only to some extent different from "normal" data modelling. This means that you should feel free to use your existing repertoire of techniques for describing the static information in an application domain. A good example is the use of text-analysis techniques to generate a first set of possible concepts, relations, and attributes.

Chapter 13 contains a number of special guidelines for working with subtype hierar- chies. In Chapter 8 you will find a number of specialized techniques for domain-knowledge elicitation. In this chapter we have only included a couple of guidelines about the relation between inference and domain knowledge.

Guideline 7-27:   A DOMAIN-KNOWLEDGE TYPE THAT IS USED AS A STATIC ROLE BY
AN INFERENCE IS NOT REQUIRED TO HAVE EXACTLY THE "RIGHT" REPRESENTATION
NEEDED FOR THIS INFERENCE
Rationale: Getting the "right" representation is typically a design issue, and should not worry the knowledge engineer too much during knowledge modelling. The key issue is that the knowledge is in principle available.

Guideline 7-28:   THE SCOPE OF THE DOMAIN KNOWLEDGE IS TYPICALLY BROADER
THAN WHAT IS BEING COVERED BY THE INFERENCES
Rationale: Domain-knowledge modelling is partly carried out independently of the model
of the reasoning process. This is a good strategy with respect to reuse (see Chapter 13),
but will almost always give rise to domain-knowledge types that are not directly relevant
to the final method(s) chosen for achieving the task. Also, the communication model may
require additional domain knowledge, e.g., for explanation purposes.

7.5   Knowledge Refinement

7.5.1   Activity Overview

During knowledge refinement two activities are carried out:

1. Validate the knowledge model, usually with the help of a simulation technique;
2. Complete the knowledge bases by adding domain-knowledge instances.

The second activity is only carried out if the validation is at least partly successful.

7.5.2   Activity 3.1: Validate Knowledge Model

Validation can be done both internally and externally. Some people use the term "verification" for internal validation ("is the model right?") and reserve "validation" for validation
against user requirements ("is it the right model?").

Checking internal model consistency can be done through various techniques. Standard structured walk-throughs can be appropriate. Software tools exist for checking the
syntax. Some of these tools also point at potentially missing parts of the model, e.g., an
inference that is not used in any task method.

External validation is usually more difficult and more comprehensive. The need for
validation at this stage varies from application to application. Several factors influence this
need. For example, if a large part of the model is being reused from existing models that
were developed for very similar tasks, the need for validation is likely to be low. Task
templates that are less well understood are more prone to errors or omissions.

The main method of checking whether the model captures the required problem-
solving behavior is to simulate this behavior. This simulation can be done in two
ways:

1. **Paper-based simulation**   This method resembles a structured walk-through. Define
   in advance a number of typical scenarios that reflect the required system behavior,
   and use the knowledge model to generate a paper trace of the scenario in terms of the
   knowledge model constructs. This can best be done in a table with three columns.
   The left column describes the steps in the scenario in application-domain terminology.

Domain	Model	Explanation
The user says: "the car does not start".	DIAGNOSIS: **complaint**: engine-behavior.status = does-not-start	A complaint is received, for which a diagnostic task is started.
A possible cause is that the fuel tank is empty.	**cover**: hypothesis; fuel-tank.status = empty	One of the three possible causes is produced by this inference. The other two are "fuse blown" and "battery low".
In that case we would expect the gas indicator to be in the lowest regions.	**predict** expected-finding: gas-dial.value = zero	The expected finding provides us with a way of getting supporting evidence for this hypothesis.
System: "Can you tell which value the gas dial indicates?". User: "It looks normal to me".	OBTAIN: actual-finding: gas-dial.value = normal	This is not what we expected, so we can rule out this possible fault.
The values differ, so it cannot be an empty fuel tank..	**match**: **result** = not-equal	The test to find supporting evidence fails.
We go and look for another possibility.	**cover**: **hypothesis** = battery.status == low	We repeat the process with a second possible solution.
And so on	.....	The task-control loop continues.

Table 7.1
Paper simulation of the reasoning process in knowledge-model terms (see the middle column). The scenarios used here should have been predefined (i.e., in the identification phase). The first column indicates what happens in domain-specific terms; the second column describes the corresponding knowledge-model action; the final column gives a short explanation.

The middle column indicates how each step maps onto a knowledge-model element, e.g., an inference is executed with certain roles as input and output. The right column can be used for explanations and comments. Table 7.1 shows an example of a paper simulation for a scenario of the car-diagnosis application.

2. **Simulation through a mock-up system**   An environment that can be used for a mock-up simulation is described in Chapter 12. Such an environment needs to have facilities for loading the knowledge-model specification plus a minimal set of implementation-specific pieces of code, such that the simulation can be done within a short time period (hours or days instead of weeks).

The simulation should provide answers to the following questions:

- How well does the model fit?
- Are possible differences between the model and the scenario on purpose?
- Where should the model be adapted?

7.5.3   Activity 3.2: Complete Knowledge Bases

During the knowledge-specification stage we are mainly concerned with the domain schema. This schema contains two kinds of types:

1. Domain types that have instances that are part of a certain case. One can view these as "information types"; their instances are similar to instances ("rows") in a database .
2. Domain types that have instances that are part of a knowledge base. These can be seen as "knowledge types": their instances make up the contents of the knowledge base(s).

Instances of the "information types" are never part of a knowledge model. Typically, data instances (case data) will only be considered when a case needs to be formulated for a scenario. However, the instances of the "knowledge types" need to be considered during knowledge-model construction. In the knowledge-specification stage a hypothesis is formulated about how the various domain-knowledge types can be represented. When one fills the contents of a knowledge base, one is in fact testing whether these domain-knowledge types deliver a representation that is sufficiently expressive to represent the knowledge we need for the application.

Usually, it will not be possible to define a full, correct knowledge base at this stage of development. Knowledge bases need to be maintained throughout their lifetime. Apart from the fact that it is difficult to be complete before the system is tested in real-life practice, such knowledge instances also tend to change over time. For example, in a medical domain knowledge about resistance to certain antibiotics is subject to constant change.

In most cases, this problem is handled by incorporating into the system editing facilities for updating the knowledge bases. These knowledge editors should not use the internal system representations, but communicate with the knowledge maintainer in the terminology of the knowledge model.

Various techniques exist for arriving at a first, fairly complete version of a knowledge base. One can check the already available transcripts of interviews and protocols, but this typically delivers only a partial set of instances. One can organize a structured interview, in which the expert is systematically taken through the various knowledge types. Still, omissions are likely to persist. A relatively new technique is to use automated techniques to learn instances of a certain knowledge type, but this is still in an experimental phase (see the references in the next chapter).

Guideline 7-29:   IF IT TURNS OUT TO BE DIFFICULT TO FIND INSTANCES OF CERTAIN KNOWLEDGE TYPES, RECONSIDER THIS PART OF THE SCHEMA
Rationale: Sometimes, we define a domain-knowledge type, such as a certain rule type, on the basis of just a few examples, under the assumption that there are more to be found. If this assumption turns out be wrong, it may well be that this part of the schema needs to be reconsidered. One can see a domain-knowledge type as a *hypothesis* about a useful structuring of domain knowledge. This hypothesis needs to be empirically verified: namely, that in practice we can adequately formulate instances of this type for our application domain.

Guideline 7-30:   LOOK ALSO FOR EXISTING KNOWLEDGE BASES IN THE SAME DO-
MAIN
Rationale: Reusing part of an existing knowledge base is one of the most powerful forms
of reuse. This really makes a difference! There is always some work to be done with
respect to mapping the representation in the other system to the one you use, but it is often
worth the effort. The quality is usually better and it costs less time in the end.

7.6   Some Remarks about Knowledge-Model Maintenance

The basic idea underlying the CommonKADS model suite is that it provides a correct
and full view of the status of application development. The models can be developed in
parallel. The project work should ensure that the models are up-to-date and consistent with
each other. Because knowledge is not static but changes over time, the process is best seen
as continuous development.

Maintenance of the knowledge model is thus not essentially different from its development. The main difference is that, for organizational reasons, it is often done by other
people. This is one of the reasons we pay so much attention to elaborate specifications of
the reasoning process in the vocabulary of the application domain and task. The knowledge
model for an application should be understandable to newcomers on the team.

If the knowledge model of an application is good and the domain is stable, one can expect the majority of maintenance to be concerned with activity 3.2 ("complete the knowledge bases"). Typically, sets of rule instances will need to be updated, because knowledge
tends to evolve over time. One of the advantages of using rule types is that it makes maintenance of the knowledge base much easier through its decomposition of the knowledge
base into sets of knowledge elements sharing a similar structure. One can in fact construct
an interface for a domain expert such that he can do this job himself.

When we talk about system design and implementation in Chapter 11 and 12 you
will see that this principle of continuous development also influences the link between
analysis and design. Systems are constructed in such a way that they contain in fact all
the analysis information (including the full knowledge model) to support clear routes for
system maintenance.

7.7   Documenting the Knowledge Model

7.7.1   Knowledge-Model Specification

The prime outcome of knowledge-model construction is the actual knowledge-model. Although it is recommended that the final full specification is written in the language described in the appendix, a more restricted specification may suffice. The minimal specification consists of the following elements:

Knowledge Model	Worksheet KM-1: Checklist Knowledge-Model Documentation Document
Document entry	**Description**
KNOWLEDGE MODEL	Full knowledge-model specification in text plus selected figures.
INFORMATION SOURCES USED	Listing of all the information sources about the application domain that were consulted. This list is first produced during the identification stage.
GLOSSARY	Listing of application-domain terms together with a definition, in textual form or other. Using Internet technology, one can create a glossary with hyperlinks to text and pictures that explains the terms.
COMPONENTS CONSIDERED	List of potentially reusable components that were considered in the identification stage, plus a decision and a rationale for why the component was or was not used. The components are typically of two types: task-oriented (e.g., task templates) and domain-oriented (e.g., ontologies, knowledge bases).
SCENARIOS	A list of the scenarios for solving application problems collected during the model-construction process.
VALIDATION RESULTS	Description of the result of validation studies, in particular paper-based simulation and/or computer simulations (prototyping).
ELICITATION MATERIAL	Include material gathered during elicitation activities (e.g., interview transcripts) in appendices.

Table 7.2
Worksheet KM-1: Checklist for the "knowledge-model documentation document".

- A diagram of the full domain schema
- An inference-structure diagram
- A list of knowledge roles (both dynamic and static) with their domain mappings
- Textual specifications of the tasks and task methods

This set of specifications, although it lacks some of the textual detail, is in practice often sufficient to be understood without problems by the other project members.

7.7.2   Additional Material

It will be clear that in building a knowledge model a large amount of other material is gathered that is useful output as a kind of background documentation. It is therefore worthwhile to produce a "domain documentation document" containing at least the full knowledge model plus the following additional information:

- A list of all information sources used
- A listing of domain terms with explanations (= glossary)
- A list of model components that were considered for reuse plus the corresponding decisions and rationale
- A set of scenarios for solving the application problem
- Results of the simulations undertaken during validation

In addition, add the transcripts of interviews and protocols as appendices to this document. Worksheet KM-1 (see Table 7.2) provides a checklist for generating the document.

7.8   Bibliographical Notes and Further Reading

Work on guidelines to support the knowledge-engineering process (and software engineering in general) has always been scarce. There have been a few other process models proposed for model-based knowledge engineering. We mention the MIKE approach (Angele et al. 1998).

Over the years quite a number of languages have been developed for CommonKADS. Some languages have been aimed at a direct implementation of the knowledge model. In our view this approach cannot be recommended because the operationality requirement of the language makes it by definition less expressive and therefore not well suited for knowledge modelling. A number of languages focus on the specification aspects and use a variety of formal specification techniques to this end. A good survey of these languages is given by Fensel and van Harmelen (1994).

8

Knowledge-Elicitation Techniques

Key points of this chapter:

- Knowledge elicitation is the process of getting the data needed for knowledge modelling.
- A number of elicitation techniques exist.In this chapter we discuss a small set of frequently used techniques, namely interviews, protocol analysis, laddering, concept sorting, and repertory grids.
- Different techniques are useful for different types of expertise data.
- In a scenario we show how these techniques can be applied to the knowledge-modelling activities described in Chapter 7.

8.1   Introduction

This chapter discusses the problem of knowledge elicitation. Knowledge elicitation comprises a set of techniques and methods that attempt to elicit knowledge of a domain specialist through some form of direct interaction with that expert. The domain specialist, usually called the "expert," is a person that possesses knowledge about solving the application task we are interested in (cf. the "knowledge provider" role in Figure 2.6).

We begin by reviewing the nature and characteristics of the elicitation activity. Next, we consider the different types of expert who may be encountered. We then look at a range of methods and techniques for elicitation. We illustrate the use of these techniques with an example of an elicitation scenario. In this example it will become clear how elicitation techniques can be used to support the knowledge-modelling activities described in Chapter 7. The example concerns an application in which offices are assigned to employees. In the example we make use of an knowledge-elicitation tool set named PC-PACK, which supports the use of the techniques. This scenario and a demo version of the PC-PACK tools can be downloaded from the CommonKADS website.

Throughout, the emphasis is on practical ways and means of performing elicitation. The use of an example will show how different techniques and tools can be used together synergistically, within the context of a knowledge-modelling methodology such as CommonKADS.

8.2   Characteristics of Knowledge Elicitation

Elicitation can be seen as providing the material for knowledge modelling. The material is not completely "raw": the result of applying an elicitation technique is usually some structured form of data, e.g., markups, diagrams, lists of terms, formulas, informal rules, and so on. It is important to realize that one should not try to get real formal descriptions out of an elicitation technique. Imposing formal representations on elicitation typically leads to strong biases in the elicitation process and often results in bad data. Elicitation should be focused and structured, but also as open as possible. It is the task of knowledge modelling to convert the elicited material into a more formal description of the problem-solving process.

The people who carry out knowledge elicitation and analysis, the knowledge engineers (also called "knowledge analysts"), are typically not people with a deep knowledge of the application domain. In the simplest case, the knowledge engineer may be able to gather information from a variety of nonhuman resources: textbooks, technical manuals, case studies, and so on. However, in most cases one needs actually to consult a practicing expert. This may be because there isn't the documentation available, or because real expertise derives from practical experience in the domain, rather than from a reading of standard texts. Few knowledge models are ever built without recourse to experts at some stage. Those models not informed by actual expert understanding and practice are often the poorer for it. Two questions dominate in knowledge elicitation:

1. How do we get experts to tell us, or else show us, what they do?
2. How do we determine what constitutes their problem-solving competence?

The task is enormous, particularly in the context of large applications. There are a variety of circumstances which contrive to make the problem even harder. Much of the power of human expertise lies in laid-down experience, gathered over a number of years, and represented as heuristics. A *heuristic* is defined as a rule of thumb or generally proven method to obtain a result given particular information. Often the expertise has become so routinized that experts no longer know what they do or why.

There are obviously clear commercial reasons to try to make knowledge elicitation an effective process. We would like to be able to use techniques that will minimize the effort spent in gathering, transcribing, and analyzing an expert's knowledge. We would like to minimize the time spent with expensive and scarce domain specialists. And, of course, we would like to maximize the yield of usable knowledge.

There are also sound engineering reasons why we would like to make knowledge elicitation a systematic process. We would like the procedures of knowledge elicitation to become common practice and conform to clear standards. This will help ensure that the results are robust, that they can be used on various experts in a wide range of contexts by any competent knowledge engineer. We also hope to make our techniques reliable. This will mean that they can be applied with the same expected utility by different knowledge engineers. But however systematic we want to be, our analysis must of necessity begin with the expert.

8.3   On Experts

Experts come in all shapes and sizes. Ignoring the nature of your expert is a potential pitfall in knowledge elicitation. A coarse guide to a typology of experts might make the issues clearer. Let us take three categories we shall refer to as "academics," "practitioners," and "samurai." In practice experts may embody elements of all three types. Each of these types of expert differs along a number of dimensions. These include the outcome of their expert deliberations, the problem-solving environment they work in, the state of the knowledge they possess (both its internal structure and its external manifestation), their status and responsibilities, their source of information, and the nature of their training.

8.3.1   Three Types of Expert

On the basis of these dimensions we can distinguish three different types of expert:

1. The *academic* type regards his domain as having a logically organized structure. Generalizations over the laws and behavior of the domain are important to the academic type. Theoretical understanding is prized. Part of the function of such experts may be to explicate, clarify, and teach others. Thus they talk a lot about their domains. They may feel an obligation to present a consistent story both for pedagogic and professional reasons. Their knowledge is likely to be well structured and accessible. These experts may suppose that the outcome of their deliberations should be the correct solution of a problem. They believe that the problem can be solved by the appropriate application of theory. They may, however, be remote from everyday problem-solving.

2. The *practitioner* class on the other hand is engaged in constant day-to-day problem-solving in the domain. For them specific problems and events are the reality. Their practice may often be implicit and what they desire as an outcome is a decision that works within the constraints and resource limitations in which they are working. It may be that the generalized theory of the academic is poorly articulated in the practitioner. For the practitioner heuristics dominate and theory is sometimes thin on the ground.

3. The *samurai* is a pure performance expert — the only reality is the performance of action to secure an optimal performance. Practice is often the only training and responses are often automatic. Samurai usually explicate their knowledge verbally.

One can see this sort of division in any complex domain. Consider, for example, medical domains where we have professors of the subject, busy house staff working the wards, and medical ancillary staff performing many important but repetitive clinical activities.

The knowledge engineer must be alert to these differences because the various types of expert will perform very differently in knowledge-elicitation situations. The academics will be concerned about demonstrating mastery of the theory. They will devote much effort to characterizing the scope and limitations of the domain theory. Practitioners, on the other hand, are driven by the cases they are solving from day to day. They have often compiled or routinized any declarative descriptions of the theory that supposedly underlie their problem-solving. The performance samurai will more often than not turn any knowledge-elicitation interaction into a concrete performance of the task — simply exhibiting their skill.

8.3.2   Human Limitations and Biases

But there is more to say about the nature of experts and this is rooted in general principles of human information processing. Psychology has demonstrated the limitations, biases, and prejudices that pervade all human decision-making — expert or novice. To illustrate, consider the following facts, all potentially crucial to the enterprise of knowledge elicitation.

It has been shown repeatedly that the context in which one encodes information is the best one for recall. It is possible, then, that experts may not have access to the same information when in a knowledge-elicitation interview as they do when actually performing the task. So there are good psychological reasons to use techniques which involve observing the expert actually solving problems in the normal setting. In short, protocol analysis techniques may be necessary, but will not be sufficient for effective knowledge elicitation.

Consider also the issue of biases in human cognition. One well-known problem is that humans are poor at manipulating uncertain or probabilistic evidence. This may be important in knowledge elicitation for those domains that require a representation of uncertainty. Consider the rule:

```
    IF      the engine will not turn over AND
            the lights do not come on
    THEN    the battery is flat with probability X
```

This seems like a reasonable rule, but what is the value of X — should it be 0.9, 0.95, 0.79? The value that is finally decided upon will have important consequences for the working of the system, but it is very difficult to decide upon it in the first place. Medical diagnosis is a domain full of such probabilistic rules, but even expert physicians cannot accurately assess the probability values.

In fact there are a number of documented biases in human cognition which lie at the heart of this problem (Kahneman et al. 1982). People are known to undervalue prior probabilities, to use the ends and middle of the probability scale rather than the full range, and to anchor their responses around an initial guess. Cleaves (1987) lists a number of cognitive biases likely to be found in knowledge elicitation, and makes suggestions about how to avoid them. However, many knowledge engineers prefer to avoid the use of uncertainty wherever possible.

Cognitive bias is not limited to the manipulation of probability. A series of experiments has shown that systematic patterns of error occur across a number of apparently simple logical operations. For example, *modus tollens* states that if "A implies B' is true, and "not B" is true, then "not A" must be true. However, people, whether expert in a domain or not, make errors on this rule. This is in part due to an inability to reason with contrapositive statements. Also in part it depends on what A and B actually represent. In other words, they are affected by the content. This means that one cannot rely on the veracity of experts' (or indeed anyone's) reasoning.

All this evidence suggests that human reasoning, memory, and knowledge representation is rather more subtle than might be thought at first sight. The knowledge engineer should be alert to some of the basic findings emanating from cognitive psychology. While no text is perfect as a review of bias in problem-solving, the book by Meyer and Booker (1991) is reasonably comprehensive.

8.4   Elicitation Techniques

The techniques we will describe are methods that we have found in our work to be both useful and complementary. We can subdivide them into natural and contrived methods. The distinction is a simple one. A method is described as natural if it is one an expert might informally adopt when expressing or displaying expertise. Such techniques include interviews or observing actual problem-solving. There are other methods we will describe in which the expert undertakes a contrived task. The task elicits expertise in ways that are not usually familiar to an expert.

It is worth noting that Schweikert et al. (1987) found an expert's own opinion of the worth of a technique no guide to its real value. In methods such as sorting we have a situation in which the expert is trying to demonstrate expertise in a nonnatural or contrived manner. He might be quite used to chatting about his field of expertise, but sorting is different and experts are suspicious of it. Experts may in fact feel they are performing badly with such methods. However, on analysis one finds that the yield of knowledge is as good and sometimes even better than for noncontrived elicitation techniques (Shadbolt and Burton 1989).

In this chapter we discuss five types of techniques:

1. Interviewing
2. Protocol analysis
3. Laddering
4. Concept sorting
5. Repertory grids

The first two elicitation methods are both natural under the definition above. The other three techniques — laddering, concept sorting, and repertory grids — are more contrived. In the rest of this section we discuss the individual techniques. In the following section the use of these techniques is demonstrated in a practical example.

8.4.1   Interviewing

Almost everyone starts knowledge elicitation with one or more interviews. The interview is the most commonly used knowledge-elicitation technique and takes many forms, from the completely unstructured interview to the formally planned, structured interview.

Unstructured interview   Unstructured interviews have no agenda (or, at least, no detailed agenda) set either by the knowledge engineer or by the expert. Of course, this does not mean that the knowledge engineer has no goals for the interview, but it does mean that she has considerable scope for proceeding: there are few constraints. The advantages of this approach stem from this lack of constraints. First, the approach can be used whenever one of the goals of the interview is that the expert and the knowledge engineer establish a good relationship. There are no formal barriers to the discussion, ranging as either participant sees fit. Second, the engineer can get a broad view of the topic easily; she can "fill in the gaps" in her own perceived knowledge of the domain, thereby making herself more comfortable with her mental model. Third, the expert can describe the domain in a way with which he is familiar, discussing topics that he considers important and ignoring those he considers uninteresting.

The disadvantages are clear enough. The lack of structure can lead to inefficiency. The expert may be unnecessarily verbose. He may concentrate on topics whose importance he exaggerates. The coverage of the domain may be too patchy. The data acquired may be difficult to integrate, either because the data do not form a unity, or because there are inconsistencies. This last will be an even more likely occurrence if the information provided by several experts is to be collated.

Structured interview   The structured interview is a formal version of the interview in which the knowledge engineer plans and directs the session. The structured interview has the advantage that it provides structured transcripts that are easier to analyze than unstructured chat.

Probe code	Question template	Effect
P1	*Why would you do that?*	Converts an assertion into a rule
P2	*How would you do that?*	Generates lower-order rules
P3	*When would you do that?* *Is <the rule> always the case?*	Reveals the generality of the rule and may generate other rules
P4	*What alternatives to <the prescribed action/decision> are there?*	Generates more rules
P5	*What if it were not the case that <currently true condition>?*	Generates rules for when current condition does not apply
P6	*Can you tell me more about <any subject already mentioned>?*	Used to generate further dialogue if expert dries up

Table 8.1
Probes to elicit further information in structured interviews.

The formal interview we have specified here constrains the provider-elicitor dialogue to the general principles of the domain. Experts do not work through a particular scenario extracted from the domain by the elicitor; rather the experts generate their own scenarios as the interview progresses. The structure of the interview is as follows.

1. Ask the expert to give a brief (10-minute) outline of the target task, including the following information:

   a. An outline of the task, including a description of the possible solutions or outcomes of the task;
   b. A description of the variables which affect the choice of solutions or outcomes;
   c. A list of major rules which connect the variables to the solutions or outcomes.

2. Take each rule elicited in stage 1; ask when it is appropriate and when it is not. The aim is to reveal the scope (generality and specificity) of each existing rule, and hopefully generate some new rules.

3. Repeat stage 2 until it is clear that the expert will not produce any new information.

The task selection is important. The scope of the task should be relatively small and should typically be guided by an initial model selection (e.g., a task template). It is also important in this technique to be specific about how to perform stage 2. We have found that it is helpful to constrain the elicitor's interventions to a specific set of probes, each with a specific function. Table 8.1 contains a list of probes which will help in stage 2.

The idea here is that the elicitor engages in a type of slot/filler dialogue. Listening out for relevant concepts and relations imposes a large cognitive load on the elicitor. The provision of fixed linguistic forms within which to ask questions about concepts, relations, attributes,and values makes the elicitor's job very much easier. It also provides sharply focused transcripts which facilitate the process of extracting usable knowledge. Of course, there will be instances when none of the above probes are appropriate (such as the case when the elicitor wants the expert to clarify something). However, you should try to keep these interjections to a minimum. The point of specifying such a fixed set of linguistic probes is to constrain the expert into giving you all, and only, the information you want.

The sample of dialogue below is taken from a real interview of this kind. It is the transcript of an interview by a knowledge engineer (KE) with an expert (EX) on fault diagnosis of a visual display unit (VDU). Also, the type of probe by the knowledge engineer is indicated. In the transcripts we use the symbol + to represent a pause in the dialogue.

```
EX          I actually checked the port of the computer
KE [P1]     Why did you check the port?
EX          If it's been lightning recently then it's a good idea to
            check the port + because lightning tends to dam-
age the ports
KE [P4]     Are there any alternatives to that problem?
EX          Yes, that ought to be prefaced by saying do that if it was
            several keys with odd effects + not necessar-
ily all of them,
            but more than two
KE [P1]     Why does it have to be more than two?
EX          Well if it was only one or two keys doing funny things then
            the thing to do is check they're closing properly + speed
            would affect all keys, parity would  af-
fect about half the keys
```

This is quite a rich piece of dialogue. From this section of the interview alone we can extract the following rules.

```
IF          there has been recent lightning
THEN        check port for damage

IF          there are two or fewer malfunctioning keys
THEN        check the key contacts

IF          about half the keyboard is malfunctioning
THEN        check the parity

IF          the whole keyboard is malfunctioning
THEN        check the speed
```

Of course, these rules may need refining in later elicitation sessions, but the text of the dialogue shows how the use of the specific probes has revealed a well-structured response from the expert. A possible second-phase elicitation technique would be to present these rules back to the expert and ask about their truthfulness, scope and so forth. One can also apply the teach-back technique of Johnson & Johnson (1987). This involves creating an intermediate representation of the knowledge acquired, which is then "taught back" to the expert, who can then check or, if necessary, amend the information.

Potential pitfalls   In all interview techniques (and in some of the other generic techniques as well) there exist a number of dangers that have become familiar to knowledge engineers.

One problem is that experts will only produce what they can verbalize. If there are nonverbalizable aspects to the domain, the interview will not recover them. This can arise from two causes. It may be that the knowledge was never explicitly represented or articulated in terms of language (consider, for example, pattern recognition expertise). Then there is the situation where the knowledge was originally learned explicitly in a propositional or language-like form. However, in the course of experience it has become routinized or automized. We often use computing analogy to refer to this situation and speak of the expert as having compiled the knowledge.

This can happen to such an extent that experts may regard the complex decisions they make as based on hunches or intuitions . Nevertheless, these decisions are based upon large amounts of remembered data and experience, and the continual application of strategies. In this situation they tend to give black box replies: "I don't know how I do that....", "It is obviously the right thing to do.... ."

Another problem arises from the observation that people (and experts in particular) often seek to justify their decisions in any way they can. It is a common experience of the knowledge engineer to get a perfectly valid decision from an expert, and then to be given a spurious justification.

For these and other reasons we have to supplement interviews with additional methods of elicitation. Elicitation should always consist of a program of techniques and methods. We discuss a set of techniques in the remainder of this section.

When to use   Unstructured interviews are usually only carried out in the early stages of the modelling process, e.g., during organizational analysis or at the start of the knowledge identification phase. The structured interview is particularly useful in the knowledge refinement stage, in which the knowledge bases need to be "filled." The probes direct the search for missing knowledge pieces. The structured interview also provides useful information in the later phases of knowledge identification and during initial knowledge specification, e.g., to get information about key concepts and relations.

A good guideline is to tape every structured interview and to create a transcript from it. During unstructured interviews one can just take notes, although a transcript can have an added value, e.g., for creating a glossary. The transcript can be used in knowledge-analysis tools such as PC-PACK to create markups in order to identify potential concepts, properties, and relations.

8.4.2   Protocol Analysis

Protocol analysis (PA) is a generic term for a number of different ways of performing some form of analysis of the expert(s) actually solving problems in the domain. In all cases the engineer takes a record of what the expert does — preferably by video- or audiotape — or at least by written notes. Protocols are then made from these records and the knowledge engineer tries to extract meaningful structure and rules from the protocols.

Getting data for protocol analysis   We can distinguish two general types of PA, namely online and offline. In on-line PA the expert is being recorded solving a problem, and concurrently a commentary is made. The nature of this commentary specifies two subtypes of the online method. The expert performing the task may be describing what he or she is doing as problem-solving proceeds. This is called *self-report* (or "thinking aloud"). A variant on this is to have another expert provide a running commentary on what the expert performing the task is doing. This is called *shadowing*.

Offline PA allows the expert(s) to comment retrospectively on the problem solving session — usually by being shown an audiovisual record of it. This may take the form of retrospective self-report by the expert who actually solved the problem, it could be a critical retrospective report by other experts, or there could be group discussion of the protocol by a number of experts, including its originator. In the case in which only a behavioral protocol is obtained, then obviously some form of retrospective verbalization of the problem-solving episode is required.

Requirements for a session   Before PA sessions can be held, a number of preconditions should be satisfied. The first of these is that the knowledge engineer is sufficiently acquainted with the domain to understand the expert's tasks. Without this the elicitor may completely fail to record or take note of important parts of the expert's behavior.

A second requirement is the careful selection of problems for PA. The sampling of problems is crucial. PA sessions may take a relatively long time, only a few problems can be addressed (Shadbolt and Burton 1989)). Therefore, the selection of problems should be guided by how representative they are. Asking experts to sort problems into some form of order (Chi et al. 1981) may give an insight into the classification of types of problems and help in the selection of suitable problems for PA (see also the next two sections on concept sorts and laddering).

A further condition for effective PA is that the expert(s) should not feel embarrassed about describing their expertise in detail. It is preferable for them to have experience in thinking aloud. Uninhibited thinking aloud has to be learned in the same way as talking to an audience. One or two short training sessions may be useful, in which a simple task is used as an example. This puts the expert at ease and familiarizes them with the task of talking about their problem solving.

Analyzing the transcript   Where a verbal or behavioral transcript has been obtained we next have to contemplate its analysis. Analysis might include the encoding of the transcript into "chunks" of knowledge (which might be actions, assertions, propositions, key words, etc.), and should result in a rich domain representation with many elicited domain features together with a number of specified links between those features.

There are a number of principles that can guide the protocol analysis. For example, analysis of the verbalization resulting in the protocol can distinguish between information that is attended to during problem-solving, and that which is used implicitly. A distinction can be made between information brought out of memory (such as a recollection of a similar problem solved in the past), and information that is produced on the spot by inference. The knowledge chunks referred to above can be analyzed by using the expert's syntax, or the pauses he takes, or other linguistic cues. Syntactical categories (e.g., use of nouns, verbs) can help distinguish between domain features and problem-solving actions and so on.

In trying to decide when it is appropriate to use PA, bear in mind that it is alleged that different knowledge-engineering techniques differentially elicit certain kinds of information. With PA it is claimed that the sorts of knowledge elicited include the "when" and "how" of using specific knowledge. It can reveal the problem-solving and reasoning strategies, evaluation procedures,and evaluation criteria used by the expert, and procedural knowledge about how tasks and subtasks are decomposed. A PA gives you a complete episode of problem solving. It can be useful as a verification method to check that what people say is what they do. It can take you deep into a particular problem. However, it is intrinsically a narrow method since usually one can only run a relatively small number of problems from the domain.

Finally, when performing PA it is useful to have a set of conventions for the actual interpretation and analysis of the resultant data. Ericsson & Simon (1993) provide the classic exposition of protocol analysis although it is oriented toward cognitive psychology.

Coding scheme   Traditionally, psychologists analyze think-aloud protocols with the use of a coding scheme. The coding scheme consists of a predefined set of actions and/or concepts that one should use to classify text fragments of the protocol. In knowledge modelling, the selected task template can fulfill the role of a coding scheme. The analyst marks where a certain inference is made, a certain task is started, or a knowledge role is used. Because task templates are useful as a coding scheme for expertise data, these templates have also been called "interpretation models."

Guidelines for PA sessions   When eliciting data for protocol analysis through a self-report or other means, the following are a useful tips to help enhance its effectiveness:

Guideline 8-1:   PRESENT PROBLEMS AND DATA IN A REALISTIC WAY
Rationale: The way problems and data are presented should be as close as possible to a real situation.

Guideline 8-2:   TRANSCRIBE THE PROTOCOLS AS SOON AS POSSIBLE
Rationale: The meaning of many expressions is soon lost, particularly if the protocols are not recorded. In almost all cases an audio recording is sufficient, but video recordings have the advantage of containing additional and disambiguating information.

Guideline 8-3:   AVOID LONG SELF-REPORT SESSIONS
Rationale: Because of the need to perform a double task the process of thinking aloud is significantly more tiring for the expert than being interviewed. This is one reason why shadowing is sometimes preferred.

Guideline 8-4:   IN GENERAL, THE PRESENCE OF THE KNOWLEDGE ENGINEER IS RE-
QUIRED IN A PA SESSION
Rationale: Although the knowledge engineer adopts a background role, her very presence suggests a listener to the interviewee, and lends meaning to the thinkaloud process. Therefore, comments on audibility, or even silence, by the knowledge engineer are quite acceptable.

Potential pitfalls   Protocol analyses share with the unstructured interview the problem that they may deliver unstructured transcripts which are hard to analyze. Moreover, they focus on particular problem cases and so the scope of the knowledge produced may be very restricted. It is difficult to derive general domain principles from a limited number of protocols. These are practical disadvantages of protocol analysis, but there are more subtle problems.

Two actions, which look exactly the same to the knowledge engineer, may be the result of two quite different sets of considerations. This is a problem of impoverished interpretation by the knowledge engineer. The knowledge engineer simply does not know enough to discriminate the actions. The obverse to this problem can arise in shadowing and the retrospective analyses of protocols by experts. Here the expert(s) may simply wrongly attribute a set of considerations to an action after the event. This is analogous to the problems of misattribution in interviewing.

A particular problem with self-report, apart from being tiring, is the possibility that verbalization may interfere with performance. The classic demonstration of this is for a driver to attend to all the actions involved in driving a car. If one consciously monitors such parameters as engine revs, current gear, speed, visibility, steering wheel position and so forth, the driving invariably gets worse. Such skill is shown to its best effect when performed automatically. This is also the case with certain types of expertise. By asking the expert to verbalize, one is in some sense destroying the point of doing protocol analysis — to access procedural, real-world knowledge.

Having pointed to these disadvantages, it is also worth remembering that context is sometimes important for memory — and hence for problem solving. For most nonverbalizable knowledge, and even for some verbalizable knowledge, it may be essential to observe the expert performing the task. For it may be that this is the only situation in which the expert is actually able to perform it.

When to use   As mentioned above, PA is particularly useful in analyzing dynamic reasoning behavior. This means that PA is most helpful in the specification of task and inference knowledge. PA is often used for template selection, e.g., by using protocols to generate an annotated inference structure. Also, it can provide information for the specification of task-method control. If no template is suitable, PA can be used to construct a task/inference description more or less from scratch. This will typically increase the number of elicitation sessions needed. In addition, protocol analysis is used for knowledge-model validation, either by finding out whether a fully specified model fits the data, or as an information source for validation scenarios.

An example of using protocol analysis for template selection is described in the scenario further on.

8.4.3   Laddering

Laddering is a somewhat contrived technique, and you will need to explain it fully to the expert before starting. The expert and the knowledge engineer construct a graphical representation of the domain in terms of the relations between domain and problem-solving elements. The result is a qualitative, two-dimensional graph where nodes are connected by labeled arcs. The graph takes the form of a hierarchy of trees. No extra elicitation method is used here, but expert and elicitor construct the graph together by negotiation.

The key point is that, having acquired some of the key terms in the domain, organizing them into some sort of structure is a natural thing to do. Laddering is a very straightforward means.

The laddering technique is typically used to construct some initial, informal hierarchies. One can see a laddering tool as a scruffy tool for hierarchical ordering without imposing too many semantic restrictions. The objects in the ladders can be of many different types. The terms "concept" and "attribute" should be interpreted loosely in the context of laddering. For example, no strict distinction needs to be made yet between "concepts" and "instances" (something that is difficult in the early phases of knowledge modelling). We will see that the tool used in the scenario supports laddering of any type of object. Object types can be defined by the user and are available as text markers.

When to use   Laddering is used mostly in the early phases of domain exploration. It is the groundwork for the more formal representation in the knowledge model.

8.4.4   Concept Sorting

Concept sorting is a technique that is useful when we wish to uncover the different ways an expert sees relationships between a fixed set of concepts. In the simplest version an expert is presented with a number of cards on each of which a concept word is printed. The cards are shuffled and the expert is asked to sort the cards into either a fixed number of piles or into any number of piles the expert finds appropriate. This process is repeated many times.

Using this task one attempts to get multiple views of the structural organization of knowledge by asking the expert to do the same task over and over again. Each time the expert sorts the cards he should create at least one pile that differs in some way from previous sorts. The expert should also provide a name or category label for each pile of each different sort.

Variants of the simple sort are different forms of hierarchical sort. One such version is to ask the expert to proceed by producing first two piles; on the second sort, three; then four, and so on. Finally we ask if any two piles have anything in common. If so you have isolated a higher-order concept that can be used as a basis for future elicitation.

The advantages of concept sorting can be characterized as follows. It is fast to apply and easy to analyze. It forces into an explicit format the constructs which underlie an expert's understanding. In fact it is often instructive to the expert. A sort can lead the expert to see structure in his view of the domain which he himself has not consciously articulated before. Finally, in domains where the concepts are perceptual in nature (e.g., x-rays, layouts, and pictures of various kinds), then the cards can be used as a means of presenting these images and attempting to elicit names for the categories and relationships that might link them.

There are, of course, features to be wary of with this sort of technique. Experts can often confound dimensions by not consistently applying the same semantic distinctions throughout an elicitation session. Alternatively, they may oversimplify the categorization of elements, missing out on important caveats.

An important tip with all of the techniques we are reviewing is always to audiotape these sessions. An expert makes many asides, comments, and qualifications in the case of sorting ranking and so on. In fact one may choose to use the contrived methods as a means to carry out auxiliary structured interviews. The structure this time is centered around the activity of the technique.

When to use   Concept sorting can discover new concepts and attributes, and is therefore particularly helpful in constructing a domain schema in unfamiliar domains. The technique is able to uncover many different viewpoints from which one can look at an application domain. Concept sorting requires some prestructuring of the data, e.g., thorough markups of interview transcripts. The technique is complementary to repertory grids.

8.4.5   Repertory Grids

The final technique we will consider is the repertory grid. This technique has its roots in the psychology of personality (Kelly 1955) and is designed to reveal a conceptual map of a domain in a fashion similar to the card sort, as discussed above (see Shaw and Gaines (1987) for a full discussion). The technique as developed in the 1950s was very time-consuming to administer and analyze by hand. This naturally suggested that an implemented version would be useful.

Briefly, subjects are presented with a range of domain elements and asked to choose three, such that two are similar and different from the third. Suppose we were trying to uncover an astronomer's understanding of the planets. We might present him with a set of planets, and he might choose Mercury and Venus as the two similar elements, and Jupiter as different from the other two. The subject is then asked the reason for differentiating these elements, and this dimension is known as a construct. In our example "size" would be a suitable construct. The remaining domain elements are then rated on this construct.

This process continues with different triads of elements until the expert can think of no further discriminating constructs. The result is a matrix of similarity ratings, relating elements, and constructs. This is analyzed using a statistical technique called cluster analysis. In knowledge engineering, as in clinical psychology, the technique can reveal clusters of concepts and elements which the expert may not have articulated in an interview. The repertory grid is built up interactively, and the expert is shown the resultant knowledge. Experts have the opportunity to refine this knowledge during the elicitation process.

When to use   This technique can be seen as the statistical counterpart of concept sorting. Like the latter, the repertory grids is particularly useful when trying to uncover the structure of an unfamiliar domain. It is used mainly to support the specification of the domain schema, both in its initial and in its more advanced stages.

8.4.6   Other Techniques

Table 8.2 summarizes the main features of the techniques discussed above. The five categories of techniques are just a selection from the available elicitation techniques. For example, rule-induction techniques (Michalski et al. 1983, Carbonell 1989) can be used to derive domain rules automatically. Such a tool can also used to discover rule patterns, leading to specification of rule types in the knowledge model.

8.5   An Elicitation Scenario

In this scenario we show how the elicitation techniques described above can be applied to a sample problem. The problem domain concerns the assignment of offices to employees of a department of a research institute. In this scenario we make use of the PC-PACK system. PC-PACK is a tool set that supports the use of elicitation techniques. A demo version of this tool set plus this scenario can be downloaded from the CommonKADS website. Tool sets such as PC-PACK are helpful aids for knowledge analysts. In the near future we will see integrated elicitation and modelling tools. At the moment such tools are not yet on the market.

Technique	Used for	Tool support
Unstructured interview	Familiarization with organization and application domain	Markup tools; text analysis
Structured interview	Knowledge-identification activities; initial knowledge specification; completing the knowledge bases	Markup tools; rule editor (when used for completing the knowledge base)
Protocol analysis	Checking a task template Generating an inference/task specification (in case of unfamiliar application domains, for which no models exist yet)	Marking up a transcript with inference and/or task markers
Laddering	Preparatory work for domain-schema specification with respect to useful hierarchies and concept attributes	Graphical support for constructing multiple hierarchies
Concept sorting	Domain-schema specification in unfamiliar domains	Graphical support tool for creating piles and new features
Repertory grid	Domain-schema specification in unfamiliar domains	Graphical grid presentation/editing plus cluster analysis software

Table 8.2
Summary of the elicitation techniques discussed.

The scenario shows how elicitation techniques can be used to get the data required by the knowledge-modelling activities described in Chapter 7. In this scenario we assume that an initial knowledge-identification phase has been conducted. The results of this phase are described in the next subsection. In the scenario we go through the initial activities in the knowledge-specification phase (see Figure 7.1).

8.5.1   The Sample Problem: Office Assignment

Problem context   The members of a research group of a computer science laboratory are moved to a new floor of their building. Due to funding cuts, they get a limited number of rooms. The problem is to build a system which can allocate the members to a suitable office. There is a constraint, however. It is important that the system also provides a cognitive model of the expert. In other words, the resulting system must be able to replicate the expert's problem-solving and solve new problems as the expert would have solved them.

Available information   Within the group, there are a number of different types of workers. Thomas is head of the research group. Eva does the administrative management of the group. Monika and Ulrike are the secretaries. Hans, Katharina, and Joachim are heads of research projects. The other people are employed as researchers.

	Action by the expert		Self-report transcript (stylized)
1	Put Thomas D. into office C5-117	1a	The head of group needs a central office so that s/he is as close as possible.to all the members of the group . This should be a large office.
		1b	This assignment is defined first, as the location of the office of the head of group restricts the possibilities of the subsequent assignments.
2	Monika X. and Ulrike U. into office C5-119.	2a	The secretaries' office should be located close to the head of group. Both secretaries should work together in one large office. This assignment is executed as soon as possible, as its possible choices are extremely constrained.
3	Eva I. into C5-116	3a	The manager must have maximum access to the head of group and to the secretariat. At the same time he/she should have a centrally located office. A small office will do.
		3b	This is the earliest point at which this decision can be taken.
4	Joachim I. into C5-115.	4a	The heads of large projects should be close to the head of group and the secretariat. There really is no reason for the sequence of assignments of Joachim, Hans, and Katharina.
5	Hans W. into C5-114.	5a	The heads of large projects should be close to the head of group and the secretariat.
6	Katharina N. into C5-113.	6a	The heads of large projects should be close to the head of group and the secretariat.
7	Andy and Uwe T. into C5-120.	7a	Both smoke. To avoid conflicts with nonsmokers they share an office. Neither of them is eligible for a single office. This is the first twin-room assignment as the smoker/nonsmoker conflict is a severe one.
8	Werner L. and Jürgen L. into office C5-123.	8a	They are both implementing systems, both nonsmokers. They do not work on the same project, but they work on related subjects. Members of the same projects should not share offices. Sharing with members of other projects enhances synergy effects within the research group.
		8b	There are really no criteria for the sequence of twin-room assignments.
9	Marc M. and Angi W. into office C5122.	9a	Marc is implementing systems; Angi isn't. This should not be a problem. Putting them together would ensure good cooperation between the RESPECT and the KRITON projects.
10	Harry C. and Michael T. into office C5-121.	10a	They are both implementing systems. Harry develops object systems. Michael uses them. This should create synergy.

Table 8.3
Stylized transcript of a self-report protocol.

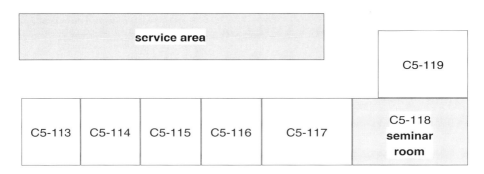

Figure 8.1
Floor plan of the sample problem.

The floor of the building where the group moves to is depicted in Figure 8.1. The shaded rooms are not available as office space. C5-117 and C5-119 to C5-123 are large rooms which can hold two people. The others are rooms for single-person use.

In Table 8.3 we have listed part of a transcript in which the expert solves the allocation problem in a self-report setting. This protocol constitutes the main "raw material" we use in this elicitation scenario.

8.5.2   Creating the Initial Domain Schema

Several elicitation techniques are useful when building an initial domain schema, particularly when the knowledge engineer does not have some data model or domain schema she can reuse. In this subsection we show the use of the following techniques:

- **Protocol analysis**   A simple mark-up tool can be used to find the relevant domain terms in a transcript and in other information sources.
- **Laddering**   Laddering is used to create some initial domain hierarchies.
- **Concept sorting and repertory grid**   Both these tools can be used to discover domain features that were not directly apparent from the domain material, such as a new concept or attribute.

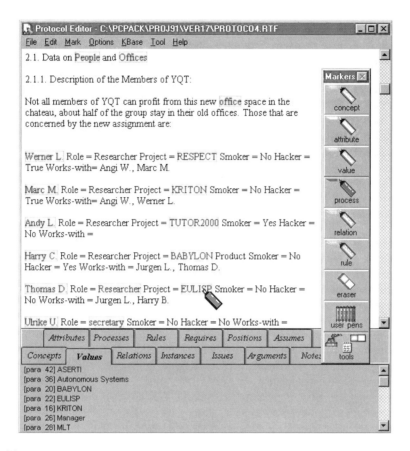

Figure 8.2
Marking up domain terms in the office-assignment material.

Marking up the protocol In using PC-PACK on the example, we need to use a so-called protocol editor to mark-up appropriate words. There are various color-coded markers available. In Figure 8.2 a snapshot of the protocol editor is shown. For the moment, only the concept, attribute, and value markers are used.

In the introductory material we can markup terms such as "office" and the terms related to the type of work: **head-of-group**, **head-of-project**, **manager**, **secretary**, and **researcher**. These terms are marked as concepts. In addition, individual people and offices are marked as concepts. At this stage we are not yet making a distinction between concepts and instances. The term "concept" is used here in a sloppy way.

Other terms can be marked as potential "attributes," such as the **project** a person is working on, whether someone is a **smoker**, and the **size** and **location** of a room. Within this tool, the attributes are just identified and not connected to concepts yet. In fact, this should really be seen as a first structuring of raw material. An attribute could easily become a relation in the final domain schema (e.g., the "project" attribute).

Finally, some terms can be marked as attribute values. In this scenario example values are `large`, `single`, and `does-not-smoke`, Again, these values might well become full concepts in the final schema.

Sometimes when marking up a protocol there is a need to add small annotations, perhaps to clarify why a particular marking-up choice was made or to elaborate on a topic. PC-PACK's protocol editor supports this by providing Post-it-type annotations for terms.

Laddering tool   PC-PACK contains a tool for performing laddering. The first task in the example will be to create a concept tree to form a useful knowledge structure from the concepts identified. The resulting diagram is shown in Figure 8.3. First, a hierarchy of people, with the management structure and people's roles, has been created by dragging and dropping the appropriate lower-level concepts marked up in the protocol. A similar method is followed to place all of the room names under the superclass "Offices."

The next task is to use the laddering tool to structure the attributes elicited from the protocol. For this purpose the laddering tool has an "attribute" mode (see Figure 8.4). The attributes are represented through a parent node, with possible attribute values as children. Not all values may be present as markups in the domain material, but the knowledge analyst is free to add additional attributes and values.

In Figure 8.4 we see five attributes that have been identified: **role**, **smoker**, **gender**, **size**, and **location**. "Gender" was entered directly by the knowledge engineer. The same holds for the attribute "role," which was added to model information also represented in the management hierarchy,

The other attributes stem from markups in the material. For some attributes only one value is mentioned in the transcript, e.g., `central` for the "location" attribute. It is usually easy to come up with alternative values through common sense (e.g., `non-central`). This can also be noted as a specific question for the next structured interview ("can you tell me what kind of locations you distinguish for rooms?"). This is typical of elicitation: the (provisional) knowledge structures the analysts build are subsequently used to focus the elicitation of expertise data.

The newly defined attributes can now be used in the previously defined concept ladder. Three attributes (smoker, gender, and role) can be attached to the **person** concept; the other two attributes (size, location) contain information related to offices.

Card-sort tool   The card sort tool supports the concept sorting technique. A snapshot of this tool is shown in Figure 8.5. The card sort tool is most effective when sorting an entire set of concepts along a new dimension. As an example, we can add a new dimension to the

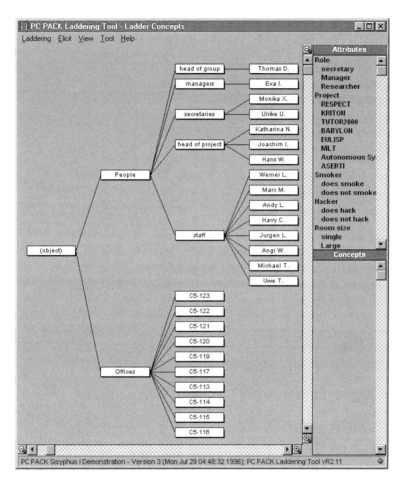

Figure 8.3
A ladder of objects involved in the office-assignment problem.

knowledge base: **hacker**. This dimension is suggested by protocol fragment 8a, in which the expert considers personal features related to implementing systems. New sorting piles must now be elicited for the values of "hacker." These values are `does-hack` and `does-not-hack`. The result is shown in Figure 8.5. The new dimension is added as an attribute to the existing set of attributes.

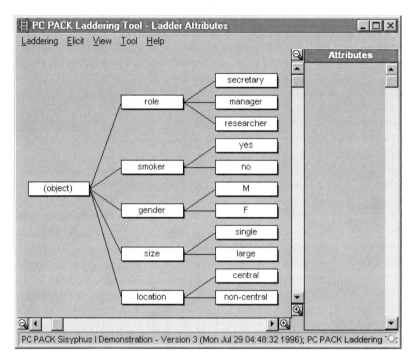

Figure 8.4
A ladder of objects involved in the office-assignment problem.

Repertory-grid tool In Figure 8.6 we see a sample grid for the office-assignment task. Along the horizontal axis we see a set of concepts within which we want to find some new distinguishing features. Along the vertical axis we see a selection of attributes that are thought to be relevant to this group of concepts. Not all attributes identified in the laddering tool will necessarily be relevant to the grid being constructed. For this example we can use smoker, hacker, gender, and role.

With all the constructs added, you are now ready to begin rating the elements. The process of rating each construct is as simple as clicking in the box at the desired point along the scale. Using the information from the protocol text, go through the constructs rating the values. For binary constructs, such as smoker/nonsmoker, it is usual to give a score at one of the poles. However, it can be seen that under certain circumstances, for example, if more knowledge were available, binary constructs like smoking can become more continuous, for instance, a rating of number of cigarettes smoked per day. For the "role" construct a way to rate secretary, manager, head of group, head of project, and researcher must be

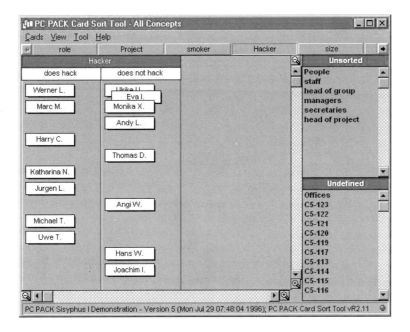

Figure 8.5
Using the card-sort tool. The piles suggest a new attribute named "hacker" to be added to the ladder.

found. In this case the construct is chosen to rate the amount of involvement in research, from secretary (no research) through to researcher (only research).

When all elements have been rated for all four constructs, the repertory grid can be displayed, see Figure 8.6. The constructs are plotted against the elements and the score given is displayed in the grid. The real power of the repertory grid, however, comes from the dendrogram. This part of the diagram, so named because of its resemblance to a tree-like structure, shows at a glance the similarity hierarchy of both elements and constructs. Figure 8.6 for example, shows that Katharina and Uwe are very similar (both females, smokers, and hackers), as are Ulrike and Monika (the two secretaries). Eva is also very similar to this group, which is not surprising since she is the manager and has a lot in common with the secretaries. In a dendrogram, the nearer to that diagram that the branches join, the more similar the elements (or constructs). Thus we can see that broader groupings also exist; for example, the male smokers Andy and Hans form a close subgroup, yet still ultimately join up with the largest group of nonsmoking, male, hacker researchers.

The repertory grid tool appears to elicit similar knowledge to the other tools, the dendrogram resembling the structure of the personnel hierarchy. However, it is only on the

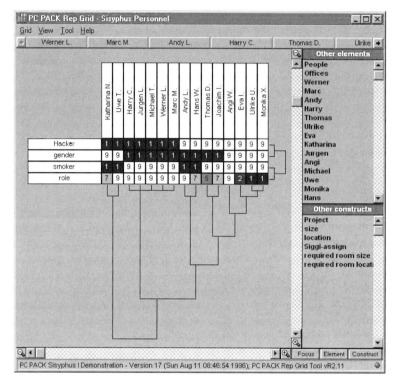

Figure 8.6
Focused repertory grid.

constructs and entities that are chosen. The grid updates automatically as these are added or removed from the analysis, and this provides a very powerful way to see the effect of different attributes on the knowledge model.

8.5.3   Choosing the Task Template

We have seen that the most appropriate technique for eliciting knowledge about the reasoning *process* is protocol analysis of a transcript resulting from a think-aloud session, such as a self-report. In this scenario we show how we can analyze the self-report of the allocation expert to find an appropriate task template. We have classified the task as an assignment task. The fact that the task is called "office assignment" already suggests this, but in practice this is not a guarantee. However, if we look at the definition of assignment (two groups of objects, etc.),it is clear that it matches our current application task. Therefore, we can

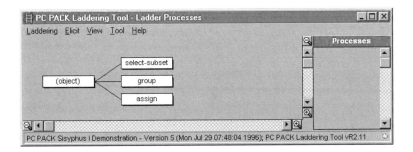

Figure 8.7
Process ladder. The three inferences of the assignment template (select, group, assign) are defined as PC-PACK processes, and can subsequently be used for markups.

propose the assignment template described in Chapter 6 (cf. Figure 6.20)) as a candidate specification of the task and inference knowledge.

We can now use this template as a coding scheme for the protocol, to find out whether the model indeed fits with this application. For this purpose, we have defined the three inferences as PC-PACK "processes," which we subsequently can use to mark up the transcript. The three process are shown as a process ladder in Figure 8.7.

In Figure 8.8 we see again a snapshot of the PC-PACK protocol editor. At the right-hand side of the figure you can see that we now have three "process" markers, respectively, for the inferences select-subset, group, and assign. The text fragments marked in this figure are all related to the select-subset inference. We can look at a listing of the "select" fragments at the bottom. The text fragments marked all concern the order in which the assignment process is performed.

Figure 8.9 shows some additional markups, in this case for the group inference. We can see that the text fragments are all concerned with the way researchers are grouped together in double rooms.

It is clear that the protocol provides a good "fit" with the task template. This is sufficient to incorporate the task template for assignment with some confidence into the knowledge model for the office-assignment application. In Figure 8.10 we have included an annotated inference structure that can be constructed on the basis of the results of protocol analysis. We now have an already quite detailed initial knowledge model and can safely continue with completing the knowledge-model specification.

8.5.4   Further Knowledge Modelling

Several techniques are useful for detailed knowledge specification. There is a group of techniques that can be used to derive rules automatically or manually from domain data.

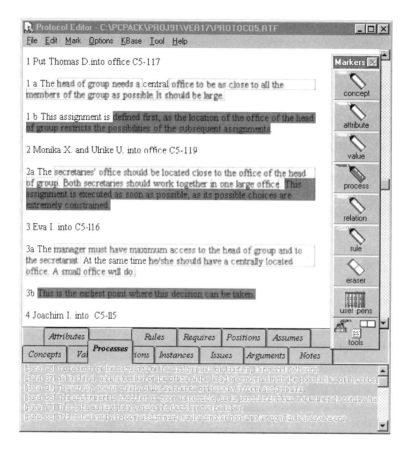

Figure 8.8
Markups in the transcript, indicating inference steps of the assignment template. The inferences act as a coding scheme for the transcript. The markups in this figure are related to the "select" process.

This technique is known as *rule induction*. Rule-induction techniques are useful for generating sample rules for the knowledge bases. and are often applied in an exploratory fashion to discover patterns that can be represented with rule types. In addition, these rule-discovery techniques can be applied in the knowledge refinement phase, when the contents of the domain models (= knowledge bases) needs to be completed.

The subject of rule induction and discovery lies outside the scope of the present work. The reader is referred to other sources, such as the PC-PACK documentation, for more details on these issues. An alternative method of acquiring rules is to mark them up with a tool such as the PC-PACK protocol editor tool. The process of marking up rules is identical

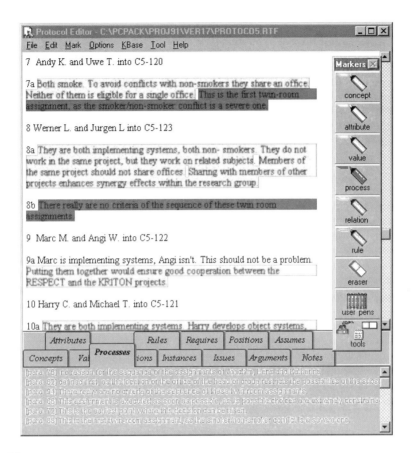

Figure 8.9
Markups in the transcript for the "group" process.

to marking up concepts, Attributes, and values. In fact, a user can define her own set of custom markers.

8.6   Some Final Remarks

The problem of knowledge elicitation is a subtle and complex one. This chapter has described some of the techniques that are used in this enterprise and indicated where software support for the process is becoming available. But we have also sought to provide an indication of the difficulties inherent in doing this kind of work. At present, knowledge

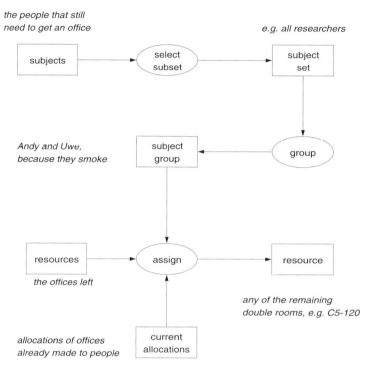

Figure 8.10
Inference structure for assignment together with domain-specific annotations for the office-assignment problem.

elicitation is itself a form of expertise. Experienced knowledge engineers come to recognize the subtleties of expert thinking. They develop skills that allow them to capture an expert's knowledge despite the many obstacles they face. Methodologies such as CommonKADS, and suites of knowledge-acquisition software such as PC-PACK, are essential means to codify and organize such knowledge-elicitation expertise.

8.7   Bibliographical Notes and Further Reading

An excellent review of the psychology of expertise is Chi et al. (1988). Several texts provide an overview of elicitation techniques, e.g., Meyer and Booker (1991) and McGraw and Harrison-Briggs (1989). The book by Van Someren, Barnard and Sandberg (1993) provides a good and practical introduction to the self-report technique.

The data about the office-assignment problem were provided by Marc Linster (1994).

Modelling Communication Aspects

Key points of this chapter:

- The communication model specifies the information exchange between tasks carried out by different agents.
- How to construct a communication model step by step, by means of three consecutive layers: overall communication plan, individual transactions, detailed information exchange specification.
- The communication plan describes the full dialogue between two agents.
- Transactions are the basic building blocks for a dialogue, and act as the go-between of two tasks carried out by different agents.
- Transactions in their turn may consist of one or more messages which are detailed in the information exchange specification. Predefined communication types and patterns allow the buildup of message protocols in a structured way.
- Various techniques are available to verify and validate a communication model.

9.1 Role and Overview of the Communication Model

To become effective, produced knowledge has to be transferred to the various parties that use it to perform their own tasks. It is the purpose of the CommonKADS communication model to specify the information exchange procedures to realize the knowledge transfer between agents. Figure 9.1 gives an overview of the main components of the communication model and how it relates to the other CommonKADS models.

In brief, a task that is carried out by one agent may produce results in the form of information objects that need to be communicated to other agents. A simple example is the basic system-user interaction, where the knowledge system presents reasoning results

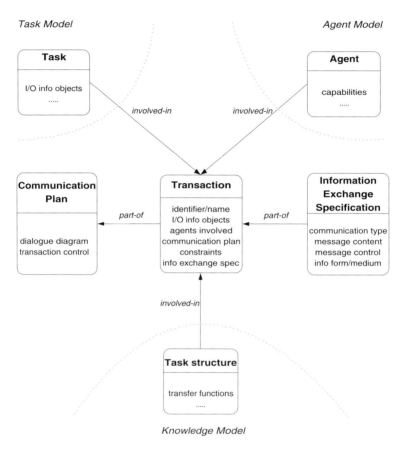

Figure 9.1
Overview of the communication model and how it relates to the other CommonKADS models.

to the user, or, alternatively, the user provides input data to the knowledge system. The description of the agents involved, together with their capabilities, stems from the agent model. The tasks, as well as their (input/output) information objects and their assignment to the various agents, originate from the task model. If tasks are knowledge intensive, they are usually refined in the knowledge model. The latter has a special leaf subtask type called a transfer function, indicating that input or output reasoning information has to be obtained from or delivered to another agent.

The key communication-model component describing such communicative acts is called a *transaction*. A transaction tells what information objects are exchanged between what agents and what tasks. It is, so to speak, the go-between of two tasks carried out by different agents. Transactions are the building blocks for the full dialogue between two agents, which is described in the communication plan. Transactions themselves may consist of several messages, which are then detailed in the information exchange specification. This specification is based on predefined communication types and patterns, which make it easy to build up message protocols in a structured way.

Accordingly, the process of constructing the CommonKADS communication model goes in terms of three subsequent layers, from global to detailed specifications, as follows (see also Figure 9.1):

1. the overall communication plan, which governs the full dialogue between the agents;
2. the individual transactions that link two (leaf) tasks carried out by two different agents;
3. the information exchange specification that details the internal message structure of a transaction.

This chapter explains this stepwise construction process, offers a number of specific techniques, and discusses how to verify and validate the communication model. We illustrate the main points through an application coming from the energy distribution industry.

9.2   The Communication Plan

In constructing the CommonKADS communication model, it is easiest to begin with the overall communication plan. The entry point of the communication analysis is: consider two agents that carry out a shared or distributed top task. For successful completion, they need to communicate and exchange information. The communication plan aims to give an overview of all the needed exchanges. Thus, it covers the *full top-level dialogue* corresponding to performing this shared top task. For example, if a knowledge system and its human user are the considered two agents, the communication plan gives the human-computer dialogue — in this case typically consisting of data input, asking or answering questions and presentation of reasoning results — associated with a single but complete session with the system.

9.2.1   Constructing the Dialogue Diagram

Since the entry point of the analysis is a top task distributed over more than one agent, it is evident that constructing the communication model crucially depends on information from other CommonKADS models. In order to start with communication modelling, the following information needs to be available:

- From the task model, the list of tasks carried out by the considered agent. For the communication model, we are interested in the leaf tasks, i.e., those that are not decomposed further, together with their input/output information objects.

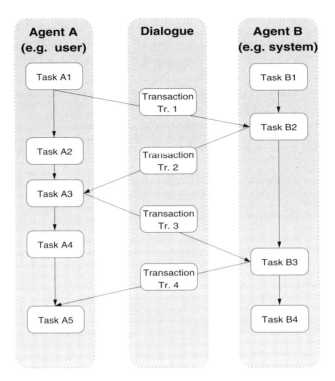

Figure 9.2
The general layout of a dialogue diagram. It forms the central part of the communication plan, as it shows the overall information flow related to agent communication.

- From the knowledge model, the set of so-called transfer functions, that is, leaf nodes in the task/inference structure that depend on data from or deliver reasoning results to the outside world. (Recall that a task/inference structure in the knowledge model is a refinement of a nonleaf, knowledge-intensive task stemming from the task model).
- From the agent model, the description of relevant agents, with their knowledge (or more generally, capabilities), responsibilities and constraints. The communication model must be constructed such that it satisfies the ensuing agent requirements, but in its turn it may also add requirements for communicative capabilities of an agent.

This is depicted in Figure 9.1. Thus, normally the knowledge engineer will have already done a significant part of task, agent, and knowledge analysis, before starting with communicating modelling. This also follows by looking at the main steps in constructing the communication plan.

1. Go through all task-model leaf tasks and knowledge model transfer functions. Make a list of all tasks that have input or output information objects that must be exchanged with another agent. Do this for each agent.

2. From this list, identify the set of associated agent-agent transactions. Here, a transaction is simply defined as the communication link needed between two leaf tasks (including transfer functions) carried out by two different agents. Transactions are the basic building blocks of the communication plan. Give each transaction an understandable name. Typically, this is a verb-noun combination indicating the communicative act performed with the information object (e.g., present diagnostic conclusions to the user).

3. The results of the previous two steps can be conveniently combined in a so-called dialogue diagram, where in a single picture we see an overview of all transactions and the tasks they are linking for every agent. The general form of a dialogue diagram is shown in Figure 9.2. The dialogue diagram presents the complete information-flow part of the communication plan.

4. Finally, the communication plan is completed by adding control over the transactions. This may be done in pseudocode or state-transition diagram form. In basic practical cases it is often a simple sequence that follows straightforwardly from the information flow. But when, for example, exception or outside event handling is involved, a control specification is usually needed.

9.2.2   Control over Transactions

The dialogue diagram shown in Figure 9.2 is useful for displaying the flow of discourse between two agents. But it does not show control. In strongly reasoning-oriented tasks, control over transactions is often a quite simple sequence that follows the flow of information objects. However, this is not good enough in situations where, for example, external events occur that conditionally trigger tasks or transactions. In such cases, we need some way to describe control over transactions. In the CommonKADS communication model we do this in a conventional way, either by means of some kind of structured control language or pseudocode, or by means of state diagrams.

As these are well-known techniques from software and information engineering, there is no need to give a long-winded elaboration of them. For state diagrams in the communication model we can employ the object-oriented Unified Modelling Language (UML) notation. Likewise, Table 9.1 contains the constructs, i.e., basic communication operators and control constructs, specialized to the communication model. We note that this approach to control will be used both for specifying the control over transactions and for specifying control within transactions, the internal structure of which may contain different messages of different types (as we will see later on in discussing the third layer of the communication model). Below we discuss a practical industrial application.

Communication model	Specifying control over transactions and messages	
Construct	Arguments	Description
SEND	(transaction or message)	*Elementary communication operator*
RECEIVE	(transaction or message)	Elementary communication operator
CARRY-OUT	(transaction)	SEND/RECEIVE combination
WAIT-until/while	(condition)	Represents the null action in communication
PROCESS	(task)	Part of an agent's tasks *outside* the communication model
;	(transaction-1; transaction-2)	SEQUENCE operator, elementary control construct (similarly for messages)
REPEAT-until/while	(condition)	Elementary control construct
IF THEN ELSE	(condition) (transaction-1) (transaction-2)	Elementary control construct (similarly for messages)
&	(transaction-1 & transaction-2)	AND operator (similarly for messages)
|	(transaction-1 | transaction-2)	CHOICE operator, denoting exclusive either/or operation (similarly for messages)
∨	(transaction-1 ∨ transaction-2)	OR operator, denoting nonexclusive either/or operation (similarly for messages)
, ·		Syntactic separators for the control specification

Table 9.1
Specifying control over transactions and messages in the communication model by means of basic communication operators and control constructs in pseudocode form.

9.3   Case: Homebots — A Multiagent System for Energy Management

9.3.1   Industrial Context

Due to the deregulation of the European energy market, the electric utility industry is in a transition from being a regulated and rather monopolistic power generation industry, to a business operating in a dynamic and competitive free market environment. For the utility industry a new business paradigm is therefore emerging. The usual business of generating, distributing, and billing customers for kilowatt hours — essentially a pure product-oriented delivery concept — is being transformed into offering different kinds of new value-added

Figure 9.3
Paradigm shift in energy utilities due to the new information society: from a pure product delivery concept to two-way customer-oriented services.

customer services (Figure 9.3). These vary from automated metering and billing-at-a-distance, advice on optimizing energy use, tailored rates and contracts, to home automation, home energy management, and demand-side management at the customer's premises. This paradigm shift will open up new opportunities, but will also necessitate new ways of thinking for most utilities, as it requires two-way communication between the utility and the customer. Here, utilities are facing the fact that proper utilization of information and knowledge is a key component in a competitive market. The traditional power distribution net must be supplemented with an information network allowing for extensive two-way communication between customers and the utility, in order to provide the new services mentioned above. Information and communication technologies (ICTs) are crucial enablers here.

Recent advances in ICTs have made it technologically and financially possible to equip many different types of nodes in the electrical network (including 230V and other substations, industrial loads and even household equipment) with significant communication (230V power grid, radio, cable TV, conventional copper lines, etc.) as well as computing capabilities of their own. In this way, nodes in the electrical network will obtain the capabilities to act as intelligent and interacting agents on behalf of the customer and the utility. There are quite a number of different advanced information technologies that jointly act as enablers here, such as: (a) cheap programmable chips that can be built in into many types of equipment; (b) advanced telecommunications technology; (c) knowledge and software engineering: object and knowledge technology and multiagent systems; and (d) emerging facilities and standards for using the power grid (also) as an integrated information infrastructure.

In Sweden, a large project called ISES (Information Society Energy System) has performed research and development for new services based on these recent advances in ICTs. One of the new service applications that are foreseen is that the electric network nodes themselves act as intelligent agents to take care of energy management. Such intelligent agents we call "Homebots" This energy management would lead (a) for the utility, to a better utilization of the power grid as a result of reduction of peak (valley) loads of the power net; and (b) for the customer, to a minimization of the overall energy cost, while maintaining a specified (individual) comfort level.

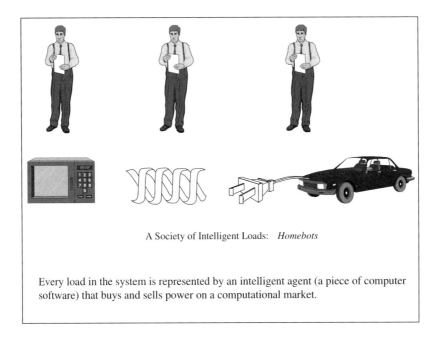

A Society of Intelligent Loads: *Homebots*

Every load in the system is represented by an intelligent agent (a piece of computer software) that buys and sells power on a computational market.

Figure 9.4
Devices and loads are equipped with smart small software programs. These software agents communicate, act, and cooperate as representatives assisting the customer, to achieve given goals such as power load management.

This provides the supplying utility with new opportunities for power load management and demand saving in the distribution grid. Better load management and demand saving have a significant impact on reducing and postponing investments by utility industries. At the same time, they serve the customer's interest, since they allow for cost reduction by taking advantage of tailored and more flexible tariffs and client contracts.

9.3.2   Intelligent Multiagent System Solution

Existing forms of energy load management are limited to a low number of large facilities since manual control still plays an important part. The benefits of multiagent systems for load management are a higher level of automation, a much larger scale, and more flexibility and distributedness.

An innovative approach is to achieve dynamic and automatic load balancing by means of software agent technology. Devices can now be equipped with communication and information-processing capabilities, by supplying them with networked, communicating

Figure 9.5
Distributed load management is implemented in terms of an auction, whereby software agents representing the utility and the customers bid and negotiate to buy and sell power demand.

microprocessors together with smart software running on top of them, as depicted in Figure 9.4. In everyday language, it is now technologically possible for software-equipped communicating devices to "talk to," "negotiate," "make decisions," and "cooperate" with each other over the low-voltage grid and other media. This enables radically new approaches to utility applications. We use this concept to achieve distributed load management in a novel fashion: by a cooperating "*society of intelligent devices*." Knowledge plus communication are the ingredients of intelligence in systems.

Every device or load, such as heaters, radiators, and boilers in a household, is represented by a software agent responsible for efficient and optimal use of energy, while taking the customer preferences into account. We call these agents Homebots. A key idea is that the communication and cooperation between devices for the purpose of load management takes the form of a computational market where they can buy and sell power demand. Individual equipment agents communicate and negotiate, in a free-market bidding-like manner, to achieve energy and cost savings for both the utility and the customer. The market models adapted from business, such as auctions, offer promising concepts to automatically manage large distributed technical systems. This is a decentralized way to reduce unwanted peak loads.

Informally, the task distribution over agents is as follows. To begin with, a software agent representing the utility (say, at the level of a transformer station) announces the start of a load management action to the customer agents (which may represent a smart electricity meter in a household or plant, or equipment beyond that such as radiators). For example, if its goal is to reduce current energy consumption, it may offer a price or tariff different from the usual one. The customer agents then determine to what extent they are interested in participating in the load management action. This is based on the customer's preferences and is, of course, also changeable and programmable by the customer. On this basis, the customer agents prepare bids to sell some power (that is: to postpone or reduce energy use) in return for a financial rebate as offered by the utility, cf. Figure 9.5.

The totality of bids is then assessed in an auction as in a free competitive market. The auction results in a reallocation of the available power. In our system, power is treated as any resource or commodity that is traded on a market. In a load management action there is a certain (limited) supply of it. Both the utility and the customer agents also have a certain demand for it, for which they are willing to pay a certain price. How much everyone gets, and at what price, is determined automatically in the auction.

In realizing an auction on the computer, we employ long-established formal theory on the functioning of competitive markets, which is available from economic science (especially from the field known as micro-economic theory). Customer preferences are in this framework expressed in terms of so-called utility functions. They represent the value for the customer for getting a certain amount of power in a numerical way: the higher the number, the higher the demand. Due to its rigorous mathematical form, this theory is readily adaptable for implementation on a computer. The corresponding algorithms that calculate the market equilibrium have been adapted from numerical analysis and optimization (since market mechanisms can be reformulated as a kind of optimum search problems).

Market negotiation and computation continues until a market equilibrium is established. This is the case when supply becomes equal to demand in the auction process. Then, each participating agent achieves the best possible deal in terms of obtaining power use versus spending financial budget. Economic market equilibrium can be shown to correspond to the optimum allocation of available power over all involved equipment agents. No agent will then gain any further by buying or selling power, and so the load management action as a market process is completed.

After the auction has been completed, its outcomes — that is, the allocation of power corresponding to the market equilibrium — are awarded and communicated to all agents involved. Next, the loads are scheduled in accordance with the awarded power over some agreed period (say, the next hour). This is implemented through appropriate on/off switching of the involved loads, whereby telecommunication over the power line will play a role. Finally, agreed results as well as implemented outcomes are monitored by all parties, providing a database of the facts needed in the contracts between utility and customer. This whole process is carried out automatically.

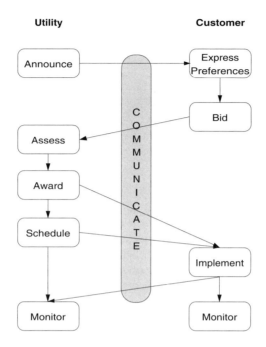

Figure 9.6
Dialogue diagram of the Homebots system: tasks in the power auction for electricity load management, with their communication links.

9.3.3 Homebots Agent Communication Plan

This informal task description leads us to a top view of the communication plan in the Homebots system in a straightforward way, as seen in the dialogue diagram of Figure 9.6. The important transactions, with their input/output information objects, in this announce-bid-award computational market scheme are the following:

1. *kickoff the auction*: sends a trigger signal to the customer agents to commence a load management action;
2. *submit the bids*: transmits the bids from the customer agents to the auctioneer for further processing;
3. *present the awarded power allocation*: informs the customer agents about the results of the auction;
4. *present the associated real-time schedule*: provides the customer agents with the calculated schedule that implements the awarded allocation;

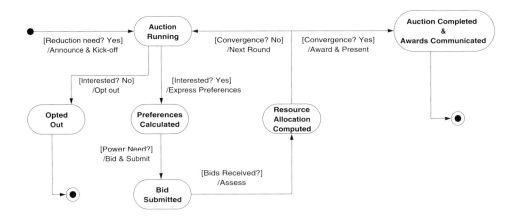

Figure 9.7
Communication plan control in the auction process of the Homebots system in state diagram form. The UML
state-diagram notation has been used here.

5. *receive the resulting real-time implementation data*: transmits the actual metering data.
   This is needed for billing as well as for assessment of the need for further load management actions.

For simplicity, we have given the simplest possible task distribution and agent architecture. Other architectures and scenarios are very well possible. For example, it is probably
preferable to separate the utility agent (representing the interests of the utility) from the actual auctioneer agent supervising the bidding process. In large-scale applications, customer
agents will be hierarchically ordered. The initiative of various tasks can also be different.
In so-called direct load management, the initiative to an auction lies with the utility agent,
but in indirect load management the customer may take the initiative, though within a pre-
set contractual framework. Also, the scheduling task can be allocated to agents in different
ways. The computational market approach is very flexible in this respect. Figure 9.6 thus
only intends to show the basics of a power load management scenario.

In this basic scenario, control within the communication plan is straightforward, as
it follows the information flow from the subtasks. The top-level control is shown in Figure 9.7 with the help of a state diagram. Information about the UML state diagrams can
be found in Section 14.3. As an notational extension, agent task-transaction pairs are indicated by an ampersand (Announce & Kick-off, Bid & Submit, Award & Present). Only
the auction part of the load management action has been given in the figure. Generally, a
state-based representation is convenient, as the formal semantics of agent communication
languages such as KQML and FIPA-ACL is based upon agent states.

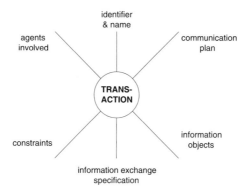

Figure 9.8
The components that together specify a transaction in the CommonKADS communication model.

9.4   Transactions between Agents

When we have finished the communication plan, we have the agent-to-agent dialogue, in terms of the transactions that form the communicative go-betweens linking two tasks. At this point, we do have the set of transactions, the related communication flow of information objects, and the control over the transactions. However, we have not yet specified much about the individual transactions themselves, other than that they have an identifier and name stating what their communicative purpose is. Hence, the second layer of the communication model contains a description of the properties of individual transactions.

9.4.1   Specification of Individual Transactions

The elements needed to specify an individual transaction are shown in Figure 9.8. For the specification itself we can use the transaction description (worksheet CM-1) displayed in Table 9.2. Most of it is rather self-explanatory. Collecting all this information within a single worksheet helps to make the transaction description self-contained, and thus more suitable for inspection and review.

   If the communication plan has been properly constructed, some components of the transaction description easily follow from the dialogue diagram: in particular the name of the transaction, and the agents and tasks it links. In addition to a name, it is helpful to give a brief explanation of purpose and context of the transaction. The heart of a transaction, of course, is transmitting some information object, and this is noted in the worksheet as the core information object (as we shall see later on, there may also be auxiliary, noncore

Communication model	Transaction Description Worksheet CM-1
TRANSACTION IDENTIFIER/NAME	A transaction is to be defined for each information object that is output from some leaf task in the task model or in the knowledge model (i.e., a transfer function), and that must be communicated to another agent for use in its own tasks. The name must reflect, in a user-understandable way, what is done with this information object by the transaction. In addition to the name, give a brief explanation here of the purpose of the transaction.
INFORMATION OBJECT	Indicate the (core) information object, and between which two tasks it is to be transmitted.
AGENTS INVOLVED	Indicate the agent that is sender of the information object, and the agent that is receiving it.
COMMUNICATION PLAN	Indicate the communication plan of which this transaction is a component.
CONSTRAINTS	Specify the requirements and (pre)conditions that must be fulfilled so that the transaction can be carried out. Sometimes, it is also useful to state post-conditions that are assumed to be valid after the transaction.
INFORMATION EXCHANGE SPECIFICATION	Transactions can have an internal structure, in that they consist of several messages of different types, and/or handle additional supporting information objects such as explanation or help items. This is detailed in worksheet CM-2. At this point, only a reference or pointer needs to be given to a later info exchange spec.

Table 9.2
Worksheet CM-1: Specifying the transactions that make up the dialogue between two agents in the communication model.

information items that have a facilitating role). Furthermore, we indicate the communication plan of which this transaction is a component. Note that this is of course trivial when there is only one communication plan. However, in multiagent systems, for example, there might be several communication plans covering different groups and types of agents.

The worksheet component concerning constraints is used to specify the preconditions that must be fulfilled before the transaction can be carried out. This might be various things, such as the availability of certain data measurements needed as input, a needed agent capability (e.g., sensory capabilities related to sound or vision) when relevant information comes in a certain form or medium, or the occurrence of an outside triggering event as is often the case in real-time embedded systems. Sometimes, it is also useful to state postconditions that are assumed to be valid after the transaction. In state administration and legal matters, it is usually assumed that "every citizen knows the law" in all its often intricate detail, whether this is actually true or not. Likewise, a transaction may simply suppose that a transmitted information object is correctly received and processed by the receiving agent, without actually asking for an acknowledgment. That this is a nontrivial postcondition, and therefore worth reflecting about in communication modelling, is something we all are familiar with from lost letters in both regular and electronic mail.

The final component of a transaction description is called the information exchange specification. Basically, it gives the type, content and form of the message that "packages" the information object that is transmitted. In very simple cases, e.g., when only data strings are exchanged between two systems, it can be sufficient to give the content of the message as a proposition or predicate statement here. However, it is well possible that a single transaction contains more than one message. For example, this occurs in a buying/selling negotiation task running between two parties. Then there is one transaction linking the buy and sell tasks, but this transaction has an internal structure consisting of a bid-react-rebid pattern of messages. Moreover, it is sometimes necessary to be able to state in what form or through which medium information in a transaction is conveyed. For all these reasons, the information exchange specification is usually not given directly as a basic component in worksheet CM-1, but a reference is given instead to a separate (worksheet) description. How to describe this detailed information exchange specification is discussed in the next section.

9.5   Detailing the Information Exchange

After the communication plan and the transaction description, the information exchange specification constitutes the third layer of the communication model. It contains the lowest level of detail. As such, it provides several important inputs for the design model and associated knowledge system implementation, concerning agent communication protocols, messages, and human-computer interaction and interfacing.

9.5.1   Information Exchange Specification

An information exchange specification refines the transaction description discussed previously, in two ways. First, it gives the internal message typing and structure of the transaction. Second, it gives syntactic form and medium information about the messages. This is done by means of a separate information exchange specification (*worksheet CM-2*), given in Table 9.3.

Some of the information in this worksheet is already available in the transaction description, such as transaction name and involved agents. It is mainly incorporated to make the specification self-contained, and easier for review and inspection. Also, the core information object that is to be transferred is already found in the transaction description. This is, however, not the case with the so-called supporting information items. In many cases it is helpful to not only transmit the core information object that is needed in the agents' task structure but also to facilitate better understanding of the transaction. This can be achieved by means of additional explanations, help texts, and the like. This covers, for example, traces of how reasoning conclusions were reached by a knowledge system, explanatory texts related to complex domain-knowledge items, wizard-like help in answering posed questions and retrieving information from other agent sources (e.g., a connected database), or system notifications or warnings to the user who is manipulating system information. These are all supporting information items, and they are specified as such, including the

Communication model	Information Exchange Specification Worksheet CM-2
TRANSACTION	*Give the transaction identifier and the name of which this information exchange specification is a part.*
AGENTS INVOLVED	1. **Sender**; agent sending the information item(s)
	2. **Receiver**: agent receiving the information item(s)
INFORMATION ITEMS	List all information items that are to be transmitted in this transaction. This includes the ('core') information object the transfer of which is the purpose of the transaction. However, it may contain other, supporting, information items, that, for example, provide help or explanation. For each information item, describe the following:
	1. **Role**: whether it is a *core* object, or a *support* item.
	2. **Form**: the syntactic form in which it transmitted to another agent , e.g., data string, canned text, a certain type of diagram, 2D or 3D plot.
	3. **Medium**: the medium through which it is handled in the agent-agent interaction, e.g., a pop-up window, navigation and selection within a menu, command-line interface, human intervention.
MESSAGE SPECIFICATIONS	Describe all messages that make up the transaction. For each individual message describe:
	1. **Communication type**: the communication type of the message describing its intention ("illocutionary force," in speech-act terminology), according to Table 9.4 and Figure 9.9.
	2. **Content**: the statement or proposition contained in the message.
	3. **Reference**: in certain cases, it may be useful to add a reference to, for example, what domain knowledge model or agent capability is required to be able to send or process the message.
CONTROL OVER MESSAGES	Give, if necessary, a control specification over the messages within the transaction. This can be done in pseudocode format or in a state-transition diagram, similar to how the control over transaction within the communication plan is specified. See for this Figure 9.7 and Table 9.1. The difference is just the level of detail.

Table 9.3
Worksheet CM-2: Specifying the messages and information items that make up an individual transaction within the communication model.

syntactic form and medium through which they are conveyed. Evidently, this is crucial information directly related and input to design model, system implementation and user-interface issues.

9.5.2   Typing the Intention of Messages and Transactions

The most characteristic element of our information exchange specification, however, is the way in which the messages that make up the transaction are described. The reason is that transaction sentences are often composite and convey, in one shot, different types of information.

As an everyday example, let us consider the following sentence, viewed as a transaction between two agents: "I'm getting cold, so could you please shut the window?" If we think about it, it becomes clear that this sentence actually consists of several messages that, moreover, have a different intent. Specifically:

1. The first part, "I'm getting cold," is, strictly speaking, no more than a bare *information or notification* message, stating that the speaking agent apparently does not find the current temperature comfortable anymore. Note that this notification message does not necessarily imply any action on the part of either agent.
2. In contrast, the second part, "Could you please shut the window?," is directly aimed at eliciting activity by the other agent, here in the form of a *request* for action.

So, within one transaction sentence, we have two messages here, differing in content as well as intent. That this is a rather general situation will be clear upon reflecting about variations of the sketched transaction. Take, for example, the alternative sentence: "I'm getting cold, why were you so stupid to open the window?" Or consider alternative answers to the original question such as "Of course, dear" vs. "I'm watching this world champion football match on TV, so why don't you do it yourself?" Note also that in all these cases the connective *"so"* has nothing to do with any form of logical deduction. This is why such statements have to be broken down into more than one message. To do otherwise even feels very artificial. It is easy to come up with other illustrations that are quite interesting from a communication model viewpoint. As an example, we leave it as an exercise to the reader to make a communication analysis of the following message: "It's the economy, stupid!"

It goes without saying that the pragmatics of human communication is often quite delicate. We believe, however, that considerations like those above are also relevant in the modelling of communication where information and knowledge systems are concerned. Nowadays, systems that involve multiagent communication, such as information systems based on the Internet or the World Wide Web, have to confront such issues. In such systems, agent communication is often inspired by the so-called speech act theory, which distinguishes between the actual content ("locutionary nature") of a speech act or message — what is actually being said — and its intended effect ("illocutionary force") upon the other agent.

This distinction is employed in many agent communication models and languages, and also in CommonKADS. This can be practically done by associating each message with a set of *predefined communication types*, which must be filled in as indicated in worksheet CM-2, cf. Table 9.3.

A possible set of communication types is presented in Table 9.4. We do not pretend any originality here: this set is a basic and simplified version of communication types found in various agent communication languages, a currently very active and still changing research area. In organizing the communication types, we use two dimensions: the first dimension is the purpose of a message — task delegation, task adoption, or pure information exchange —, whereas the second dimension indicates the degree of commitment or strength one is exerting this purpose. So, in a nutshell one may say that for typing the intention of a

Communication model	Predefined communication types		
Task delegation			
Request	Require	Order	Reject-td
Task adoption			
Propose	Offer	Agree	Reject-ta
Pure information exchange			
Ask	Reply	Report	Inform

Table 9.4
Predefined communication types, used in specifying the intention (intended effect on the receiving agent) with which a message is sent.

message, we have that *intention = purpose × commitment*. In the table, this leads to 3×4 = 12 predefined basic communication types. The semantics of the communication types in Table 9.4 is as follows:

- *Request/Propose:* refer to a message sent by an agent that sees a potential for cooperation, but wishes to negotiate on the terms of this cooperation. Loosely: "I have an interest, but not yet a commitment."
- *Require/Offer:* refer to a message indicating that the sending agent already has made a precommitment, and intending to prompt the receiving agent for its commitment. This type thus denotes a conditional commitment.
- *Order/Agree:* the message types indicating that the agent has made a commitment, and thus will act accordingly in carrying out its tasks.
- *Reject-td/ta:* denote that the agent does not want to commit or cooperate in task delegation (td) or adoption (ta).
- *Ask/Reply:* evidently refer to messages that have as intent a query for information from another agent, and delivery of such information in return.
- *Report:* types a message sent after an agent has acted toward a (previously) agreed-upon task goal, with the intention of letting the other agent know the status of achievement (e.g., success, failure, outcome of the action).
- *Inform:* refers to a message type that just delivers, provides or presents information objects to another agent. It indicates an independent informative action, where no previous request or agreement is involved (in contrast to reply or report messages).

We see that we now have at our disposal a rather rich vocabulary to specify the intention of messages. (Other, and richer proposals exist in the agent software literature, but the present one does cover a wide range of practical knowledge systems.) It is also seen that only giving the (propositional) content of messages is very limited, and that additional, explicit specification of intention greatly improves the understanding of communicative acts. And this is what the communication model aims at. This is further magnified by realizing that the above communication types are not only suitable for characterizing sep-

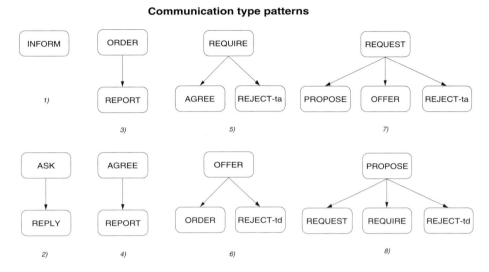

Figure 9.9
Library of message patterns, built from the predefined communication types. Branching arrows indicate (exclusive) alternatives.

arate messages. The communication types lend themselves very well to construct typed patterns or chains of messages that naturally belong together. A possible library of such patterns, adapted on software agent work done at Daimler-Chrysler, is presented in Figure 9.9. These communication patterns also constitute a currently very active and open agent research area; they are sometimes known as *conversation policies*.

Question/answer patterns are a straightforward example occurring in many knowledge systems. Negotiation tasks and associated bidding protocols provide another, more complex, pattern. In the following section we show an example of this, relating to our market-based program for energy management.

9.6   The Homebots System Example Continued

The Homebots system contains several transactions, as discussed above. Some are rather simple, especially the transaction linked to the *announce* task serving to kickoff the auction (cf. Figures 9.6 and 9.7). The second transaction, whereby the bids are calculated (*bid* task carried out by the customer agents) and subsequently submitted to the auctioneer, is much more interesting. For reasons of space, we only treat this transaction in some detail, see Table 9.5.

Communication model	Transaction Description Worksheet CM-1: Homebots System
TRANSACTION IDENTIFIER/NAME	*Transaction 2: Submit-the-bid*: transmits the bids from the customer agents to the auctioneer for further processing. The auctioneer then does intermediate calculations (of the going price and/or the going allocation), and in its turn transmits these to the customer agents to enable bid revision.
INFORMATION OBJECT	Linking the *bid* and *assess* tasks: (1) customer bids; (2) intermediate auctioneer calculations (going price or going allocation).
AGENTS INVOLVED	Customer agents, sending bids and receiving the going market data; the auctioneer agent (in base version identified with the utility agent) receiving bids and sending out the going market data.
COMMUNICATION PLAN	Homebots (base version).
CONSTRAINTS	During the transaction a decision procedure (e.g., how often to retry and how long to wait) is needed telling what to do when agents do not submit bids, as this might be due to a communication failure. A post-condition derives from the convergence condition for market equilibrium (e.g., all agent bid prices must have become the same).
INFORMATION EXCHANGE SPECIFICATION	see the worksheet CM-2 below.

Table 9.5
Worksheet CM-1: The submit-the-bid transaction in the Homebots system.

We thus see that the submit-the-bid transaction is composite. It is a single transaction because it is an exchange link between two tasks, but it handles more than one core information object. Both types of agents are problem-solving and reasoning agents, both are acting as sender and receiver in this transaction, and both hold part of the overall initiative. This is a typical multiagent situation that contrasts with the one usually encountered in conventional knowledge systems. A more detailed specification of the information exchange is given in Table 9.6.

For the control specification of the submit-the-bid transaction in worksheet CM-2, we now use the pseudocode format as presented in Table 9.1. The specification is shown in Figure 9.10.

In multiagent systems, transactions related to task adoption and delegation come into play. In contrast, conventional knowledge systems that have an advisory function (e.g., assessment of housing applications, or diagnosis of technical systems) are characterized by the fact that most communication refers to basic information exchange. Core information objects are either simply provided or delivered (INFORM message type), or exchanged through a question-and-answer pattern (ASK/REPLY communication types). Supporting information items such as help and explanation texts belong to a different type, however. Since such items are only presented as an open option to the user, the related support item messages are typically of the OFFER communication type. Hence, for intelligent multiagent systems we indeed need a richer repertoire in communication modelling.

Communication Model	Information Exchange Specification Worksheet CM-2: Homebots system
TRANSACTION	*Transaction 2: Submit-the-bid*
AGENTS INVOLVED	1. **Sender** (customer): bid. 2. **Receiver** (auctioneer): bid. 3. **Sender** (auctioneer): going market data. 4. **Receiver** (customer): going market data.
INFORMATION ITEMS	We have for bids as well as for going market data (price and/or allocation): 1. **Role**: both are *core* information objects. No support items are defined in this transaction. 2. **Form**: both are normally numerical data strings (real). Depending on the problem-solving method chosen, they might be scalar, or a pair of reals. Several variants are possible, and this has an impact on computational efficiency and communication speed. 3. **Medium**: not of interest here, as the agent-agent interaction is fully electronic within a standard software environment and communication protocol.
MESSAGE SPECIFICATIONS: 1. BID-MESSAGE	Type: PROPOSE Content: bid (structure depends on reference theory) Reference: market theory. From: customer agents To: auctioneer
2. OPT-OUT-MESSAGE	Type: REJECT-ta Content: no further participation in bidding From: customer agents To: auctioneer
3. AUCTION-DATA-MESSAGE	Type: INFORM Content: going market data (see reference theory) Reference: theory underlying market protocol From: auctioneer To: customer agents
4. NEXT-ROUND-MESSAGE	Type: REQUEST Content: trigger signal for new round of the auction From: auctioneer To: customer agents
Control over messages	See pseudo-code specification given in main text.

Table 9.6
Worksheet CM-2: The submit-the-bid messages and their communication types in the Homebots system.

```
REPEAT
WHILE <market convergence condition not satisfied>
   IF <interest in load management>
      THEN PROCESS(bid-task);
           SEND(BID-MESSAGE)
      ELSE SEND(OPT-OUT-MESSAGE)
   END-IF
   IF <bids received>
      THEN PROCESS(assess-task)
      ELSE PROCESS(decision sub-procedure [e.g. WAIT...])
   END-IF
   SEND(AUCTION-DATA-MESSAGE)
   &
   SEND(NEXT-ROUND-MESSAGE)
END-REPEAT

PROCESS(award-task)
(et cetera).
```

Figure 9.10
Control specification of the submit-the-bid transaction.

9.7   Validating and Balancing the Communication Model

Various techniques are available to verify and validate a communication model. We discuss
some simple but useful ones below.

9.7.1   Communication Plan Walk-through

A very straightforward technique to validate a communication model is a communication
plan walk-through. Walk-throughs are encountered in software engineering at many points
and in many guises. A walk-through is a form of peer group review: colleagues of the
responsible knowledge engineer or developer undertake to evaluate the communication
plan and give their comments back to the knowledge engineer.

A walk-through is a suitable technique to validate the communication model in an
early stage, as it is well possible to "mentally simulate" the flow of transactions in a communication plan, and it is helpful that this is done by (relative) outsiders. This procedure
is useful in order to:

- check the adequacy of the transaction structure;
- identify whether the list of information objects is complete;
- detect the need for additional help or explanation items.

Different, more or less formal, setups can be used for a walk-through session. One
possibility is to do it in the form of a prepared meeting, with a starting presentation by the

- Present a simple and natural dialogue.
- Speak the user's language.
- Minimize the user's memory load.
- Maintain consistency in terminology.
- Give feedback about what is going on.
- Show clearly marked exits from unwanted states.
- Offer shortcuts for the experienced user.
- Give help, explanations, and documentation.
- Provide good error messages.
- Even better: design to prevent errors.

Table 9.7
Nielsen's heuristic evaluation guidelines for usability.

knowledge engineer, and a round of commentary and discussion, finalized by short formal minutes with recommendations from the reviewers.

9.7.2   The Wizard of Oz

The "Wizard of Oz" is an experimental technique to validate communication with a knowledge system. In a Wizard of Oz experiment, a human expert plays the role of a (prospective) knowledge system and mimics its behavior toward an end user. In order to make the validation experiment as realistic as possible, the expert and the user sit in separate rooms, and communicate with each other only via a computer terminal.

A Wizard of Oz setup is ideally suited to test the question-and-answer patterns that often occur in knowledge systems. In such cases, it is helpful that the relevant parts of the task and knowledge models have been developed before, and that the expert's repertoire and actions are constrained accordingly. The communication model in the discussed Homebots case study may, of course, be tested in a Wizard of Oz setting with nonexperts (since even intelligent heaters remain rather dumb systems compared to humans). Alternatively, in that case the communication generated by the negotiations could also be tested directly by means of *mock-up* software.

The Wizard of Oz technique will help to ensure that the end user understands and accepts the shared task-inference structures and their knowledge contents. The technique is more elaborate than the communication plan walk-through, but has the potential to reveal more and deeper information concerning the handling of knowledge by the end users. Note also that the technique may be very well used *before* any system development has taken place.

9.7.3   Engineering for Usability: Heuristic Evaluation

Clearly, a significant part of the communication model will often be tied in with user-interface issues. As this constitutes a whole computer science field in itself, we will not treat these issues here but refer instead to the vast literature on user interface design. Nevertheless, we would like to list a number of heuristics and guidelines presented by Nielsen in his book *Usability Engineering* (1998). His approach is called "heuristic evaluation" of usability. The associated guidelines are shown in Table 9.7. They may, for example, serve as a set of evaluation criteria to be used in inspection sessions, like the communication plan walk-through discussed previously. Empirical studies have shown that one should have several evaluators, and a number of about five seems to give the best cost-benefit ratio.

9.7.4   Guidelines for Balancing the Communication Model against Other Models

The relation of the communication model to the other models has been explained in the introduction to this Chapter, and is also shown in Figure 9.1. On this basis, we have defined a number of rules and guidelines for what the boundaries and connections should be of the communication model vis-à-vis the other models. These rules and guidelines are:

- Leaf tasks from the task model as well as the knowledge model are key inputs to the communication model, insofar as they handle information objects that must be exchanged between agents. (Such leaf tasks in the knowledge model are called transfer functions.) The foremost rule for communication modelling says that a separate transaction must be defined for each information object exchanged, *and* for each distinct pair of leaf tasks.
- The agent model describes the agent capabilities (knowledge), responsibilities, and constraints. Check whether these are compatible with the constraints for the transactions in the communication model. It may be that communication requires additional capabilities from an agent. If so, add these by revising the agent model.
- As a double-check, verify whether the communication plan is compatible with structure, power/culture, process, and resources in the organization model.
- The rule of structure-preserving design in the design model also holds for the communication model constructs, in the same way as it holds for the knowledge-model structure.
- A borderline case between the design and communication models are the syntactic form and media aspects of information items in the detail information exchange specification. They might belong to either one. The demarcation criterion is that if there is an *intrinsic* conceptual reason that information items take on a certain form or are carried by a certain medium, this is to be modelled in the communication model. Otherwise, it is a matter of implementation choice, as a consequence of which it belongs to the design model. For example, some information objects "must" come with a certain form or medium. For example, a signature authorizing a purchase or expense might not be considered legally valid if it is given in electronic form. Such a constraint is part of the communication model. The general rule is to model form and media aspects in the design model, unless there is a good conceptual reason *not* to.

1. Identify the core information objects to be exchanged between agents. Do this by checking, for each agent, the list of leaf tasks from the task model and the knowledge model (the transfer functions).
2. Identify the associated list of transactions, as exchange links between two tasks, and give each transaction a suitable, i.e., user-understandable, name.
3. Now, construct the dialogue diagram so that you have a pictorial overview of the overall communication plan. If needed, add a specification of the control over the transactions. This yields a complete communication plan.
4. Describe all individual transactions, following the format given in Figure 9.8 and worksheet CM-1.
5. Describe the internal structure of each transaction where necessary, by filling in the information exchange specification according to worksheet CM-2.
6. Validate and balance the communication model according to the techniques and guidelines given.

Table 9.8
Steps in communication-model construction.

• Decisions as to what supporting information items to introduce belong to the communication model, and not to the design model, because they are a matter of user task support, not system implementation.

9.8   A Structured Process for Communication Modelling

We have outlined how the communication model specifies the information exchange between tasks carried out by different agents. It is constructed stepwise by means of three consecutive layers: overall communication plan, individual transactions, and detailed information exchange specification. The communication plan describes the full dialogue between two agents. Transactions are the basic building blocks for a dialogue, and act as the go-between for two tasks carried out by different agents. Transactions in their turn may consist of one or more messages which are detailed in the information exchange specification. Predefined communication types and patterns, features familiar from agent communication languages, allow the buildup of message protocols in a structured way. We have shown how to break down communication modelling into natural steps, and for all steps in communication modelling we have presented simple and practical techniques such as worksheets and diagrams. So, we have outlined how the specification of agent communication is approached in CommonKADS as a structured analysis process, necessary for building quality system applications.

As a summary, we list in Table 9.8 the guidelines for communication model development laying out the various activities that need to be undertaken by the system developer:

9.9   Bibliographical Notes and Further Reading

The growing capabilities of electronic communication such as the Internet and the World Wide Web currently have a strong influence on developments in knowledge engineering and management. There is increased attention for distributed enterprises and associated information-system applications, exemplified in new concepts such as virtual organizations, chain management, information and knowledge sharing, distributed intelligence, intelligent agents, and multiagent technology. These developments try to come to grips with the fact that knowledge processes are becoming more and more inherently distributed.

In the software world, this leads from large and relatively monolithic information and knowledge systems to relatively independent interacting software agents. A recent collection on software agents can be found in Bradshaw (1997). Modelling of communication in intelligent agent systems is of prime importance, but significantly more complex than in conventional knowledge systems. Bradshaw's book contains a chapter on the KQML agent communication language referred to in this chapter. The mentioned Daimler-Chrysler work on communication in distributed intelligent systems is found in Haddadi (1995). The original version of the CommonKADS communication model was developed by Waern et al. (1993) for conventional knowledge systems; the report contains a good case study of a conventional single-system/single-user expert system for diagnosis of telecommunication equipment in the field. The version of the CommonKADS communication model expanded to intelligent multiagent systems presented in this chapter was developed by Akkermans et al. (1998). More information related to the Homebots case study is found elsewhere (Akkermans et al. 1996, Ygge 1998).

10

Case Study: The Housing Application

Key points of this chapter:

- We illustrate the use of the CommonKADS analysis models in a simple application.
- The domain concerns the assignment of rental residences to applicants.
- The knowledge-intensive task we focus on concerns assessing whether an applicant satisfies the criteria for a certain residence.
- We show parts of the organization, task, agent, knowledge, and communication models developed for this application.

10.1 Introduction

In this chapter we describe a small case study to illustrate the analysis models and methods discussed so far. The case study concerns a domain in which rental houses are assigned to applicants. A short description of this domain is given in in the next section.

10.2 Application Domain: Rental Residence Assignment

In the Netherlands rental residences are allocated by the government to people in need of a residence. Residence distribution is done by the local government. People that want to rent a residence have to register as a potential "applicant." Every two weeks a magazine is published which contains a listing of residences for which registered applicants can apply. There is a published procedure for deciding which applicant will get the residence (mainly based on the length of time people have been waiting). A summary of the key figures related to residence assignments is published in the next magazine. This information can

Allowed income for a single-person household			
Up to 22 years	23–64 years	65+ years	Rent
fl. 0–27,999	fl. 0–24,999	fl. 0–21,999	Less than fl. 545
fl. 28,000–31,999	fl. 25,000–29,999	fl. 22,000–24,999	Less than fl. 750
fl. 32,000–35,999	fl. 30,000–34,999	fl. 25,000–28,999	Less than fl. 1047
fl. 35,000–44,999	fl. 35,000–44,999	fl. 29,000–44,999	Fl. 600 or more
et cetera			

Table 10.1
Part of the table that indicates the relation between rent and income.

be used by applicants to adapt their application strategy (e.g., by applying next time for a house in a less popular area). To be eligible for a residence, applicants have to satisfy a number of criteria. There are four types of eligibility criteria. First, people have to apply for the right residence category. Second, the size of the household of the applicant needs to be consistent with requirements on minimum and maximum habitation of a certain residence. The third criterion is that there should be a match between the rent of the residence and the income of the applicant. Table 10.1 shows some sample rent-income criteria. Finally, there can be specific conditions that hold for one particular residence.

Currently, assessing whether applicants satisfy these criteria is done manually by civil servants of the local government. This manual checking takes a lot of time, and you are asked to develop a system for automatic assessment of residence applications. Input to the system are the data about a particular application: data about an applicant and a residence. The system output should be a decision about whether the application is in line with the criteria yes or no. The system has to communicate with a database system containing data about residences and applicants, and with another program that computes a priority list of applicants for each residence.

10.3 Organization Model

In this section we describe the organization model by going though the sequence of worksheets.

10.3.1 OM-1: Problems, Solutions, and Context

Table 10.2 shows the first worksheet OM-1, which lists the perceived organizational problems, characterizes the organization context (which for the purpose of the current analysis is assumed to be invariant), and provides a list of possible solutions.

Two problems are listed: (1) the fact that assessment of individual residence applications takes too much time, and (2) the fact that there is not enough time to handle urgent cases, for which specialized rules and regulations apply. It seems normal to think that there is some causal connection between these two problems, and that solving one will

Organization Model	Problems and Opportunities Worksheet OM-1
PROBLEMS AND OPPORTUNITIES	* Assessment of individual applications takes too much time * There is not sufficient staff for handling urgent cases
ORGANIZATIONAL CONTEXT	Mission: * Enable people to take as much as possible themselves responsibility for finding a suitable home. * Enable insight into the dynamics of the rental housing market External factors: * Local council. * National regulations. * Applicants / public opinion. * Rental agencies. Strategy: * Provide high quality for a reasonable price. * Move to (semi-)private service company. * Broaden scope, e.g., include lower segment of privately owned residences.
SOLUTIONS	Solution 1: * Develop an automated system for application assessment * Set up a training program for a group of assigners to specialize in urgency handling

Table 10.2
Worksheet OM-1: Problems, organizational context, and possible solutions.

thus also solve the other. This is in practice often dangerous. For example, if the first problem is solved through automation, it might be the case that the human resources that become available do not have the skill to carry out the other task. The solution listed on the worksheet is typical in the sense that it does not consist of a single item (building a software system), but combines software development with organizational measures (training personnel, creating new organizational roles, reorganizing the business process).

Although often a project is initiated with a particular target system already in mind (in this case a system for automatic assessment of residence applications), it is useful to make an explicit note of the problems the system is supposed to solve, and also to look at possible alternative solutions and other measures. As we see in this worksheet, the solution proposed is in fact a "package" of which the software system is just one element. This is typical of many projects.

The second row of worksheet OM-1 describes the organizational context. These elements are assumed to stay the same during the project at hand. This means that we assume that the mission and goals of the organization are fixed as far as the project is concerned. It might well be that the project comes to conclusions which could affect the organizational goals, but this process lies outside our current scope. The mission and goals in this case study reflect the fact that this organization is a recently privatized department of the local administration and is moving in the direction of a "real" business. The people working in the organization used to be civil servants.

Organization Model	Variant Aspects Worksheet OM-2
STRUCTURE	See Figure 10.1.
PROCESS	See Figure 10.2.
PEOPLE	See Figure 10.1: roles of people are specified for each part of the organization structure.
RESOURCES	**Database**: existing database of applicants and residences. **Priority calculator**: program for computing a priority list of applicants for a residence.
KNOWLEDGE	**Assessment criteria**: knowledge for judging correctness of individual applications (e.g., rent-income table). **Assignment rules**: knowledge used for selecting an applicant for a particular house. **Urgency rules**: special rules and regulations for urgent cases (e.g., handicapped people).
CULTURE & POWER	* Hierarchical organization. * Employees view the future with some trepidation. * Management style is still based on history as civil servant department.

Table 10.3
Worksheet OM-2: Variant aspects of the housing organization.

OM-2: Description of Focus Area in the Organization   The second worksheet describes the part of the organization on which the project focuses. The worksheet contains six slots. The first two slots, "structure" and "process," are usually best shown in a graphical way.

Figure 10.1 shows the current organization structure. This figure combines the "structure" slot with the "people" slot, indicating the roles of people in the organization. In many organizations the roles of people are tightly connected to their physical position: in such cases this kind of combination makes sense. Here we see that the organization is structured in a hierarchical fashion. The directorate forms the top level of the hierarchy. There are four departments. The "public service" department is responsible for producing the bi-weekly magazine, as well as answering questions of the public. The "residence assignment" department carries out the actual assignment work. This assignment work can be split up into two parts: standard cases and urgent cases. The computer department maintains the databases and other software. The policy department assists the directorate in the formulation of the long-term policy of the organization.

Figure 10.2 shows the main business processes in the organization. As in the social security domain (cf. Chapter 3) we distinguish a primary process and a secondary process. The primary process is responsible for delivering the "product" (in this case an assignment of a residence); the secondary process describes support activities for the primary process. Such a division into primary and secondary is probably useful in many application domains.

The primary process in this case study consists of four steps. The process is carried out in bi-weekly cycles. First, a magazine is produced which is distributed to the public

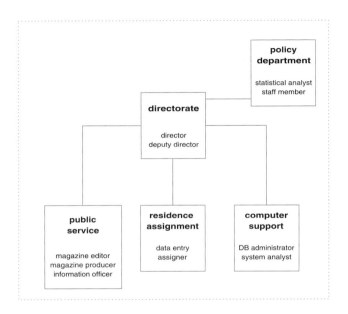

Figure 10.1
Structure and people in the current situation.

and which contains the available residences in a particular cycle as well as the results of the previous cycle. Second, incoming applications (e.g., through posted paper forms) are entered into the database. This data-entry task performs a check on whether the registration number of the applicant and the number of the residence are indeed valid numbers. The third task looks at each individual application and checks whether the applicant is applying for a residence she is entitled to (see the criteria described at the beginning of this chapter). This assessment task is responsible for the first problem mentioned in worksheet OM-1. Finally, the available residences are assigned to one of the correct applications for this house.

Guideline 10-1:   CONSIDER SPLITTING THE BUSINESS PROCESS INTO AT LEAST TWO SUBPROCESSES: A PRIMARY PROCESS AND A SECONDARY PROCESS
Rationale: Most organizations have one (or more) main processes that deliver the product (this could be something physical like a car, but can also be a service) and some other "support" processes, such as training, evaluation, and so on.

CommonKADS does not prescribe a fixed graphical notation for the figures constructed in the course of organizational analysis. In Figure 10.2 the UML notation for

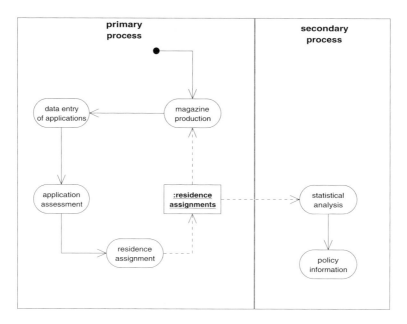

Figure 10.2
Primary and secondary business processes in the current situation. The notation used is that of a UML activity diagram.

activity diagrams is used. Unless you have your own favorite, this is probably a good default notation standard.

The other entries in worksheet OM-2 contain information about resources, knowledge as well as culture and power. Some relevant existing computer programs are listed as resources. Three types of knowledge are listed: these are further detailed in worksheet OM-4. The short description in the "culture & power" slot provides hints about the working and management style.

10.3.2   OM-3: Main Tasks in the Business Process

In this worksheet we describe the main tasks that appeared in the "process" slot in OM-2. We have limited the tasks in this worksheet to the tasks in the primary process of Figure 10.2. As we see, two of the four tasks are knowledge intensive, namely the assessment and the assignment task. For each task we also indicate its significance. It is worthwhile to note that "significance" is an elusive concept and hard to quantify. A typical quantitative yardstick is the workload of a task, as can be seen in the social-security case in Chapter 3. However, most of the time we have to be content with a qualitative estimate, such as a five-

Organization Model		Process Breakdown Worksheet OM-3				
No.	Task	Per-formed by	Where?	Knowl-edge asset	Inten-sive?	Signifi-cance
1	Maga-zine produc-tion	Magazine editor / magazine producer	Public service		No	3
2	Data entry of applica-tions	Data typist / automated telephone number	Residence assignment		No	2
3	Applica-tion assess-ment	Assigner	Residence assignment	Assessment criteria	Yes	5
4	Resi-dence assign-ment	Assigner	Residence assignment	Assignment rules Urgency rules	Yes	5

Table 10.4
Worksheet OM-3: Process breakdown.

point scale. Here, we see that the two knowledge-intensive tasks also score high in terms of significance. This is an indication that is useful to consider automation of the task.

10.3.3 OM-4: Knowledge Assets in the Housing Domain

The fourth worksheet gives a short description of the main knowledge assets in the part of the organization we are focusing on. In the housing case three knowledge assets are listed (see also OM-2). The first knowledge asset concerns knowledge about assessment criteria for applications. The main issue concerned with this asset refers to its form: we would like to have it in electronic form in order to make it available for automation. The knowledge concerning assignment rules has no associated problems. This is not a surprise, because it is possessed by a program that uses this knowledge.

The knowledge concerning urgent cases is apparently the most difficult to get a grip on. The reason for this is that it consists of rules and regulations from different sources at different periods in time. Also, the criteria and definitions used are open to interpretation. The project we describe here has refrained from tackling a task in which this type of knowledge is featured. However, in a future project it might useful to develop this type of knowledge, e.g., to increase its quality. Worksheet OM-4 is a typical focus point for knowledge-management activities in which we are interested in describing knowledge at a coarse-grained level and defining strategies for knowledge development and distribution in the organization (see also Chapter 4).

Organization Model		Knowledge Assets Worksheet OM-4				
KNOWL-EDGE ASSET	POS-SESSED BY	USED IN	RIGHT FORM?	RIGHT PLACE?	RIGHT TIME?	RIGHT QUALITY?
Assess-ment criteria	Assigner	3. Applica-tion assessment	No: paper-form → electronic	Yes	Yes	Yes
Assign-ment rules	Priority calculator / assigner	4. Residence assignment	Yes	Yes	Yes	Yes
Urgency rules	Assigner	4. Residence assignment	Yes	Yes	Yes	No: often incom-plete, ambigu-ous, inconsis-tent

Table 10.5
Worksheet OM-4: Knowledge assets.

10.3.4   OM-5: Judging Feasibility

In the final worksheet OM-5 we indicate the feasibility of potential solutions for perceived organizational problems. The worksheet for the housing application describes the feasibility of the solution we proposed in worksheet OM-1, namely automating the application-assessment task plus retraining staff. When discussing business feasibility it is often dangerous to expect large paybacks in terms of cost reduction. Even if a system saves labor effort, it might well be that from a social perspective it will be impossible to fire people. It is usually more realistic to use the knowledge system for quality improvement.

In the housing case the technical feasibility appears to be high, mainly because assessment problems are well understood and the knowledge is already present in an explicit (paper) form. For the project feasibility you have to carefully consider the availability of the required software-development expertise. In particular, the availability of the expert is often an important bottleneck to consider. In the housing case this appears (luckily) not to be a problem.

All in all, the proposed solution is judged to be feasible provided it is backed by people in the organization. Therefore, the first action proposed is to inform the staff involved of the plans and to elicit their explicit support. Such actions depend of course on the local traditions, and in this case might be typical of the "consensus" culture in the Netherlands.

Organization Model	Checklist for Feasibility Decision Document: Worksheet OM-5
BUSINESS FEASIBILITY	Automation of the application assessment will cost approximately $150,000 for development costs and $10,000 per year for maintenance. This investment is cost-effective if we assume that fewer than three persons will be needed to do the application-assessment work. From a human-resource management perspective it would be best if most of these resources (say two persons) would get a different type of job with the explicit purpose of working on existing bottlenecks in the organization, in particular urgency handling. The net cost reduction of one person is easier to "sell" to the staff, but means also that payback time will be longer. Also, additional costs such as training costs will have to be taken into account. The investment will provide a higher quality if we assume the program will make fewer errors than the humans. This is important for the public image of the organization.
TECHNICAL FEASIBILITY	Assessment tasks are well understood. Many existing system tackle this task type. The knowledge needed for assessment is explicitly available.
PROJECT FEASIBILITY	There is no real "expertise" is this domain. This minimizes the well-known risk of the limited availability of the expert. Skills needed on the project team are: experience in building an assessment application, knowledge about the database, and knowledge about the priority calculator.
PROPOSED ACTIONS	* Set up a project team and a schedule for system development. * In parallel: start with the required organizational changes, namely training assigners as "urgency handler". * But first: liase with the residence-assignment and computer departments to get their support for the proposed new organization structure.

Table 10.6
Worksheet OM-5: Feasibility of the solution "automation of the application-assessment task in combination with retraining staff for urgency handling".

10.4   Task Model

Assuming we have decided that solution 1 in worksheet OM-1 is feasible, the task model (TM) explores the "application-assessment" task in more detail. The task model has two associated worksheets. The first one enables us to do a first task analysis of the task we are focusing on. The second worksheet takes a closer look at the knowledge involved in the this task.

10.4.1   TM-1: First Task Analysis

Worksheet TM-1 in Table 10.7 contains a description of application assessment. The description is at a more detailed level than in the organization model. In the task model we are "zooming in" on a task. We describe both the internals of a task (control information, data manipulated), as well as external information such as the goal of the task, performance requirements, quality criteria, and constraints. The worksheet lists some typical examples of task information for the assessment task.

Task Model	Task Analysis Worksheet TM-1
TASK	3. Application assessment
ORGANIZATION	Primary business process; carried out in the residence-assignment department by the assigner.
GOAL AND VALUE	This task should ensure that applicants are treated in a fair and equal manner. The task is essential to delivering the assignment service at the required quality level.
DEPENDENCY AND FLOW	*Input tasks*: 1. Magazine production; 2. Data entry *Output tasks*: 4. Residence assignment
OBJECTS HANDLED	*Input objects*: Application, data about residences and applicants *Output objects*: Validated application *Internal objects*: –
TIMING AND CONTROL	Carried out for every application delivered by the data entry task Each time a new application is received from data entry, this task can be carried out. The residence-assignment task for a certain residence can only be carried out if the assessment task has validated all applications for this residence. Applications that fail the validation test can be thrown away without notification of the applicant. It would be good to keep a log of all task activations plus a summary of the results.
AGENTS	In the new situation: knowledge system
KNOWLEDGE AND COMPETENCE	Assessment criteria
RESOURCES	–
QUALITY AND PERFORMANCE	The task is not time-critical, but it is expected that assessment will be quick (at most a few seconds). System availability should be at least 95%. In case the system is not available, the applications that need to be validated should be placed in a queue.

Table 10.7
Worksheet TM-1: First analysis of the application-assessment task.

Often, we can link in relevant analysis descriptions made for other applications. For example, Figure 10.3 and Figure 10.4 show respectively a data-flow diagram and a state-transition diagram that have been taken from prior system-development work in this domain. Also, existing database schemas are often useful to link in here. The database schema for the database of applicants and residences is shown in the section on knowledge modelling (see Figure 10.6).

10.4.2   TM-2: Knowledge Bottleneck Identification

In the task model we also take a closer look at the knowledge assets involved in the task. Worksheet TM-2 is used for this purpose. In this worksheet we characterize the nature of a knowledge asset in terms of a number of attributes related to nature, form, and availability of the knowledge. Table 10.8 is an instance of this worksheet for the knowledge asset "assessment criteria." We see that the nature of this type of knowledge is formal and/or

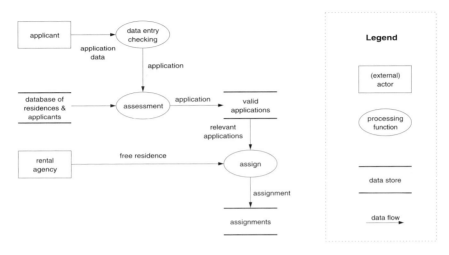

Figure 10.3
Data-flow diagram for the main processes, data flow and data stores of the application-assessment task, as well as directly related tasks.

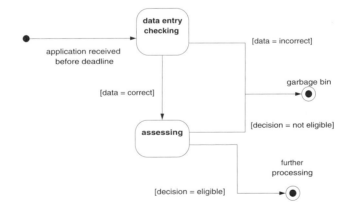

Figure 10.4
State diagram for the main flow of control during a single execution of the application-assessment task and the preceding "data-entry" task.

Task Model	Knowledge Item Worksheet TM-2	
NAME	Assessment criteria	
POSSESSED BY	Assigner / knowledge system	
USED IN	3. Application assessment.	
DOMAIN	Government rules and regulations	
Nature of the knowledge		**Bottleneck / to be improved?**
Formal, rigorous	X	
Empirical, quantitative		
Heuristic, rules of thumb		
Highly specialized, domain-specific	X	
Experience-based		
Action-based		
Incomplete		
Uncertain, may be incorrect		
Quickly changing	X	X
Hard to verify		
Tacit, hard to transfer		
Form of the knowledge		
Mind		
Paper	X	
Electronic		
Action skill		
Other		
Availability of knowledge		
Limitations in time		
Limitations in space		
Limitations in access		
Limitations in quality		
Limitations in form	X	X

Table 10.8
Worksheet TM-2: Knowledge asset characterization plus identification of bottlenecks.

rigorous, highly specialized, and quickly changing. The form of the knowledge is paper. This is in itself not a problem (the paper description is in fact quite precise and unambiguous), but if we look at availability we see that there is a problem connected with the form. We would like to have the knowledge in electronic form so that it can be made available to a computer program. Finding bottlenecks is a central issue in knowledge analysis at this course-grained level. Improving bottlenecks related to knowledge is what really helps an organization. Bottlenecks are thus a focus point for all knowledge-management activities.

The worksheet acts as a checklist. For example, the fact that the assessment criteria have the feature "quickly changing" was something not mentioned before. The worksheet help us in asking the right questions in an interview.

Agent Model	Agent Worksheet AM-1
NAME	assigner
ORGANIZATION	Residence-assignment department, plays role in the primary business process.
INVOLVED IN	3. Application assessment 4. Residence assignment
COMMUNICATES WITH	Database: data of applicants and residences Priority calculator: software program that supports residence assignment Rental agencies: companies that actually rent out the residence
KNOWLEDGE	Assessment criteria Assignment rules Urgency rules
OTHER COMPETENCES	Ability to handle problematic cases (often related to urgency).
RESPONSIBILITIES AND CONSTRAINTS	Make sure people are treated equally (no favors). This has been a problem in the past.

Table 10.9
Worksheet AM-1: The "assigner" agent.

10.5   Agent Model

As was remarked in Chapter 3, the agent model does not add much new information to the stuff already contained in the organization and task models. The agent model reorganizes the information so that we can look at it from the perspective of the agents involved. The agents will eventually have to do their (new) jobs in the organization. The success of the system depends on their willingness and ability to cooperate. In Table 10.9 we see worksheet AM-1 for the "assigner" agent. This is the human role in the organization most affected by the proposed solution. Her work is likely to change dramatically. Information added to this worksheet relates mainly to the skills and competencies required for the agent. In this case we see that social skills are required, in particular for handling the urgent cases. Given the proposed organizational changes, there will be more need for such in the future.

10.6   Summary of Proposed Solution and Its Effects

We complete the context analysis with filling in worksheet OTA-1, which summarizes the proposed organization changes, improvements, and actions. The worksheet for the housing case is shown in Table 10.10.

10.7   Knowledge Modelling

We use the process model of Chapter 7 to describe how the knowledge model of the housing application was constructed. We consider identification, specification, and refinement activities in sequence.

Organization, Task, Agent Models	Checklist for Impact and Improvement Decision Document: Worksheet OTA-1
IMPACTS AND CHANGES IN ORGANIZATION	1. A new software agent is introduced into the organization. This agent (the knowledge system) is expected to take over the bulk of work related to task 3 "application assessment". The knowledge system will need to be integrated with two other software agents: the applicants/residences database and the priority calculator. 2. A new human role "urgency handler" is created.
TASK/AGENT-SPECIFIC IMPACTS AND CHANGES	1. Assigners may have to do other work. Define how much work is saved, and how much additional effort for urgency handling will/should become available. 2. The computer-support group will get more responsibility.
ATTITUDES AND COMMITMENTS	Management thinks the changes will be received positively by the agents whose work changes. This has to be verified though interviews and/or other means.
PROPOSED ACTIONS	1. Propose preliminary plan for full development. 2. Conduct interviews with agents affected by the new situation and define accompanying measures in case of negative attitudes. Reconsider the project if there is a negative attitude among these agents. 3. Select staff for retraining as "urgency handler". 4. Plan the training program.

Table 10.10
Worksheet OTA-1: Summary of organizational changes, improvements, and actions.

10.7.1   Identification Activity: Domain Familiarization

A number of information sources were scanned. In this case, the written information turned out to be extremely helpful. The reason for this was that one of the goals of the new business process for residence assignment was to make it as transparent as possible to the public. People should be able to see which criteria were applied. The bi-weekly magazine with the available houses also contained an explicit description of the assessment criteria and of the full procedure. Additional sources of information were a few transcripts of interviews with assigners and a document describing information about urgent cases.

10.7.2   Identification Activity: List Potential Model Components

From the task point of view we have to look at templates for the assessment task. The template described in this book (see Chapter 6) is of course a candidate, but there are also others. For example, the CommonKADS library book (Breuker and Van de Velde 1994) contains a chapter on assessment models.

From the domain point of view we can get information from the existing database of residences and applicants. The data model of this database is a candidate for (partial) reuse. This also simplifies the realization of the connection between the assessment system and the database.

10.7.3   Specification Activity: Choose Task Template

For the housing application we chose the task template for assessment described in Chapter 6. There are two reasons for this choice:

1. The inference structure appears to fit well with the application. A good technique for establishing such a fit is to construct an "annotated inference structure." An example is shown in Figure 10.5. The dynamic roles have been annotated with application-specific examples. We see that the role "norm" can be played by a "rent-fits-income" criterion. The knowledge needed for the evaluation of this norm can be found in the decision table (cf. Table 10.1). If it is easy to find examples that cover the domain well, the chances are high that the template is useful. One can see it as a hypothesis that needs to be verified in the remainder of the knowledge-modelling process, e.g., by filling the static knowledge roles and simulating the knowledge model. It can be the case that the inference structure needs some adjustment. For example, in the housing application we need an additional input for the evaluate inference, because it turns out that there are sometimes special rules connected to a particular residence. This addition is shown as a shaded area in Figure 10.5. In most domains some tuning of the task template is necessary.

2. A second reason for choosing the task template of Chapter 6 is that it already contains a domain schema. This schema gives us a head start in domain modelling. In general, it can be said there are still considerable differences between the available reusable components. These concern scope, level of detail, and formality. Although there is a considerable research effort in arriving at standard descriptions, this is still something for the future. For the moment the knowledge engineer has to cope with a heterogeneous set of reusable components.

10.7.4   Specification Activity: Construct Initial Domain Schema

As suggested by a guideline in Chapter 7, this activity should be carried out in parallel with the previous one to ensure that the "task" view does not bias the "domain" view too much, and vice versa. For the initial domain conceptualization the data model of the existing database turned out to be the major source of information.

Residences and applicants   In the housing domain, we find two central object types which can be modelled with standard data-modelling techniques, namely **residence** and **applicant**. Both can be specified through a concept with a collection of attributes. Figure 10.6 shows these two concepts graphically. The value types for attributes can be chosen from the predefined list (see the appendix), but one can also define a customized value type. The definition below is an example of a value-type specification for the attribute **household-type** of the concept **applicant** (see Figure 10.6).

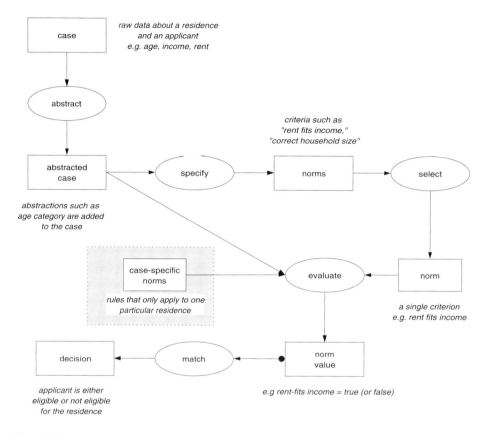

Figure 10.5
Annotated inference structure for the residence-assessment problem. The shaded area is an addition needed for this application. The rest is taken directly from the task template for assessment.

```
VALUE-TYPE household-type-value;
    TYPE: NOMINAL;
    VALUE-LIST: {single-person, multiple-persons};
END VALUE-TYPE household-type-value;
```

The **TYPE** slot indicates whether or not an ordering is assumed on the values in the list. The type **nominal** says that no ordering is assumed. For another value type, namely **age-category**, an ordering exists and thus the type will get the value **ordinal**.

Between the two concepts a relation named **residence-application** is defined. Each instance ("tuple") of the relation denotes a request of a particular applicant (a person or a family) for a particular residence. The numbers at the end points of the relation line specify

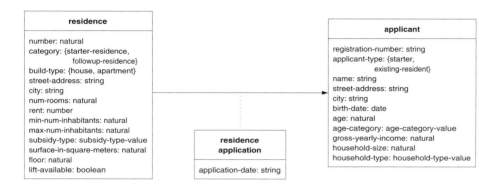

Figure 10.6
Representation of the two central domain concepts in residence assessment: "residence" and "applicant".

the cardinality of the relation: **applicants** can apply for at most two residences, and for a **residence** any number of people can apply.

A relation can freely be used as a complex object type in its own right. This is typically the case when the relation has attributes of its own, or if the relation is used as an argument in another relation. In knowledge modelling this type of "second-order" relation is a frequently used modelling tool, because it is a convenient way of handling the complex information items that tell us something about other information items (cf. our intuitive definition of knowledge as "information about information"). The graphical representation stresses the potential use of relations by allowing the relation to be represented in a similar way as a concept (see Figure 10.6).

Housing criteria   In addition to the information about residences and applicants, the notion of criterion stands out as an important concept in this domain. Assessment is all about criteria. We saw in the domain description in Section 10.2 that for this system we need to distinguish four types of criteria:

1. Has the applicant applied for the right category of residences?
2. Does the size of the applicant's household fit with the limitations set for the residence?
3. Does the applicant's income fit with the rent of the residence?
4. Does the applicant satisfy the other residence-specific constraints (if any)?

These four criteria can be true or false for a particular case. We represented this by defining four subtypes of a concept **residence-criterion** (see Figure 10.7). The criteria all have a attribute **truth-value**, which can be used to indicate whether a criterion is true or false.

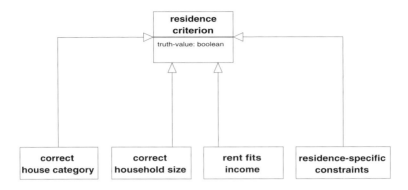

Figure 10.7
Subtype hierarchy representing the four types of criteria.

For the moment we limit the domain schema description to the **residence**, **applicant**, and **criteria** definitions. In the next activity we add additional domain-knowledge types, in particular the rule types which are needed to model the domain knowledge for assessment.

10.7.5 Specification Activity: Complete Knowledge-Model Specification

In Chapter 6 we learned that this task is an instance of the task type *assessment*. Because the task templates provided such a good covering of the knowledge components for this application (see the activity concerning the choice of a task template), the construction process can take the form of the "middle-out" approach described in Chapter 7. We can assume that the inferences in Figure 10.5 are at the right level of detail and start modelling from there. The full knowledge-model specification in textual format can be found in the appendix.

Task knowledge   The task and task-method specifications can almost directly be copied from the default method for assessment described in Chapter 6. The main distinction is that we decided here to structure the method as a composite task with two subtasks. This is a somewhat stylistic decision, and is typical for small variations and adjustments introduced by a knowledge engineer for a particular application. The resulting task-decomposition diagram is shown in Figure 10.8. The figure shows in a graphical form all tasks plus their methods and the inferences they are ultimately linked to.

   The top-level task is named ASSESS-CASE. The task definition in Figure 10.9 describes the I/O of this task. It is common to give tasks a domain-independent name. However, in the textual specification we can (optionally) add a domain-specific name (ASSESS-RESIDENCE-APPLICATION in Figure 10.9). Note that the input and output is also de-

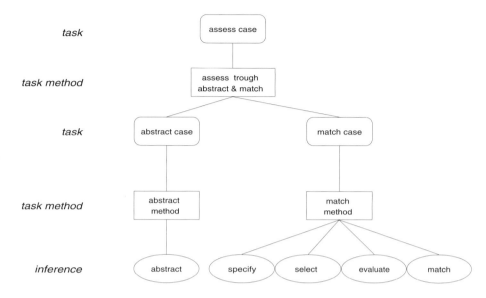

Figure 10.8
Tasks and task methods in the residence-assessment domain. The task methods at the lowest level of decomposition refer to inferences (the ovals).

scribed in a domain-independent vocabulary. We use a term such as **case-description** instead of **residence-application**. The task method for the top-level assessment task structures the reasoning process into two steps:

1. **Abstracting the case description**   The decision knowledge in assessment is usually phrased in terms of case characteristics that abstract from individual cases and provide useful categories of cases that need to be distinguished for assessment purposes. An example in the housing domain is the notion of **household-type**. The concept **applicant** has an attribute **household-size**. In assessment we abstract all cases into two groups of cases: households with one person (single) or with more than one. In this way a relatively large set of cases is transformed into two sets. In this application the abstractions are of a simple nature: they concern only the age-category and the household type. In general, abstractions are an integral part of many knowledge-intensive applications. The power of abstraction seems to be an important element of (human) expertise. It is a technique that helps us to cope with the intrinsic complexity of reality.

2. **Matching the (abstracted) case against the decision knowledge**   Once the case is in the right (abstracted) form, we can see how it matches with the assessment criteria. The result of this match is a decision.

```
TASK assess-case;
    DOMAIN-NAME: asses-residence-application;
    GOAL: "
        Assess whether an application for a residence by a certain
        applicant satisfies the criteria.";
    ROLES:
      INPUT:
        case-description: "Data about the applicant
                           and the residence";
        case-specific-requirements: "Residence-specific criteria";
      OUTPUT:
        decision: "eligible or not-eligible for a residence";
END TASK assess-case;

TASK-METHOD assess-through-abstract-and-match;
    REALIZES:
        assess-case;
    DECOMPOSITION:
        TASKS: abstract-case, match-case;
    ROLES:
      INTERMEDIATE:
        abstracted-case: "Original case plus abstractions";
    CONTROL-STRUCTURE:
        abstract-case(case-description -> abstracted-case);
        match-case(abstracted-case + case-specific-requirements
                -> decision);
    END TASK-METHOD assess-through-abstract-and-match;
```

Figure 10.9
Specification of the top-level task "assess-case." For the housing application we structured the task knowledge into one overall task and two subtasks.

The task control within the ASSESS-CASE task is a simple sequence of the two subtasks. The task method introduces one additional role, namely **abstracted-case**. This is an example of an intermediate reasoning result, introduced by the decomposition.

Domain knowledge   We can now look at the domain schema provided with the assessment template (see Figure 6.7). We can see the following relationships between this schema and the housing domain:

- A **case-datum** is in fact an attribute of **residence** or **applicant** (cf. Figure 10.6). A case as a whole is in fact one instance of the residence-application relation.
- A norm corresponds in this domain to one of the four criteria shown in Figure 10.7.
- For the three rule types (i.e., abstraction rules, criteria requirements, and decision rules), we discuss in the following paragraphs whether and in which form these exist in the housing domain.

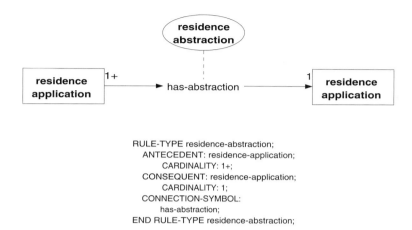

```
RULE-TYPE residence-abstraction;
    ANTECEDENT: residence-application;
        CARDINALITY: 1+;
    CONSEQUENT: residence-application;
        CARDINALITY: 1;
    CONNECTION-SYMBOL:
        has-abstraction;
END RULE-TYPE residence-abstraction;
```

Figure 10.10
The rule type for abstractions. The arrows go from antecedent to consequent. Note that the intended meaning is that the antecedent and the consequent consist of expressions about feature values of the concepts indicated (in this case "residence application").

Abstractions   The abstractions that are required for this particular assessment model are simple. Basically, we need to abstract the age of applicants into a value indicating one of three possible **age-category** values, and we also need to abstract the number of family members into a value for **household-type** (single or not). Both abstracted values are used later on in the evaluation of the norm `rent-fits-income` (see also the rent-income table in Section 10.2).

The abstraction knowledge can be represented using a "rule type" as shown in Figure 10.10. This rule type is in fact a domain-specific version of the rule type defined in Figure 6.7. As explained earlier, rule types are a sort of relation in which the arguments are not object instances but *expressions* about features of an object. An example of an abstraction rule (i.e., an instance of the rule type) would look like this:

```
residence-application.applicant.household-size > 1
    HAS-ABSTRACTION
residence-application.applicant.household-type = multiple-persons;
```

The antecedent and the consequent are separated through the connection symbol **has-abstraction**. The idea is that this connection symbol is chosen in such a way that it provides a meaningful name for the dependency between the antecedent and the consequent. One can see that both antecedent and consequent are expressions *about* attribute values of applicants. This is typical of rules, and distinguishes them from relation instances. Note that we define the expressions that can be part of a rule somewhat implicitly. The statement

```
ANTECEDENT: residence-application;
    CARDINALITY: 1+;
```

in the abstraction rule type means that the antecedent of a rule instance of this type consists of at least one expression (but possibly more) about a feature of **residence-application**. We use the term "feature" to refer to both concept attributes and relations in which the concept is involved. For both, the "dot" notation (`concept.feature`) is used.

For the rule expressions we assume that a standard set of expression operators is available, depending on the value type of the operand. For example, if the expression concerns a numeric attribute, the standard operator set is $=, \neq, >, \geq, <, \leq$.

Criteria requirements The largest part of the domain knowledge is concerned with logical rules that specify when a certain criterion is true or false. These rules specify the *requirements* that need to be met for a criterion. The rule type **residence-requirement** (see Figure 10.11) defines this requirement knowledge in a schematic way. Again, this rule type is a domain-specific version of the rule type defined in Figure 6.7. An instance of this type is a rule in which the antecedent consists of expressions about a residence application (could concern both the residence and the applicant). The consequent is an expression about the truth value of a criterion.

All cells in the first three columns of the rent-income table (see Table 10.1) correspond to an instance of this rule type. For example, the first cell in the first column corresponds to:

```
residence-application.applicant.household-type = single-person
residence-application.applicant.age-category = up-to-22
residence-application.applicant.income < 28000
residence-application.residence.rent < 545
    INDICATES
rent-fits-income.truth-value = true;
```

Requirements for other criteria can be expressed in similar ways.

Decision knowledge Finally, we need some domain-knowledge types concerning decisions knowledge. The decision itself can be represented through a concept definition with an attribute **value** indicating whether a certain applicant is eligible for a certain residence. In addition, we need a way to express the logical dependency between criteria and the decision. In our domain these decision rules are very simple: only if all criteria are true for a certain case is the applicant **eligible** for the residence she applied for. Again, the decision rule type can be derived from the rule type that comes with the task template (cf. Figure 6.7).

Domain schema overview Figure 10.11 shows the domain schema for the housing application. The domain schema resembles in many aspects the default assessment domain

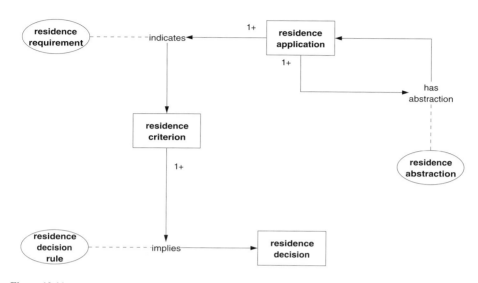

Figure 10.11
Domain schema for the housing application. The attributes and subtypes defined in previous figures have been left out.

schema shown in Figure 6.7. The main difference is that here the types have domain-specific names.

Knowledge bases   In knowledge modelling, unlike data modelling, we are usually interested in the "instances" of some of the object types. This concerns in particular those types of which the instances represent the static knowledge used in the reasoning process (cf. the "static roles" of inferences). The knowledge bases are the vehicles for writing down such knowledge "instances."

Figure 10.12 shows the specification of the two knowledge bases we identified for this domain. For historical reasons these two knowledge bases have been called respectively the **system-description** and the **measurement-system**:

1. The knowledge base **system-description** contains the abstraction knowledge about applicants. The USES clause at beginning of the knowledge base tells us what kind of knowledge instances can be placed in the knowledge base. This definition is always of the form **DOMAIN-TYPE from SCHEMA-NAME**. We have defined only one schema, but as we discuss in Chapter 13, there can be a need to define multiple domain schemas.
2. The knowledge base **measurement-system** can contain instances of two different domain-knowledge types: norm requirements and decision rules.

```
KNOWLEDGE-BASE system-description;
    USES:
        applicant-abstraction FROM assessment-schema,
    EXPRESSIONS:
        applicant.household-size = 1
            HAS-ABSTRACTION
        applicant.household-type = single-person;

        applicant.household-size > 1
            HAS-ABSTRACTION
        applicant.household-type = multi person;
END KNOWLEDGE-BASE system-description;

KNOWLEDGE-BASE measurement-system;
    USES:
        residence-requirement FROM assessment-schema,
        residence-decision-rule FROM assessment-schema;
    EXPRESSIONS:
        /* sample requirement for norm ''rent fits income'' */

        applicant.gross-yearly-income >= 70000 AND
        residence.description.rent > 1007
            INDICATES
        rent-fits-income.truth-value = true;

        /* sample decision rule */

        rent-fits-income.truth-value = false
            IMPLIES
        decision.value = not-eligible;
END KNOWLEDGE-BASE measurement-system;
```

Figure 10.12
Knowledge bases for the residence-assessment application. The first knowledge base "system-description" contains the abstraction rules. The second knowledge base "measurement-system" contains both the static residence requirements, as well as the final decision rules. Only some sample rules are listed.

The **EXPRESSIONS** slot of the knowledge base contains knowledge instances. These instances should belong to the types listed in the **USES** slot. In Figure 10.12 only a few sample rule instances are listed. During knowledge-model specification we typically do not yet try to list all the instances in the knowledge bases, but are satisfied with a few typical examples. In the knowledge refinement phase, the knowledge bases can be completed (see further).

Having defined the tasks and their methods, as well as full domain schemas plus partial knowledge bases, we can now connect these two by completing the specification of the inferences of Figure 10.5.

Inference knowledge   We identified five inferences that are needed to realize the assessment tasks:

1. **Abstract:**   This inference is able to take some case data, i.e., data about an applicant and a residence, as input and produce a new abstracted case datum as a result.
2. **Specify:**   This inference generates a list of norms that could be evaluated for a certain case. In the housing domain, there are four norms: correct residence category, correct household type, rent consistent with income, and (optionally) additional residence-specific requirements.
3. **Select:**   This inference selects one norm from the list. The selection can be done randomly, or be based on heuristics like "first the most likely one to fail."
4. **Evaluate:**   This inference evaluates a particular norm for the case at hand, and returns a truth value, indicating whether the norm holds for this case. An example output of this inference would be that for a particular case the norm `rent-fits-income` is true.
5. **Match:**   The match inference takes as input all results of norms evaluation, and succeeds if a decision can be reached. In the housing domain, the decision `not-eligible` can be reached as soon as one of the four norms turns out to be false. The decision `eligible` can only be reached after all norms have been evaluated and are true.

The inferences provide the link between the tasks and their methods on the one hand and the domain schema on the other hand. The main distinction with a task is that an inference does not have a "method" associated with it. The inference is assumed to be completely specified through its input, output, and static knowledge (the dynamic and static role definitions). No internal control is specified for the inference.

For each role used in the inference, a mapping is defined from the role to the domain objects that can play this role. In this way the functional names (the roles) provide an indirect link between the "functions" themselves (tasks and inferences) and the "data" (the domain schema).

Figure 10.13 shows the textual specification of two of the inferences, namely abstract and evaluate. In Figure 10.14 the corresponding knowledge roles are specified. The textual specification of knowledge roles is richer than the graphical representation in an inference structure. The main additional piece of information concerns the domain-mapping for each knowledge role.

Take, for example, the specification of abstract. In this inference three knowledge roles are used. The knowledge-role specifications show the domain mappings of inference roles to domain-knowledge constructs. The input role **case-description** is mapped onto the domain-knowledge relation **residence-application**. This means that all objects of **residence-application** can play the role of case description. Remember that **residence-application** is in fact a relation between an applicant and a residence. One can see a **residence-application** object as a conglomerate of attribute values about a certain residence and a certain applicant. This is indeed precisely what constitutes a case description in this domain. The static role **abstraction-knowledge** is mapped onto the domain-knowledge

```
INFERENCE abstract;
    ROLES:
      INPUT:
        case-description;
      OUTPUT:
        abstracted-case;
      STATIC:
        abstraction-knowledge;
    SPECIFICATION: "
        Input is a set of case data. Output is the same set of
        data extended with an abstracted feature that can be
        derived from the data using the corpus of abstraction
        knowledge.";
END INFERENCE abstract;

INFERENCE evaluate;
    ROLES:
      INPUT:
        norm,
        abstracted-case,
        case-specific-requirements;
      OUTPUT:
        norm-value;
      STATIC:
        requirements;
    SPECIFICATION: "
        Establish the truth value of the input norm for the given
        case description. The underlying domain knowledge consists
        of the requirements in the knowledge base and of additional
        case-specific requirements (which are part of the task
        input).";
END INFERENCE evaluate;
```

Figure 10.13
Textual specification of two of the inferences.

type **residence-abstraction**. For static roles, it is common to indicate also the knowledge base in which the knowledge is stored, in this case the knowledge base **measurement-system**.

The second inference evaluate is defined in a similar manner. Note the use of **SET-OF** to indicate that the role consists of a set of domain objects. The use of **SET-OF** is not necessary for static roles, where by default we assume that it concerns a set. Note-worthy is also that the roles **norm** and **norm-value** both map onto the same domain type **residence-criterion**. The difference between the two roles is that the value for the **truth-value** attribute is filled in, but this difference is something that we cannot express in our notation. However, the difference in meaning should be clear intuitively.

```
KNOWLEDGE-ROLE case-description;
    TYPE: DYNAMIC;
    DOMAIN-MAPPING:
        residence-application;
END KNOWLEDGE-ROLE case-description;

KNOWLEDGE-ROLE case-specific-requirements;
    TYPE: DYNAMIC;
    DOMAIN-MAPPING:
        SET-OF residence-requirement;
END KNOWLEDGE-ROLE case-specific-requirements;

KNOWLEDGE-ROLE abstracted-case;
    TYPE: DYNAMIC;
    DOMAIN-MAPPING:
        residence-application;
END KNOWLEDGE-ROLE abstracted-case;

KNOWLEDGE-ROLE norm;
    TYPE: DYNAMIC;
    DOMAIN-MAPPING:
        residence-criterion;
END KNOWLEDGE-ROLE norm;

KNOWLEDGE-ROLE norm-value;
    TYPE: DYNAMIC;
    DOMAIN-MAPPING:
        residence-criterion;
END KNOWLEDGE-ROLE norm-value;

KNOWLEDGE-ROLE abstraction-knowledge;
    TYPE: STATIC;
    DOMAIN-MAPPING:
        residence-abstraction FROM system-description;
END KNOWLEDGE-ROLE abstraction-knowledge;

KNOWLEDGE-ROLE requirements;
    TYPE: STATIC;
    DOMAIN-MAPPING:
        residence-requirement FROM measurement-system;
END KNOWLEDGE-ROLE requirements;
```

Figure 10.14
Textual specification of knowledge roles used in the "abstract" and "evaluate" inferences.

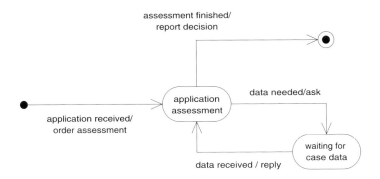

Figure 10.15
State diagram representing the communication plan for the assessment task.

10.7.6   Refinement Activity: Fill Knowledge Bases

Filling the knowledge bases for the housing case was not difficult. All information about abstractions, requirements and decision rules was included in the bi-weekly. A full listing of the domain knowledge for the knowledge bases can be found in the appendix. These rules will typically need regular updating. For example, the rent-income table is likely to be changed every year or so.

10.7.7   Refinement Activity: Validate Knowledge Model

In the housing case study, knowledge-model validation was done by building a prototype system containing only the reasoning stuff. This prototype is shown as an example implementation in Chapter 12 (see the system traces in Figures 12.5–12.8). Based on the traces provided by such a running system one can detect faults, inconsistencies, and further improvements. In this activity the scenarios drawn up earlier are useful as sample material for the prototype.

10.8   Communication Model

The communication model for this application is rather simple. The overall communication plan can be described in a single diagram. Figure 10.15 shows the main states and transitions involved in this task.

Once a new application is received, a transaction ORDER APPLICATION ASSESSMENT becomes active. This brings the system in the "assessing" state. For carrying out an assessment, the system will need information about the applicant and the residence she is

Communication Model	Transaction Description Worksheet CM-1
TRANSACTION	ORDER APPLICATION ASSESSMENT
INFORMATION OBJECT	A residence application
AGENTS INVOLVED	Data entry + knowledge system (+ assigner)
COMMUNICATION PLAN	See Figure 10.15. The transaction can become active as soon as a new application arrives.
CONSTRAINTS	In the prototyping phase, the system will interact with the assigner, a human agent. In the future, the system will be part of a fully automated system and interact with the data entry system.
INFORMATION EXCHANGE SPECIFICATION	This transaction is of the **order** type. No detailed information exchange specification is required.

Table 10.11
Worksheet CM-1: Transaction "order application assessment" details.

Communication Model	Transaction Description Worksheet CM-1
TRANSACTION	OBTAIN APPLICATION DATA
INFORMATION OBJECT	Attribute-value pairs of an applicant and residence, e.g., age of a certain applicant
AGENTS INVOLVED	Database + knowledge system
COMMUNICATION PLAN	See the transitions connected to the "waiting-for-data" state in Figure 10.15.
CONSTRAINTS	Ensure correct mapping of the data request onto the data format required by the database.
INFORMATION EXCHANGE SPECIFICATION	This transaction is of the **ask-reply** type.

Table 10.12
Worksheet CM-1: Transaction "obtain application data" details.

applying for. This gives rise to a second transaction which consists of a ask/reply pattern: a request for data is sent to the database, and the system goes into a "waiting for data" state. When the case data are received, the system returns to the "assessing" state. When assessment has finished the system makes a transition to its final state. During this transition the transaction "report decision" is carried out. This transaction ensures that, for example, a valid application is inserted into the database used by the priority calculator.

Thus, the figure contains three transactions:

1. Order application assessment
2. Obtain application data
3. Report decision

These transactions can be described in more detail with the help of worksheet CM-1. Table 10.11 and Table 10.12 show the worksheets for the first two transactions.

In this chapter we have seen how a simple knowledge-intensive application can be analyzed and modelled using the CommonKADS modelling framework. One important point to note is that the knowledge model for assessment described in this chapter was not developed from scratch, but is in fact a small variation on an existing model that we were able to reuse.

Designing Knowledge Systems

Key points of this chapter:

- In design we construct a specification of a software system based on the requirements provided by the knowledge model and the communication model.
- The preferred design approach is structure-preserving design, meaning that the information contained in the analysis models is maintained during system design.
- Applying this principle delivers a reference architecture for CommonKADS systems. This architecture is a powerful support mechanism in the design of CommonKADS-based systems.
- The design process can be split into four steps, each of which is recorded in a separate worksheet.

11.1   Introduction

In this chapter we look at the problem of turning requirements specified in the analysis models into a software system. The major input for the design process in CommonKADS is the knowledge model, which can be viewed as a specification of the problem-solving requirements. Other inputs are the external interaction requirements (defined in the communication model), and also a set of "nonfunctional" requirements (defined in the organization, task, and agent models) typically related to budget, software. and hardware constraints. Based on these requirements, the CommonKADS *design model* describes the structure of the software system that needs to be constructed in terms of the subsystems, software modules, computational mechanisms, and representational constructs required to implement the knowledge and communication models.

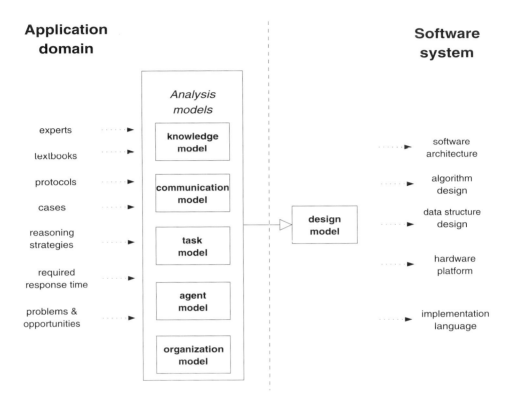

Figure 11.1
The design model, contrary to the other five CommonKADS models, is part of the software world.

In system design, a radically different viewpoint and vocabulary are used when compared to the other models. System design is concerned with *software* and its internal organization. It is as if we turn our head from the application domain, and start looking at the other side: the resulting system. The other models, in particular the knowledge and communication models, can be seen as setting the requirements for this design process. This change of viewpoint is shown somewhat intuitively in Figure 11.1.

Design of knowledge-intensive systems is essentially not much different from the design of any complex information system. We assume that you have background knowledge of design methods in general software engineering. A good overview of the software design process can be found in the textbook by Sommerville (1995). Here, we mainly focus on design issues that are specific to knowledge-intensive systems.

Central to the design process is the *software architecture*. A software architecture describes the structure of the software in terms of subsystems and modules, as well as the control regimen(s) through which these subsystems interact. In this chapter we present a *reference architecture* that can be used for CommonKADS-based knowledge-intensive systems. A reference architecture is a skeletal form of an architecture that can be instantiated for a class of systems. A reference architecture predefines a number of architectural design decisions. A reference architecture is a powerful way of supporting the design process. The CommonKADS reference architecture makes use of an important modern design principle, namely the principle of *structure-preserving design*. This principle dictates that both the *content and the structure* of the information contained in the analysis models (in particular the knowledge model and the communication model) are preserved during design. As we shall see, this principle facilitates transparency and maintainability of the design, and therefore ensures a high design quality.

Similar to earlier chapters, we document the design model through a number of worksheets that act as a checklist for the design decisions that need to be taken. This chapter starts off with a more detailed discussion about the principle of structure-preserving design, because it is considered central to design in CommonKADS. We then give an overview of the design process in the form of four typical design steps that one needs to take. Subsequently, these four steps are described in greater detail. Each step has an associated worksheet. We finally look at two special cases of design, namely design of prototypes and design of distributed systems.

11.2   Structure-Preserving Design

11.2.1   Design Quality

As a general rule, realizing a system will be simple and transparent if the gap between application and architecture specification is small, meaning that the knowledge and communication constructs map easily onto computational primitives in the architecture. For example, although it is in principle possible to map the knowledge model onto a first-generation rule-based architecture, such a design would result in loss of the distinctions between the various types of knowledge. All knowledge types would be mapped onto the flat rule base. This approach reduces maintainability and reusability.

In principle, the designer is free to make any set of design decisions that result in meeting the requirements formulated during analysis. However, from a methodological viewpoint a *structure-preserving design* should be strongly favored. By "structure-preserving" we mean that the *information content and structure* present in the analysis models is preserved in the final artifact. For example, it should be possible to retrieve from the final system both the domain-knowledge structures specified during analysis as well as their relations to knowledge roles. In other words, design should be a process of *adding* implementation detail to the analysis models.

Thus, the basic principle behind this approach is that distinctions made in the analysis models are maintained in the design and the implemented artifact, while design decisions that add information to the knowledge and communication models are explicitly documented. Design decisions specify computational aspects that are left open during analysis, such as representational formats, computational methods used to compute inferences, dynamic data storage, and the communication media. The advantage of a structure-preserving design is that the knowledge and communication models act as a high-level documentation of the implementation and thus provide pointers to elements of the code that must be changed if the model specifications change.

Preservation of information is the key notion. Structure-preserving design ensures that the design process meets quality criteria. These quality criteria are:

- **Reusability of code**   Structure-preserving design prepares the route for reusability of code fragments of a knowledge system, because the purpose and role of code fragments are made explicit. Reusable code fragments can be of various types and grain size, ranging from implementations of inferences to implementations of an aggregation of inferences plus control knowledge. The layered structure of CommonKADS knowledge models facilitates this type of reusability.

- **Maintainability and adaptability**   The preservation of the structure of the analysis model makes it possible to trace an omission or inconsistency in the implemented artifact back to a particular part of the model. This considerably simplifies maintenance of the final system. It also facilitates future functionality extensions. Experience with systems designed in a structure-preserving fashion indicates that they are indeed much easier to maintain than conventional systems.

- **Explanation**   The need to explain the rationale behind the reasoning process is a typical feature of knowledge-intensive systems. A structure-preserving approach facilitates the development of explanation facilities that explain the reasoning process in the vocabulary of the knowledge model. For example, for some piece of domain knowledge it should be possible to ask:

  - in which elementary problem-solving steps it is used and which role it plays;
  - when and why it is used to solve a particular problem.

  As the knowledge model is phrased in a vocabulary understandable to a human observer, a structure-preserving design can provide the building blocks for "sensible" explanations.

- **Knowledge-elicitation support**   Given a structure-preserving design, the knowledge-model description can fulfill the role of semantic information about pieces of code of the artifact. This additional information can be used to support knowledge elicitation, debugging and refinement in various ways. Some examples:

  - One can construct editors for entering domain knowledge directly into the system which interact with the user in the vocabulary of the model.

- One can build debugging and refinement tools which spot errors and/or gaps in particular parts of a knowledge base by examining its intended usage during problem-solving.
- It is possible to focus the use of machine-learning techniques to generate a *particular type* of knowledge, e.g., abstraction and specification knowledge.

Structure-preserving design is currently also being advocated in software engineering in general, especially in the area of object-oriented modelling and design. The motivation there follows a similar rationale, with an emphasis on reusability and maintenance.

11.2.2   Overview of the Design Process

A typical design process starts with a specification of the software architecture. Once the general structure of the software is defined though the architecture, a detailed architecture specification can be made. This serves as the basis for the actual application. In addition, design decisions need to be taken with respect to the hardware and software platforms designated for implementation. As these latter decisions might influence the rest of the design process, these decisions should be taken early on in the design process.

This leads to a design process consisting of four steps:

Step 1: Design the system architecture   In the first step we specify the general architecture of the system. Typically, this step is largely predefined by the reference architecture provided by CommonKADS (see the next section), and can therefore be carried out quickly.

Step 2: Identify the target implementation platform   In this step we choose the hardware and software that should be used for system implementation. This choice is made early on in the design process, because choices in this area can seriously affect the design decisions in steps 3 and 4. Often, the choice is largely or completely predefined by the customer, so there is in reality not much to choose from.

Step 3: Specify the architectural components   In this step the subsystems identified in the architecture are designed in detail. Their interfaces are specified and detailed design choices with respect to representation and control are made. CommonKADS provides a checklist for the design decisions that need to be made here.

Step 4: Specify the application within the architecture   In the final step we take the ingredients from the analysis models (e.g., tasks, inferences, knowledge bases, transactions) and map those onto the architecture. As we will see, the strength of the CommonKADS reference architecture is that it already predefines to a large extent how this mapping should be performed.

The design process is graphically summarized in Figure 11.2. The next four sections describe the four steps in more detail. Each section defines a worksheet that acts as a

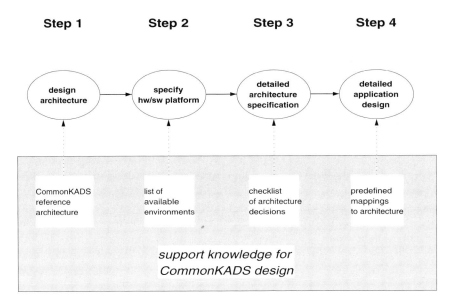

Figure 11.2
The four steps in system design. The lower part of the figure shows the support knowledge provided by CommonKADS to help in constructing the design model.

documentation of the design step. Together, the filled-in worksheets constitute the design model of an application.

At this point it might be useful to make a note about the ordering of steps in the design process. As we all know, design is a creative process. When humans perform a design activity, they hardly ever do this in a purely rational top-down fashion. Designers design in an ad hoc fashion, mixing bottom-up with top-down design at will. This is all normal and should not be regarded as "bad." However, in *documenting* the design it is wise to write it down *as if* the design had been done in a rational way. This makes the design much more understandable to outsiders. The reader is referred to the paper entitled "A Rational Design Process: How and Why to Fake It" by Parnas and Clements (1986) for a convincing argument in favor of this approach.

11.3 Step 1: Design System Architecture

The system architecture defines the general structure of the software you are constructing. An architecture description typically consists of three elements (Sommerville 1995, chapter 13):

1. a decomposition of the system into *subsystems*:
2. the overall *control regimen*;
3. the decomposition of subsystems into *software modules*.

For CommonKADS we have defined a *reference architecture* that can be used in most applications. This architecture is described at two levels of granularity.

11.3.1 Global System Architecture

We first describe the architecture of the system as a whole. The architecture is based on the Model-View-Controller (MVC) metaphor (Goldberg 1990). The MVC architecture was developed as a paradigm for designing programs in the object-oriented programming language SmallTalk-80. In this architecture three major subsystems are distinguished:

- **Application model** This subsystem specifies the functions and data that together deliver the functionality of the application. In the case of a CommonKADS-based system, the application model contains the reasoning functions. The "data" in the application model are the respective knowledge bases and the dynamic data manipulated during the reasoning process.
- **Views** The "views" subsystem specifies external views on the application functions and data. Typically, these views are visualizations of application objects on a user-interface screen, but it could also be a view of a data request in terms of a SQL query. Views make static and dynamic information of the application available to external agents, such as users and other software systems. The separation of application objects from their visualizations is one of the important strengths of an MVC-type architecture. Application objects are decoupled from their visualizations, and built-in update mechanisms are used to ensure the integrity of the visualizations. Typically, there can be multiple visualizations of the same object. The original MVC architecture focused mainly on views as user-interface objects, but they can equally well be used to interface with other software systems.
- **Controller** The controller subsystem is the central "command & control" unit. Typically, it implements an event-driven control regimen. The controller contains handles for both external and internal events, and may also have a clock and start a system process in a demon-like fashion. The controller activates application functions, and decides what to do when the results come back. The controller defines its own view objects to provide information (e.g., on a user interface) about the system-control process. The controller implements the communication model, in particular the control information specified in the communication plan and within the transactions.

Although this architecture was originally developed in an object-oriented environment, there is nothing "inherently" object-oriented about it. In fact, one can see it as a functional decomposition of groups of objects. However, realizing this architecture might indeed be

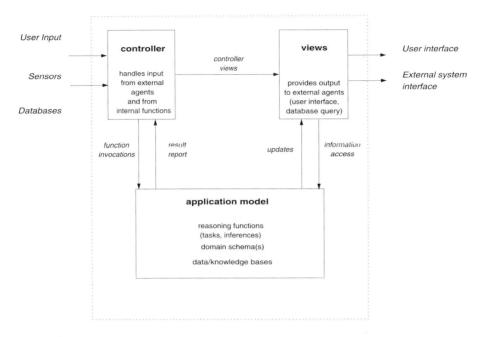

Figure 11.3
Reference architecture for a CommonKADS system. The architecture is essentially an instantiation of the MVC
(Model-View-Controller) architecture.

easier in an O-O programming language, because the control regimen lends itself well to a
message-passing approach. The message-passing control paradigm also fits well with the
way communication is modelled in CommonKADS (see Chapter 9).

   This global system architecture is depicted graphically in Figure 11.3. System inputs
are handled by the controller. The controller can send activation messages to one or more
application functions, which in the CommonKADS case are typically reasoning functions
(i.e., the activation of a task).

   The "application model" subsystem has itself a more fine-grained architectural description, as we will see in the next section. Further on in this chapter, we discuss in more
detail the detailed specification of this architecture (step 3) and how one can design the
application within it (step 4).

11.3.2   Architecture of the "Application-Model" Subsystem

The application model contains the software components that should realize the functions
and data specified during analysis. In CommonKADS terms, the application model con-

tains the reasoning functions (the tasks and inferences) and the information and knowledge structures (the domain knowledge). The reference architecture of this subsystem is shown in Figure 11.4. The architecture is based on the following principles:

1. The architecture should follow the principle of "structure-preserving design," and thus supports an easy mapping of analysis material onto design, and also provides hooks for the necessary design-specific refinements.
2. For several reasons we have opted for an object-oriented decomposition of the architectural components of this subsystem:

   a. Although some of the analysis components have a functional character (e.g., task, inference), their description during analysis is that of an information object. Tasks and inferences are described in a declarative way, which easily maps onto an object specification.
   b. Integration and/or coordination with other systems becomes more important in the design stage. As O-O is the prevailing paradigm in contemporary software engineering, an O-O-based design of a knowledge-intensive system will make an integration easier.
   c. Also, because many implementation environments use an object-oriented approach, the mapping onto such an environment will be easier.

The basic idea behind the objects in Figure 11.4 is that we incorporate the structure of the knowledge model into the design and add implementation-specific details. For example, we see in Figure 11.4 that the object "inference method" is introduced. This object does not occur during analysis, because inferences are specified as a black box. However, during design we have to specify a method (algorithm) for implementing the inference, using the roles specified for this inference. Other objects in the architecture come directly from analysis, but contain additional design-specific details. For example, the dynamic roles have an associated datatype as well as a number of access/modify operations, which enable the use of the dynamic roles as the "working memory" of the reasoning system. In the section on step 3 of the design process, we go through the full list of design-specific extensions, and outline the options from which the designer has to choose.

Worksheet DM-1 (see Table 11.1) summarizes the outcome of this first step in the design process. In Table 11.2 one can find an instantiated version of this worksheet based on the decisions taken for the reference CommonKADS architecture described in this section. This sample sheet can be used as the point of departure for system design. Deviations from the reference architecture should be clearly reported in this worksheet.

11.4   Step 2: Identify Target Implementation Platform

Theoretically, one can carry out a design completely independent of the implementation platform that will be used. We can make a complete object-oriented design and implement

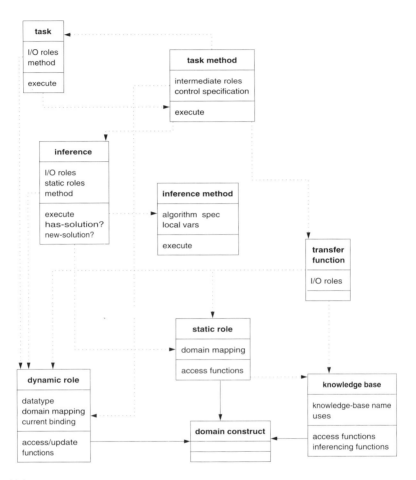

Figure 11.4
Architecture of the "application-model" subsystem. The subsystem is decomposed in an object-oriented way and follows the structure-preserving design principle. The dotted lines indicate method-invocation paths; the solid lines are information-access paths.

it in COBOL. It will usually take more time than if we had chosen an object-oriented implementation language, but in principle there is no inherent limitation. In practice, however, it matters.

For this reason it is usually a good idea to identify early on in the project what the constraints are with respect to the implementation platform. In particular, if the platform is fixed in advance by the customer, you have to be careful.

Design Model	Worksheet DM-1: System Architecture
Architecture decision	**Format**
SUBSYSTEM STRUCTURE	Refer to diagram with subsystems. *One can also refer here to standard subsystem structures such as a repository model, a client-server model, MVC model, abstract machine model, ...*
CONTROL MODEL	Characterization of the overall system control regimen. *E.g., event-driven, centralized control, call-return model, ...*
SUB-SYSTEM DECOMPOSITION	Refer to diagrams in which subsystems are being decomposed. *Indicate for each decomposition the paradigm underlying the decomposition, e.g., object-oriented or function-oriented.*

Table 11.1
Worksheet DM-1: System architecture description. The structure of this worksheet is based on the description of a system architecture given by Sommerville (1995, Chapter 13).

Design Model	Worksheet DM-1: System Architecture
Architecture decision	**Format**
SUBSYSTEM STRUCTURE	See Figure 11.3. The architecture is a variation of the MVC model.
CONTROL MODEL	Centralized control with a "manager" that handles incoming events and that may have its own internal clock and agenda.
SUBSYSTEM DECOMPOSITION	The subsystem "application model" is decomposed into modules in Figure 11.4. This decomposition follows object-oriented principles.

Table 11.2
Worksheet DM-1: Instantiation for the reference CommonKADS architecture. This sheet can be used as a template in which deviations from the reference architecture should be clearly reported.

Guideline 11-1:   IF THERE ARE NO EXTERNAL CONSTRAINTS FOR THIS STEP, DEFER IT TO AFTER STEP 3
Rationale: Steps 2 and 3 influence each other. If you are free in selecting a platform, you can select the one that suits best your architectural decisions.

Nowadays, the choice of an implementation platform is mainly a software choice. The number of widely used hardware platforms has decreased considerably, and most popular software is available on different platforms. Therefore, we concentrate here on the software choice.
The following characteristics are relevant to the software choice:

- **Availability of a library of "view" objects**   Absence of such a facility will undoubtedly imply much extra implementation work. A pure offline batch-processing system could be an exception.
- **Declarative knowledge representation**   The knowledge in the system (often in the form of "rules") needs to be available in a form in which it can be easily managed, updated, and refined. Therefore, a declarative representation of knowledge is best. This is sometimes a problem in O-O environments.

- **Standard interfaces to other software**   Often, access to databases is needed. You then need to use a protocol for interacting with the database, e.g., ODBC. For a distributed system, a standard CORBA-type interface is desirable.
- **Language typing**   Given the O-O nature of the architecture design, an object-oriented typing of software objects simplifies the mapping of analysis and design onto code. In a language like Prolog with hardly any typing, the designer has to build her own type representation.
- **Control flow**   Does the environment support a message-passing approach? It is possible to have multiple threads of control?
- **CommonKADS support**   Does the software provide an implemented CommonKADS architecture, e.g., through a library package? Does it support a link with a CASE tool for CommonKADS analysis, e.g., reading in knowledge-model and communication-model descriptions? Both facilities can speed up the implementation considerably and are particularly useful if prototyping is required.

Worksheet DM-2 (see Table 11.3) provides a checklist for the selection of a software environment. In the next chapter we look at two sample software environments each of which could be a reasonable choice. It is not meant as a limitative list, but more as typical examples of a class of software environments. The two environments are:

1. A Prolog environment is described as an example of the class of traditional knowledge-system programming languages. We have chosen a Prolog with an add-on O-O package of predefined view objects. Its main disadvantage is the weak language typing.
2. The Aion-8 system is a dedicated object-oriented environment for knowledge-intensive systems. It is a richer environment than Prolog, but also less flexible.

11.5   Step 3: Specify Architectural Components

In step 3 of the design process we define the architecture components in more detail. In particular we define the interfaces between the subsystems and/or system modules. In this section we describe for each component which generic architectural facilities can be provided, and what kind of options the designer has in making these design decisions. For the components involved we refer back to Figures 11.3 and 11.4.

Some platforms may actually provide you with a CommonKADS architecture in which the decisions have been predefined. That has advantages (step 3 hardly takes any time), but destroys your potential for creativity (if there was a need for that anyway).

11.5.1   Controller

The controller realizes an event-driven control approach with one central control component. It can be viewed as the implementation of the communication model. The fol-

Design Model	Worksheet DM-2: Target Implementation Platform
SOFTWARE PACKAGE	Name of the software package
POTENTIAL HARDWARE	Hardware platforms the package runs on
TARGET HARDWARE	Platform the software will actually run on
VISUALIZATION LIBRARY	Library available? Facilities for views: automatic updates, etc.
LANGUAGE TYPING	Strong vs. weak typing. Full O-O typing? Including multiple inheritance?
KNOWLEDGE REPRESENTATION	Declarative or procedural? Possibility to define rule sets?
INTERACTION PROTOCOLS	Protocols supported for interacting with the outside world: ODBC, CORBA, ...
CONTROL FLOW	Message-passing protocol? Multiple threads of control?
COMMONKADS SUPPORT	Does the software provide an implemented CommonKADS architecture, e.g., through a library package? Does it support a link with a CASE tool for CommonKADS analysis, e.g., reading in knowledge-model and communication-model descriptions?

Table 11.3
Worksheet DM-2: Specification of the facilities offered by a software environment in which the target system will be implemented.

lowing is a list of typical design decisions that need to be taken in connection with the controller:

- Decide on an interface of an event handler, both for external events (incoming data or requests) and internal events (return values of application-model functions).
- Decide whether the controller should be able to perform demon-like control, in which case an internal clock and an agenda mechanism need to be designed for the controller.
- Should interrupts be possible, e.g., of the execution of tasks?
- Is there a need for concurrent processing?

Guideline 11-2: BE CAREFUL WITH ALLOWING INTERRUPTS AND/OR CONCURRENCY
Rationale: Specification of control in either case is both difficult and error-prone. Make yourself familiar with the specialized literature on this subject.

The need for complex architectural facilities for the controller depends heavily on the complexity of the communication model. A system with a highly interactive style such as the Homebots system used as an example in Chapter 9 will require elaborate facilities. On the other hand, a system performing the assessment of residence applications discussed in Chapter 10 (which is mainly a batch-processing system) have only very few demands. The following facilities are typically needed:

- Event handlers for activating application-model functions asked for by an external agent (an external event).

- Event handlers for receive transfer functions in the application model.
- Event handlers for internal events, in particular events generated by transfer functions of the type obtain. This may also require *suspend* and *resume* operations on application-model functions.
- Event handlers for providing information about the reasoning process: tracing information, what-if scenarios, printing reports, and so on.
- Event handlers for aborting execution of a function.

Typically, each transaction will be implemented as an event handler or as a combination of event handlers. The controller defines its own view objects to represent "meta" information about the system-control process.

11.5.2   Application Model: Task

For the **task** object we need to define two operations: (1) an *initialize* operation that can be used to set values for the input values of the task, and (2) an *execute* operation, which should invoke the corresponding task method. For the latter operation one has to decide whether it has a boolean return value, indicating success or failure of the task method. This decision depends on the type of control used in the operationalization of the control structure (see below).

11.5.3   Application Model: Task Method

The two main decisions for the design of a task method are concerned with the operationalization of the control structure. The first decision concerns the control language used. Control in knowledge models is usually specified in an imperative form, but is still defined in informal pseudocode. The designer has to decide on a set of control constructs for implementing the control structures. You need at least sequencing, selection (if ... then ... else) and iteration (repeat ... until, while ... do, for ... do). You may also want to consider control constructs for concurrent processing and synchronization. Part of the control language is provided by invocation of operations on other architecture objects, such as dynamic roles (working memory operations), tasks, inferences, and transfer functions (all subfunction calls).

The second decision is concerned with the place where the control structure is defined. In an O-O approach it seems natural to view this as the implementation of an *execute* operation, but this destroys the declarative nature. For example, it would then not be easy to define a view that shows the flow of control. The alternative is to "objectify" the whole control structure, which implies a significant amount of work. This decision is typically strongly influenced by the target implementation platform. We will see example solutions in Chapter 12.

11.5.4 Application Model: Inference

Like a task, the design of the **inference** object is largely based on the information contained in the knowledge model. In design we usually assume that an inference has an "internal memory" for the solutions found. This memory is "reset" each time a task in which the inference is involved terminates. An inference execution fails if no *new* solution is found. The design decisions with respect to inferences are related to the definition of operations that enable inference execution. We usually need three operations, namely:

- The *execute* operation retrieves the static and dynamic inference inputs and invokes the inference method. If a new solution is found, it should be stored in some internal state variable.
- The *has-solution?* and *new-solution?* operations are tests that can be used in the task-method control language and "try" an inference method without actually changing the state of working memory. Implementation of these operations might actually benefit from a truth-maintenance mechanism for the operations on dynamic roles (see below).

In the implementation there is ample room for efficiency improvement, in particular by storing intermediate results of inference-method invocations. The design of inferences is usually easy within a logic-programming environment (e.g., Prolog), because inference execution behaves very much like backtracking in this type of language.

11.5.5 Application Model: Inference Method

Inferences do *not* specify *how* the inference will be achieved. This *how* description is typically something that has to be added during design. During analysis, the knowledge engineer often takes what one could call an *automated-deduction view* of a particular inference: the knowledge engineer specifies an inference in such a way that she knows that it is possible to derive a conclusion, given the available knowledge, no matter how complex such a derivation might be in practice. In analysis, the emphasis lies on a competence-oriented description: can I make this inference in principle, and what is the information I need for making it happen? An inference method specifies a computational technique that actually does the job. Some example inference methods are constraint satisfaction, forward and backward chaining, matching algorithms, and generalization.

One can take the view that inference methods are part of inferences (i.e., included in the implementation of the *execute* operation) and thus should not have the status of separate architectural components. However, the relation between inferences and inference methods is typically not one-to-one. Several inferences may apply the same inference method, but for different purposes. The reverse can also be true, namely that one inference is realized through multiple methods. Thus, incorporating inference methods into inference prevents making full use of reusability. To enable reuse, inference methods should not have direct access to the dynamic and static roles, but rather receive these as input arguments when the method is invoked by an inference. This makes it possible for designers to keep a catalog of inference methods available that can be used for many tasks. In practice it turns out that many applications just require some simple rule-chaining methods plus some set-selection methods.

11.5.6   Application Model: Dynamic Role

For dynamic roles two architectural design decisions need to be taken:

1. Which *datatypes* do you support for dynamic roles? Example datatypes are **element** (single role filler), **set** (unordered, no duplicates), **bag** (unordered, duplicates allowed), and **list** (ordered, duplicates allowed).
2. What *access* and *modification* operations do you support for each datatype? For example, for sets you can think of **select** (retrieve a random member from the set), **add** (add elements to a set), **subtract** (delete elements from a set), and **empty?** (a test to see whether the set has any members).

In addition, you might want to provide some mechanisms for truth maintenance, which would support "what-if" questions and the test operations on inferences (*has-solution?* and *new-solution?*). The need for truth maintenance might be a factor influencing the choice of a target implementation platform.

11.5.7   Application Model: Static Role

For the static role object, the architecture needs to provide access functions. They can typically be of three kinds:

1. Give all instances of a knowledge role.
2. Give a single knowledge instance of the role.
3. Does a certain knowledge instance exist?

The first request is by far the most common access function and is for most applications sufficient. The access functions typically delegate the request to the access functions defined for the corresponding knowledge base.

11.5.8   Application Model: Knowledge Base

For the knowledge bases three decisions have to be taken:

1. We have to decide on the representational format for the instances of rule types. Note that this need not necessarily be a production rule formalism. Sometimes, a relational table-like formalism can suffice. Dedicated environments such as AionDS provide a rule formalism together with some associated inference methods. In programming

languages such as Prolog and Java, this will have to be constructed by the designer and, subsequently, the implementer.

2. We have to define some access and modify functions. These access functions typically match the needs of the access functions of the static role object (see above).
3. We are likely to need knowledge-base modification and/or analyze functions. These functions are related to the editor functions that allow a knowledge maintainer to update, debug, and/or refine the system knowledge bases.

11.5.9 Application Model: Domain Constructs

The domain constructs such as concepts, relations, and rule types are usually only included for documentation purposes, and do not require any additional architectural facilities.

11.5.10 Views

Views realize the presentation of the system to external agents. In the architecture we have to provide two types of facilities for realizing views:

1. a number of view types, such as windows, menu types, browsers, figures, and so on;
2. architectural facilities for linking an application-model object to one or more views, and ensuring integrity of the views by sending update messages to the relevant views at the moment an application-model object changes.

With respect to view types for user interfaces, the current state of the art is to use a number of predefined graphical user-interface methods. Most implementation environments provide a standard set of those facilities. Also, views to present information to other software systems have been standardized. For example, most implementation environments can handle SQL output to other systems.

Two types of user interfaces are typically required for knowledge-intensive systems, namely (1) the interface with the *end user(s)*, and (2) the interface with the *expert(s)*. We briefly discuss the architectural facilities for both interfaces.

End-user interface Typically, the end user is not the same person as the domain expert that helped to develop the system. In most cases the system goal is to make the expert's knowledge available to (relatively speaking) laypersons.

For this end-user interface the main architectural design decision is whether the target environment delivers you with sufficient "view" power. Does it provide the facilities required? The state of the art is a graphical direct-manipulation interface. However, if you want to have speech recognition and/or generation, then special facilities may need to be designed.

Expert interface   Assuming the domain experts are not the end users of the system, we usually need an additional interface to allow the experts to interact with the system. This expert interface typically consists of two components:

1. An architectural facility that allows the expert to trace the reasoning process of the system in the terminology of the knowledge model. This allows the expert to see the reasoning subsystem "in action" and to identify errors and/or gaps in the underlying knowledge.
2. Facilities to edit, refine, and extend the knowledge bases. An example would be a dedicated rule editor, which in the ideal case would be specialized for specific rule types.

In Figure 11.5 an archetype of a tracer interface for the reasoning component is shown. The window contains four areas:

1. In the upper-left part the control structure of the task method that is currently being executed is shown. The current locus of control is shown in highlighted form.
2. The upper-right box shows the inference structure. Inferences blink when these are executed.
3. In the lower-left quadrant the current bindings are shown of the active dynamic roles. Each role is shown as a "place" with the name of the role and a listing of the domain instance(s) that currently play(s) this role.
4. Finally, the lower-right part shows the static role for the (last) inference being executed. The instances listed are typically rules of a certain knowledge base.

Such a tracer facility can be of great help in the knowledge refinement stage.

11.5.11   Summary of Architecture Specification

Worksheet DM-3 (see Table 11.4) provides a checklist for the decisions that need to be taken during architecture specification.

11.6   Step 4: Specify Application within Architecture

Finally, the design needs to be completed by specifying the application-specific parts within the architecture. We can distinguish two steps in this process:

Step 4a: Map the analysis information on the architecture specified in the previous step.

Step 4b: Add additional details needed for application design.

We discuss these two steps in turn.

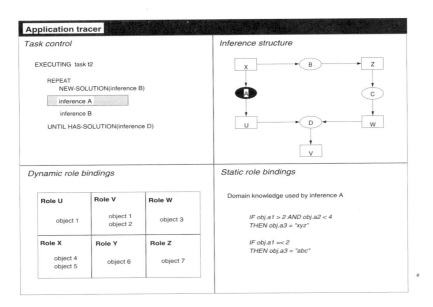

Figure 11.5
Archetype of a tracer interface for the reasoning components. The window contains four areas. In the upper-left the control structure of the task method that is currently being executed is shown. The current locus of control is shown in highlighted form. The upper-right box shows the inference structure. Inferences blink when these are executed. In the lower-left quadrant the current bindings are shown of the active dynamic roles. Each role is shown as a "place" with the name of the role and a listing of the domain instance(s) that currently play(s) this role. Finally, the lower-right part shows the static role for the (last) inference being executed. The instances listed are typically rules of a certain knowledge base.

11.6.1 Step 4a: Map Analysis Information

From the reference architecture it will be clear that the analysis information, in particular the knowledge model, can be mapped easily onto architecture components, thus creating a number of architecture component instances (tasks, inferences, etc.). For example, for each task in the knowledge model a corresponding architectural task object needs to be created. This mapping process can be done manually or through some automatic means. The latter approach is preferred, because it reduces the chance of errors. One criterion for implementation environment selection is therefore whether the target environment has some mapping support tools. Information about available mapping tools can be found on the CommonKADS website (see the preface).

The scope of the mapping tools may vary. In particular, the following ingredients might or might not be present:

Design Model	Worksheet DM-3: Architecture Specification
Architecture component	Typical decision points
CONTROLLER	Mechanisms for internal/external event handling. Concurrency? Interrupts possible? Allow what-if scenarios? User control over reasoning strategy?
TASK	Can a task fail? Initialization method.
TASK METHOD	Language for control structure. Define where and in what way the internal method control is specified: declarative or procedural.
INFERENCE	Define internal state variable; when should this variable be reset, e.g., after task completion? Define operations for execution and "probe" tests (has-solution?, new-solution?).
INFERENCE METHOD	Many-to-many mapping from inference to inference method. Algorithm should be selected. Catalog of inference methods?
DYNAMIC ROLE	Data types for roles. Access/modification operations for each data type.
STATIC ROLE	Define access operation: give-all, give-one, exists-one?
KNOWLEDGE BASE	Decide about rule-instance representation. Define access and modify/analyze methods. Cf. the domain-expert interface.
VIEWS	Standard graphical direct-manipulation interface? Special facilities required (e.g., natural language production)? Different interface: end-user, expert-user. Provide generic tracing facilities?

Table 11.4
Worksheet DM-3: Checklist of decisions with respect architecture specification.

- Automatic creation of the control-structure specification
- Automatic creation of the rule instances
- Automatic creation of controller objects

For controller objects CommonKADS does not provide much in terms of standardized object descriptions, which means that extensive mapping support is unlikely to be present for this part.

11.6.2   Step 4b: Add Design-Specific Details

In this section we list the additional design decisions that need to be made for a certain application. The decisions are discussed in connection with the component involved. Three components are not mentioned, because they do not require any further application design after their mapping in step 4a: tasks, static roles, and domain constructs.

Controller   As we saw in step 4a, in most cases the designer will have to do some hand-work to transform the communication model into a controller specification. . The amount of work needed depends heavily on the facilities required here. As a minimum, a bootstrapping procedure is needed for starting the system. Event handlers for obtaining user information are almost always necessary as well.

Some complicating factors for controller design are:

- Complex external interaction (cf. Homebots system).
- Strong user control over the reasoning process. An example of such a system is the system developed by Post et al. (1996), which supports the dispatching of ambulances by emergency call operators. Due to potential time constraints, the system control needed to be extremely flexible and adaptive.
- Need for "what-if" scenarios.
- Need for concurrent reasoning processes.
- Need for demon-like behavior. In this case you have to define when the system should become active through an agenda mechanism.

In case of a real-time system, the designer should become familiar with the specialized literature on this subject.

Task method   Formalize the method control structure in the control language provided by the architecture.

Inference   Write a specification of the invocation of an inference method. This method invocation should show how the dynamic and static roles map onto arguments of the inference method. Often, some "massaging" of the inputs is necessary, as the representation of roles is purposely not optimized for reasoning purposes.

Inference method   For each inference the designer needs to specify or select an inference method. These methods can be reasoning methods described in the AI literature, or simple standard algorithms (sorting, subset selection, etc.).

Dynamic role   Choose a datatype for each role. This choice is constrained by the datatypes provided by the architecture. Use real role sets (instead of lists) whenever possible, as it leads to more natural dynamic behavior (random selection of set elements and therefore more reasoning-behavior variation).

Views   The choice of the type of view (e.g., a browser or a menu) is guided by general user-interface design principles, which are already described adequately in other works. Chapter 17 of Sommerville (1995) is a good starting point and provides a set of useful guidelines. In the case of the end-user interface the choice of the view types should be strongly guided by available application-domain representations.

Guideline 11-3:   CHOOSE VIEWS THE END USER IS ALREADY FAMILIAR WITH
Rationale: Still too often computer scientists try to impose on end users representations that they like themselves. Typically, each application domain has its own "views" of information, which have developed over the years and have proved their worth in practice. It is usually best to try to base your views as much as possible on these existing representations. It considerably raises your chances of user acceptance.

Design Model	Worksheet DM-4: Application Design	
Element	**Design decision**	**Comments**
CONTROLLER	Translate communication-plan control plus the transactions into event handlers.	*Need for real-time behavior? Need for concurrency? Need for user control over reasoning?*
TASK METHODS	Formalize control structure.	*Strongly constrained by control language provided by the architecture. Some mapping tools already do this task for you.*
DYNAMIC ROLES	Choose a datatype for each role.	*Constrained by datatypes provided by architecture. Use real role sets (instead of lists) whenever possible, as it leads to more natural reasoning behavior (random selection).*
INFERENCES	Write a specification of the invocation of the inference method(s).	*This method invocation should show how the dynamic and static roles map onto arguments of the method. Often, some "massaging" of the inputs is necessary, as the role representation of (static) roles are purposely not optimized for reasoning purposes.*
INFERENCE METHODS	Specify or select inference methods.	*Choose an appropriate reasoning technique or algorithm. Limit the number of methods by trying to use a method for more than one inference.*
KNOWLEDGE BASES	Translate knowledge-base instances into the representational format provided by the architecture.	*Some mapping tools already do this task for you.*
VIEW OBJECTS	Select appropriate views for the application-model and the controller objects.	*For the end-user interface: use as much as possible domain-specific representations.*

Table 11.5
Worksheet DM-4: Checklist for application-design decisions.

11.6.3 Summary of Application Design

Worksheet DM-4 (see Table 11.3) provides a checklist for the various application-design decisions that need to be taken.

11.7 Design of Prototypes

"Rapid prototyping" has a bad reputation because the term has been used to refer to quick-and-dirty partial implementations that never scale up. However, in modern project-management (see Chapter 15) prototyping is a well-articulated technique to try out a "risky" or poorly understood part of the prospective system. We briefly discuss two types of prototype design.

11.7.1   Prototype of the Reasoning System

There are two standard situations in which it may be useful to develop a prototype of the reasoning part (without an elaborate controller or user interface) :

- The knowledge model is not based on an existing task template, but is constructed "by hand." In this case there is usually a risk that the reasoning behavior will be different from what the analyst expects.
- There seem to be gaps in the domain knowledge but it not clear what these gaps precisely are.

Prototypes of the reasoning engine should allow us to trace the reasoning process in knowledge-model terms and therefore need an interface such as sketched in Figure 11.5. Such a reasoning trace can give the expert or the knowledge engineer a deeper insight into the "knowledge-model dynamics" and reveals problems or errors that are not apparent from the static knowledge-model description.

To carry out this type of prototyping without spending a large amount of time (and resources) on it, it is important to have some tools available for supporting the prototype generation. In particular, the knowledge-model mapping tools are important in addition to an implementation environment with a "CommonKADS package." With the right tools designing and implementing a prototype should normally be achievable within a matter of days.

11.7.2   Prototype of the User Interface

Often, it is also useful to build early on a prototype of the user interface, containing both "controller" and "view" objects. In particular, if either the views or the controller require complex representations, such prototypes are useful. In case of complex user-system requirements, such a prototype plus some associated user experiments might be the only way of getting the information necessary for a proper communication model. Again, see the work of Post et al. (1996) for an example of this type of prototyping.

11.8   Distributed Architectures

Increasingly, applications are built in a distributed fashion. With "distributed" we mean that subsystems of a single application are spread over multiple physical sites. This is not the place for a detailed discussion on this topic. We limit the discussion to three potential ways in which knowledge-system components can be used in a distributed architecture.

1. **Reasoning service**   The most straightforward way of distributed usage is to make the bare reasoning engine available as a "service" without any real user interface and

without event handlers. For example, the residence-assessment application could be made available such that only the "knowledge-model" elements are implemented. This application could be accessed by potential applicants to test the residences they want to apply for. It is fair to say that this approach is only in a limited way "distributed."

2. **Knowledge-base/ontology server**   There is a growing need to standardize, share, and exchange knowledge descriptions. For example, efforts are underway to build "knowledge-rich" thesauri to define the relevant terms in diverse fields such as medicine and art. The domain descriptions can be modelled with the CommonKADS domain-knowledge constructs. We can then implement a broker that delivers on request a domain-knowledge element, such as a standardized description of a Chinese vase of a certain period. The first generation of these systems is currently being built. A good example of the possibilities is the terminology server for art objects built in the context of the European research project GRASP (Wielinga et al. 1997). The server is part of a distributed system that assists in finding the rightful owners of stolen art objects.

3. **Method service**   One can imagine that implementation of the various task templates can be used as services in a distributed system. The domain knowledge would in that case be provided by the client, who may actually be able to get this domain knowledge from another server (see the previous point). The practical use of this type of service is, however, still a research issue.

If you are seriously considering building an application with distributed characteristics, you will want to choose an implementation language in step 2 that supports a protocol for distributed systems. A popular protocol is the CORBA architecture (Ben-Natan 1995).

11.9   Bibliographical Notes and Further Reading

There is not much literature on design of knowledge systems. The best approach to get a background in this field is to study a modern text on software design in general, and to specialize this for design of knowledge systems.

Knowledge-System Implementation

Key points of this chapter:

- CommonKADS really works: you can actually build a running system.
- System implementation can still be hard work, but is relatively straightforward once you have done your CommonKADS groundwork.
- We show two implementations of the housing case. The languages were chosen for convenience: other choices could work equally well.
- The first implementation in Prolog follows the design rules set out in Chapter 11 strictly, and shows a full structure-preserving implementation.
- The second implementation in AionDS 8.0 shows how a CommonKADS application can be realized in a popular O-O-based environment used in business.

You might have wondered while reading about all this model stuff in previous chapters: does this paperwork ever lead to something that works? The answer is yes! In fact, implementation of CommonKADS models is usually relatively straightforward. It may still be a reasonable amount of work, particularly if there are specific user-interface requirements, but there should not be any major obstacles left.

In this chapter we show how you can implement a CommonKADS analysis and design in two sample implementation environments. One is a public domain Prolog environment and is particularly targeted to the academic community. The other environment is Platinum's AionDS version 8.0 (nicknamed Aion), an environment which integrates an object-oriented and a rule-based approach and is used in business practice. However, we should stress that our choice is in a sense arbitrary and is based on convenience (in particular, availability). The sample application is the housing application, the analysis of which is described in Chapter 10. The source code of both implementations can be found at the

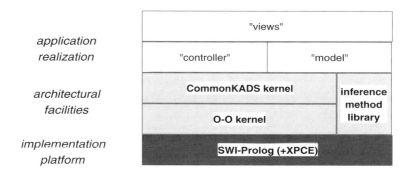

Figure 12.1
Software architecture of the Prolog implementation. The software on top of Prolog can be conceived of as consisting of three layers. The first layer implements object-oriented concepts on top of Prolog and implements the underlying view-update facilities required for the MVC architecture. The second layer implements in a generic way the mapping of CommonKADS objects on the MVC architecture. The third layer is the implementation of the actual application. The inference-method library is an additional architectural facility that provides implementations of algorithms frequently used for realizing inferences, e.g., rule-based reasoning. This library is implemented directly on top of Prolog.

CommonKADS website (see the preface). For the Prolog implementation a link is added to the download site of the Prolog system used.

12.1 Implementation in Prolog

12.1.1 Overview

The implementation described here uses the public domain SWI-Prolog system (Wielemaker 1994) which runs on Windows95 and UNIX platforms (see the CommonKADS web-site for more information). The implementation is intended purely for educational purposes. No efforts have been made to add gadgets such as syntax checking, editors, and so on. Detailed analysis of the code will undoubtedly reveal places where the implementation contains bugs or can be improved. Still, we hope it serves its role as an insightful example of an implementation.

Figure 12.1 shows the main elements of the software architecture of the Prolog implementation. The software can be conceived of as consisting of three layers, i.e., two architectural layers and one application layer:

1. The first layer implements object-oriented concepts on top of Prolog and provides the underlying view-update facilities required for the MVC architecture (the O-O kernel in Figure 12.1).

2. The second layer contains class, attribute, and operation definitions for generic CommonKADS objects (the CommonKADS kernel in Figure 12.1). These definitions provide the building blocks for realizing a CommonKADS application in an MVC-like architecture.
3. The third layer is the implementation of the actual application: it constitutes a specialization of the generic objects of the CommonKADS kernel. It implements the "model," "view," and "controller" objects of the actual application.

The next subsections discuss these three layers in more detail. The inference-method library is an additional architectural facility that provides implementations of algorithms frequently used for realizing inferences, e.g., rule-based reasoning. This library is implemented directly on top of Prolog and is used in the realization of the housing application.

12.1.2   Baseline Architecture

We first implemented a small set of O-O primitives on top of Prolog. The primitives provide a simple typing system on top of Prolog. The purpose of these primitives is to simplify the mapping from the CommonKADS design as shown in Figure 11.4 onto the Prolog code. Thus, it is meant to ensure a transparent structure-preserving implementation.
The object-oriented primitives fall into three classes:

1. *definitions* of classes, attributes, and operations;
2. *actions* such as creating an object, changing attribute values, and invoking operations;
3. *queries* such as asking for the current value of an attribute and checking the superclasses of a class.

Figure 12.2 gives an overview of the main O-O primitives. For more details the reader is referred to the source code. The O-O layer also provides architectural facilities for the separation of application objects from their visualization. This is done by including a mechanism that broadcasts any change in an object state. Such state changes can be the creation of an object or a change of an attribute value. As we will see, the view subsystem can catch such messages to update object visualizers.

12.1.3   Implementing the CommonKADS Architecture

Using the O-O primitives discussed above, we implemented the CommonKADS architecture described in the previous chapter. This architecture should allow an easy mapping of the communication model onto the "controller" subsystem and of the knowledge model onto the "model" subsystem. The architecture of the latter subsystem is in fact a more or less direct implementation of the subsystem decomposition shown in Figure 11.4. The classes, attributes, and operations defined in the CommonKADS Prolog architecture are shown in Figure 12.3.

```
% DEFINITIONS

def_class(+Class, +ListOfSuperClasses)
def_attribute(+Class, +Attribute, +ValueType, +Cardinality).
def_operation(+Class, +Operation, +ListOfArgumentTypes, +RetrunType).
def_value_type(+ValueType, +NominalOrOrdinal, +ListOFValues).

method(+Class, +Operation, +Object, +Input, -Output).
method(+Class, +Operation, +Input, -Output).

% ACTIONS

create(+Class, ?ObjectID, +ListOfAttributeValues).
put_attribute_value(+ClassOrObject, +Attribute = +Value).
invoke(+ObjectOrClass, +Operation, +Input, -Output).

% QUERIES

get_attribute_value(+ClassOrObject, +Attribute = -Value).
has_base_class(+ObjectOrClass, ?Class).
is_a(+ObjectOrClass, ?Class).
. . . . . . . . . .
```

Figure 12.2
Informal specification of the main predicates available in the O-O layer on top of Prolog. The plus indicates
that the argument needs to be bound when the predicate is called; the minus indicates that the variable will be
bound by execution of the predicate; arguments preceded by ? can either be bound or unbound. For example, the
predicate "is-a" can be used both to find an immediate superclass of an object (second argument is unbound) or to
check whether this the case for a particular superclass (second argument is bound). Operations may have a void
return type: in that case the "invoke" predicate will return an empty list [].

The classes shown contain the information contained in the knowledge and communication model. This is in accordance with the structure-preserving principle. In addition,
these class definitions contain implementation-specific extensions. We distinguish two
types of extensions:

1. *architecture-specific extensions* which concern code that can be written generically (the
   same for each application);
2. *application-specific extensions* which point to the code that needs to be added for each
   individual application.

Our goal is to keep these *application-specific extensions as minimal as possible*. This enables fast construction of prototype systems. In the Prolog architecture we have included
only simple facilities for handling the communication model. It only supports (like Prolog
itself) a single thread of control. Therefore, the transactions need to be implemented as
standard procedure invocations. The Prolog environment has limited use in highly interactive systems and is mainly intended for prototyping of the knowledge model.

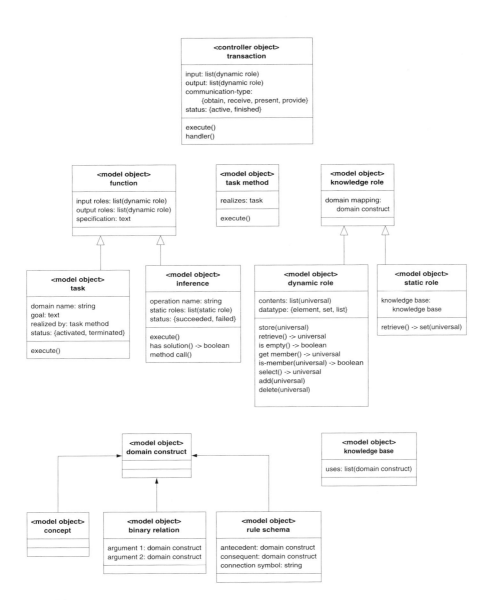

Figure 12.3

Classes for the "model" and the "controller" subsystem of the Prolog architecture. Only one controller class is included: "transaction." The signature of operations is defined in a sketchy manner. The keyword "universal" stands for any object.

Architecture-specific extensions   Architecture-specific extensions need only be defined once for the architecture. The application builder does not need to be concerned with these extensions. An example of such an extension is the implementation of the *execute* operation defined on a **task**. The implementation of this operation can be defined at the architecture level, because it just invokes the *execute* operation of the corresponding task method. Note that this assumes we have defined only one possible method per task. In case of multiple task methods (see Chapter 13) the operation implementation needs to be defined by the application to indicate how a specific task method is chosen.

Another example of a architecture-specific extension is the addition of a **status** attribute to **transaction**, **task**, and **inference**. As we will see, the value of this attribute is used by the trace facility in the "view" subsystem. This is a typical implementation-specific extension: during knowledge analysis this attribute is not of interest.

Application-specific extensions   A number of extensions need to be defined for each application. This can be considered the "real" implementation work for an application. At least the following extensions need to be defined for implementing an application:

- For each transaction in the communication model: define an implementation of the *handler* operation.This handler should implement the information transfer in and out of the system. For example, the "get-case" transaction contains the code for retrieving data about a case that needs to be assessed from a database of cases.
- For each task method: define an implementation of the *execute* operation. This code should implement the control structure of the task method using the control primitives provided by the architecture.
- For each inference: define an implementation of the *method-call* operation. This operation is responsible for specifying how the inference is realized using existing or newly coded inference methods. The Prolog architecture has a small catalog of predefined inference methods, including a rule interpreter which can handle backward and forward reasoning.
  The implementation of the *method-call* operation can contain any "hack" you want, because the internals of an inference are assumed to be of no interest to the user.
- For each dynamic role: specify the value of the **datatype** attribute. In the Prolog architecture this value can be an `element`, `set` (unordered collection, no duplicates), or `list` (ordered collection, duplicates allowed).

In the next subsection we see how these three types of application-specific extension are defined for the housing application.

12.1.4   Realizing the Housing Application

As we saw in Chapter 11, realizing the application in fact consists of carrying out three implementation activities:

1. mapping analysis objects onto the architecture;
2. coding the implementation-specific extensions of the analysis objects (see the list of four items in the previous section);
3. coding the required application views to realize the user interface and possibly other interfaces.

Mapping the analysis objects This step is carried out by specializing the CommonKADS-specific classes defined in the architecture. Thus, the task ASSESS-CASE is defined as a specialization of the class **task**. The reader is referred to the Prolog code at the CommonKADS website for examples. This mapping process form knowledge model to implementation should typically be supported by an appropriate CASE tool that handles the code generation from the knowledge-model specification. Manual transformations are tiresome and error-prone, and should be avoided as much as possible.

Coding the implementation-specific extensions In this second step one has to write additional code for the four items identified earlier: (1) defining data types for dynamic roles, (2) writing an implementation for each *method-call* operation for each inference, (3) writing an implementation of the *execute* method of each task method, and (4) writing handlers for each transaction. Examples of this code for the housing application are shown in Figure 12.4. The implementation of the method call for the inference evaluate is a typical example of what one has to do when implementing an inference.

The implementation consists of the following steps (see Figure 12.4):

1. The various inputs for the inference are retrieved using operation calls on the respective dynamic and static roles. This particular inference is in fact a bit more complex than usual, because part of its dynamic input is in fact a rule set (the case-specific requirements). The implementation joins the static and the dynamic rule sets into one rule set (see the `append` clause). The first two retrievals concern the two other dynamic input roles.
2. The rule interpreter is invoked. This is a predefined method which can do forward as well as backward reasoning. For the evaluate inference, backward reasoning is used (cf. the first argument of the predicate). The second and third arguments are, respectively, the rule set and the data set used for backward reasoning. Finally, the fourth argument of the predicate is the goal that needs to be proved by backward reasoning. In this case the goal is to find a truth value for a norm. We can see that for this inference the operational interpretation is apparently that successful execution of the "requirement" rules means the norm is true. Only in case no rule is successful does the norm get a "false" value.
3. Finally, the result is placed in the output role **norm-value**.

The implementation of the *execute* operation for the task methods should be more or less a direct implementation of the control structure of the task method. For example,

```
/*
    Step 4b: Adding implementation-specific decisions
*/

% data types of dynamic roles

def_class_value(norm, data_type = element).
def_class_value(norm_value, data_type = element).
def_class_value(norms, data_type = set).

% linking inferences to method calls (here: the rule interpreter)

method(evaluate, method_call, [], []) :-
  invoke(norm, retrieve, [], Norm),
  invoke(abstracted_case, retrieve, [], Case),
  invoke(requirements, retrieve, [], StaticRules),
  invoke(case_specific_requirements, retrieve, [], DynamicRules),
    union(StaticRules, DynamicRules, Rules),
    if(rule_interpreter(backward,Rules,Case,Norm:truth_value=true),
      then(invoke(norm_value, store, Norm:truth_value = true, [])),
      else(invoke(norm_value, store, Norm:truth_value = false, [])))).

% implementation of control structures of tasks

method(match_method, execute, [], []) :-
  invoke(specify, execute, [], []),
  repeat(
    ( invoke(select, has_solution, [], true),
      invoke(evaluate, execute, [], []),
      invoke(norm_value, retrieve, [], NV),
      invoke(evaluation_results, add, NV, [])),
     until(invoke(match, has_solution, [], true)))).
```

Figure 12.4
Application-specific code for the housing system.

compare the code at the bottom of Figure 12.4 with the control structure of the MATCH method in the knowledge model. The main difference is that I/O is done "behind the scenes" (an implementation detail).

The reader is referred to the source code for details of the implementation of the transactions (which were kept simple in the housing case).

Coding the views   Finally, we need to write the required view implementations. In our sample system we only included some simple views to allow tracing the system execution. Most of the views currently in the Prolog code are generic: they can be used for other applications as well. Views often have a compositional structure. For example, in the Prolog implementation there is one large application window frame, consisting of three

Figure 12.5
Starting the assessment of a residence application. The data of the case to be assessed are shown at the right. For this case, there are no case-specific requirements.

subviews. These subviews are represented as text windows which show information about transaction, task, and inference activity, as well as changes in dynamic role values. The views are shown in the next section (Figures 12.5–12.8).

12.1.5   Running the Application

Included are a number of screen dumps that give the flavor of the Prolog housing application in action. In Figure 12.5 we see the start of the assessment process for a particular residence application. The data of the case to be assessed are shown at the right. For this case, there are no case-specific requirements. The interface used here is a simple generic tracer that is used for validation prototypes. The application window consists of three areas. In the upper-left text area state changes of transactions and tasks (i.e., activation, termination) are written. In the lower-left area the success and failure of inference execution is reported. The text area at the right is used to report changes in the contents of dynamic knowledge roles. The system halts each time some new piece of information is

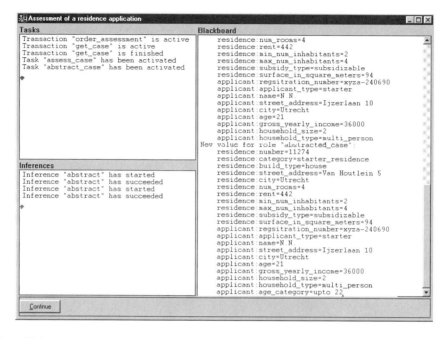

Figure 12.6
The task "abstract-case" has finished. It has produced two new case attributes: the age category and the household type (see the last two lines of the role "abstracted-case-description").

written in one of the text areas, and waits for the user to press the `continue` button (see bottom of the window).

In the second figure (Figure 12.6) the task ABSTRACT-CASE is being carried out. As we see in the lower-left box, the abstraction inference has succeeded two times and produced two new case attributes: the age category and the household type (see the last two lines of the role **abstracted-case-description**. Once the inference fails, the abstraction task will be terminated.

In Figure 12.7 we see that the MATCH-CASE task has been activated. Four norms have been specified as being relevant to this case. One norm has been (randomly) selected, namely `correct-household-size`. This norm is evaluated and turns out to be true for this case. The match inference does not deliver a decision. This means that the select-evaluate-match loop needs to be repeated for other norms.

Finally, in Figure 12.8 we see the termination of the assessment process for the sample case. All norms have been evaluated and have been found to be true for this case (see the role **evaluation-results**). This leads to the decision that the applicant is eligible for the

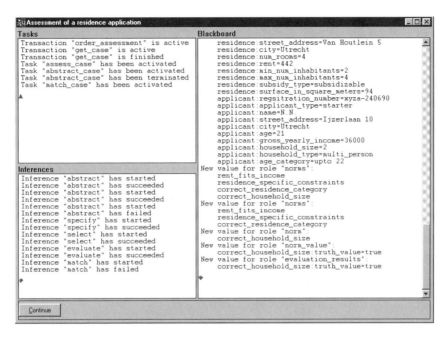

Figure 12.7
The match case task has been activated. One norm has been (randomly) selected, namely "correct-household-size." This norm is evaluated and turns out to be true for this case. The match inference does not deliver a decision, so the process needs to be repeated for other norms.

residence in question. The execution of the "report-decision" transaction is the final system action.

12.2   Implementation in Aion

12.2.1   Overview

The second CommonKADS implementation of the housing application uses the implementation environment AionDS. This environment is used in business practice. The 8.0 version (also called Aion) has an object-oriented basis (classes, attributes, methods) with rule-based extensions, such as rule-definition formats and rule-execution methods. The code of the implementation can be downloaded from the CommonKADS website. You will require the Aion environment to be able to run it.

Although the environment is a different one, the implementation is in essence quite similar to the Prolog implementation described in the previous section. Figure 12.9 gives

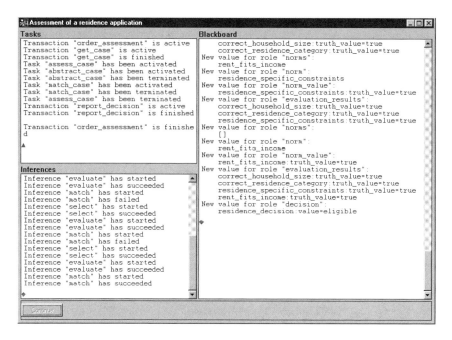

Figure 12.8
The termination of the assessment process. All norms have been found to be true for this case (see the role "evaluation-results"), so the decision is that the applicant is eligible for the house in question.

an overview of the architecture. Each box in this figure represents an Aion library. The architecture consists of four layers:

1. Framework layer   This layer provides the basic architectural facilities underlying the implementation. The application was built in such a way that it constitutes a *framework* for realizing task-oriented applications. CommonKADS-based applications fall into this category. The design principles of this framework are discussed in the next subsection. This layer is implemented as a single Aion library (the `framelib`).

2. CommonKADS layer   This layer is in many respects similar to the CommonKADS layer in the Prolog architecture. It provides a set of Aion object classes which can be used to implement the CommonKADS analysis objects. For the moment, the Aion implementation is limited to knowledge-model objects. This layer is also implemented as a single Aion library (the `commonkadslib`).

3. Task-template layer   The architecture has a special layer for constructing implementations of task templates. These can be seen as generic implementations of tasks, which

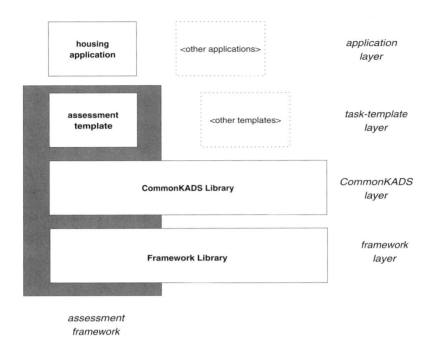

Figure 12.9
Architecture of the Aion implementation. The solid boxes have been implemented. The dashed boxes are possible additions.

have to be "instantiated" for a particular application. For this application the assessment template has been implemented. Other templates can be added at will. Each template is implemented as a separate Aion library (in this case the `assessmentlib`).

4. Application layer   The uppermost layer contains the actual application-specific code for the system. Each application is implemented as a separate Aion library. Because the need for class specialization is avoided (see further), task templates can be connected to empty applications. The source code at the website contains the library file for the housing application (the `housinglib`).

Compared with the Prolog implementation, the Aion implementation has one additional layer: the "task-template" layer. The Aion system is in this respect more sophisticated, as it supports more refined forms of reuse. The Aion implementation splits the "model" subsystem of the MVC architecture into two subparts: a domain-independent, task-specific part (i.e., the implemented task template) and a part containing the model elements that represent knowledge specific to the application domain. This makes it easier

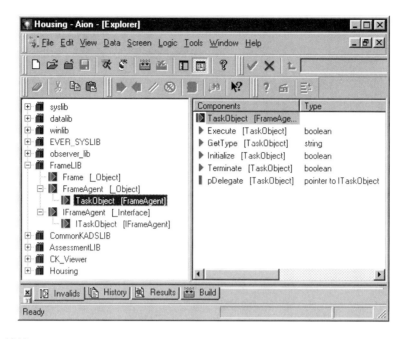

Figure 12.10
Aion screen showing classes and interfaces of the framework library.

to use part of the "model" for other applications that incorporate the same template. In the following each of the respective layers is described in more detail. The final subsection shows traces of the running system.

12.2.2   Framework Layer

Frameworks in general   The implementation is realized in the form of a *framework*. An object-oriented framework is defined as an extendible subsystem for a set of related services (D'Souza and Wills 1998). A framework consist of a cohesive set of classes that collaborate to provide services. A framework typically uses a control regimen based on the so-called Hollywood principle: "don't call us, we'll call you." This call-back mechanism enables the system developer to construct an application in the framework by supplying application-specific code for the hooks provided by the framework. The framework provides, wherever possible, default implementations for the hooks (see further).

Two types of frameworks are being distinguished: (1) domain-oriented frameworks that are aimed at the information structure in a domain and, (2) agent-oriented frameworks that are applicable if the work of an actor or a task needs to be implemented. Implementing CommonKADS requires an agent-oriented framework. The knowledge model and the communication model are in fact descriptions of the possible behaviors of an agent carrying out a knowledge-intensive task.

Framework for the housing application   The Aion housing application is implemented as an agent-oriented framework. The framework layer provides the basic facilities for realizing an application framework. It defines a general notion of **frame-agent** representing an active actor-like object class. The frame agent is subsequently specialized within the class **task**. A notion of task does not exist in Aion, and therefore had to be added. To the class **TaskObject** methods are attached for starting and terminating tasks,

The implementation of the framework makes heavy use of the concept of "interface." An interface in Aion is similar to an interface in the programming language Java. It is best viewed as a class definition without definitions of internals of the class. Interfaces are effectively used to overcome the limitations of single inheritance, allowing class and behavior patterns to be added to existing classes. The interfaces specify the *roles* that need or can be played by application objects. In the following sections we show some examples of how interfaces can be used to define CommonKADS classes. Figure 12.10 shows classes and interfaces defined in the framework library.

The framework layer includes one small other library, namely a coded form of the "observer" pattern. This design pattern (Gamma et al. 1995) defines a generic way to monitor the state changes in classes. The observer pattern has been used as basis for a CommonKADS-specific trace facility.

12.2.3   CommonKADS Layer

Similar to the Prolog implementation, the CommonKADS layer of the Aion system defines a number of classes for CommonKADS objects. Inferences and tasks are defined as subclasses of the **frame-agent** class hierarchy in the framework library. Inferences and tasks are thus the "active" objects that can have a status such as "activated" or "terminated" (cf. the status attribute for the same objects in the Prolog system). Dynamic roles are introduced as interfaces, i.e., `IDynamicRole` (the "I" character at the beginning is the convention used here to denote interfaces), as these require a binding to an application object.

Figure 12.11 shows a part of the Aion classes defined in the CommonKADS layer. The interface mechanism described in the previous section is used to provide for each class definition a specialization hook such that the application can refine or override the generic code provided by this layer. For example, for the class **inference** an interface is defined, in this case **IInference**. The purpose of this interface is to allow the application developer to write an object class definition that implements the role defined by the interface, and in this way extend or overwrite the generic implementation of an inference.

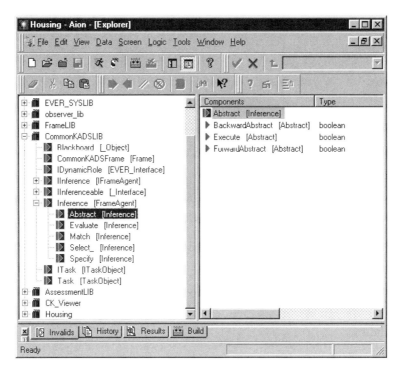

Figure 12.11
Aion classes and interfaces defined for the CommonKADS layer.

The CommonKADS layer also contains a number of predefined inferences. So far, only the inferences that are used in the assessment template are included, but more inferences could easily be added. Typically, one would want to supply default implementations for all inferences that occur in the inference catalog of this book (cf. Chapter 13). These default inference implementations are a example of the principle of maximizing both support as well as flexibility. One could argue that these generic inference implementations should be part of the task-template layer, but the developers quite understandably decided that most are applicable in a wider context than just a single task. The interfaces of type **IInferenceable** specify the roles for the generic inference implementations.

In addition to the CommonKADS model classes (as said before, the communication model was outside the scope of this system) the CommonKADS layer also provides the generic facilities for tracing the behavior of the active objects (i.e., task, inferences, and dynamic roles) in the implementation. This CommonKADS tracer uses a generic implementation of the **observer** pattern (see above). The CommonKADS tracer displays in a

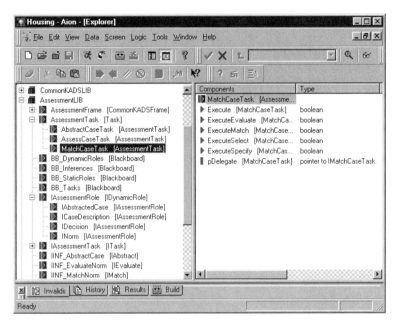

Figure 12.12
A number of sample classes in the assessment library. This library is part of the task-template layer of the Aion framework for implementing CommonKADS systems. Each library in this layer should provide a default implementation of a certain task type.

similar manner to the Prolog tracer an account of the reasoning process in terms of the behavior of tasks and inferences, as well as the state changes of dynamic roles. In the examples of the running Aion system you will see this CommonKADS tracer in action.

12.2.4 Task-Template Layer

This layer, which is not present as a separate entity in the Prolog system, makes use of the notion of template knowledge model in CommonKADS. Here one can see clearly the parallel with design patterns in O-O. The task templates are precisely what one would expect from a pattern for a knowledge-intensive task.

The task-template layer offers an implementation for a certain task type. At the moment, only a library has been built for the assessment template, but it would be only a matter of putting in more work to add other templates. Figure 12.12 shows a number of classes defined in the assessment library. This layer defines concrete tasks, such as the top-level task ASSESSMENT, as subclasses of the general **task** class. The same is true

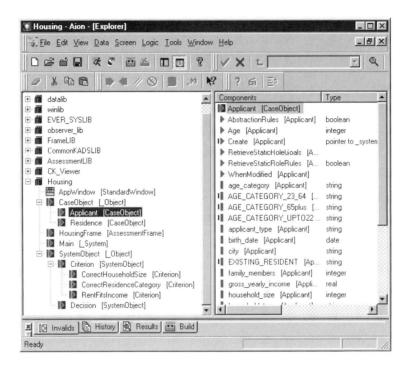

Figure 12.13
Classes for the application library of the housing system.

for knowledge roles and inferences. Again, interface definitions are used to provide application developers with a hook to provide different behavior of the assessment library (for inferences as well as tasks).

12.2.5   Application Layer

The application layer is the focus point for an application developer. For each application the developer should define a separate library, and indicate how classes and interfaces from the lower layers are used in the implementation. Each application typically includes the framework library as well as the CommonKADS library. In addition, a task-template module needs to be included. An application may actually include several task templates. In that case, the application has to indicate how these templates are used together to reach the overall goal. In other words, the application should have strategic knowledge (cf. Chapter 13) about how to combine tasks to reach a certain goal. The application developer will have to code the following parts:

- **Domain-knowledge representation**   The concepts and relations in the knowledge model will need to be represented as, respectively, classes and associations in Aion. Instances of concepts and relations can be represented with static instances in Aion. For rule types no Aion construct is available. The rule instances can be represented through the Aion rule formalism.
- **Template extensions**   The template needs to be mapped to the application. An example is to connect knowledge roles to domain concepts. The framework distinguishes two types of template extensions:

  1. *Obligatory* extensions: these are minimally required to get a running application.
  2. *Optional* extensions: these can be used to refine the application, or to override default implementations.

The extensions mainly concern mappings of domain classes to roles in the template. In addition, the implementation of the inference methods may need to be coded. For the latter, the framework provides a number of standard method implementations (typically rule-based), as well as default implementation of concrete inferences (abstract, select, etc.).

A number of sample classes coded for the housing application are shown in Figure 12.13. The extensions that need to be coded are similar to those required for the Prolog system. As in the latter system, ideally a large part of this coding should be supported by a CASE tool that performs (semiautomatically) the mapping from a knowledge-model specification to Aion code. Also, one could think of a wizard guiding a application developer through the process of attaching a task template to an application.

12.2.6   Running the Aion Application

The CommonKADS tracer, specified in the `CK-viewer` library (connected to the CommonKADS layer) can be used to generate a trace of the reasoning process. This trace is similar to the tracer developed for the Prolog system; only the window organization is slightly different. Such a tracer turns the running system into a white box, providing the developer with a debugging tool. The tracer is also useful if one wants to demonstrate the reasoning part to a domain expert.

The Aion tracer puts its information on three sheets: one for status information about tasks, one for status information about inferences, and one for changes in dynamic roles (the "blackboard"). Figures 12.14 and 12.15 show the housing application in action. The state of the reasoning process in Figure 12.14 corresponds to the state shown in Figure 12.6, i.e., at the point when the abstraction task is finished. Similarly, Figure 12.15 corresponds to the system state in Figure 12.7 (one norm has been evaluated).

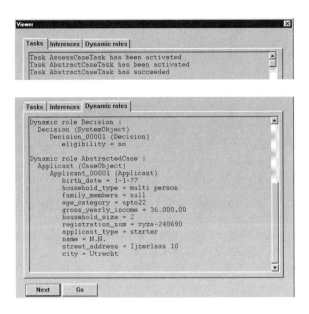

Figure 12.14
Trace of the running housing application in Aion. The abstraction task has just finished. The generic CommonKADS tracer puts its information on three sheets: one for status information about tasks, one for status
information about inferences, and one for changes in dynamic roles (the "blackboard"), The figure shows the
trace information on the task and the dynamic roles sheets.

12.3   Bibliographical Notes and Further Reading

There is not much literature about a structured design and implementation process for
knowledge systems. Many approaches still go directly from high-level model to code. The
MIKE approach (Angele et al. 1998) is one of the few exceptions. Fensel and van Harmelen (1994) give a overview of languages for implementing CommonKADS-like knowledge
models.

The implementation described in Section 12.2 was provided courtesy of Leo
Hermans and Rob Proper of Everest, 's Hertogenbosch, the Netherlands (e-mail:
l.hermans@everest.nl).

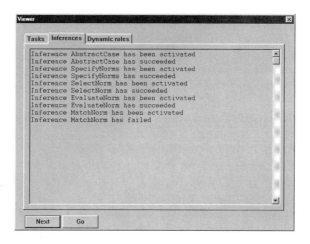

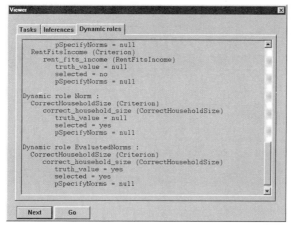

Figure 12.15

This trace of the running housing application shows the situation where a norm has been selected and is now being evaluated. In this figure the inference and the dynamic roles sheets are shown.

Advanced Knowledge Modelling

Key points of this chapter:

- Knowledge modelling of complex applications often requires more sophisticated tools and techniques than those presented in Chapter 5. We offer here a number of advanced modelling techniques.
- Advanced domain-modelling constructs comprise multiple subtype hierarchies, aggregates, formulas, and schema modularization.
- Inference standardization is not feasible, but we can provide you with a catalog of structured descriptions of inferences.
- Several ways exist to introduce more flexibility in the task knowledge, such as multiple methods for the same task and supporting strategic reasoning about task combinations.

13.1 Introduction

In Chapter 5 we introduced a basic set of knowledge-modelling techniques. However, in complex applications the knowledge engineer will be in need of a larger set of modelling tools. Here, we provide some of those techniques.

We dive deeper into the modelling of domain, inference, and task knowledge. In the first section we discuss some advanced domain-modelling constructs that you might find useful. Most of these constructs are not unique to knowledge modelling: they are also used in advanced data modelling. Examples of advanced constructs are:

1. specification of the precise meaning of subtype relations;
2. the possibility of defining for a single concept multiple subtype hierarchies along several dimensions, which are termed "viewpoints";
3. a built-in part-of construct that can be used to model "natural" part-whole relations;

4. inclusion of a mathematical-modelling language to specify logical and mathematical constraints and formulas;
5. schema modularization through an "import" mechanism, thus enabling grouping of similar constructs in a single schema.

For the inference knowledge we present a small catalog of inference descriptions. This is not meant as a formal theory, but provides a guideline which novice CommonKADS users can consult. In the section on task knowledge we discuss techniques for introducing more flexibility in task activation. We also discuss other reusable components, such as problem-solving methods.

13.2   Domain Knowledge

13.2.1   Semantics of the Subtype Relation

Subtype relations are often-used constructs in modelling a domain. The generalizations captured in a subtype hierarchy are attractive to analysts who are always looking for ways of grasping the main concepts of a domain in a parsimonious way.

Two features of subtype relations deserve special attention, because they provide us with useful additional information about the meaning (or "semantics") of a subtype relation. These two features are:

1. *Disjointedness.* A subtype relation is "disjoint" if each instance of the supertype belongs to *at most* one subtype. If multiple participation in subtypes by a single instance is possible, we call this subtype relation "overlapping."
2. *Completeness.* A subtype relation is "complete" if each instance of a supertype participates in *at least one* subtype. If participation in the subtype is optional, the subtype relation is called "partial."

The default way of introducing a subtype is to include a **SUBTYPE-OF** statement in the subtype. However, when one wants to define these two semantic properties for the subtype relation, one needs to add also a **SUPERTYPE-OF** definition in the supertype. A typical example is shown in Figure 13.1. The figure shows the definition of the type **employee**. The intended meaning of the definition is that instances of **employee** can optionally also be instances of one or more of the subtypes. Thus an employee can be both a system analyst and a project manager, but also neither of those. The specification of completeness and disjointedness is restricted to the textual definition. The graphical format is freed on purpose from this type of detail, in order to preserve an easy and intuitive understanding of the diagrams.

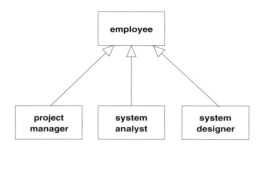

```
CONCEPT employee;
    SUPER-TYPE-OF:
            system-analyst,
            system-designer,
                project-manager;
        SEMANTICS:
            DISJOINT: NO;
            COMPLETE: NO;
    ......
END CONCEPT employee;
```

Figure 13.1
Disjointedness and completeness are specified at the level of the supertype. This requires an explicit supertype-of declaration in the textual specification, followed by the definition of the semantics properties (see above). No graphical format is provided. The example shows the supertype "employee." The intended meaning of the definition is that instances of this concept can optionally also be instances of one or more of the subtypes.

13.2.2   Multiple Subtype Hierarchies

Constructing subtype hierarchies is usually seen as an important activity in data modelling in general, and thus also in domain-knowledge modelling. Subtypes provide the analyst with a powerful abstraction mechanism, and have the well-known advantages of parsimony (through attribute inheritance) and reuse (through domain generalization). In some domains such as classification of a flora species, the knowledge engineer will find large pre-defined hierarchies. However, in most domains, these hierarchies need to be constructed by the knowledge engineer.

There are usually several possible ways to organize a subtype hierarchy. Figure 13.2 shows a typical example of a problem frequently encountered in hierarchy organization. The figure shows a small fragment of a hierarchy of infections organized in two different ways. In the left tree, pneumonia has viral pneumonia and bacterial pneumonia as its immediate subtypes. One level lower, the distinction between acute and chronic is made. In the tree fragment at the right, these two levels are inverted. The problem is often

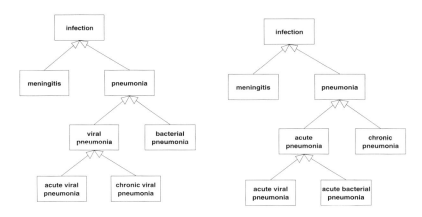

Figure 13.2
A fragment of two alternative subtype hierarchies.

that neither tree is satisfactory. For example, in the tree on the left we cannot talk about `acute pneumonia`; the same is true for `viral pneumonia` in the tree on the right.

The problem lies in the fact that levels in a subtype tree are often not really subordinate to each other. For example, the distinction between "acute" and "chronic" infections has an equal standing when compared to "viral" and "bacterial" infections. Both can be seen as *dimensions* along which subtypes are defined. In fact, each level in Figure 13.2 can be viewed as such a dimension:

- The first distinction between the diseases is made on the basis of *localization* of the infection: the meninges of the brain (meningitis) or the lung (pneumonia).
- The second and third dimensions are the time factor (acute vs. chronic) and the causal agent (viral vs. bacterial, also called "etiology" in medicine).

If there is not a clear ordering of the dimensions in a particular domain, it is usually better to define these dimensions at the same level of abstraction. CommonKADS provides the notion of viewpoint for this purpose. The term "viewpoint" is used here because a dimension is a way to "view" a certain object. A **VIEWPOINT** definition is similar to a **SUPERTYPE-OF** definition. The main difference is that the dimension along which the subtypes are defined is explicitly stated. Figure 13.3 shows an alternative definition of `infection` and its subtypes. The convention is that we use **supertype-of** to define the main or dominating subtype dimension. In the case of `infection` we decided to make localization the main dimension. Alternatively, we could have defined this dimension also as a third viewpoint, thus giving all dimensions the same status. The graphical representation of this definition is shown in Figure 13.4. Using these three dimensions we can now

```
CONCEPT infection;
    SUPER-TYPE-OF:
        meningitis, pneumonia;
    VIEWPOINTS:
        time-factor:
            acute-infection, chronic-infection;
        causal-agent:
            viral-infection, bacterial-infection;
END CONCEPT infection;
```

< definitions of meningitis, viral-infection, etc. >

```
CONCEPT acute-viral-meningitis;
    SUB-TYPE-OF:
        meningitis, acute-infection, viral-infection;
END CONCEPT acute-viral-meningitis;
```

Figure 13.3
Defining viewpoints in CommonKADS. Each viewpoint is defined through a dimension such as "causal agent" (or "etiology") along which subtypes are organized. These subtypes can subsequently be used to define concepts through multiple inheritance (see "acute-viral-meningitis").

define an infection subtype such as `acute-viral-meningitis` as a subtype of three concepts. Note that in Figure 13.4 we have introduced a number of new concepts that we were not able to represent in the first hierarchy in Figure 13.2: `acute-infection`, `chronic-infection`, `viral-infection`, and `bacterial-infection`.

Subtype dimensions occur in almost any domain. For example, in the house assignment domain described in Chapter 10 one encounters two subtype trees of houses (see Figure 13.5). A **residence** can be both characterized in terms of its building type (**house** or **apartment**) or through the type of "ownership" (**rented residence**, etc.).

13.2.3 Aggregates

In many applications we encounter part-whole relations. For example, a personal computer consists of a processor, internal memory, a hard disk, and so on. Of course, we can model these relations by introducing a relation with a name such as "consist-of." But this still leaves the intended meaning of the relation open. Because part-whole relations are often important notions in capturing the structure of a domain, we introduce a special language construct for it.

Figure 13.6 shows an example of a part-whole specification. In a concept definition we can introduce a **HAS-PART** slot to indicate that the concept is actually an aggregate entity consisting of subparts. Such parts need not be "real" physical parts, but also can be of a more conceptual nature. The main rationale for using **HAS-PART** is that a term such as "part-of" or "consist-of" is intuitively appealing from an application-domain point of view.

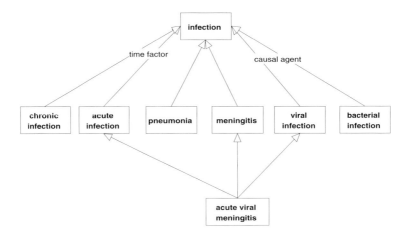

Figure 13.4
Graphical representation of the viewpoints defined on "infection" and their use in multiple inheritance.

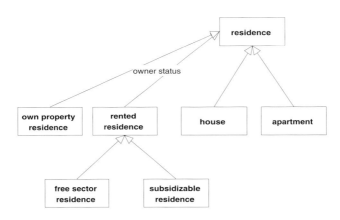

Figure 13.5
Two sets of subtypes of "residence." The left part of the tree is defined along the "owner status" dimension.

```
CONCEPT patient-visit-record;
    PROPERTIES:
        date-of-visit: DATE;
        attending-physician: NAME;
    HAS-PARTS:
        patient-data;
        anamnesis;
        physical-examination;
        test;
            CARDINALITY: 0+;
            ROLE: test-done;
END CONCEPT patient-visit-record;
```

Figure 13.6
Specification of a part-whole relation through the "has-parts" construct. The default cardinality is precisely one, meaning that each instance of the aggregate has exactly one instance of the part. Thus, a patient-visit-record consists of precisely one instance of patient-data, anamnesis and physical-examination, and of any number of tests. Each part can be given a role name.

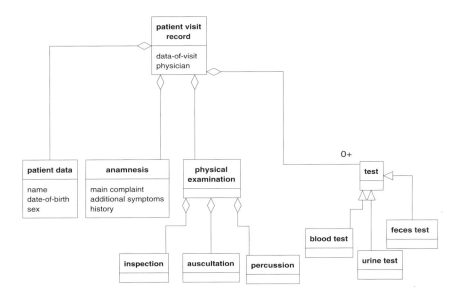

Figure 13.7
An example of a part-whole relation in a medical domain. The part-whole relation is visualized by adding a diamond symbol to the "whole" side of the relation. On the "part" side the cardinality of the part-whole relation can be indicated in the usual manner.

The default cardinality is precisely one, meaning that each instance of the aggregate has exactly one instance of the part. Each part can be given a role name, similar to the general relation construct. The default role names are "part" and "whole."

Figure 13.7 shows a graphical representation of the specification in Figure 13.6. The part-whole relation is visualized by adding a diamond symbol to the "whole" side of the relation. On the "part" side the cardinality of the part-whole relation can be indicated in the usual manner. In the example, a **patient-visit-record** consists of **patient-data**, **anamnesis**, **physical-examination** and any number of **test**s. As one can see, **physical-examination** itself is an aggregate concept consisting of three subparts.

It most applications it is intuitively clear what the part-whole relations should be. If in doubt, refrain from using it and use the more neutral relation construct instead.

13.2.4   Expressions and Formulas

In many domains there is a need to express some mathematical domain theory. The standard data-modelling primitives do not support the specification of such theories very well. Therefore, we imported into the CommonKADS knowledge-modelling language a format for writing down equations, expressions, and complete mathematical models. The format we use is the neutral model format (NMF).

NMF is a language for expressing mathematical models. The main objectives of NMF are (1) to make a distinction between a model and the simulation environment in which the model can be executed, and (2) that models should be easy to understand and express for nonexperts. Standardization of NMF is in progress. NMF is currently used by the American Society of Heating, Refrigerating, and Air-Conditioning Engineers.

In NMF one can express mathematical formulas and mathematical models (with parameterization). One of the ideas is that the models are stored in reusable libraries and can thus be shared.

Most of the equation syntax of NMF will be familiar to programmers. Consult the appendix for details on how to use the NMF syntax and how it is embedded into the CommonKADS knowledge-modelling language.

13.2.5   Rule Types and Rule Instances

Rule types   The notion of rule type is an important modelling technique in CommonKADS knowledge models. It is there that most of the the real differences with traditional data models reside. It is worth taking the following guidelines into account when using rule types:

Guideline 13-1:   SPEND TIME TO FIND APPROPRIATE NAMES FOR THE RULE TYPE ITSELF AND FOR THE CONNECTION SYMBOL

Rationale: Choosing the right names can greatly enhance the understandability of the domain-knowledge specification. It is hard to underestimate this name-giving enterprise. The rule-type name (the label of the ellipse in the graphical notation) should be a name applicable *to the rule as a whole*. The connection symbol should enable readability of the rule: it should make a logical connection between the antecedent and the consequent.

Guideline 13-2:   WHEN A SHORT NAME CANNOT BE FOUND, DO NOT BE AFRAID OF LONG NAMES
Rationale: Our human vocabulary is targeted at things that we see or talk about every day. For that reason it is usually simple to find appropriate names for simple information entities (age, person, employee, company), but much more difficult for complicated concepts used in reasoning processes. We just do not have words for them! That means that a proper name will always be some sort of circumscription of the thing we want to model, e.g., "potential causal dependency."

Guideline 13-3:   RULE TYPES MODEL REAL-WORLD "RULES" OR DEPENDENCIES, NOT AN IMPLEMENTATION CONSTRUCT
Rationale: Rule types specify some knowledge-rich dependency between concepts and/or relations. This is what we often call a rule in conversation. This notion of rule is quite different, and actually much broader, than the notion of rule as an implementation construct. Be careful not to confuse these two.

One variation of a rule-type definition was not mentioned in Chapter 5. Sometimes, we have knowledge about a certain type of concept without a clear antecedent or consequent. An example is knowledge about restrictions of attribute values of a component in a configuration-design task. This type of knowledge is usually called "constraints." The rule-type definition allows you to specify constraints. The textual and graphical notations are simple and straightforward. An example of a constraint definition is shown in Figure 13.8. This rule type models a set of logical formulas concerning a component. The notation is simpler, because a connection symbol is not required.

Rule instances   In this book we use an semiformal notation for writing down instances of rule types. As an example, let's take the "requirement" rule from Chapter 10:

```
residence-application.applicant.household-type = single-person
residence-application.applicant.age-category = up-to-22
residence-application.applicant.income < 28000
residence-application.residence.rent < 545
    INDICATES
rent-fits-income.truth-value = true;
```

If one takes a close look at this rule from a formal point of view, it turns out that it contains at least two tacit assumptions:

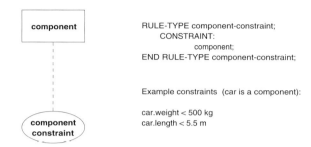

RULE-TYPE component-constraint;
    CONSTRAINT:
        component;
END RULE-TYPE component-constraint;

Example constraints (car is a component):

car.weight < 500 kg
car.length < 5.5 m

Figure 13.8
Graphical and textual notation for constraints: rule types which model expressions about one type of concept.

1. The statements about **residence-application** in the antecedent should be interpreted as universally quantified statements about residence applications in general. Thus, we really want to say in this rule:

```
FORALL x:residence-application
        x.applicant.household-type = single-person
        x.applicant.age-category = up-to-22
        x.applicant.income < 28000
        x,residence.rent < 545
            INDICATES
        rent-fits-income.truth-value = true;
```

The symbol x is here a logical variable of the type **residence-application**.

2. The statement about the `rent-fit-income` criterion says something about a value of concept (i.e., class). The universal quantification is not applicable here.

In fact, we are here at crossroads. From a formal point of view, the sloppy notation is ambiguous and even inconsistent. However, from a pragmatic point of view it turns out that statements such as the first rule above *hardly ever lead to ambiguities*. In fact, most people have more problems understanding the correct formal representation than the (technically speaking) incorrect intuitive rule representation!

Our advice is simple: keep to the representation with which you are most familiar, but be wary of complicated formal representations as *the only* representation of knowledge in a knowledge model. The reason for this is that a knowledge model is a communication vehicle: it should serve as documentation of your modelling work, and inform newcomers of what has been done.

Please note that this statement is not a condemnation of formal techniques. On the contrary, formal techniques have a clear role, particularly in model verification (van Harmelen 1998). But usually it is a good idea to complement a formal knowledge representation with a less formal, more intuitive format.

The intuitive format used in the rule above works well, as long there is no need to talk explicitly about different instances of the same type. If the latter is the case, the implicit universal quantification becomes ambiguous. You will have to introduce variables to be able to reference certain instances in your rule. The following rule shows the use of variables in defining the concept of "smoker / nonsmoker" conflict in a room allocation problem:

```
/* ambiguous rule */
employee.smoker = true AND
employee.smoker = false
     IMPLIES-CONFLICT
smoker-and-non-smoker.truth-value =true;

/* use of variables to remove the ambiguity */

VAR x, y: employee;

x.smoker = true AND
y.smoker = false
     IMPLIES-CONFLICT
smoker-and-non-smoker.truth-value =true;
```

The first rule really does not convey the meaning we want to attach to the rule. Here we really need to introduce variables to understand the intended meaning of the rule.

The CommonKADS conceptual modelling language supports a syntax for specifying rule instances within knowledge bases. The rules above and also the rules in the sample knowledge model in the appendix comply with this syntax. The syntax has the NMF format (see above) for equations as its basis, with a number of rule-specific extensions. You will have to consult the BNF syntax definition in the appendix for details.

Rule types and knowledge bases   In most cases knowledge bases will contain instances of rule types. You can follow the guideline that there should be a separate knowledge base for each rule type. In general, however, there can be many-to-many relationships between rules and knowledge bases. Rules of similar types or role can be placed together, particularly if rule sets are small. One should take care that rule types in the same knowledge base have different connection symbols. Otherwise, the rule types cannot be distinguished. Also, rules of the same type may be spread over several knowledge bases if they play different roles in the reasoning process. This means that the structure of knowledge bases is much more bound to the structure of the reasoning process than the rule types.

13.2.6   Schema Modularization through the Import Mechanism

If a domain schema gets too large, it is good engineering practice to split it up into parts or modules. A guideline one can use here is the size of the schema:

Guideline 13-4:   IF THE SCHEMA DIAGRAM DOES NOT FIT ON A SINGLE PAGE, THEN
CONSIDER SPLITTING THE SCHEMA INTO MODULES
Rationale: This is an extremely pragmatic guideline. People like figures, and we should
be able to tell the full story of a schema in one figure. If this cannot be done, it makes
sense to break down the element (in this case, the domain schema) into parts. Be careful
not to cheat, e.g., by decreasing font sizes. This only has the undesirable effect of making
the figure unreadable, and makes matters worse.

Schema modularization can be achieved with the USES construct. For each domain-
schema we can define which other schemas are being used. There are two options:

1. A full domain schema is imported into the current schema. This has the effect of
    making all definitions of the **used** schema also part of the **using** schema.
    The syntax is:

    ```
    DOMAIN-SCHEMA system-connections;
        USES: system-components;    /* The imported schema  */
        .....
    ```

2. A selected set of definitions of a certain schema is included in the current domain
    schema. This makes only those definitions part of the **using** schema.
    The syntax is:

    ```
    DOMAIN-SCHEMA liver-disease;
        USES:
            disease FROM general-medical-concepts;
            finding FROM general-medical-concepts;
            organ FROM general-medical-concept;

        .....
    ```

The USES construct is a first step in schema organization. In the next section we see
more ways of working with multiple schemas.

13.2.7   Domain-Schema Generalization

One can describe a domain schema at several levels of abstraction. For example, if we
model a computer system we can describe it in terms of specific elements such as "CPU,"
"memory," and "screen." We can also generalize from this description, and introduce an
abstract notion such as "component." In knowledge analysis one is often interested in
making schema generalizations, because these make the schema more general and thus
more widely applicable.

There are different ways in which one can generalize a domain schema, based on
different types of generalizations. We can distinguish four types of domain schemas:

1. **Domain-specific schema** . Domain-specific schemas are domain schemas that are specific for a particular type of system or artifact. Examples of domain-specific schemas could be domain schemas for ships, cars, rental housing, or electrical networks. A domain-specific schema generalizes over particular application tasks in that domain. Thus, a domain-specific schema for ship design could be used by both a design-assessment application as well as by a design-construction application. In the housing domain we could say that the part of the schema concerning applicants and residences is domain-specific, as it may well be used in other applications in the same organization.

2. **Generic domain schema** . A generic domain schema describes a "top-level category." One can see a generic domain schema as a basic mechanism for "carving up the world." It is related to the Aristotelian notion of categories. The main difference is that as a knowledge engineer we are not aiming at a complete set of generic domain schemas, but are only interested in those categories that frequently occur and repeatedly prove to be of use in practical applications. Examples of useful top-level categories that have been identified are notions such as physical, functional, and behavioral entities, connectedness, part-whole, and topology. Although in principle generic domain schemas are extremely useful, their use in current practice is limited. The "distance" between the generic concepts and applications terms just seems to be too large. However, this view might well change in the near future, as there are numerous research projects active in this area.

   In the short term, the most promising generic domain schemas are probably those which generalize over particular artifacts, and describe general features of artifacts. Such generic domain schemas usually define a viewpoint related to some physical process type: flow, heat, energy, power, electricity. Such processes reappear in many different technical domains. For example, flow processes occur in many technical systems as well as biological systems.

3. **Method-specific domain schema** . The method-specific domain schema contains the conceptualizations required by a certain method for realizing a task. It is the most specific domain schema from the *use* perspective. This perspective is important, because the way we look at knowledge is often dependent on its use. The domain schemas in Chapter 6 are examples of such method-specific domain schemas. As you may have noticed, these schemas do not contain any domain-specific terms. For example, the assessment schema is in many respects similar to the schema for the housing application (see Chapter 10), but all domain-specific concepts have been replaced by domain-neutral terms. This makes it easier to reuse the domain-knowledge schema in combination with the task template in a new assessment domain.

4. **Task-specific domain schema** . In Chapter 6 we have given only one method per task type, sometimes with slight variations. If one would compare different method-

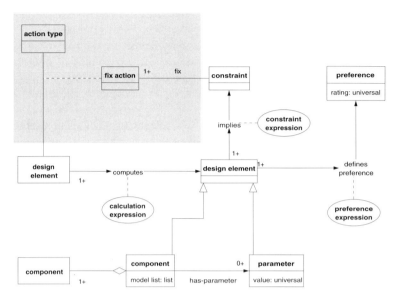

Figure 13.9
The domain schema of the propose-and-revise method revisited. The nongray part can be seen as the "representation core" needed by every configuration-design task, and thus constitutes the task-specific domain schema for configuration design. The gray area denotes the method-specific extensions required for the propose-and-revise method.

specific domain schemas for the same task type, we would note that there is a general core of knowledge types. This "intersection" of all method-specific domain schemas is called the task-specific domain schema. This domain schema contains the *minimal* conceptualizations required to carry out a certain type of task. For example, a study in configuration design (Schreiber and Birmingham 1996) showed that part of the domain schema in Figure 13.9 (see Chapter 6) is actually such a task-specific domain schema for configuration. This domain schema is shown in Figure 13.9. The figure is derived from the domain schema for the propose-and-revise task method described in Chapter 6 (see Figure 6.18). The nongray area represents the task-specific domain schema for configuration design. Thus, components, parameters, constraints and calculations are needed for every configuration-design problem. The knowledge types within the grey area are the method-specific extensions required by the propose-and-revise method: fixes and corresponding actions to modify the design (see the method description in Chapter 6).

Now, you might be wondering, what kind of domain schemas are the car-diagnosis schema and the house-assessment schema in earlier chapters? These contain both domain-specific terms (e.g., **house**, **applicant**), but also task-specific terms (e.g., **decision**, **requirement**). Domain schemas for particular applications are in fact amalgamates of different types of domain schemas. Such an amalgamation is not a bad thing in itself. The application actually requires this tight coupling of domain schemas in order to be able to make a system work. For this amalgamation of domain- and use-specific knowledge types, we use the term *application domain schema*.

Using multiple schemas for knowledge sharing and reuse   One program of work in current knowledge-engineering research is to study the nature of types of schema generalizations. Generalized domain schemas are called "ontologies," a term borrowed from philosophy. Ontologies are supposed to contain an explicit description of the semantics ("meaning") of the types introduced. The aim of ontology research is, roughly speaking, twofold:

1. To reuse ontologies in other application domains or tasks. If applicable, the availability of such reusable ontologies can speed up the knowledge-engineering process considerably. The method-specific ontologies in Chapter 6 can be seen as a small step in this direction.
2. Knowledge bases cost a lot to develop, but in practice are difficult to reuse. One purpose of ontologies could be to use these as semantic descriptions of knowledge bases, thus enabling a better understanding of the meaning of knowledge pieces in a knowledge base. In a special issue of the International Journal of Human-Computer Studies (Schreiber and Birmingham 1996) one can find efforts to enable reuse of a large knowledge base with the help of a configuration-design ontology.

Ontologies should be seen as a "natural next step" on the road to more expressive information modelling. In this new era, where there is a tremendous need for more intelligent, knowledge-intensive search, storage, and communication facilities, this type of development is crucial. In particular, knowledge management will increasingly be dealing with constructing, sharing and reusing organization-wide ontologies.

13.3   Inference Knowledge

13.3.1   Inference Standardization

Inferences are important components of knowledge models. Inferences act as the building blocks of the reasoning process. From the start, people have been interested in getting a standard set of these building blocks. There is a parallel here with design tasks. As we pointed out in Chapter 6, a design task can only be automized if the design is made up from predefined building blocks of a sufficiently large grain size. The same holds more or less for knowledge engineering itself. If we would have a standard set of inferences, the knowledge-modelling problem would be a much easier task.

Unfortunately, no such standard set exists to date. Several proposals have been put forward. A good overview and discussion of the issues involved can be found in the work of Aben (1995). Still, when we choose names for inferences we do so carefully, trying to be as precise as possible. In this book we have tried to keep the same intuitive interpretation whenever an inference was used at more than one place. However, there is no formal theory behind it.

For the moment, the best we can do is offer you a small catalog of the inferences used in this book. This catalog is a structured textual description. For each inference we briefly indicate the following characteristics:

- **Operation**: A description of the sort of input and output the inference operates on.
- **Example**: An example of the inference in some application.
- **Static knowledge**: A characterization of the domain knowledge typically used to make the inference.
- **Typical task types**: The types of tasks the inference typically occurs in.
- **Used in template**: The task templates in Chapter 6 in which this inference occurs.
- **Control behavior**: How is the computational behavior of the inference? This behavior can be described through the following two characteristics:

    1. *Does the inference always produce a solution?* If the inference can fail, we can use the control primitive HAS-SOLUTION (see Chapter 5) when invoking the inference in the control structure of a task method.
    2. *Can the inference produce multiple solutions, given the same input?* If the answer is yes, the inference can be used in a loop, using the control primitive NEW-SOLUTION.

- **Computational methods**: What computational methods are likely to be used when realizing this inference during design and implementation?
- **Remarks**: Remarks about the inference, which could not be made under any of the previous headings.

We make no claim that the catalog is complete. Some people may also want to attach a different meaning to an inference. The catalog is meant as a rough guideline for a novice CommonKADS user.

13.3.2   Inference Catalog

Abstract

Operation:	Input is some data set, output is either a new given abstracted from the data set, or the input set plus an abstracted given (i.e., the updated input set). The choice between these two options is a mainly stylistic.
Example:	Data abstraction in medical diagnosis: any body tempera-

ture higher than 38.0°C is abstracted to "fever."

Static knowledge:	Abstraction rules, subtype hierarchy.
Typical task types:	Abstraction occurs mainly in analytic tasks. In this book the inference is found in the assessment task template and is mentioned as a typical extension in diagnosis.
Used in templates:	Assessment.
Control behavior:	This inference typically may succeed more than once. Make sure to add any abstraction found to the data set to allow for chained abstraction.
Computational methods:	Forward reasoning with abstraction rules, generalization in a subtype hierarchy.
Remarks:	Although theoretically abstraction is reduction of information, in knowledge-engineering practice it is in effect an addition of information, because the system keeps the old data and uses the abstraction as additional information.

Assign

Operation:	This inference is concerned with a resource that is assigned to an actor, a unit, or similar "active" objects.
Example:	Assign a room to an employee.
Static knowledge:	This inference uses a mix of constraints and preferences.
Typical task types:	The inference is rather specific for synthetic tasks; it is hard to think of an example of assignment in an analytic task.
Used in templates:	Assignment, scheduling.
Control behavior:	This inference may fail. It also can produce more than one solution from the same input (e.g., room assignments with the same preferences).
Computational methods:	In simple cases a rule-based approach can be chosen. More complex problems may require the use of constraint-satisfaction algorithms.
Remarks:	In some cases the "assign" inference comprises simply the computation of a formula. In such a case we advise you to use the inference compute instead. The inference assign is different from the task ASSIGNMENT. The latter is a task that comprises a number of different inferences, including the actual assignment (cf. the assignment task in the housing case study (see Chapter 10), in which the assignment turned out to be algorithmic).

Classify

Operation:	Associate an object description with a class it belongs to.
Example:	Classify a discrepancy as being "minor" or "major."
Static knowledge:	Class definitions, consisting of necessary and sufficient features. For example, a Grey Reinet apple should have a rusty surface (a necessary condition).
Typical task types:	Although this inference is most common in analytic tasks, it can also be used in synthetic tasks, e.g., classifying a design to be of a certain type.
Used in templates:	Monitoring.
Control behavior:	This inference typically produces precisely one solution (cf. its use in the monitoring template).
Computational methods:	Mostly simple pattern matching.
Remarks:	When a classify inference comes up in an application, one should always ask oneself: is this a full knowledge-intensive task in its own right or is it just a simple inference? One can take this decision by looking at the domain knowledge. If the classification is a simple deduction from class definitions, then one can view it safely as an inference. This requires typically the presence of sufficient conditions for the classes. If this is not the case, the inference process is more complex, and one should consider modelling this as a separate task (and thus introduce a complete classification task template). Also, if the output can be a set of possible classes, it is likely this function needs to be specified as a task in its own right.

Compare

Operation:	Input is two objects. The inference returns `equal` if the two objects are the same. If this is not the case, the inference returns either `not-equal` (in case of two symbols) or some numerical value, indicating the difference.
Example:	Comparison of two findings: the one predicted by the system and the one actually observed.
Static knowledge:	In simple cases, no domain knowledge is required, because the comparison is purely syntactic. In other cases, domain knowledge may need to come into play to make the comparison. For example, if the objects are characterized by numerical values, the domain knowledge could

provide knowledge about intervals within which two values are assumed to be equal.

Typical task types:	Mainly analytic tasks.
Used in templates:	Diagnosis (Chapter 5), monitoring.
Control behavior:	Produces precisely one solution.
Computational methods:	Often requires only simple techniques.

Cover

Operation:	Given some effect, derive a system state that could have caused it.
Example:	Cover complaints about a car to derive potential faults.
Static knowledge:	This inference uses some sort of behavioral model of the system being diagnosed. A causal network is the most common candidate.
Typical task types:	This inference is specific for diagnosis.
Used in templates:	Diagnosis.
Control behavior:	This inference produces multiple solutions for the same input.
Computational methods:	Abductive methods are used here. These can range from simple to complex, depending on the nature of the diagnostic method employed.
Remarks:	This is an example of a task-specific inference. Its use is much more restricted than, for example, the select inference.

Critique

Operation:	Given a proposed solution, generate one or more problems with it. The purpose is usually to find ways of improving the solution.
Example:	Critique the design of an elevator.
Static knowledge:	The knowledge used by this inference is usually domain-specific; there is hardly any general critiquing knowledge for design. Its character tends to be heuristic and context-dependent.
Typical task types:	This inference is found in synthetic tasks.
Used in templates:	Configuration design.
Control behavior:	In the configuration-design template, it succeeds precisely once. However, one can think of situations where multiple outputs can be generated for the same design.

Computational methods:	The computational methods tend to be domain-specific.
Remarks:	The critique inference is an important step in the propose-critique-modify methods for design described by Chandrasekaran (1990).

Evaluate

Operation:	Input is a set of data and a norm. Output is a truth value indicating whether or not the data set complies with the norm. If the evaluation always concerns the same norm, the norm can be omitted as a dynamic input role (cf. the scheduling template).
Example:	Evaluation of criteria in the housing case.
Static knowledge:	A norm is usually some symbol such as "enough money." The domain knowledge should indicate how the truth value can be derived from the data set. Requirements for norms can often be represented in a decision-table format.
Typical task types:	This inference is widely applicable.
Used in templates:	Assessment, scheduling.
Control behavior:	The inference produces precisely one solution for a particular data set.
Computational methods:	Backward reasoning, using the norm as the goal.

Generate

Operation:	Given some input about the system (system features, requirements), provide a possible solution.
Example:	Generate a possible rock class to which a rock sample may belong.
Static knowledge:	When used for analytic tasks: knowledge about all the possible solutions (the solutions are enumerable for analytic tasks). When used for synthetic tasks: system-composition knowledge, e.g., plan elements and possible ways of connecting these (in sequence, in parallel).
Typical task types:	This inference can be used in all kinds of tasks. The output therefore varies depending on the type of task in which it occurs. If used in diagnosis, generate produces a fault category that could explain the faulty behavior. If the inference is used in planning, it would produce a possible plan.
Used in templates:	Classification, synthesis.

Control behavior:	Can produce multiple solutions for the same input. Sometimes, this inference is defined as producing a set. In that case, the inference succeeds precisely one time, namely with the set of all possible solutions. This is a stylistic matter.
Computational methods:	In analytic tasks: simple look-up. In synthetic tasks: algorithm for computing all possible combinations.
Remarks:	This is a generic inference that occurs in many domains. The inference is typically associated with a "generate & test" approach, in which there is some "blind" generation of possible solutions to the problem. The inference cover can be seen as a specific form of generate.

Group

Operation:	Input is a set; output is a aggregate object containing two or more elements of the input set
Example:	Grouping of employees for joint assignment to an office.
Static knowledge:	Domain-specific knowledge about positive and negative preferences for grouping. For example, in the office-assignment application criteria may act as positive or negative preferences. A combination of a smoker and a non-smoker is a typical example of a high-priority conflict. Such strong conflicts are usually considered to be enough to rule out certain solutions. The preferences are often ordered, but the ordering scale varies.
Typical task types:	Mainly synthetic tasks.
Used in templates:	Assignment.
Control behavior:	Can provide multiple solutions.
Computational methods:	Constraint satisfaction; generate full combination space and then use negative and positive preferences for repeated subset filtering (Schreiber 1994).
Remarks:	In earlier descriptions of inference typologies the name "assemble" was used for a similar inference.

Match

Operation:	Given a set of inputs, see whether these together lead to a combined result.
Example:	Match the norms for which values have been established to see whether it leads to a decision.

Static knowledge:	Rules that indicate whether a combination of findings or results leads to some joint conclusion.
Typical task types:	Mainly confined to analytic tasks.
Used in templates:	Assessment.
Control behavior:	Inference fails or succeeds a single time.
Computational methods:	Forward reasoning.
Remarks:	This is a difficult one. The name "match" has several different meanings. We have opted here for a quite specific definition, without actually committing to one particular task.

Modify

Operation:	This inference takes a system description as both input and output. An optional input is the actual modification action that needs to be carried out.
Example:	Modifying the design of an elevator by upgrading the machine model.
Static knowledge:	Knowledge about the action: one-time action or repeatable action, e.g., upgrading a component or increasing a parameter value.
Typical task types:	Mostly synthetic tasks.
Used in templates:	Configuration design, scheduling.
Control behavior:	Delivers one output.
Computational methods:	Simple update.
Remarks:	It is possible to use this inference in diagnosis, e.g., in case of a reconfiguration test.

Operationalize

Operation:	Given some requirements for a system, transform these requirements into a format which can be used in a reasoning process.
Example:	Transform requirements like "fast computer" to parameter values such as "at least Pentium processor of 266 hertz."
Static knowledge:	This is a tricky step in a design process. Knowledge tends to be heuristic. The choices made here may need to be revisited during the design.
Typical task types:	Synthetic tasks.
Used in templates:	Configuration design, synthesis.

Control behavior:	It is preferable that this inference proposes several alternative operationalizations.
Computational methods:	Forward reasoning.
Remarks:	Most methods for synthetic tasks leave this step out, because it is difficult to automize. Yet, it is a crucial (if not the most crucial) step in artifact design.

Propose

Operation:	Generate a new element to be added to the design.
Example:	Propose a hard disk model for a PC configuration.
Static knowledge:	Dependencies between component choices; component preferences.
Typical task types:	Synthetic tasks.
Used in templates:	Configuration design.
Control behavior:	May succeed multiple times.
Computational methods:	Forward reasoning, preference algorithm.
Remarks:	This inference is in some ways similar to generate. Here, only part of the solution is generated. The inference may also use search-order knowledge to guide the order of proposals, although in that case it is worth considering moving it from an inference to a task, mainly because there is some form of interesting control inside the function.

Predict

Operation:	Given a description of a system, generate a prediction of the system state at some point in the future.
Example:	Predict the blood pressure of a patient.
Static knowledge:	Requires a model of the system behavior. This model will be either quantitative or qualitative
Typical task types:	At the moment, mainly analytic tasks. The inference is often used in model-based diagnosis.
Used in templates:	Diagnosis.
Control behavior:	One time.
Computational methods:	Qualitative reasoning, mathematical algorithm.
Remarks:	Prediction can be a knowledge-intensive task in its own right.

Select

Operation:	Input is a set or a list. Out is one element or a sub-set/sublist.
Example:	Select a diagnostic hypothesis from the disease differential.
Static knowledge:	Often, the domain knowledge provides selection criteria.
Typical task types:	Found in all tasks. Some synthetic tasks can be formulated almost completely as consisting of subset selection, namely when the design space is relatively small.
Used in templates:	All templates.
Control behavior:	Produces multiple solutions.
Computational methods:	Standard selection algorithms. If the selection is from a set, the inference should produce the output in a random order.
Remarks:	This is a very general and commonly used inference. The inference can range in complexity from a simple, trivial selection to the application of complex selection criteria. The select inference is often a good candidate for gradual refinement, e.g., start with random selection (no static knowledge role) and later on include selection knowledge to optimize reasoning behavior.

Sort

Operation:	Input is a set of elements. Output is a sorted list containing the same elements
Example:	Sorting a set of valid designs based on the preferences (e.g., cheapest first).
Static knowledge:	Comparison function that decides on the relative order of two elements.
Typical task types:	This inference is most frequently encountered in synthetic tasks, where it is used to apply preferences to a set of possible designs. It can also be used in analytic tasks, e.g., for ordering a set of hypotheses (e.g., by using knowledge about the *a priori* likelihood of the hypothesis).
Used in templates:	Synthesis.
Computational methods:	Use standard sorting methods.
Control behavior:	This inference succeeds precisely one time with one particular input.

Remarks:	The name of this inference has a very computational flavor, but it is in fact an effective way of describing certain expert reasoning patterns. Sorting is used by experts to structure the search space. The sorting knowledge is often some form of search-control knowledge. Sometimes, sorting is modelled as a repeated invocation of a knowledge-intensive select inference.

Specify

Operation:	This inference takes as input an object and produces as output a new object that in some way is associated with the input object.
Example:	Specify an observable for a hypothesis.
Static knowledge:	Domain-specific rules that make a direct association. These rules can be either heuristic or be based on a domain theory.
Typical task types:	This general inference occurs in many different tasks.
Used in templates:	Assessment, diagnosis, monitoring, configuration design, scheduling.
Control behavior:	Could fail and/or provide multiple solutions.
Computational methods:	Forward reasoning.
Remarks:	The inference is the "vaguest" one in this catalog. It is difficult to pinpoint its exact meaning. The output should be something "new." Still, the inference is used frequently.

Verify

Operation:	Input is a description of a system which is being tested. Output is a truth value, indicating whether the system has passed the test. An optional output is the name of a violation (only if the verification failed).
Example:	Verify the design of a computer.
Static knowledge:	For analytic tasks: knowledge indicating consistency of a hypothesis with a set of data. For synthetic tasks: internal and external constraints ("hard requirements").
Typical task types:	This inference can occur in any type of task. It is most often found in methods that apply a "generate & test" approach.
Used in templates:	Diagnosis, configuration design.
Control behavior:	The inference succeeds precisely once.
Computational methods:	Forward reasoning.

13.4   Task Knowledge

13.4.1   Organization-Specific Task Templates

Larger organizations will typically have a variety of knowledge-intensive applications. Often, there is quite some overlap between the task types of these applications. For example, a governmental body for handling several types of social benefit claims will typically have a range of assessment applications. Similarly, a company in the process industry may have multiple applications in which a production process needs to be designed.

In such situations it makes sense to start keeping a record of the tasks and methods used in each application. In such a way, one can build up an organization-specific set of task templates. The advantage of such a catalog is that the terminology can be tailored to the domain, and therefore the resulting templates are easier to understand for other people in the company or for newcomers. Initiating, developing, and maintaining such a catalog of organization-specific task templates are typically activities which should fall under the responsibility of the knowledge manager. In addition, there will often be a need to harmonize the domain schemas used by these applications.

13.4.2   The Notion of Problem-Solving Method

The default methods for task types described in Chapter 6 are similar to what is called a *problem-solving method* (PSM) in the research literature. The main difference between a task method in the knowledge model and a PSM is the fact that a PSM description is usually not yet directly linked to an application task. A task method is thus best seen as an *instantiation* of a PSM for a task. In current knowledge-engineering research PSMs are an important object of study, but in this book we do not discuss their full implications in depth (for more information see the bibliographical notes below).

PSMs offer both advantages and disadvantages when compared with task methods. The major advantage is that one can exploit the fact that in many task-specific methods the same patterns reoccur. For example, in many methods an "empirical-validation" pattern can be identified: some hypothesis is posed about the state of affairs in the world, this hypothesis is subsequently tested through some data-gathering method, and then the hypothesis is accepted or rejected based on the comparison between the hypothesis and actual observations. Most of the analytic task templates in Chapter 6 contain such a pattern. A PSM allows one to capture this pattern, without committing to task-specific jargon. A PSM has therefore in principle a higher reusability potential.

As usual, in the advantage also lies the disadvantage. Because a PSM is so general and does not commit to a particular task, its description tends to be abstract and difficult to understand. Therefore, PSMs may pose a usage problem in daily knowledge-engineering practice because people do not understand what a PSM may do. Another disadvantage is that the grain size of a PSM is usually smaller than that of a task template. A task template is in fact a package of methods tailored to a task type. This method-configuration process needs to be done by the knowledge engineer, if one decides to construct the task-knowledge specification from PSMs.

13.4.3   Multiple Methods for a Task

In Chapter 5 we assumed that the knowledge engineer chooses one particular method for realizing a certain task. The choice of a particular method for a task is fixed in the specification. For some applications this approach is too rigid. This is particularly true of systems developed in a changing or varying environment. One can think of a diagnostic system for which the data about the malfunctioning system are of varying quantity or grain size. In one environment the system may get detailed system data, and a model-based diagnosis method can be used. In another environment the data are just some global indicators, ruling out any detailed behavioral analysis. In the latter case a classification method might be called for.

One way of modelling this situation is to allow the definition of multiple task methods for a single task. In addition, one would need to specify a "decision" function for handling the method choice.

However, we recommend using a less complicated solution which avoids the introduction of new modelling constructs:

1. Introduce an intermediate "task-selection task."
2. In the control structure of the method for this task, specify one or more special inferences or transfer functions, the output of which enables in some way the selection of one of the methods.

Figure 13.10 shows a task-decomposition diagram for handling the problem mentioned above with this work-around. The example concerns the introduction of multiple "hypothesis generation" methods. The method GENERATION-STRATEGY has two subtasks and one transfer function of the obtain type. The idea is to ask an external agent (who that is is defined in the communication model) what the grain size is of the data. Based on this information, the system will opt for one of the two generation methods.

13.4.4   Combining Tasks: Strategic Knowledge

In Chapter 6 we saw that application tasks often consist of a number of task types. Table 6.3 lists typical task combinations. But in Chapter 5 we suggested that a knowledge model concerns one particular knowledge-intensive task. The question therefore arises: how can we combine several task types and define how these together solve the application task?

We can use a similar work-around as mentioned for the problem of multiple methods: defining the application task as a supertask of the tasks corresponding to one task type.

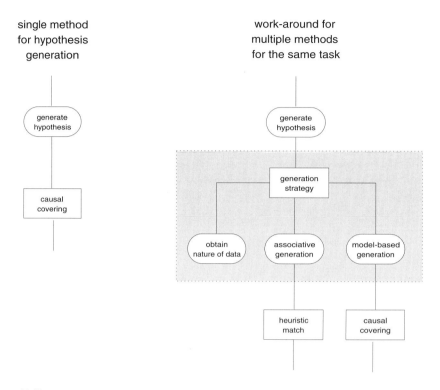

Figure 13.10
Example for the work-around when you want to be able to handle multiple methods for a task. A separate decision task is used as an "in-between." The example concerns the introduction of multiple "hypothesis generation" methods. The method "generation-strategy" has two subtasks and one transfer function of the "obtain" type. The idea is to ask an external agent (who that is, is defined in the communication model) what the grain size is of the data. Based on this information, the system will opt for one of the two generation methods.

The task method of this supertask then defines how the tasks need to be combined to solve the overall problem.

This approach works. However, you will sometimes find it is not optimal. You may discover that the reasoning process about how to combine tasks is a full knowledge-intensive task in its own right. It is a task with a metalevel flavor. Reasoning about combining tasks to achieve a goal is called "strategic reasoning." The reader is referred to the literature for references to work on strategic reasoning. Dynamic method configuration can also be seen as strategic reasoning. This is certainly an area for further development.

13.5 Bibliographical Notes and Further Reading

The work of Gruber (1993, 1994) provides a good introduction to ontology research. Also, two special issues of the International Journal of Human-Computer Studies (Guarino 1995, Gaines 1997) provide useful sources of information.

Catalogs of inferences have been proposed at a number of places. The first KADS project published a generic set of inferences (Breuker et al. 1987). In the context of the work on Role-Limiting Methods, work on a catalog of "mechanisms" has been undertaken (Klinker et al. 1991). The notion of "mechanism" is similar to that of inference. As mentioned in this chapter, Aben (1995) gives a good overview of formal methods for inference characterization.

A recent special issue of the International Journal of Human-Computer Studies (Benjamins and Fensel 1998) gives a good overview of work on problem-solving methods. The use of multiple methods was already part of early work on the Components of Expertise approach to knowledge modelling (Vanwelkenhuysen and Rademakers 1990). "Strategic knowledge" was viewed as a fourth knowledge category in early versions of KADS, in addition to task, inference and domain knowledge. Work in the context of the REFLECT project (van Harmelen et al. 1992) approached strategic reasoning as a separate knowledge-intensive task, which reasons at a metalevel. This work has recently been followed up in work on dynamic method selection and configuration (ten Teije et al. 1998).

UML Notations Used in CommonKADS

Key points of this chapter:

- UML is a set of standard notations for methodology developers, originated from an object-oriented viewpoint.
- The UML subset used within CommonKADS comprises activity diagrams, state diagrams, class diagrams (in adapted form) and, to a lesser extent, use-case diagrams.
- This chapter provides background information on these four UML notations.
- The chapter can be used as a reference each time a notation is used in a previous chapter.

14.1 UML Background

During the 1990s a number of object-oriented analysis approaches have become popular, particularly the methods of Booch (1994), Rumbaugh et al. (1991), and Jacobson et al. (1992). Although there were many commonalities, there were also many differences in both coverage and notation used. This led leading researchers in this field to work on a joint notation for O-O analysis and design models. The idea was to set a standard for object-oriented analysis and design. The result is the UML notation, which has already gone through a number of versions. UML stands for "Unified Modelling Language" (not "Universal," which would have been a bit presumptuous).

UML has received worldwide attention. It is being supported by a large number of companies in the software industry. It is important to realize that UML is in itself *not* a methodology. For example, UML does not provide a life cycle of software-development activities. UML can best be viewed as a proposal for a set of standard notations that have turned out to be useful in software modelling and design. The UML notations should typically be imported into software development methodologies. An example of such a methodology is Catalysis (D'Souza and Wills 1998), which uses a subset of the UML analysis notations.

CommonKADS follows a similar approach. In this chapter we describe the UML notations used within CommonKADS. These notations have already been mentioned at various places in this book:

1. Activity diagram
2. State diagram
3. Class diagram
4. Use-case diagram

For each diagram we describe the basic elements, their notation, and for what purposes the diagram can be used within CommonKADS. We have not striven for a full coverage of the UML diagrams. In particular, some detailed notations for class diagrams have been left out.

This chapter has been written as a reference text for the UML notations. For this reason we have made the text more or less self-contained, and therefore the description of the class diagram overlaps at some points with the domain-schema description in Chapter 5. The glossary at the end of this book provides a quick reference to the UML notations used.

14.2   Activity Diagram

14.2.1   Purpose

An activity diagram models the control flow and information flow of a procedure or process. Activity diagrams are best used if the procedure is not, or only to a limited extent, influenced by external events. This means that the control flow should be largely synchronous. If external events dominate and create asynchronous control, a state diagram is a more appropriate modelling technique.

Activity diagrams can be used at various levels of abstraction. For example, one can use an activity diagram to model the main tasks or activities in a business process. Alternatively, they can be used to model an algorithm.

Activity diagrams are a useful diagramming technique in the context of CommonKADS. Two model components are most likely to benefit from this notation:

1. Modelling the organization process (worksheet OM-2)   Activity diagrams are well suited for modelling the business process at a high level of abstraction. The notation is flexible because it can model both control flow and information flow, and also the "location" where the process takes place. The business process drawn up for the housing case (see Figure 10.2 in Chapter 10) is a good example of the use of an activity diagram.

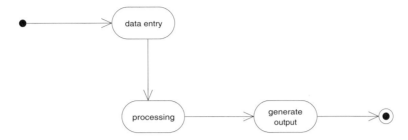

Figure 14.1
Notation for activity states and activity-state transitions.

2. Modelling the control structure of a task method   In CommonKADS it is common practice to use a form of limited pseudocode to model the control and information flow within a method. This is done in the control structure of a task method. The activity diagram provides an alternative graphical notation for describing this control structure. An example of using activity diagrams for method control modelling is given in Figure 5.24. This activity diagram models the control flow described for the simple diagnostic method diagnose-through-generate-and-test (see the car-diagnosis example in Chapter 5).

14.2.2 Activity States and State Transitions

The basic ingredient of an activity diagram is an *activity state*. An activity state is a state in which some work (activity, task) is carried out. The state terminates when the work is finished. This is the main difference with states in a state diagram: these typically terminate when certain (external) events take place. An activity is modelled graphically as a rounded box. The name of the activity state should be indicative of the activity or task being carried out in the state. Examples of activity states are shown in Figure 14.1.

After termination an activity state can lead to another activity state. This is modelled through an activity-state transition. The graphical notation is a solid line with an open arrow. Two special circular symbols are used to model the start and stop states of the procedure. If no stop state is present, the process is cyclic (e.g., an indefinite loop).

14.2.3 Decision

State transitions are not always deterministic. It may be the case that control is transferred to one state or another depending on the outcome of the previous state. We can model this selection process with a *decision*. Figure 14.2 shows an example decision.

A decision has an incoming state transition and two or more outgoing state transitions. A condition (or "guard") on the outgoing arrow defines the situations in which this

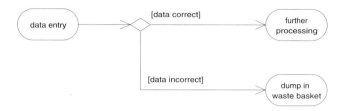

Figure 14.2
Notation for a decision.

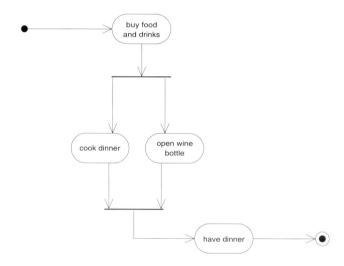

Figure 14.3
Notation for concurrent activity states.

branch is taken. The data involved in the condition should involve some piece of internal information.

14.2.4   Concurrency

In some cases activity states can be active in parallel. This type of concurrent activity can be specified with the split/join notation for control. An example is shown in Figure 14.3.

The horizontal bar is used for splitting and joining control threads. In the example of Figure 14.3 we see four activity states related to having a dinner. We see that the activities of cooking dinner and choosing and opening an appropriate bottle of wine can be carried

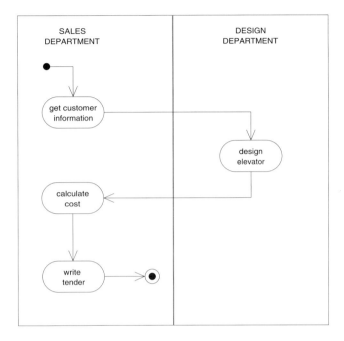

Figure 14.4
Notation for swim lanes in an activity diagram. The example concerns part of a business process of a company selling elevators.

out in parallel. Only when both activities have been completed successfully can we enjoy our dinner.

14.2.5   Swim Lanes

In modelling a process in an organization it is sometimes useful to split the process into a number of areas. For example, when we want to model the process within a library it could be useful to separate the subprocesses concerning lenders from those in which the library staff is involved. For this purpose "swim lanes" are used in activity diagrams. Swim lanes are simply represented as rectangular boxes in which activity states are placed that belong to a particular subprocess. The agent or organizational unit to which the subprocesses belong is placed as a text label at the top of the box. State transitions can cross box borders. One activity state always belongs to one swim lane.

Figure 14.4 shows an activity diagram in which two swim lanes are used to model part of the business process of a company selling elevators. The first swim lane describes

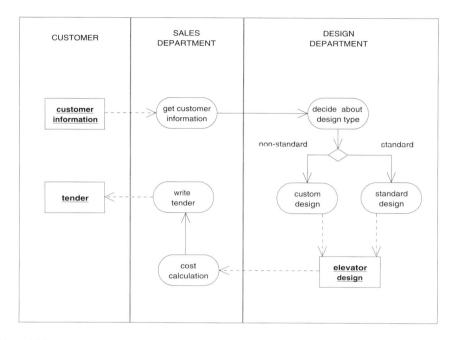

Figure 14.5
Notation for object flow. Object flows are attached to transitions between activity states. The flow itself is shown
as a dashed line extending from or leading to a state transition.

activities related to the sales department of the company; the second swim lane concerns
the design department of the company.

14.2.6   Object Input/Output

Modelling information input/output is not required in activity diagrams, but it is often
useful to include this type of information. Because UML does not support (unlike its
predecessor OMT) the traditional data-flow diagram (DFD) notation, this is in fact the
only way in UML to show data dependencies between related processes.

Figure 14.5 shows the notation for object flows. It was already included in Chapter 3,
but is repeated here for convenience. This figure is a refined representation of the process
modelled in Figure 14.4. We added an additional swim lane for the customer and included
the major information objects involved in the process.

As we see, object flows are attached to transitions between activity states. The flow
itself is shown as a dashed line extending from or leading to a state transition. The notation
:class-name stands for an anonymous object of the specified class (for details see the

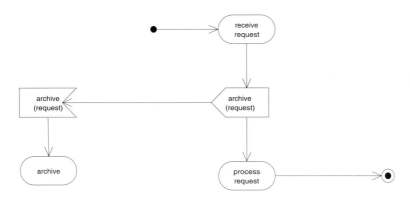

Figure 14.6
Sending and receiving signals in an activity diagram. Signals typically introduce the notion of external control into an activity diagram.

section on class diagrams). It is common in activity diagrams to add an additional status label to an object (such as "entered" or "placed") if the object occurs more than once in an activity diagram. An object flow starting from a transition indicates that the object is created as a result of the activity state. An example is the object **:tender**, which is created as a result of the **write tender** activity. If one attaches an object input flow to a state transition (e.g., **:customer-information** in Figure 14.5) this means that the transition is dependent on the existence of this object.

If the transition from one activity state to another is completely determined by the production of a certain object, the state transition can be replaced by introducing the object as an intermediate input-output flow between two activity states. An example of this is the placement of the **:elevator-design** object between two activities in Figure 14.5.

14.2.7   Signals

Activity diagrams typically show control within a certain process or procedure, without any limitations posed by the "outside world" (which is effectively everything outside the scope of the activity diagram). Interaction with the external world can be included in an activity diagram through the use of *signals*.

UML distinguishes two kinds of signals: *sending* signals and *receiving* signals. A sending signal is shown as a side effect of an activity-state transition. The notion used for a sending signal is a convex hexagon; for a receiving signal it is a concave hexagon (see Figure 14.6). Signals come in pairs: sending signals should have receiving counterparts. If in the transition from one activity state to another a signal is sent or received, this is shown through two sequential state-transition lines. The intended meaning is that there is in fact a direct transition between the two states with the signal as an explicit side effect of the transition.

Signals are a way of showing how events influence the control of a process. If extensive use is made of signals, then consider changing the diagram format into a state diagram. State diagrams are the prime modelling method if external events govern process control.

14.3   State Diagram

14.3.1   Purpose

A state diagram is a technique which helps to model the dynamic behavior of a system that is influenced by external events. The UML state-diagram notation is used in the communication model to specify the communication plan control. In addition, state diagrams can be used in the task model to describe task control, in particular asynchronous control.

14.3.2   State

A *state* models the state a system is in *over a period of time*. In object-oriented analysis one usually assumes that a state is always a state of some object class. Not all objects have "interesting" states. A good guideline is to develop state diagrams for all object classes with significant dynamic behavior.

During a state activities and actions can be performed. An *activity* takes time, and can be interrupted by events that cause a state transition. An *action*, on the other hand, is assumed to be instantaneous from our modelling point of view. Actions, in contrast to activities, cannot be interrupted. Within states we can define three types of actions:

1. *entry* actions, which are always carried out when a state is entered;
2. *exit* actions, which are done whenever the state is terminated;
3. event-based actions: some event occurs which does not trigger a state transition, but only the execution of an action. An example is the `insert(coin)` event in Figure 14.9.

Figure 14.7 shows the UML notation for states: a rectangle with rounded corners. The first compartment contains the state name. This name should typically be a verbal form that indicates a time duration (usually ending with "-ing" such as "waiting" or "checking"). The second compartment contains any state variable you may want to introduce. A timer is a frequently encountered state variable in state diagrams. The third compartment contains the actions and activities connected to the state. The following syntax is used:

```
entry    / <action>
<event>  / <action>
do       / <activity>
exit     / <action>
```

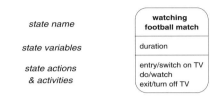

Figure 14.7
Notation for a state.

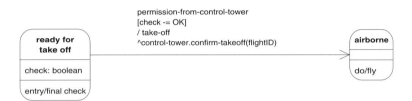

Figure 14.8
Notation for a state transition. The state diagram describes an airplane departing from an airport.

14.3.3   State Transition

Over time, system objects can go from one state to another. This is modelled with a *state transition* link between states. The nature of the state transition can be described with a textual annotation of the transition. The syntax of this text string is:

```
<event> [ <guard> ] / <action> ^send-message(<class>)
```

An *event* causes a state transition to occur. If no event is specified, the state transition occurs once the activities carried out within the state are completed. A state without outgoing events is thus the same as an activity state in an activity diagram. Events come from "outside the diagram," e.g., from other objects or from external agents.

A *guard* is a condition on the transition. Only if this condition is true, does the transition take place. Guards typically refer to state variables and represent different outcomes of processing performed within a state.

An *action* is some process that always occurs when the state transition takes place. If all actions going out of a state have the same associated action, this action can also be placed as an exit action within this state (see earlier). Vice versa, if all incoming actions

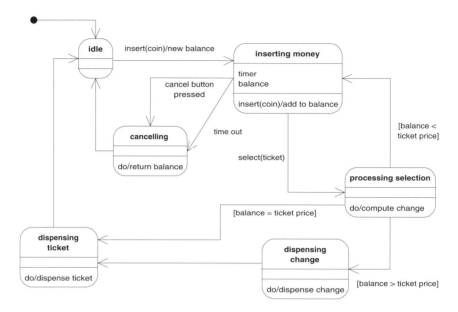

Figure 14.9
State diagram for a ticket machine.

into a state have the same associated action, the action can be placed as an entry action in this state.

Finally, the *send-message* clause sends a message to some other object. Such a message will be received by the other object as an event. A send-event pair in a state diagram is the same as a sending-receiving signal pair in an activity diagram.

An example of a state transition with a label containing all four ingredients is shown in Figure 14.8. The transition from the state **ready-for-takeoff** to the state **airborne** occurs when permission is received from the control tower (an event), under the condition that the final instrument check is OK (a guard). The action **takeoff** is executed when the transition occurs. The transition has the side effect of sending a message to the control tower confirming the takeoff.

Similar to activity diagrams, state diagrams can contain start and stop states. The same symbols are used in both diagrams. State diagrams model possible behavioral states of an object of a certain class. As an example, a state diagram of a simple ticket machine is shown in Figure 14.9.

The initial state is the **idle** state. There is no stop state. The process is modelled as a cycle. A new cycle starts when a coin is inserted. This leads to a state in which more coins can be inserted and in which one can select a particular ticket type. Once a ticket type is selected the system goes into a state in which the transaction requested is checked. There are three possible outcomes of this **processing selection** state, which are all represented as guards. Based on the outcome the system will proceed with dispensing the ticket (and possibly some change) or return to the **inserting money** state. If the customer presses the cancel button, the system returns the balance. The same happens if no action is performed by the customer during a certain time period. Note that the states in the lower part of the diagram have no outgoing events. This means that the state transitions take place automatically once the work to be done (see the "do" activity) is completed.

14.3.4   Aggregate States and Substates

UML state diagrams have facilities for defining both aggregate states and generalized states. In the first case the aggregate stands for a set of concurrent substates. In case of a generalized state the system is in one of the possible substates.

The official UML notation prescribes that substates are placed within the box of the aggregate state or superstate (consult the glossary or a UML textbook for details). In practice, we mainly use concurrent states without an explicit name for the aggregate state, and for this type of concurrency one can use the same notation as used in the activity diagram: a horizontal bar. Figure 14.10 shows an example of two concurrent states. The diagram models a cash machine in which card and cash are ejected in parallel (some cash machines do this in sequence).

Concurrency is an important feature of object-oriented models. In practice, it also has become more important because the current generation of programming languages (Java, Ada) has built-in constructs for concurrency. This makes the implementation of concurrent processes much more feasible than it used to be.

14.4   Class Diagram

14.4.1   Purpose

The purpose of a class diagram is to describe the static information structure of the application domain. The class diagram is in fact an extension of traditional entity-relationship modelling. The extensions reflect the increasing requirements that are placed on the expressivity of information models.

The diagram is part of the system analysis process and therefore should be phrased in domain terminology. The analyst should take care to avoid any commitment toward design details. The class diagram notation is the richest UML notation. Here, we only discuss the core elements of the class-diagram notation.

The graphical notation for a domain schema in the knowledge model (see Chapter 5) is based on the UML class-diagram notations. There are three differences between a domain schema and a class diagram:

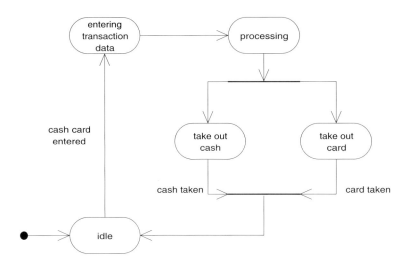

Figure 14.10
Notation for state concurrency. The diagram models a cash machine in which card and cash are ejected in parallel.

1. In CommonKADS the specification of information structure is decoupled from the specification of processes. Therefore, CommonKADS classes (i.e., concepts) do not specify operations (see further). This implies that we leave the third compartment empty, or omit it altogether.
2. In a domain schema we introduce one additional notation for modelling knowledge structures, namely the "rule type". This is a typical extension needed from the perspective of knowledge-intensive applications.
3. Finally, there are two terminological differences:

   a. "classes" in UML are called "concepts" in the domain schema;
   b. "associations" in UML are termed "relations" in the domain schema.

   These terminological differences have a historical background. In fact, it should not be a real problem. You can use "concept" for a class without operations. You can use relation and association interchangeably, because it cannot give rise to ambiguities.

   Taking these differences into account, class-diagram notations can be used freely in a CommonKADS knowledge model. The class diagram can also used in the task model to describe the general information types involved in a certain task or business process.

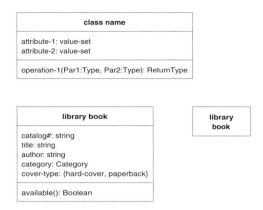

Figure 14.11
Notation for classes.

14.4.2   Class

Classes are the central objects in class diagrams. Classes represent groups of objects in the application domain that share a similar information structure. Classes are shown as boxes with three compartments:

1. The top compartment contains the name of the class (in boldface type). This name should be as precise as possible. Choosing the right names is an important skill for an analyst.
2. The middle compartment contains a specification of the attributes of the class. An *attribute* is some simple piece of information that is common to all objects belonging to a class. For each attribute a value set is specified, indicating the range of possible values of the attribute.
3. The lower compartment specifies operations that can be carried out on objects of the class. Operations may have parameters and a return type, but neither is necessary. The ID of the object is always implicitly assumed to be a parameter, and need not be listed explicitly. The syntax for the specification of operations is as follows:

$$\text{operation-name}(\text{parameter : type} <, \text{more parameters} >) : \text{return-type}$$

Figure 14.11 summarizes the graphical notation for classes. We usually assume a number of predefined value types that can be used in the attribute compartment and as parameter types:

- *string*: list of printable characters, started and ended with a double quote
- *number*: any numeric value

General notation for association

Notation for a binary association

Figure 14.12
Notation for an association. The diamond notation is the general one. The diamond symbol can be omitted in case of a binary association.

- *integer*: value belongs to the subset of integer numbers
- *boolean*: value is either "true" or "false"
- *date*: value is some calendar date
- *universal*: any value is allowed

You can also define your own value set. Enumeration types are most frequent (see the "{hard-cover, paperback}" example for the attribute **cover-type** of class **library-book** in Figure 14.11).

14.4.3 Association

An *association* defines a relationship between classes. In a way, an association is similar to an attribute: it can be used to define a characteristic of an object in a class. Loosely speaking, associations are attributes whose values refer not to atomic values but to other objects.

A typical example of an association is a **married-to** relation between a woman and a man. This sample association is shown in Figure 14.12. In the general notation for associations a diamond symbol is introduced and linked with the object classes to be associated. The diamond symbol can be omitted if it concerns a binary association. A binary association is an association in which two object classes are involved. In that case, a direct line can be drawn between the object classes involved in the association. The object classes participating in the association are called "arguments" of the association. A number of features can be specified for an association:

- **Direction** Names of an association may indicate a certain direction. For example, the association **owned-by** between a car and a person is directional: it can only be read as "car X is owned by person Y." The **married-to** association on the other hand does not imply a direction. Directionality of an association is indicated by carets attached to the association name[1] (see the associations in Figure 14.13). A direction only makes sense for binary relations.
- **Cardinality** The cardinality indicates the number of times an object of an argument class can participate in the association. This is also called "multiplicity." Cardinality is specified as a textual annotation along the association line close to the argument type it refers to. In the case of the **married-to** association the cardinality is in both directions "0–1" meaning that both a man and a woman can have zero or one **married-to** associations, which is more or less consistent with the Western view of marriages (always be aware of the context in which your models are valid). If no cardinality is specified, the default cardinality of "precisely one" is assumed. It is a good modelling guideline to challenge any "precisely one" association. Figure 14.13 shows some additional examples of cardinality specification. Central is the **student** object class. The diagram defines that a particular student can be enrolled in any number of courses, has precisely one major subject, should have at least one address, and may optionally be married.
- **Argument role** When we specify an association, it can be useful to specify the *role* played by objects in the association. The **married-to** association provides a clear example of roles: "husband" and "wife" are roles played by the **man** and **wife** objects in this association. The roles "employer" and "employee" in the **works-for** association in Figure 14.15 (see further) are also examples of argument roles.

14.4.4 Association Class

An interesting feature of associations is that they can have attributes of their own. For example, the wedding date is an attribute of the **married-to** association. It turns out that in many cases it is useful to treat associations as information objects in their own right. Associations act in many applications as kinds of structured, complex objects, for which one can define attributes, operations, and all the other stuff connected to object classes. In UML this can be achieved by defining an *association class*.

The graphical notation for an association class is shown in Figure 14.14. The association name is placed in a class box. This class box is linked with a dashed line to the

---

[1]In the knowledge model we used an arrow to model directionality, which is a small deviation from the UML standard. Choose the one you are comfortable with.

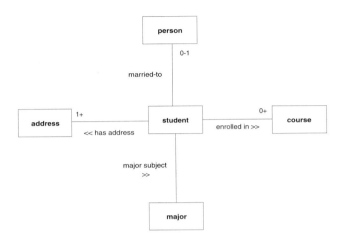

Figure 14.13
Examples of different types of cardinality in associations defined for a "student" object class.

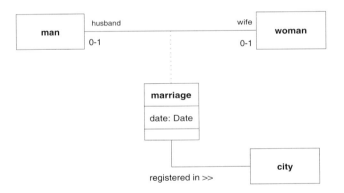

Figure 14.14
Notation for an association class.

association. The analyst is free to add attributes, methods and the like to the association class. In fact, from a modelling point of view there is no limitation on association classes when compared to "normal" classes. Association classes are an important abstraction mechanism in modelling applications and occur in almost every model with a certain degree of complexity.

   The need for an association class arises in the case where attributes cannot be placed in one of the association arguments. In the example in Figure 14.15 the attributes **salary**

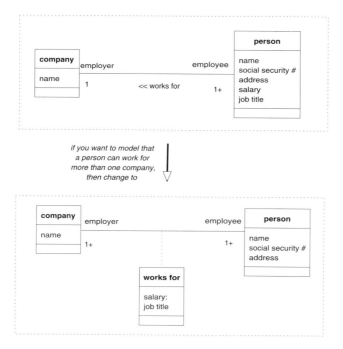

Figure 14.15
The need for an association class arises if attributes cannot be placed in one of the association arguments. In this example the attributes "salary" and "job title" can only be placed in the "person" object if we assume that a person works for just one company (this should be the intended meaning of the upper diagram). If this is not true, we have to create an association class and move the attributes to this class (cf. the lower diagram).

and **job-title** can only be placed in the **person** object if we assume that a person works for only one company. If this is not true we have to create an association class, and move the attributes to this class. Some analysts would actually say that the association class is the preferred modelling method in both cases, because it captures the domain structure better.

14.4.5 Generalization

Generalization is one of the most common constructs in class diagrams. With generalization we can build class hierarchies. We usually assume inheritance of object-class characteristics (attributes, operations, and associations) from superclasses to subclasses.

Figure 14.16 shows the notation for generalization: an open triangular arrow. In this example the association **executer-of** is inherited by all subclasses of **agent**. In Figure 14.17 you find a second example of generalization concerning paragraph types in a document.

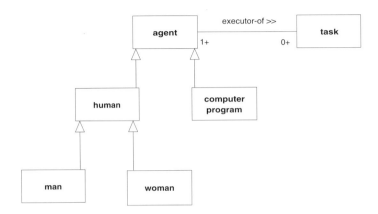

Figure 14.16
Notation for generalization. In this example the association "executor-of" is also defined for all subclasses of agent.

We see here that object attributes are specified as high as possible in the class hierarchy. By specifying an object characteristic at the right level of abstraction, we achieve parsimony and avoid information redundancy.

In many applications it turns out that one single hierarchy is too limitative to capture adequately the information structure in the domain. Therefore, UML offers a number of advanced techniques for generalization, including multiple inheritance and the specification of multiple hierarchies along different dimensions. These issues are treated in more depth in Chapter 13.

14.4.6   Aggregation

An aggregation can best be viewed as a predefined binary association in which one argument plays the role of "aggregate" or "whole," and the other argument constitutes the "part." Part-whole relations occur in many domains. These relations can be used to model both physical as well as conceptual aggregates. An example of an aggregation is shown in Figure 14.18.

The notation used is that of a line with a diamond symbol attached to the "whole" side of the association. Like any other association, cardinality can be specified for an aggregation relation. In the case of the audio system shown in Figure 14.18 we see that the system should have an amplifier, may have either two or four speakers, and optionally includes a set of headphones.

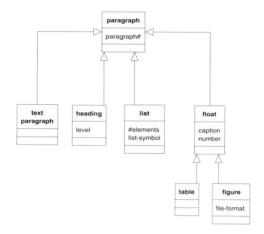

Figure 14.17
Subclasses of paragraph in a document. Attributes of the superclass are being inherited by the subclass, meaning that all paragraphs have a paragraph number. For some subclasses new attributes are being introduced.

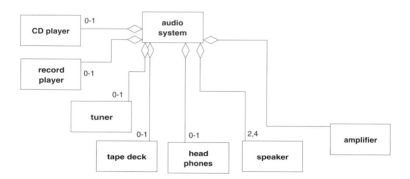

Figure 14.18
Notation for aggregation. The example concerns an old-fashioned audio system consisting of a number of different components.

Figure 14.19
Notation for composition.

Composition   Composition is a strong form of aggregation. If we define an aggregation as being a composition, we state that the "part" cannot exist without the aggregate. If the aggregate is deleted, all parts cease to exist. The graphical notation used to denote a composition is a black aggregation symbol. An example of composition is shown in Figure 14.19. A document is composed of an arbitrary number of paragraphs. Paragraphs derive their existence from being part of a document and cannot "live" as separate entities.

Note that composition is typically a viewpoint from an application. Whether paragraphs "really" cease to exist after deletion of a document they are part of is a matter of viewpoint. The discipline of "mereology" (the science of the part-whole relations) has a lot to say about this topic, but this falls outside the scope of the present work.

Combined generalization and aggregation   In practice, analysts often use a combination of aggregation and generalization to model complex objects. Figure 14.20 shows an example of the combined use of these techniques. The figure is a refinement of Figure 14.18. In the combined figure we can specify that at least one of the four input systems for sound carriers needs to be a part of the audio system, a fact that was difficult to express in Figure 14.18.

14.4.7   Object

Objects of a certain class are sometimes useful to include in class diagrams[2]. The notation used is shown in Figure 14.21. The object name is bold underlined and followed by a colon and the name of the class it belongs to. One can also define an anonymous object by just writing **:class-name** in the object box. The object notation is also used in other diagrams, such as the activity diagram.

---

[2]Strictly speaking, these diagrams are called object diagrams.

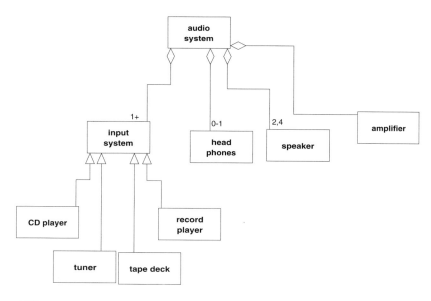

Figure 14.20
Combining aggregation and generalization often provides an elegant modelling method. In this figure we can show that at least one of the four input systems for sound carriers needs to be a part of the audio system.

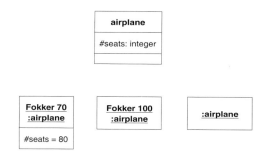

Figure 14.21
Notation for class objects.

Figure 14.22
Notation for use cases. Left: General notation for use cases and system. Right: Use cases in a library system.

14.5   Use-Case Diagram

14.5.1   Purpose

Use-case diagrams are typically used in the early phases of system development. The diagrams show what kind of services a customer and/or user can expect from the system to be developed. Therefore, use-case diagrams are mainly a tool for the initial requirement-engineering phase. The diagrams describe the system functionality from the outsider's point of view. It is useful as a communication vehicle between the developer and the customer.

The diagram fits well with the agent model (see Chapter 3), where it can be used as a summary of agent interactions with the prospective system. Use-case diagrams can also be used as a technique to present the proposed solution to the customer or to other stakeholders.

14.5.2   Use Case

A *use case* is a service provided by a system[3]. The system can be a software system or some other system in the world. Use cases interact with actors (see further) who are not part of the system. A use case is shown graphically as an ellipse with the name of the use case as a label. A use case is always placed in a rectangular box denoting a particular

---

[3]Our advice for people having problems with understanding the term "use case" (like ourselves): replace it in your mind with "service."

Example actors:

actor   lender   librarian

Figure 14.23
Notation for actors.

system. The name of the system is written in the upper part of the box. Figure 14.22 shows examples of the notation.

14.5.3   Actor

Actors are agents (i.e., humans or computer programs) that interact with the system. An actor makes use of services provided by the system or provides information for system services. Actors are defined at the "class" level, meaning that an actor stands for a group of actor objects. In a library system example actors would be "lender" and "librarian," but not individual lenders or librarians. Figure 14.23 shows the UML notation for actors. The name of the actor class is placed at the bottom of the actor icon.

14.5.4   Relationships

The most common relationship in use-case diagrams is the *interaction* relation between an actor and a use case. This is shown as a simple solid line between an actor and a use case. There can be many-to-many relations between actors and use cases.

Figure 14.24 shows an example of a use-case diagram for the library system. In this case the actors are human agents. Typically, actors should be seen as roles played in an application setting. One human could play multiple roles, and thus take the form of multiple actors.

In addition, the analyst can define generalization relationships. Generalization is treated in more detail in the section on the class diagram. In use-case diagrams the same notation is used (an open triangle arrow). A generalization can be defined between actors as well as between use cases. The latter is the most common form. In the case study in Section 14.7 we see an example of use-case generalization (cf. Figure 14.27).

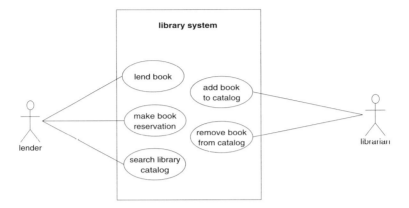

Figure 14.24
Notation for a use-case diagram.

14.6   General UML constructs

Apart from the various sets of diagrammatic notations, UML also has a number of general-purpose notations. Here we mention two of these: *stereotype* and *annotation*.

14.6.1   Stereotypes

Stereotypes are a built-in extendibility mechanism of UML. A stereotype allows the user to define a new metatype. The standard metatypes of UML are the basic constructs like *class* and *association*. Sometimes, we like to distinguish certain subsets of classes, activity states, and so on. For example, if we use activity states to model a business process, we may want to distinguish between primary and secondary processes (see, e.g., Figure 10.2). We can achieve this by introducing stereotypes. Figure 14.25 shows the notation used for stereotypes[4]. The name of a stereotype is placed above the construct involved (activity state, class, ...), enclosed in two angle brackets from each side.

Stereotypes can loosely be viewed as kinds of supertypes. They are particularly helpful in increasing the readability of UML diagrams.

14.6.2   Annotations

The UML constructs are meant to convey the maximum amount of useful information for a particular purpose (e.g., expressing the static information structure for class-diagram

---

[4]We use two angle brackets for indicating stereotypes. The official notation is to use *guillemets*, but this is not supported by many word-processing systems. The two angle brackets are a reasonable approximation.

Figure 14.25
Notation for stereotypes.

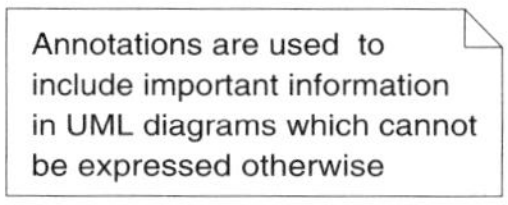

Figure 14.26
A UML annotation.

constructs). However, sometimes we feel the need to include some additional piece of information, which is not easily modelled with a predefined notational construct. For such a situation UML uses a general *annotation* construct. The graphical form is shown in Figure 14.26. Annotations can be included in every UML diagram. They do not have any formal status.

14.7 A Small Case Study

14.7.1 Problem Statement

A university department offers about thirty courses for students. Most of the students are following the major program offered by the department. In addition, students from other programs follow the courses (typically some 20%). Like many other departments, the department wants to have software for course enrollment, storing and retrieving exam results, and other administrative stuff related to courses and students. The prospective system has received the name "CAS" (for course administration support). It is the purpose of this case study to show how one can specify the data and functions for CAS, using the UML notations discussed earlier.

We have not striven in this case study for completeness. We use the case study mainly as a means of demonstrating the use of the four diagramming techniques.

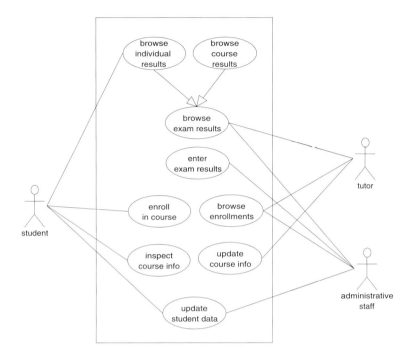

Figure 14.27
Use-case diagram for the CAS application.

14.7.2   Use-Case Model

In a use-case diagram we can express the services that are expected from the CAS system. First, we have to identify a number of actors that interact with the system. In this example we have limited the set of actors to `student`, `tutor`, and the `administrative staff` of the department.

The system is expected to provide the following services to these actors:

- **Personal student data**: A student can change his or her own personal data, such as home address and telephone number. The administrative staff should be able to do this as well.
- **Course information**: Students can access information about the courses that are being taught by the department. The tutors should be able to both access and update the course information.
- **Course enrollment**: Students can enroll in a course. Tutors and administrative staff should be able to look at the enrollment status of courses.

- **Exam results**: A student can get access to his personal exam results. The tutors and the administrative staff have access to all exam results. The exam results can only be entered by the administrative staff.

The use-case diagram in Figure 14.27 shows how these services can be represented as use cases with which actors interact. The use cases at the top of the system box are an example of the use of a generalization relation between use cases. The use case `browse exam results` is a generalization of the browsing of results on an individual basis (this is a service for all three actors) and browsing of results per course (which is only allowed for tutors and administrative staff).

14.7.3   Class Diagram

In the class diagram in Figure 14.28 we have focused on the static information structure, and not paid attention (yet) to operations. This is typical of the early phases of analysis, as operations are often only added at a later stage.

In the class diagram we see the main object classes of this domain. The class **course** is a central entity. Courses have tutors. "Tutor" is a defined here as an association between a course and a **university staff member**. From the cardinality specification we can see that the staff members may teach any number of courses (including zero), and that courses have at least one tutor, but possibly more. Courses also can be related to other courses through the **requires** association. This can be used to define prerequisites for courses.

Students and courses can be related through the **enrollment** association. We see here a typical example of an association class. An enrollment is an information object in its own right. For example, we like to store data about the enrollment date. Also, we can link an enrollment object to the exam results of a student for a course. Note that the purpose of building a class diagram is to capture an adequate view of the domain information structure. If we would design a database scheme, other considerations come into play. That is, however, not our present concern.

The diagram is somewhat simplified for presentation purposes. For example, the student information is in reality more extensive.

14.7.4   Activity Diagram

Activity diagrams are useful when modelling procedures and processes within a system. An example in the CAS example is the enrollment procedure. An activity diagram for this procedure is shown in Figure 14.29.

The first activity in this diagram is concerned with entering the enrollment request. Once this piece of work is finished, two parallel "check" activities are started, namely (1) checking whether the student has fulfilled the course preconditions, and (2) checking whether the student limit for the course is not exceeded. Both activities are followed by a

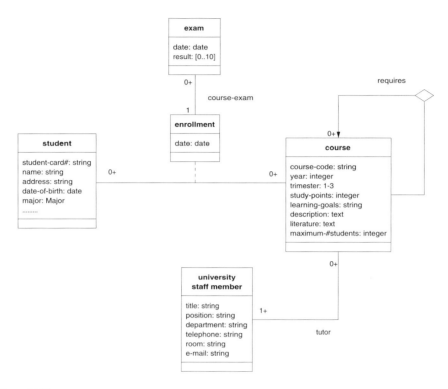

Figure 14.28
Class diagram for the CAS application.

decision point. Only if both checks are OK (see the horizontal bar for control joining) is the enrollment registered.

This enrollment is a typical process for activity modelling. The process is not governed by events from outside. If the latter is the case, it is better to use a state diagram.

14.7.5   State Diagram

The CAS system is basically a query system, and therefore from the information-processing point of view not really dominated by external events (for the user-interface side this may be different). Therefore, there is in this application not much need for state diagrams. We have included one state diagram for the "update student data" procedure. Student personal data are stored in a general university database. For this reason, the update service of the CAS system should first send a change request to the university database,

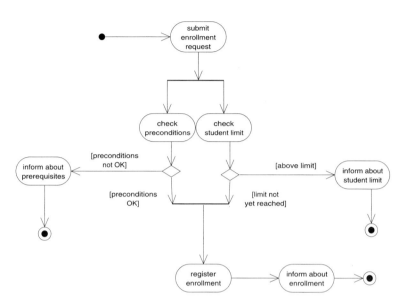

Figure 14.29
Activity diagram for course enrollment.

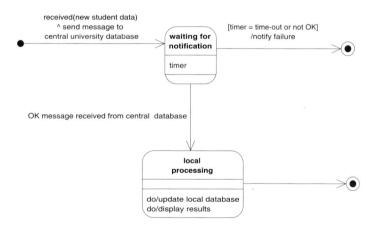

Figure 14.30
State diagram for updating personal student data.

and only change the local database if an acceptance answer is received. The corresponding state diagram is shown in Figure 14.30. We have included a state variable **timer** in the **waiting** state. If no answer is received from the university database within a certain time limit, the update process is cancelled.

This procedure could also have been modelled with an activity diagram in which two send/receive signals are placed. In case of a limited number of external events, the choice between the two types of diagrams is mainly a matter of personal preference.

14.8   Bibliographical Notes and Further Reading

Up-to-date information about UML and related subjects can be found via the website of the Rational Rose company:

```
http://www.rational.com
```

For a full UML overview the reader is referred to textbooks such as Booch et al. (1998) and Eriksson and Penker (1998).

15

Project Management

Key points of this chapter:

- Knowledge project management needs careful attention, but is otherwise based on straightforward principles rooted in common sense and systematic thinking.
- How to strike a balance between rigorous control and the need for adaptability and flexibility.
- How to decompose a project into manageable pieces: the concepts of project cycles and model states.
- How to carry out a risk analysis.
- How *not* to manage a knowledge-system project.

15.1 Control versus Flexibility: Striking the Balance

Software projects have the reputation of being difficult to control. Since much expert knowledge is tacit, this holds even more for knowledge-system projects. Notwithstanding this, there is a need for control, since projects are required to deliver expected results on time, within budget, and with prespecified quality. The question we discuss in this chapter is how one can achieve this, while at the same time knowledge projects often have something of a *learning* character, so that the structure of knowledge may turn out to deviate from what was anticipated, requirements may change in the process, and goals must accordingly be adjusted along the project route.

The classic way to control software projects is depicted in Figure 15.1. In software engineering it is known as the *waterfall* model, but it is an approach quite typical of many different areas of project management. The essential idea is to break down a project into a sequence of separate and prespecified phases, each phase resulting in its own distinct type of deliverables and associated documentation.

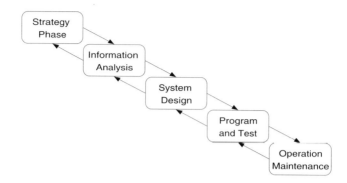

Figure 15.1
The classic "waterfall" life cycle for software engineering.

The strategy phase, for example, ends with a document outlining the results of a feasibility study, the project brief, i.e., the business goals the project is supposed to meet, and the project plan. The information analysis phase starts from here, and delivers a requirements document based on the structure, flow, and control of the information that is to be processed by the prospective system. Then the design stage turns this into a technical system specification of the architecture and software module structure in relation to the chosen software and hardware platform. Next, the system is programmed accordingly, integrated, and tested, after which it is handed over to the user organization. At this point, system development is completed, and the operational life of the system has started. From the software engineering point of view, the work done on the system is called maintenance, although in practice often many new requirements and new functionalities are introduced in the course of time. The system life cycle ends when it is phased out or decommissioned.

Thus, characteristic of the waterfall approach is its linear sequence of prefixed phases. The result of each phase has to be accepted and signed off by the customer. In project management terms, therefore, the end of each phase usually represents a milestone of the project at which a go/no-go decision is taken for the next phase. If one would carry out a knowledge system project according to the CommonKADS methodology, but within a waterfall framework, it would probably be phased as follows:

1. Scoping and feasibility study (organization model, Chapter 3);
2. Impact and improvement study (task and agent models, Chapter 3);
3. Knowledge analysis (knowledge model, Chapter 5);
4. Communication interface analysis (communication model, Chapter 9);
5. System design (design model, Chapter 11);
6. Knowledge-system implementation (Chapter 12).

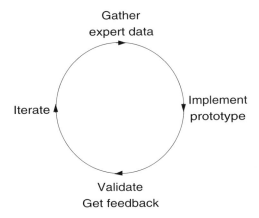

Figure 15.2
Rapid, evolutionary prototyping approach to software system development.

A strong advantage of the waterfall model is that it provides a very clear-cut handle for managerial control. However, practice has shown that it has a number of disadvantages as well:

- The early phases are mainly document-oriented, and visible and operational results in terms of software that can be tried out and judged by end users appear only rather late in the life cycle. Hence, it is sometimes difficult to see progress and to maintain the confidence in the project by stakeholders such as managers, clients and prospective users.
- Prefixed phases make changes during the project — owing to changed external circumstances, new insights gained from ongoing work in the project, changing needs and requirements — very difficult and costly. So, the waterfall model is very rigid. It is adequate for applications for which the road to go is clear well in advance, for example, yet another database or spreadsheet application that is based on many similar previous experiences within the organization. It does not work for advanced information systems or innovative projects where uncertainty or change plays a role. Therefore, it is also not very well suited for knowledge-intensive systems projects.

Other models for the software process have therefore been developed that produce useful results at an earlier stage and are more flexible in dealing with uncertainty and change. One such model, called an evolutionary or *prototyping* approach, is shown in Figure 15.2. It may be considered as the extreme opposite of the waterfall model: it aims to produce practical results quickly in a number of iterative improvements based on learning from the previous cycle. So it is highly adaptable and experimental. This is its strong

Figure 15.3
The spiral model for the software life cycle.

point as well as its weak spot: due to its lack of structure it is not really possible to come up with sound project goals and plans in advance. The prototyping approach has been en vogue for quite some time in the childhood years of expert systems, but experience has shown that it is hard to keep managerial control over such projects. Rather than being planned and controlled, they emerge and unfold organically over time. But, as with the waterfall approach, this is not what you really want for projects that aim at industry-quality knowledge systems. Neither extreme rigidity nor extreme flexibility yields the solution for knowledge projects.

A model for software development that attempts to combine the good features of both the waterfall and prototyping approaches has been proposed by Barry Boehm (1988). It stems from the area of complex large-scale information systems, as found in large government software projects, and in defense and high-tech industries such as aerospace and so on. As the straight line symbolizes the waterfall approach and the circle represents the prototyping approach, this intermediate approach is known as the *spiral* model, as depicted in Figure 15.3. The four quadrants indicate recurring and structured steps of project management activity. Through this, the aim is to achieve progress by means of subsequent cycles that may be adapted on the basis of experience from previous cycles. Depending on the situation, one may decide for analysis and design documents as in the waterfall model, but also for prototyping activities if these are judged to be more illuminating or useful. In this way, the spiral model aims at striking a balance between structured control and flexibility. The CommonKADS approach to the management of knowledge projects has grown out of this idea of a spiral development.

15.2 Project Planning: The CommonKADS Life-Cycle Model

The CommonKADS life-cycle approach is based on the following principles:

- Project planning concentrates first of all on products and outputs to be delivered, rather than on activities or phases.
- Project planning is done in a configurable and adaptive manner in terms of spiral-like cycles, which are driven by a systematic assessment of the risks to the project.
- Quality assurance is an integrated part of project management, due to the fact that quality is "engineered into" knowledge-system development through the CommonKADS methodology.

These principles are practically supported by two important elements of the CommonKADS methodology: (1) the model suite, as discussed in the previous chapters, and (2) the project management cycle, as displayed in Figure 15.4. The project management cycle consists of four activities — review, risk, plan, and monitor — that recur in every cycle of the project:

1. **Review**   This is the first stage in the project management at each cycle. The current status of the project is reviewed, and the main objectives for the upcoming cycle are established. For the initial round, cycle-0, an overall project plan, including a quality plan, is developed. Internal and external constraints on the project are reviewed and alternatives are investigated by the project manager. An important task to close off the review stage is to ensure the commitment of the various stakeholders of the project, which may include managers and decision-makers involved, customers, prospective users, experts.

2. **Risk**   The general directions for the project as set at the review stage constitutes the input for the second project management stage: risk assessment. The obstacles that are potentially in the way of success of the project are identified, and their significance is assessed. How to do this is discussed in detail in the next section. Needed counteractions are decided upon by the project manager, and fed into the subsequent stage: planning.

3. **Plan**   Given a clear view obtained in the previous two stages on objectives, existing risks, and associated actions to be undertaken, the next step is to make a detailed plan for the next cycle. This covers the standard planning activities in project management,

Figure 15.4
The CommonKADS configurable life cycle, based on the spiral model, for knowledge system projects. The four quadrants indicate the stages and activities to be carried out in project management.

including establishing a work breakdown structure in terms of tasks, a schedule of these tasks, e.g., with the help of a Gantt chart, allocating the needed resources and personnel to these tasks, and agreeing on the acceptance criteria for the work to be carried out.

4. **Monitor**   After this, the next cycle of development work commences. The progress of this work is being monitored and, where needed, steered by the project manager. The meetings with stakeholders relating to the acceptance of the work in the current cycle are being prepared, and the produced outputs are evaluated. The results of this evaluation are then fed into the next stage, the review part of the next cycle.

15.3   Assessing Risks

A salient feature of the CommonKADS life cycle is that project planning is based on a systematic consideration of the risks to the project. Therefore, before detailed planning of the next cycle begins, a stage of risk assessment takes place (see the second, lower-right quadrant in Figure 15.4). This is the second stage in the project management cycle. Here,

Project Management		Risk Assessment Worksheet PM-1			
RISK	AFFECTED QUALITY FEATURE	LIKELI-HOOD OF OCCUR-RENCE	SEVERITY OF EFFECT ON PROJECT	RANK OF RISK	COUNTER-MEASURE
Risk identifier and nature	Quality feature at stake due to risk	Very low, low, medium, high, very high	Very low, low, medium, high, very high	Ranking number, based on product of likelihood and effect	Action to be taken against risk

Table 15.1
Worksheet PM-1: Worksheet for carrying out project risk identification and assessment.

the aim is to identify what kind of risks exist that may hamper the progress of the project, to estimate how likely they are to occur, and, if so, how severe they impact the project as a whole, in order to design adequate countermeasures against the important risks. The analysis of project risks can be conveniently done with the aid of the worksheet given in Table 15.1. A list of risks commonly encountered in knowledge projects is given can be found at the CommonKADS website. This list can be used as a checklist by the project manager.

As an example, a commonly occurring risk is that the expert is difficult to get access to and has not much time available. This will endanger the intended functionality of the system (see the quality feature tree of Figure 15.6). In many situations, the probability that this risk actually will occur is quite high, and so is the severity of its impact on the overall project. Thus, this kind of risk will be ranked with a high priority, and high-level management action may be needed as a countermeasure to reduce this risk. Another example of risk is that during knowledge modelling end users of the future system have no clear idea of what exactly is going on and wonder about the usability of the system. Such a risk might be countered by deciding to develop and demonstrate a prototype for the graphical user-interface. Thus, the actions following from such a risk assessment will help to shape project planning for the next cycle.

15.4   Plan: Setting Objectives through Model States

We pointed out that the CommonKADS life-cycle approach concentrates first of all on setting objectives in terms of outputs to be delivered, rather than activities or phases. Here, the model suite plays a key role. Project objectives for a cycle are expressed and measured

Project Management	Model State Planning Worksheet PM-2
Attribute	**Description**
MODEL NAME	One of the CommonKADS models: organization, task, agent, knowledge, communication, design model.
STATE VARIABLE	A part or component(s) of the selected model on which project work is to be done (e.g., the inference layer of the knowledge model).
STATE VALUE	An indicator of the degree of completion to be achieved by the work on the selected model component(s). The following qualitative five-point range is useful: **1. Empty:** The starting state value, indicating that no work has been done yet. **2. Identified:** Basic features relating to the selected model component(s) have been listed. These may refer to essential characteristics of the model component (e.g., the task decomposition shows the typical features of an assessment type of task), identifying external requirements and inputs (e.g., listing the information sources that will be used for the work on the model). **3. Described:** The modelling or implementation work has been fully carried out. This is the level of a complete first version or draft. **4. Validated:** The work done is tested, verified, and validated with respect to outside criteria or sources (e.g., against given quality measures, external requirements, or by checking the correctness of developed models with relevant experts). **5. Completed:** The work on the model component is finished according to the established acceptance criteria (e.g., being accepted and signed off after a review with the client).
QUALITY METRICS	The quality metrics according to the quality plan that will be used to measure whether the desired model state has indeed been achieved. Also, the procedure to establish this is to be indicated here.
ROLE	This is an optional attribute of a model state. It can be used to indicate that a model state plays a specific role in a project, e.g., as a milestone at which a go/no-go decision is to be taken.
DEPENDENCIES	This is an optional attribute: sometimes it is useful to indicate that achievement of a model state critically depends on certain external inputs (e.g., a management decision to be taken, equipment to be available, or results from another part of the project to be finished).

Table 15.2
Worksheet PM-2: How to describe a model state, as an objective to be achieved by the project.

in terms of a certain degree of completion of one or more models, to be achieved as an output by the work in the upcoming cycle. This concept reflecting the degree of completion of a CommonKADS model is called the *model state*. How a model state is described is indicated in Table 15.2.

Project planning (the third, lower-left quadrant in Figure 15.4) is thus based on setting objectives for the next project cycle in terms of the model states, following the approach given in Table 15.2. In essence it is quite simple, as the project manager has to go over the following checklist of questions:

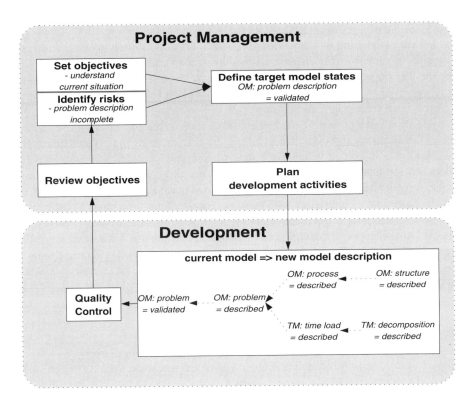

Figure 15.5
Example project management cycle with associated development activities. The arrows indicate the sequencing of activities. OM, organization model; TM, task model.

1. What model(s) are to be worked on in the next cycle?
2. On which component(s) of this model should the development work focus?
3. To what degree or extent must this be carried out in the upcoming cycle?
4. By what means, resources, development method, or technique?
5. How do we establish that the desired end state has been reached?
6. How do we measure that its quality is satisfactory?

It is important to note that the first three questions make the project life cycle *configurable and scalable*. It is at the discretion of the project manager to decide on which model, model components, and/or software modules the project will work on in the next cycle. This is based on the outcomes of previous cycles, so that the project is able to learn from experience, and can adapt to changing needs or circumstances in a flexible way.

An example of a project management cycle is depicted in Figure 15.5. Suppose we are at the very beginning of a knowledge project. Then, it is often necessary to gather relevant information from the different parties involved to understand the current situation better (review stage, upper left). A major risk may be that the problem to be solved, as it is perceived by the various parties in the organization, is not really fully clear for the project team (risk stage, middle upper left). For example, the project team may in part come from another part of the organization, as is often the case with separate IT development departments. Thus, in planning the first cycle of the project (plan stage, upper right), it is important to achieve a state whereby the problem description has been validated by the relevant outside parties to the project (e.g., the key decision-makers at the management level). Development activities are planned accordingly, for example, by scheduling meetings or interviews with those decision-makers. The bottom part indicates the monitor stage of the project management cycle, where the actual development activities are carried out. Here we see example components from organization and task modelling, as treated in Chapter 3. The results of the development work are then evaluated against the project and quality plan, after which a new project cycle begins with a new review stage (middle left). The next round of the spiral commences.

15.5   Notes on Quality and Project Documentation

Acting as a project manager requires active involvement in a wide, even disparate, variety of tasks. To summarize what a project manager should take care of it is helpful to give a concise overview of the project management documentation that is typically produced in the course of a knowledge project. We will do that in this section, along with some supporting checklists.

CommonKADS project documentation is listed in Table 15.3. The documentation of each cycle is outlined in Table 15.4.

As we may expect, much of the documentation applies generally to any project. The cycle reports constitute the project management documentation that is most specific for knowledge projects, as it follows from the CommonKADS life-cycle model. But note that similar documentation will occur in other areas of information-system development, where a spiral approach is employed as the model for project management.

The quality plan, as indicated above, is an important part of any project plan as it is developed in the initial cycle (cycle-0). Quality attributes relevant to knowledge system projects are presented in Figure 15.6. The lower part is representative of information systems in general. The upper two branches of the tree are characteristic for knowledge-oriented projects. The branch indicated as *knowledge capture* refers to the quality features of the activities of knowledge acquisition, modelling and validation as carried out by the knowledge engineers in the project team. The *knowledge usability* branch denotes the quality features of the knowledge as it will be embedded in the prospective system. Thus, this

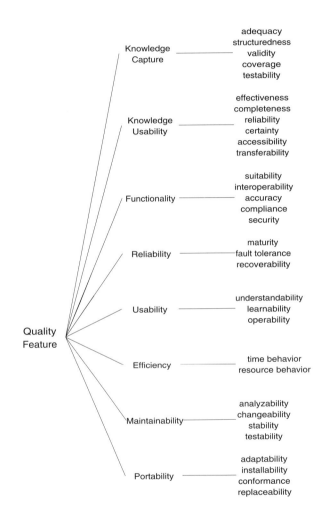

Figure 15.6
Tree of quality features.

Knowledge Project Documentation

Project plan   At the initiating cycle of the project (cycle 0) an overall project plan is developed. It is updated as necessary as the project progresses. This overall project plan will typically cover the following topics:

- Project motivation, background, scope, goals.
- Project deliverables.
- An overall work breakdown, covering the list of project cycles and an associated description of project tasks and schedule. A more detailed description for each cycle is given in the cycle documentation (see below).
- Overall resources available to the project within any established budget.
- Project organization, personnel, external dependencies, reporting relationships, training, and experience.
- References to the contract and other relevant external or background material.

Quality plan   This plan is also produced at the initiating cycle of the project (cycle 0), in conjunction with the above overall project plan. The important elements of the quality are treated separately later on in in this section.

Cycle documentation   For each cycle, a more detailed management document is produced. Its structure and content is discussed in the separate box immediately below.

Project close down report   At the end of a project, it is worthwhile to produce a document that evaluates the project as a whole. Such a report will cover the lessons learned for the organization from the project, and indicate recommendations and proposed guidelines for the future. This may refer to different areas, e.g., follow-up work, improvements to the quality system, intercompany and client cooperation, or staffing, resourcing, and training issues.

Table 15.3
Overview of project documentation.

branch represents the view of future users and beneficiaries of the knowledge, which often are mainly outside the project.

For the most part, therefore, the quality plan for knowledge projects has the same structure and covers the same topics as is the case for other information systems. Table 15.5 provides a checklist of the main elements in a quality plan.

A key element in the contract and the project plan will always be the set of deliverables that the project is required to produce. A default list is given in Table 15.6.

Note that this standard list is only to be used as a general guideline. Depending on the size and nature of the project, changes in the list will have to be made by the project manager. For example, in exploratory projects it may be that only the first two deliverables are needed. In small projects it might be useful to combine deliverables (for example, on knowledge modelling, communication, design, and test), while in large projects it may be wise to split up deliverables (for example, split up the knowledge-model document into parts regarding task structure, domain knowledge, and problem-solving methods). This possibility of breaking up or combining deliverables is precisely the idea behind a spiral

Project Cycle Documentation

At each cycle of the project, a specific cycle document is created at the start, and completed as the cycle progresses. In its structure, it follows the review-risk-plan-monitor project management activities, as we have discussed them above (cf. Figure 15.4). Hence, cycle documents will typically cover the following topics:

- **Review**

  - Position and purpose of the cycle within the overall project plan
  - Summary of the outcome of the previous cycle, defining the starting point of the current cycle
  - Cycle objectives and outline plan
  - Constraints, considered alternatives, choices made for the cycle

- **Risk**

  - List and explanation of identified risks
  - Risk assessment according to the worksheet PM-2 given in Table 15.2
  - Resulting conclusions for the cycle plan and development approach

- **Plan**

  - Cycle plan, covering task breakdown, resource allocation, cycle outputs, accounting for the risk assessment and detailing the overall project plan
  - The cycle outputs are based on the concept and definition of CommonKADS model states, according to the worksheet PM-1 given in Table 15.2
  - A description of the (agreed) acceptance criteria, on the basis of which the planned cycle outputs will be evaluated

- **Monitor**

  - Periodic progress reports, as standardly required by the organization
  - Records of acceptance assessment meetings evaluating the cycle outputs
  - Concluding review of the actual results measured against the expected project progress, as an input to the next cycle

Table 15.4
Overview of project cycle documentation.

development approach. The decision on this rests with the project manager, in agreement of course with the outside decision-makers that are involved. This is an important element in the configurability and scalability of the CommonKADS life cycle.

In the development of conventional information systems, usually a requirements document is produced that defines what the purpose and content of the system is supposed to be from the viewpoint of the client and user. In CommonKADS, essentially the model suite as a whole plays a role equivalent to that of a requirements document. Because the requirements document is such a major element in many conventional development methodologies, we show how it maps onto the CommonKADS model suite components in Table 15.7. The indicated structure of a requirements document has been adopted from standards such as the *IEEE Guide to Requirements Specification*.

1. Introduction and scope
2. Organization and responsibilities
3. Deliverables
4. Requirements tracking
5. Documentation plan
6. Standards, procedures, conventions
7. Methodology, techniques, tools
8. Subcontracting and purchasing
9. Quality features and metrics (cf. Figure 15.6)
10. Reviews of project work and management
11. Quality system and quality assurance records
12. Configuration management and change control
13. Verification and validation plan
14. Model development plan

Table 15.5
Topics covered in a quality plan.

1. Scoping and feasibility study (organization model)
2. Impact and improvement study (task/agent model)
3. Knowledge model report
4. Design report (including design and communication models)
5. Software deliverables
6. System documentation (including user manual, installation and
   maintenance guide)
7. Test report on knowledge verification and validation

Table 15.6
Default list of project deliverables.

As a final note, a major concern for project managers is always to keep control over the budget and human effort spent on the road toward achieving the project goal. In planning and managing a knowledge project, it is therefore necessary to have an advance estimate of the effort needed to carry out different activities, such as knowledge modelling, organizational analysis, design and implementation. Actual data on these aspects are currently limited, however. As in software-engineering economy in general, every organization should gather its own specific data to get a grip on the costs incurred by knowledge projects. Data that are available suggest that the economy of knowledge projects is similar to that of other advanced complex information systems. Typical, but rough, indicators are given in Table 15.8. The more knowledge intensive an application is, the more effort has to be relatively spent to knowledge acquisition, modelling, and validation. This is analogous to information systems in general, where a global rule is that information analysis and design take a greater portion of the total effort with increasing complexity of the application.

Requirements document section	CommonKADS equivalent
Introduction Scope	Project plan; scoping and feasibility report
General description Objectives Expected future enhancements	Contract; project plan Impact and improvement report
Organizational requirements	Impact and improvement report
Functional requirements	Task model
Interface requirements Human factors and human-computer interaction Explanatory requirements Hardware and software interfaces	Agent model; communication model Communication model Organization model (computing resources); communication model; design model
Information requirements	Knowledge model
Performance requirements Information storage requirements	Design model Knowledge model (domain knowledge); design model
Design constraints Development environment constraints Operational environment constraints	Design model Organization model (target); design model
Resource constraints	Contract; project plan
Quality constraints Verification requirements Attributes Acceptance testing requirements	Quality plan (verification and validation plan) Contract; quality plan Contract; quality plan (standards)
Other requirements Installation requirements Documentation requirements	Organization model; design model Contract; project plan
Glossary References	identical identical

Table 15.7
A conventional requirements document and how it maps onto the CommonKADS model suite.

Effort Distribution in Knowledge-System Development	
Activity	*Percentage*
Project management	10%
Organization-task-agent models	10%
Knowledge modelling	30%
Design and communication models	20%
Implementation and testing	25%
Quality assurance	5%

Table 15.8
Rough distribution of efforts spent in the various activities in a typical knowledge system project.

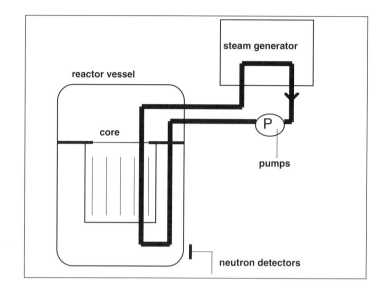

Figure 15.7
Schematic diagram of a nuclear reactor. The type shown here is a so-called pressurized water reactor.

15.6   Case: A Project on Nuclear Reactor Noise Analysis

15.6.1   Application Domain and Project Brief

Noise is a naturally occurring phenomenon in many technical and nontechnical systems, and it is found in very diverse domains, such as acoustics, mechanics, and electromagnetism. It is the joint result of a large variety of small signals caused by the various components of a working system. Noise is not only annoying but also of practical interest: its analysis can yield valuable information about the state of a system. It is the basis, for example, of seismic investigations. By comparing noise signals produced by a system with those generated by a reference system that is considered to be of excellent quality, one can distinguish between good and poor products or equipment. That's why it is used in industry for product quality control, and for condition monitoring of production process equipment for the purpose of early failure detection and predictive maintenance.

At the Netherlands Energy Research Foundation ECN, a specialist group has been working for many years on noise analysis of nuclear reactors. Figure 15.7 gives a simple schematic of a nuclear reactor. Nuclear fission reactions in the core of the reactor vessel produce heat. This heat is transported by boron-carrying coolant water that is pumped

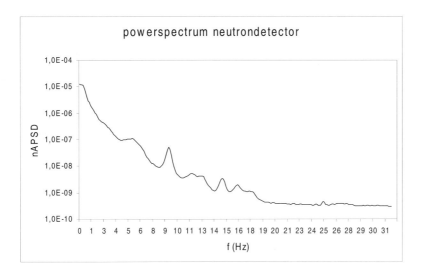

Figure 15.8
An example of a noise spectrum of a nuclear reactor, as measured by the neutron detectors.

through the core to a steam generator that drives a turbine. This creates forces on the core as a result of which it will vibrate within the reactor vessel. This generates noise that can be measured with the help of the neutron detectors located around the vessel. An example of a measured noise spectrum is displayed in Figure 15.8. It shows the energy fluctuations measured by the neutron detectors as a function of the frequency. It is the specialist's task to interpret the meaning and importance of these fluctuations.

Noise analysis of spectra such as those in Figure 15.8 enables one to infer important physical parameters of the reactor. For example, one can derive the so-called reactivity that indicates how many new neutrons are generated through the nuclear fission reactions. This parameter should remain stable and below a threshold value. For noise analysis, delicate mathematical theories, algorithms, and computer packages are available. These are limited, however. For the interpretation of the produced information in diagnostic terms it appears that noise analysis experts are usually involved. Therefore, the idea sparking off the project was that a knowledge system might be a useful tool in enhancing existing mathematical software by supporting the diagnostic interpretation of the system condition. This would make noise analysis more widely applicable. The project brief was to investigate to what extent this was indeed the case.

Project Management		Risk Assessment Worksheet PM-1: Noise-Analysis System:			
RISK	AFFECTED QUALITY FEATURE	LIKELIHOOD OF OCCURRENCE	SEVERITY OF EFFECT ON PROJECT	RANK OF RISK	COUNTER-MEASURE
Lack of acquaintance with domain	Knowledge capture	Very high	Very high	1	Study domain literature, make glossary, on-the-job training with expert group.
Unknown complexity of task	Knowledge capture	Very high	High	2	Focus knowledge acquisition with experts early on this topic by empirical scenarios.
Limited availability of expert	Knowledge capture and usability, functionality	High	High	3	Develop contacts also with other, outside experts.

Table 15.9
Worksheet PM-1: Risk analysis for the nuclear reactor noise analysis and interpretation system.

15.6.2 First Project Cycle

In the initiating cycle-0 of the project, the broad overall project goals and approach were worked out and agreed with the specialist group. In the review stage of first cycle, the central objective defined was to get a detailed understanding of the state of the art and how a knowledge system can advance this. Next, a risk analysis was carried out. It revealed the following main risks (see Table 15.9): (1) insufficient acquaintance with the domain by the knowledge engineer; (2) complexity of the noise analysis task unknown; (3) limited availability of the expert. The first and third risks are very common in knowledge-system projects. The second risk, task complexity, resulted from inspection of early knowledge elicitation data. It appeared to be ambiguous in the sense that the noise interpretation task could be quite simple like a classification task. Alternatively, it might be extremely complex as a form of heavy mathematical model-based reasoning, or it might be of intermediate complexity as in assessment-type tasks. Different parts of the elicitation data could be construed or interpreted to support either position.

As a result of this risk assessment, in the planning stage a cycle plan has been developed that incorporates the risk countermeasures listed in Table 15.9. Outputs of the cycle are in terms of CommonKADS model components and their states. The resulting plan is shown in the form of a Gantt chart in Figure 15.9, and in summary worksheet form in Table 15.10. The following activities were defined in the cycle-1 plan:

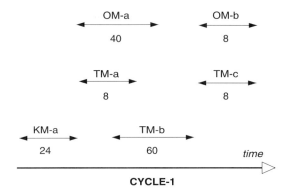

Figure 15.9
Gantt chart of the plan for the first cycle in the noise-analysis knowledge project. The numbers denote the estimated hours of effort for an activity.

KM-a As a preliminary part of the domain layer of the knowledge model, make a glossary of important domain concepts and a first-cut domain-specific ontology (cf. Chapter 7).

OM-a Develop the organization model for the current situation.

OM-b Develop the organization model for the envisaged new situation, with knowledge system introduced.

TM-a Make a first version of the task model for the existing mathematical signal-processing software system.

TM-b Make a first version of the task model for the noise interpretation tasks of the expert.

TM-c Make a first version of the task model for the envisaged knowledge system.

In the subsequent develop/monitor stage, activities were carried out following the cycle plan. Knowledge acquisition was done by means of an array of different methods, including open and structured interviews, think-aloud protocols by the expert, consulting other specialists, collecting and studying technical domain literature, and on-the-job training in the expert group by the knowledge engineer, actually processing measured real-time data from a nuclear-power station. This approach was indeed successful to counteract the risks mentioned in Table 15.9. A highly interesting conclusion was that reactor-noise interpretation is very close to an assessment type of task. So it could be concluded that, given the fact that the task is not overly complex for a knowledge system, further work on the

Project Management	Model State Planning Worksheet PM-2: Cycle 1 Noise-Analysis System
Attribute	**Description**
MODEL NAME	*KM-a:* knowledge model *OM-a/b:* organization model *TM-a/b/c:* task model
STATE VARIABLE	*KM-a:* Domain knowledge (initial domain schema) *OM-a/b:* All organization model components *TM-a/b/c:* Task type and top-level decomposition
STATE VALUE	*KM-a:* Identified *OM-a/b:* Described *TM-a/b/c:* Identified
QUALITY METRICS	Knowledge capture, evaluated by e.g., *teach back* to experts and other responsible staff

Table 15.10
Worksheet PM-2: Cycle 1 planning for the nuclear reactor noise analysis and interpretation system.

project was warranted. Second, it was concluded that further work could be based on the reusable task template discussed in Chapter 6. This turned out to be indeed the case and it made things significantly easier later on.

Even with the flexible but sound planning due to the spiral project management approach, project monitoring *is* needed during development (i.e., the fourth quadrant of the spiral) because unexpected things might happen along the road. In the noise-analysis project, although the activities did follow the cycle plan, the total effort (indicated in Figure 15.9) appeared to be underestimated. This was mainly due to the time it took to consult other experts from outside organizations. The benefit of doing this was, however, that a full second case study could be carried out, based on another nuclear reactor of a different type and situated at a different location. The results were a clear validation of the conclusion that reactor noise interpretation is an assessment type of task. Later on, it turned out to be possible to build a single generic task-inference model covering both cases, and based on the reusable assessment task template.

Another interesting experience was that initially the expectations of expert and knowledge engineer differed more than was anticipated, although they had formally agreed on project brief and approach beforehand. This became visible in the transcripts of an interview dialogue such as the following:

> *Knowledge engineer:* (shows noise spectra as in Figure 15.8) — If the reactivity differs from the expected value, is it possible to say what the possible causes are? Does it also show up in or affect the values of other physical parameters?

In response, initially the expert tended to find such questions not very relevant for developing a knowledge system, and came up with counterquestions such as:

Project Management	Model State Planning Worksheet PM-2: Cycle 2 Noise-Analysis System
Attribute	**Description**
MODEL NAME	*OM-c:* Organization model *TM-d:* Task model
STATE VARIABLE	*OM-c:* Resources and problems/opportunities components *TM-d:* Task goal/value, performance/quality, and resources components
STATE VALUE	*OM-c:* Completed *TM-d:* Described
QUALITY METRICS	Knowledge capture (coverage), knowledge usability (effectiveness), functionality (suitability, accuracy); evaluated mainly by differential or comparative analysis

Table 15.11
Worksheet PM-2: Cycle 2 planning for the nuclear reactor noise analysis and interpretation system.

> *Expert:* In what language are you going to implement the system? On a VAX or a PC?

This shows — and this is a very general experience, especially in open-ended projects as many knowledge projects are — that *expectation management* with respect to the various project parties and stakeholders is a crucial activity.

15.6.3 Second and Further Project Cycles

The first project cycle concentrated on task-domain content and complexity, as the main risks were perceived to be related to these aspects. Now that these risks were seen to be quite well under control, the second cycle of the noise analysis project focused on the economic cost-benefit aspects. The reason was that, given the technical feasibility established in the first cycle, the main risk was now considered to lie in the danger that the initial estimates of the economic feasibility might be overly crude. Thus, the cycle-2 plan aimed to cater for this by two activities: *OM-c*, detailing the organization model especially with respect to its problems/opportunities and resources components (see Chapter 3), and *TM-d*, comparing the envisaged system task model with the capabilities and associated costs of existing commercial systems on the market (see Table 15.11 and Figure 15.10, left). This resulted in a more detailed insight into added value vs. cost of the prospective noise knowledge system.

The results of the second cycle were not unequivocal. A market study done by an external company indicated the potential for significant savings on a worldwide basis. It was also clear, however, that national interests and political issues related to nuclear energy were a complicating factor, difficult to quantify in financial terms. Visits of the knowledge engineer to potential end users revealed some, not unexpected, reluctance to change existing work procedures and habits, as well as some, again not unexpected, differences in

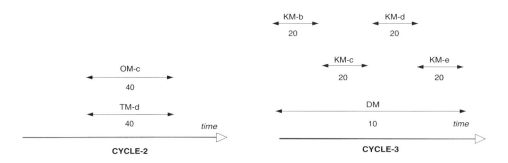

Figure 15.10
Gantt charts of the second (left) and third (right) cycles of the noise-analysis project planning. For an explanation of the activities, see the text.

attitudes between engineers on the work floor and their managers. The comparison with existing commercial systems indicated a quite clear ceiling cost of the knowledge system of some tens of thousands of dollars (a figure which was estimated to be achievable). Furthermore, gradually it became clear that there was some commercial potential in industrial sectors other than nuclear energy, such as the offshore business. Overall, a moderate further investment in noise knowledge systems was considered to be justified.

Next, the third project cycle again focused more on domain-knowledge content: the main risk seen was to ensure that the delicate and rather technical aspects of this domain could indeed be adequately converted into forms and rules suitable for computer treatment. Accordingly, the cycle-3 plan concentrated on filling in the various components of the knowledge and design models, as seen in Figure 15.10 (right). Here, the activities defined were *KM-b*: describe the assessment task instances in both cases; *KM-c*: describe the related inference structures; *KM-d/e*: describe/complete the domain models in the domain layer of the knowledge model; *DM*: identify ensuing architecture, platform, and application design decisions (cf. Chapter 11).

These activities involved some significant technical effort, but did not lead to any unexpected surprises. As the focus was on domain-knowledge content, a regular contact with the noise-analysis expert group was maintained to ensure the quality of the work. From the third cycle onward, the project life cycle became rather predictable, and could be more and more managed in the waterfall form discussed early in this Chapter. For the implementation of the noise knowledge system, it appeared that any standard rule-based software architecture and environment was suitable, with a characteristic size of several dozens of rules for a single application.

15.6.4   Reflections and Lessons Learned

The project case study described above is, we believe, quite typical of many knowledge projects. Especially in the initial stages, the project manager has to deal with a lot of unknown or uncertain factors. Here, not even the task type and complexity of the application were really clear in advance. In fact, it was taken into account that review of the first cycle could well lead to the recommendation to stop the project, because the task appears too complex for an information system.

These elements of uncertainty present a compelling case for a flexible and configurable project management approach, as the proposed CommonKADS version of the risk-based spiral model. Even a superficial look at the case study reveals that it leads to a clearly *nonwaterfall* project. In knowledge projects, iterative elements must be built in by design, often in the course of the *learning process* itself. Further testimony to this is to imagine what the project plan would have looked like if outcomes of a previous cycle had been slightly different (for example, more or less complexity of the task, more or less optimistic economic feasibility estimates, etc.).

The case study also emphasizes the importance of analyzing the business and organizational aspects of knowledge-system development and introduction. These aspects are often underestimated by computer scientists and software engineers, who tend to have a bias and preference for the content-related technical aspects. Then, the danger is often poor handling of what we have called expectation management of end users and customers. Managers, marketers and persons with a background in business administration are often more sensitive to these aspects. For them, a common pitfall is often a limited appreciation of the technical aspects of a knowledge project. As hinted at in the case study, a reasonable technical competence is needed to make adequate economic and marketing forecasts, at least in a second, more refined round of the project spiral.

Sometimes, there can be unanticipated positive surprises. Reactor noise analysis and housing application or credit card fraud assessment are obviously very disparate domains. Nevertheless, it turned out that the assessment task template, originally developed in financial and policy applications, could be reused in this highly technical noise analysis domain. Such a finding is gratifying: something a project team can hope for, strive for, but never plan for. It is a showcase for the unexpectedly wide range and potential of generic and reusable models we have argued for at several places in this book. It also points to a personal quality of good knowledge project managers: to be able to surf good project waves even if you did not expect them — as if you expected them.

15.7   How *Not* to Manage a Knowledge-System Project

To end this chapter, it would be useful to summarize lessons and guidelines for good project management. In contrast, however, it may be even more illuminating and memorable to show — based on true stories and many years of practical experience! — what to do as a project manager if you want to head for disaster in your knowledge project. Here, then, are some (only some!) of our *recipes for failure*:

1. One of the tedious aspects of being a project manager is that you have to balance the different, and often conflicting, interests of outside stakeholders such as clients, users, experts, and department managers. This is extremely time-consuming and slows down the technical progress of your project. So the best strategy is not to waste too much time on these stakeholders. Since they usually are ignorant about knowledge systems, they are not of much help to you anyway.

2. Cautious project managers live by so-called 80-20 rules. For example, 80% of the system functionality can often be delivered with only 20% of the project budget, while the final 20% of functionality consumes the remaining 80% of the budget. Such rules are used to argue in favor of modest improvements in the degree of automation. You, on the other hand, will of course make the real difference. So, go for the full 100%. If you cannot think big, you will never act big.

3. Knowledge projects are often viewed by outsiders as innovative, sometimes complex and risky. This may lead to some resistance. To overcome this, you as a project manager have to sell the project well. Do this by introducing high ambitions and expectations from all stakeholders right from the start. In this era of business process redesign, one must go for quantum leaps of improvement, not limited steps. After all, as a project manager you will be remembered only for a big success, not for a number of small ones. (The drawback to this strategy is that you may also be remembered for a big mistake.)

4. The power, image, and position of a project manager within an organization in practice depends on the budget he controls. This is why a spiral approach is not adequate: the danger is that you get your budget only in portions cycle by cycle, and that each time you have to make a case for it based on results. To improve your status in the organization, you will be better off by going for one big budget right at the start, based on big expectations.

5. We are happy to include some more real-life recipes for disaster from you . . . Of course, the above "guidelines" are meant in an ironic way. This helps, we hope, to get the message across about careful project management: because situations as indicated here are not only Dilbert-like cartoons but regrettably do really happen in projects.

15.8   Bibliographical Notes and Further Reading

A classic and still useful text on the economic aspects of the software life cycle and its planning is Boehm (1981). The spiral life-cycle model was first proposed in Boehm (1988). The CommonKADS adaptation of this, including the state-based project management approach, was developed in the KADS-II project (see the reports at the CommonKADS website). A recent, concise student text on software project management is Ricketts (1998). Related risk analysis is extensively treated in Hall (1998). System project management procedures are often a formal element in quality management systems in organizations (Peratec 1994). As pointed out in this chapter, the CommonKADS suite of aspect models constitutes a comprehensive approach to knowledge-oriented requirements engineering that includes the upfront stages before system specification. For techniques useful in the very early stages, see also Chapter 8 on knowledge elicitation. For knowledge managers and related business consultancy, Scott-Morgan (1994) is recommended additional reading. A recent good practice guide on software requirements engineering in general is Sommerville (1997). The work described in the case study was carried out by Sjaak Kaandorp at ECN.

Appendix: Knowledge-Model Language

This appendix contains detailed information about the CommonKADS language for specifying knowledge models. Section A.2 contains a full specification of the knowledge-model language using a BNF notation. Section A.3 contains the full knowledge model for the housing application (see Chapter 10).

A.1   Language Conventions

A.1.1   Syntactic Conventions

The conventions used in the syntax specification. are listed in Table A.1.

A.1.2   Low-Level Syntax

Comments   Comments are not formally part of the syntax of CML. Comments follow the C style: initiate a comment with /* and terminate with */. Comments can appear anywhere between the symbols of the CML syntax.

Names   The most frequently occurring low-level construct is a **name**. CML defines a name to start with a letter followed by letters, digits, hyphens, and underbars in an arbitrary order. If additional characters are required in a name, the entire name must be embedded in single quotes. For example, the concept *Monster of Loch Ness* is defined as follows:

```
CONCEPT 'Monster of Loch Ness';
   ...
END CONCEPT 'Monster of Loch Ness';
```

What a name refers to is suggested by the convention *Construct*-name, where *Construct* is the type of thing the name denotes. The CML parser will take this rather literally, if the parser encounters a *Concept-name*, it will create a concept of the given name if it did not already exist.

X ::= Y	The syntax of X (a nonterminal) is defined by Y.
[X]	Zero or one occurrence of X.
X*	Zero or more occurrences of X.
X+	One or more occurrences of X.
X Y ...	One or more occurrences of X separated by Y. This construct is mainly used to abbreviate comma-separated lists. For example, "Name, ..." is short for "Name ⟨, Name ⟩*".
X | Y	One of X or Y (exclusive or).
⟨ X ⟩	Grouping construct for specifying the scope of operators.
symbol	Bold: predefined terminal symbols of the language. In the syntax definition these symbols are given in lowercase. In a CML file they must be given in uppercase.
Symbol	Capitalized: user-defined terminal symbols of the language.
symbol	Lowercase: nonterminal symbols.
"Text"	Arbitrary text between double quotes. A double quote inside the text can be escaped with a backslash.
'X'	Escapes the operator symbol (e.g., *) and denotes the literal X.

Table A.1
Conventions for syntax specification.

Hyphens, underbars, and spaces   The ASCII character set has given us two symbols that are used interchangeably: the hyphen and the underbar. Some languages allow a hyphen in a name (e.g., Lisp), whereas others disallow it (e.g., C). CML allows both characters as it is language in which one may want to denote concepts which already have an established notation (e.g., *hole-in-1*). Users of CML are advised to use the notation of a concept as it appears in (public) sources. In general, the consequence is to use hyphens and spaces rather than underbars. To avoid practical problems when CML is translated into other languages, the CML parser has several options through which hyphens and spaces can be converted to underbars automatically.

A.1.3   Operators in Expressions

Table A.2 lists the operators that can be used in expressions. Note that the operator for equality is = = (and not =). The main entry point in the syntax for expressions is **equation** (Section A.2.10, p. 417). Operators are listed in order of increasing precedence. Operators of equal precedence are grouped between horizontal rules. Note that a hyphen may be used in names and is also an operator. White space around hyphens intended as a minus sign may thus be necessary.

```
CONCEPT vehicle;
  ATTRIBUTES:
    no-of-wheels: INTEGER;

  AXIOMS:
    no-of-wheels > 3;
```

Operator	Description
=	Equivalence (mathematics)
: =	Assignment (programming)
<	Less than (comparison)
< =	Less than or equal to (comparison)
>	More than (comparison)
> =	More than or equal to (comparison)
= =	Equal to (comparison)
! =	Not equal to (comparison)
- >	Implication (logical)
< -	Inverse implication (logical)
< - >	Double implication (logical)
AND	Conjunction (logical)
OR	Disjunction (logical)
XOR	Choice (logical)
+	Addition (arithmetic)
–	Subtraction (arithmetic)
*	Multiplication (arithmetic)
/	Division (arithmetic)
* *	Exponentiation (arithmetic)
–	Negation (arithmetic)
NOT	Negation (logical)
.	Dereference (programming)
'	Derivative (mathematics)
(. . .)	Grouping
[. . .]	Subscript

Table A.2
List of expression operators.

A.2   Language Syntax

A.2.1   Synonyms

Table Table A.3 lists the synonyms of terms used in the CML syntax specification. The term in the left column is used in this document, the term(s) in the right column give synonyms used in previous versions of CML and are still accepted by the CML parser.

A.2.2   Knowledge Model

```
knowledge-model           ::=   knowledge-model Knowledge-model ;
                                 [ terminology ]
                                 domain-knowledge
                                 inference-knowledge
                                 task-knowledge
                                 [ psm-knowledge ]
                                 end knowledge-model [ Knowledge-model ; ] .
```

Term	Old version (still valid)
attributes	properties
domain-schema	ontology, domain-knowledge-schema
knowledge-base	domain-model
knowledge-model	expertise-model
list-of	listof, list
rule-type	rule-schema
set-of	setof, set
specification	spec
use	uses, import
value-specification	value-spec
value-type	value-set

Table A.3
Synonyms of language terms.

It is usual for **psm knowledge** to be defined separately, for example as part of a library of PSMs.

A.2.3   Domain Knowledge

domain-knowledge   ::=   **domain-knowledge** *Domain-knowledge* ;
                                     [terminology]
                                     ⟨ domain-schema |
                                     ontology-mapping | knowledge-base ⟩ *
                                     end domain-knowledge [*Domain-knowledge* ;] .

Domain Schema

A domain-schema is defined through the specification of *types* or *constructs*. CML provides several representational primitives: **concept** (Section A.2.3, p. 407), **relation** (Section A.2.3, p. 409), and **rule-type** (Section A.2.3, p. 408).

The keyword **definitions**, to introduce the constructs defined in the schema, is no longer required.

domain-schema   ::=   **domain-schema** *Domain-schema* ;
                                 [terminology]
                                 [**use** : use-construct , ... ;]
                                 [**definitions** :] domain-construct*
                                 end domain-schema [*Domain-schema* ;] .

use-construct   ::=   *Domain-schema* |
                                 Construct **from** *Domain-schema* .

domain-construct   ::=   binary-relation | concept | mathematical-model |
                                     relation | rule-type | value-type .

Concept

The notion of *concept* is used to represent a class of real or mental objects in the domain being studied. The term concept corresponds roughly to the term *entity* in ER-modelling and *class* in object-oriented approaches.

Every concept has a *name*, a unique symbol which can serve as an identifier of the concept, possible super concepts (multiple inheritance is allowed).

concept	::=	**concept** *Concept* ;
		[terminology]
		[**super-type-of** : *Concept* , ... ;
		[**disjoint** : **yes** | **no** ;]
		[**complete** : **yes** | **no** ;]]
		[**sub-type-of** : *Concept* , ... ;]
		[**has-parts** : has-part+]
		[**part-of** : *Concept* , ... ;]
		[**viewpoints** : viewpoint+]
		[attributes]
		[axioms]
		end concept [*Concept* ;] .
has-part	::=	*Concept* ;
		[role]
		[cardinality] .
viewpoint	::=	**dimension** :
		Concept , ... ;
		[**disjoint** : **yes** | **no** ;]
		[**complete** : **yes** | **no** ;] .

Axioms

The axioms slot supports the specification of (mathematical) relationships that are defined to be true.

axioms	::=	**axioms** :
		equation ; ... .

Examples   Consider the definition of a chess-square:

```
CONCEPT chess-square;
  ATTRIBUTES:
    rank: INTEGER;
    file: INTEGER;

  AXIOMS:
    1 >= rank >= 8;
    1 >= file >= 8;
END CONCEPT chess-square;
```

This restricts the value of the rank (column) and file (row) of a chess-square to be between 1 and 8.

Attributes

Most constructs in CML can have attributes. An attribute is a (possibly multi-valued) function into a value set. A number of value sets are assumed to be predefined, see **type-range** (Section A.2.3, p. 410). The value sets can also be defined by the user, see **value-type** (Section A.2.3, p. 410). The value set of an attribute cannot be another construct, relations between constructs have to be modelled as a (binary) relation.

attributes	::=	**attributes** : attribute+ .
attribute	::=	*Attribute* : type-range ;
		[cardinality]
		[**differentiation-of** : *Attribute* (*Concept*) ;]
		[**default-value** : *Value* ;] .

Semantics. The cardinality of an attribute defines how many values that particular attribute may take. If the cardinality is omitted it is assumed to be precisely one. An attribute can be a differentiation of an attribute of a super construct, both the name and value set of the attribute can be differentiated. Consider the following example.

```
CONCEPT vehicle;
  ATTRIBUTES:
    wheels: INTEGER;
END CONCEPT vehicle;

CONCEPT human;
  ATTRIBUTES:
    legs: INTEGER;
      DIFFERENTIATION-OF: wheels(vehicle);
END CONCEPT human;
```

Rule Type

rule-type	::=	**rule-type** *Rule-type* ;
		[terminology]
		rule-type-body
		[**examples** : "Text" ;]
		end rule-type [*Rule-type* ;] .
rule-type-body	::=	constraint-rule-type | implication-rule-type .
constraint-rule-type	::=	**constraint** : user-defined-type ;
		[cardinality] .

implication-rule-type	::=	**antecedent** : user-defined-type ;
		[cardinality]
		consequent : user-defined-type ;
		[cardinality]
		connection-symbol : *Name* ; .

Mathematical Model

mathematical-model	::=	**mathematical-model** *Mathematical-model* ;
		[terminology]
		[**parameters** : parameter+]
		[**equations** : equation-list]
		end mathematical-model [*Mathematical-model* ;] .
parameter	::=	*Parameter* : type-range ; .
equation-list	::=	⟨ equation | model-reference ⟩ + .
model-reference	::=	**model** *Mathematical-model* ([function-arguments]) .

Relation

The notion of relation is a central construct in modelling a domain. In CML we allow various forms of relations to cater for the specific requirements imposed by KBSs. The relation construct is used to link any type of objects to each other, including concepts and relations. CML supports two types of relation arguments: a single concept; and a set of such objects.

relation	::=	**relation** *Relation* ;
		[terminology]
		[**sub-type-of** : *Relation* , ... ;]
		arguments : argument+
		[attributes]
		[axioms]
		end relation [*Relation* ;] .
argument	::=	argument-type ;
		[**role** : *Role* ;]
		[cardinality] .
argument-type	::=	domain-construct-type |
		set-of domain-construct-type |
		list-of domain-construct-type .
domain-construct-type	::=	built-in-type | user-defined-type .
built-in-type	::=	**object** | **concept** | **rule-type** |
		relation | **binary-relation** |
		mathematical-model | **value-type** .
user-defined-type	::=	*Concept* | *Rule-type* | *Structure* |
		Relation | *Binary-relation* | *Mathematical-model* .

.

Binary Relation

binary-relation   ::=   **binary-relation** *Relation* ;
                                           [terminology]
                                           [**sub-type-of** : *Relation* , ... ;]
                                           [**inverse** : *Relation* ;]
                                           argument-1 : argument
                                           argument-2 : argument
                                           [relation-type]
                                           [attributes]
                                           [axioms]
                                           end binary-relation [*Relation* ;] .

relation-type   ::=   **transitive** | **asymmetric** | **symmetric** |
                                           irreflexive | **reflexive** | **antisymmetric** .

Type Range

type-range   ::=   primitive-type | primitive-range |
                                           Value-type | { *String-value* , ... } .

primitive-type   ::=   **number** | **integer** | **natural** | **real** | **image** |
                                           string | **boolean** | **universal** | **date** | **text** .

primitive-range   ::=   **number-range** open-bracket *Number* ,
                                           max-number close-bracket |
                                           integer-range open-bracket *Integer* ,
                                           max-integer close-bracket .

Value Type

value-type   ::=   **value-type** *Value-type* ;
                                           [terminology]
                                           [**type** : **nominal** | **ordinal** ;]
                                           ⟨ **value-list** : { *Value* , ... } ⟩
                                           | ⟨ **value-specification** : primitive-type | `"Text"` ⟩ ;
                                           [attributes]
                                           end value-type [*Value-type* ;] .

A.2.4   Knowledge Base

knowledge-base   ::=   **knowledge-base** *Knowledge-base* ;
                                           [terminology]
                                           use : knowledge-base-use , ... ;
                                           [[**instances** :] ⟨ instance | tuple ⟩ +]
                                           [**variables** : variable-declaration ; ... ;]
                                           [**expressions** : knowledge-base-expression ... ;]
                                           [**annotations** : `"Text"` ;]
                                           [attributes]
                                           end knowledge-base [*Knowledge-base* ;] .

knowledge-base-use	::=	*Domain-schema* | *Rule-type* **from** *Domain-schema* .
variable-declaration	::=	*Variable* , ... : *Variable-type* ; .
knowledge-base- expression	::=	variable-declaration | rule-type-instance | `"Text"` .
rule-type-expression	::=	equation | type-operator rule-type-expression | rule-type-expression part-operator rule-type-expression .
type-operator	::=	**sub-type-of** | **super-type-of** | **type-of** .
part-operator	::=	**has-part** | **dimension** | **role** .

Instances

A knowledge base normally contains instances of the constructs defined in a domain schema. The constructs for which instances can be defined is listed in the following table.

Domain schema	Knowledge base	Defines
concept	**instance**	Attribute values and parts
binary-relation	**tuple**	Arguments and attribute values
relation	**tuple**	Arguments and attribute values

Instances of concepts have a name to uniquely identify them. The names of these instances can then be referred to in instances of relations. It is not necessary for names of instance to be meaningful at all, they can be arbitrary identifiers.

| instance | ::= | **instance** *Instance* ;
[terminology]
instance-of : user-defined-type ;
[**has-parts** :
⟨ *Instance* ; [**role** : *Role* ;] ⟩ +]
[**attributes** :
⟨ *Attribute* : *Value* ; ⟩ +]
end instance [*Instance* ;] . |
| tuple | ::= | **tuple**
[terminology]
instance-of : user-defined-type ;
[⟨ **argument-1** : *Instance* ;
    argument-2 : *Instance* ; ⟩ \|
⟨ **arguments** : *Instance* , ... ; ⟩]
[**attributes** :
⟨ *Attribute* : *Value* ; ⟩ +]
end tuple . |

```
DOMAIN-SCHEMA tournament-participation;

  CONCEPT player;
    ATTRIBUTES:
      name: STRING;
      nationality: STRING;
  END CONCEPT player;

  CONCEPT tournament;
    ATTRIBUTES:
      city: STRING;
      participants: INTEGER;
      dates: STRING;
      rounds: INTEGER;
  END CONCEPT tournament;

  BINARY-RELATION played-in;
    ARGUMENT-1:
      player;
    ARGUMENT-2:
      tournament;
    ATTRIBUTES:
      score: REAL;
  END BINARY-RELATION played-in;

END DOMAIN-SCHEMA tournament-participation;
```

Figure A.11
Domain schema for participation in chess tournaments.

Example   A simple domain schema for players who can participate in tournaments is shown in Figure A.11. For a particular tournament, for example the first match for the chess World Championship, we have the instances shown in Figure A.12. The example illustrates that for each instance, obviously, the construct that defines the instances must be given (with **instance-of**). The arguments of a tuple refer to the *names* of instances.

A.2.5   Inference Knowledge

inference-knowledge   ::=   **inference-knowledge** *Inference-knowledge* ;
                                        [terminology]
                                        [**use** : use-construct , ... ;]
                                        ⟨ inference |
                                            knowledge-role |
                                            transfer-function ⟩ *
                          end inference-knowledge [*Inference-knowledge* ;] .

```
KNOWLEDGE-BASE 'World Chess Championships';
  USE: tournament-participation;

  INSTANCE steinitz;
    INSTANCE-OF: player;
    ATTRIBUTES:
      name: 'William Steinitz';
      nationality: AUT;
  END INSTANCE

  INSTANCE zukertort;
    INSTANCE-OF: player;
    ATTRIBUTES:
      name: 'Johannes Zukertort';
      nationality: POL;
  END INSTANCE

  INSTANCE 'WCC 01';
    INSTANCE-OF: tournament;
    ATTRIBUTES:
      city: 'New York, St Louis, New Orleans (USA)';
      dates: 'January 3 - March 11, 1886';
      participants: 2;
      rounds: 20;
  END INSTANCE

  TUPLE
    INSTANCE-OF: played-in;
    ARGUMENT-1: steinitz;
    ARGUMENT-2: 'WCC 01';
    ATTRIBUTES:
      score: 12.5;
  END TUPLE

  TUPLE
    INSTANCE-OF: played-in;
    ARGUMENT-1: zukertort;
    ARGUMENT-2: 'WCC 01';
    ATTRIBUTES:
      score: 7.5;
  END TUPLE
END KNOWLEDGE-BASE 'World Chess Championships';
```

Figure A.12
Example instances in the chess knowledge base.

Inference

inference	::=	**inference** *Inference* ;
		[terminology]
		[**operation-type** : *Name* ;]
		roles :
		input : *Dynamic-knowledge-role* , ... ;
		output : *Dynamic-knowledge-role* , ... ;
		[**static** : *Static-knowledge-role* , ... ;]
		[specification]
		end inference [*Inference* ;] .

Transfer Function

transfer-function	::=	**transfer-function** *Transfer-function* ;
		[terminology]
		type : ⟨ **provide** | **receive** | **obtain** | **present** ⟩
		roles :
		input : *Dynamic-knowledge-role* , ... ;
		output : *Dynamic-knowledge-role* , ... ;
		end transfer-function [*Transfer-function* ;] .

Knowledge Role

knowledge-role	::=	**knowledge-role** *Knowledge-role* ;
		[terminology]
		type : **static** | **dynamic** ;
		domain-mapping :
		⟨ dynamic-domain-reference |
		static-domain-reference ⟩ ;
		end knowledge-role [*Knowledge-role* ;] .
dynamic-domain-reference	::=	domain-construct-type |
		set-of domain-construct-type |
		list-of domain-construct-type .
static-domain-reference	::=	domain-construct-type **from** *Knowledge-base* .

A.2.6   Task Knowledge

task-knowledge	::=	**task-knowledge** *Task-knowledge* ;
		[terminology]
		[**use** : *Inference-knowledge* , ... ;]
		task-element*
		end task-knowledge [*Task-knowledge* ;] .

Task

task	::=	**task** *Task*
		[terminology]
		[**domain-name** : *Domain* ;]
		[**goal** : `"Text"` ;]
		roles :
		input : role-description+
		output : role-description+
		[**specification** : `"Text"` ;]
		end task [*Task* ;] .
role-description	::=	*Task-role* : `"Text"` ; .

Task Method

The decomposition of a task method allows the specification of a function if it is not known whether the decomposition is an inference or a tasks. This facilitates the construction of flexible libraries.

task-method	::=	**task-method** *Task-method* ;
		[**realizes** : *Task* ;]
		task-decomposition
		[**roles** : **intermediate** : role-description+]
		control-structure : control-structure
		[**assumptions** : `"Text"` ;]
		end task-method [*Task-method* ;] .

A.2.7   Control Structure

control-structure	::=	pseudo-code .
pseudo-code	::=	statement+ | ⟨ { pseudo-code } ⟩ .
statement	::=	function-call ; |
		control-loop |
		conditional-statement |
		role-operation |
		`"Text"` ; .
function-call	::=	function ([proc-input] [`'->'` proc-output]) ; .
function	::=	*Task* | *Inference* | transfer-function .
proc-input	::=	*Role* `'+'` ... .
proc-output	::=	*Role* `'+'` ... .
control-loop	::=	⟨ **repeat** pseudo-code **until** control-condition ;
		end repeat ⟩ |
		⟨ **while** control-condition **do** pseudo-code **end while** ⟩ |
		⟨ **for-each** *Role* **in** *Role* **do** pseudo-code **end for-each** ⟩ .

control-condition	::=	⟨ **has-solution** function-call ⟩ |
		⟨ **new-solution** function-call ⟩ |
		⟨ **empty** *Role* ⟩ |
		⟨ control-condition **and** control-condition ⟩ |
		⟨ control-condition **or** control-condition ⟩ |
		⟨ control-condition **xor** control-condition ⟩ |
		⟨ **not** control-condition ⟩ |
		⟨ **size** *Role* comparison-operator *Integer* ⟩ |
		⟨ *Role* comparison-operator *Value* ⟩ |
		⟨ (control-condition) ⟩ |
		`"Text"` .
role-operation	::=	*Role* ' `:=` ' role-expression ; .
role-expression	::=	*Role* |
		⟨ unary-role-operator role-expression ⟩ |
		⟨ role-expression binary-role-operator role-expression ⟩ .
binary-role-operator	::=	**add** | **delete** | **subtract** .
unary-role-operator	::=	**member** | **select** | **select-random** .

A.2.8   Problem-Solving Methods

Problem-solving methods (PSMs) are generalized task methods (see Chapter 13). PSM descriptions are usually not part of a specific knowledge model of an application, but are placed in a separate library to be used by application developers. The corresponding language definitions are included here for completeness.

psm-knowledge	::=	**psm-knowledge** *Psm-knowledge*
		[terminology]
		psm-description*
		end psm-knowledge [*Psm-knowledge* ;] .
psm	::=	**psm** *Psm* ;
		[terminology]
		[**can-realize** : problem-type , ... ;]
		decomposition :
		functions : *Function* , ... ;
		roles :
		input : role-description+
		output : role-description+
		intermediate : role-description+
		control-structure : control-structure
		[**competence** : `"Text"` ;]
		[**assumptions** : `"Text"` ;]
		[**pragmatic-concerns** : `"Text"` ;]
		[**cost** : `"Text"` ;]
		[**utility** : `"Text"` ;]
		[**communication-protocol** : `"Text"` ;]
		end psm [*Psm* ;] .

| problem-type | ::= | **assessment** \| **assignment** \| **classification** \|
configuration \| **design** \| **diagnosis** \|
modelling \| **monitoring** \| **planning** \|
prediction \| **scheduling** \| `"Text"` . |

A.2.9   Ontology Mapping

Note An elaborate description of ontology mappings is the subject of further research.

| ontology-mapping | ::= | **ontology-mapping** *Ontology-mapping* ;
[terminology]
from : *Domain-schema* ;
to : *Domain-schema* ;
mappings : `"Text"` ;
end ontology-mapping [*Ontology-mapping* ;] . |

A.2.10   Equations

The equation syntax is adopted from NMF (Neutral Model Format). NMF is an emerging standard for the definition of mathematical models. The basic entry point is **equation** (Section A.2.10, p. 417). A description of the operators and their precedence is given in **operator-precedence** (Section A.1.3, p. 404).

Equation

equation	::=	' (' equation ') ' | sign-operator equation | negation-operator equation | equation arithmetic-operator equation | equation logical-operator equation | equation comparison-operator equation | equation dereference-operator equation | equation equation-operator equation | unsigned-constant | variable-expression | function-expression | conditional-expression .
variable-expression	::=	*Variable* [derivative] [subscripts] .
subscripts	::=	' [' equation , ... '] ' .
unsigned-constant	::=	*Unsigned-integer* | *Unsigned-real* | `"Text"` .
function-expression	::=	*Function* (equation , ...) .

conditional-expression	::=	**if** equation **then**
		   equation
		   [**else** equation]
		end if .

Operators

equation

equivalence-operator	::=	'='.
assignment-operator	::=	':='.
sign-operator	::=	'+' | '-'.
negation-operator	::=	**not**.
arithmetic-operator	::=	'+' | '-' | '*' | '/' | '**'.
logical-operator	::=	**and** | **or** | **xor**.
implication-operator	::=	'->' | '<-' | '<->'.
dereference-operator	::=	'.'.
comparison-operator	::=	'<' | '>' | '<=' | '>=' | '==' | '!='.
derivative-operator	::=	'''.

A.2.11 Support

Cardinality

cardinality	::=	**cardinality** : cardinality-spec ; .
cardinality-spec	::=	**any** |
		Natural |
		Natural "+" |
		Natural "-" *Natural* .

Role

role	::=	**role** : *Role* ; .

Terminology

terminology	::=	[**description** : "Text" ;]
		[**sources** : "Text" ;]
		[**synonyms** : *Name* , ... ;]
		[**translation** : *Name* , ... ;] .

A construct can be annotated with a textual description and sources (textbook, dictionary) as well as with a list of synonyms and translations.

A.3   Full Knowledge Model for the Housing Application

```
KNOWLEDGE-MODEL Housing;

/* Knowledge model for the assessment task in the housing case study.
   See for more information Chapter 10.

   AUTHOR:              Guus Schreiber, UvA
   LAST MODIFIED:       25 May 1998
*/


DOMAIN-KNOWLEDGE residence-domain;

DOMAIN-SCHEMA assessment-schema;

CONCEPT residence;
    DESCRIPTION:
        "A description of a residence in the database of the
         distribution system";
    ATTRIBUTES:
        number: NATURAL;
        category: {starter-residence, follow-up-residence};
        build-type: {house, apartment};
        street-address: STRING;
        city: STRING;
        num-rooms: NATURAL;
        rent: REAL;
        min-num-inhabitants: NATURAL;
        max-num-inhabitants: NATURAL;
        subsidy-type: subsidy-type-value;
        surface-in-square-meters: NATURAL;
        floor: NATURAL;
        lift-available: BOOLEAN;
    AXIOMS:
        min-num-inhabitants <= max-num-inhabitants;
END CONCEPT residence;

VALUE-TYPE subsidy-type-value;
    TYPE: NOMINAL;
    VALUE-LIST: {subsidizable, free-sector};
END VALUE-TYPE subsidy-type-value;

CONCEPT applicant;
    DESCRIPTION:
        "A person or group of persons (household) registered as
         potential applicants for a residence";
    ATTRIBUTES:
        registration-number: STRING;
        applicant-type: {starter, existing-resident};
        name: STRING;
```

```
        street-address: STRING;
        city: STRING;
        birth-date: STRING;
        age: NATURAL;
        age-category: age-category-value;
        gross-yearly-income: NATURAL;
        household-size: NATURAL;
        household-type:           household-type-value;
    AXIOMS:
        applicant.age = FLOOR(TODAY() - applicant.birth-date);
END CONCEPT applicant;

VALUE-TYPE age-category-value;
     TYPE: ORDINAL;
     VALUE-LIST: {'upto 22', '23-64', '65+'};
END VALUE-TYPE age-category-value;

VALUE-TYPE household-type-value;
     TYPE: NOMINAL;
     VALUE-LIST: {single-person, multi-person};
END VALUE-TYPE household-type-value;

BINARY-RELATION residence-application;
    DESCRIPTION:
        "Application of an applicant for a certain residence. ";
    ARGUMENT-1: applicant;
        CARDINALITY: 0+;
    ARGUMENT-2: residence;
        CARDINALITY: 0-2;
    ATTRIBUTES:
        application-date: DATE;
END BINARY-RELATION residence-application;

/* assessment knowledge types */

RULE-TYPE residence-abstraction;
    ANTECEDENT:
        residence-application;
            CARDINALITY: 1+;
    CONSEQUENT:
        residence-application;
            CARDINALITY: 1;
    CONNECTION-SYMBOL:
        has-abstraction;
END RULE-TYPE residence--abstraction;

CONCEPT residence-criterion;
    ATTRIBUTES:
        truth-value: BOOLEAN;
END CONCEPT residence-criterion;
```

```
CONCEPT correct-household-size;
    SUB-TYPE-OF: residence-criterion;
END CONCEPT correct-household-size;

CONCEPT correct-residence-type;
    SUB-TYPE-OF: residence-criterion;
END CONCEPT correct-residence-type;

CONCEPT residence-specific-constraints;
    SUB-TYPE-OF: residence-criterion;
END CONCEPT residence-specific-constraints;

CONCEPT rent-fits-income;
    SUB-TYPE-OF: residence-criterion;
END CONCEPT rent-fits-income;

RULE-TYPE residence-requirement;
    ANTECEDENT:
        residence-application;
            CARDINALITY: 1+;
    CONSEQUENT:
        residence-criterion;
            CARDINALITY: 1;
    CONNECTION-SYMBOL:
        indicates;
END RULE-TYPE residence-requirement;

CONCEPT residence-decision;
    ATTRIBUTES:
        value: {eligible, not-eligible};
END CONCEPT residence-decision;

RULE-TYPE residence-decision-rule;
    ANTECEDENT:
        residence-criterion;
    CONSEQUENT:
        residence-decision;
    CONNECTION-SYMBOL:
        implies;
END RULE-TYPE residence-decision-rule;

END DOMAIN-SCHEMA assessment-schema;

KNOWLEDGE-BASE system-description;
    USES:
        residence-abstraction FROM assessment-schema;
    EXPRESSIONS:
        /* Abstraction rules */

        applicant.age < 23
            HAS-ABSTRACTION
```

```
        applicant.age-category = 'upto 22';

        applicant.age >= 23 AND
        applicant.age < 65
            HAS-ABSTRACTION
        applicant.age-category = '23-64';

        applicant.age >= 65
            HAS-ABSTRACTION
        applicant.age-category = '65+';

        applicant.household-size = 1
            HAS-ABSTRACTION
        applicant.household-type = single-person;

        applicant.household-size > 1
            HAS-ABSTRACTION
        applicant.household-type = multi-person;
END KNOWLEDGE-BASE system-description;

KNOWLEDGE-BASE measurement-system;
    USES:
        residence-requirement FROM assessment-schema,
        residence-decision-rule FROM assessment-schema;
    EXPRESSIONS:
        /* Requirements */

        /* correct residence category? */

        residence.description.subsidy-type = free-sector
            INDICATES
        correct-residence-category.truth-value = true;

        residence.category = starter-residence AND
        applicant.sub-type = starter
            INDICATES
        correct-residence-category.truth-value = true;

        residence.category = follow-up-residence AND
        applicant.sub-type = existing-resident
            INDICATES
        correct-residence-category.truth-value = true;

        /* correct household size? */

        residence.description.min-num-inhabitants <=
        applicant.household-size
        AND
        residence.description.max-num-inhabitants >=
        applicant.household-size
            INDICATES
```

```
correct-household-size.truth-value = true;

/* rent fits income
   free sector residence */

applicant.gross-yearly-income >= 70000 AND
residence.description.rent > 1007
    INDICATES
rent-fits-income.truth-value = true;

/* rent fits income
   single-person upto 22  */

applicant.household-type = single-person AND
applicant.age-category = 'upto 22' AND
applicant.gross-yearly-income < 27000 AND
residence.description.rent < 524
    INDICATES
rent-fits-income.truth-value = true;

applicant.household-type = single-person AND
applicant.age-category = 'upto 22' AND
applicant.gross-yearly-income >= 27000 AND
applicant.gross-yearly-income <  35000 AND
residence.description.rent < 1007
    INDICATES
rent-fits-income.truth-value = true;

applicant.household-type = single-person AND
applicant.age-category = 'upto 22' AND
applicant.gross-yearly-income >= 35000 AND
applicant.gross-yearly-income <  45000 AND
residence.description.rent >= 600
    INDICATES
rent-fits-income.truth-value = true;

applicant.household-type = single-person AND
applicant.age-category = 'upto 22' AND
applicant.gross-yearly-income >= 45000 AND
applicant.gross-yearly-income <  70000 AND
residence.description.rent >= 810
    INDICATES
rent-fits-income.truth-value = true;

/* rent fits income
   multi-person upto 22  */

applicant.household-type = multi-person AND
applicant.age-category = 'upto 22' AND
applicant.gross-yearly-income < 38000 AND
residence.description.rent < 524
```

```
     INDICATES
rent-fits-income.truth-value = true;

applicant.household-type = multi-person AND
applicant.age-category = 'upto 22' AND
applicant.gross-yearly-income >= 38000 AND
applicant.gross-yearly-income <  46000 AND
residence.description.rent < 1007
     INDICATES
rent-fits-income.truth-value = true;

applicant.household-type = multi-person AND
applicant.age-category = 'upto 22' AND
applicant.gross-yearly-income >= 46000 AND
applicant.gross-yearly-income <  56000 AND
residence.description.rent >= 600
     INDICATES
rent-fits-income.truth-value = true;

applicant.household-type = multi-person AND
applicant.age-category = 'upto 22' AND
applicant.gross-yearly-income >= 56000 AND
applicant.gross-yearly-income <  70000 AND
residence.description.rent >= 810
     INDICATES
rent-fits-income.truth-value = true;

/* rent fits income
   single-person 23-64 */

applicant.household-type = single-person AND
applicant.age-category = '23-64' AND
applicant.gross-yearly-income < 25000 AND
residence.description.rent < 679
     INDICATES
rent-fits-income.truth-value = true;

applicant.household-type = single-person AND
applicant.age-category = '23-64' AND
applicant.gross-yearly-income >= 25000 AND
applicant.gross-yearly-income <  35000 AND
residence.description.rent < 1007
     INDICATES
rent-fits-income.truth-value = true;

applicant.household-type = single-person AND
applicant.age-category = '23-64' AND
applicant.gross-yearly-income >= 35000 AND
applicant.gross-yearly-income <  45000 AND
residence.description.rent >= 600
     INDICATES
```

```
rent-fits-income.truth-value = true;

applicant.household-type = single-person AND
applicant.age-category = '23-64' AND
applicant.gross-yearly-income >= 45000 AND
applicant.gross-yearly-income <  70000 AND
residence.description.rent >= 810
    INDICATES
rent-fits-income.truth-value = true;


/* rent fits income
   multi-person 23-64 */

applicant.household-type = multi-person AND
applicant.age-category = '23-64' AND
applicant.gross-yearly-income < 34000 AND
residence.description.rent < 679
    INDICATES
rent-fits-income.truth-value = true;

applicant.household-type = multi-person AND
applicant.age-category = '23-64' AND
applicant.gross-yearly-income >= 24000 AND
applicant.gross-yearly-income <  46000 AND
residence.description.rent < 1007
    INDICATES
rent-fits-income.truth-value = true;

applicant.household-type = multi-person AND
applicant.age-category = '23-64' AND
applicant.gross-yearly-income >= 46000 AND
applicant.gross-yearly-income <  56000 AND
residence.description.rent >= 600
    INDICATES
rent-fits-income.truth-value = true;

applicant.household-type = multi-person AND
applicant.age-category = '23-64' AND
applicant.gross-yearly-income >= 56000 AND
applicant.gross-yearly-income <  70000 AND
residence.description.rent >= 810
    INDICATES
rent-fits-income.truth-value = true;

/* rent fits income
   single-person 65+ */

applicant.household-type = single-person AND
applicant.age-category = '65+' AND
applicant.gross-yearly-income < 25000 AND
```

```
residence.description.rent < 679
    INDICATES
rent-fits-income.truth-value = true;


applicant.household-type = single-person AND
applicant.age-category = '65+' AND
applicant.gross-yearly-income >= 25000 AND
applicant.gross-yearly-income <  29000 AND
residence.description.rent < 1007
    INDICATES
rent-fits-income.truth-value = true;


applicant.household-type = single-person AND
applicant.age-category = '65+' AND
applicant.gross-yearly-income >= 29000 AND
applicant.gross-yearly-income <  45000 AND
residence.description.rent >= 600
    INDICATES
rent-fits-income.truth-value = true;


applicant.household-type = single-person AND
applicant.age-category = '65+' AND
applicant.gross-yearly-income >= 45000 AND
applicant.gross-yearly-income <  70000 AND
residence.description.rent >= 810
    INDICATES
rent-fits-income.truth-value = true;


/* rent fits income
   multi-person 65+ */

applicant.household-type = multi-person AND
applicant.age-category = '65+' AND
applicant.gross-yearly-income < 31000 AND
residence.description.rent < 679
    INDICATES
rent-fits-income.truth-value = true;


applicant.household-type = multi-person AND
applicant.age-category = '65+' AND
applicant.gross-yearly-income >= 31000 AND
applicant.gross-yearly-income <  39000 AND
residence.description.rent < 1007
    INDICATES
rent-fits-income.truth-value = true;


applicant.household-type = multi-person AND
applicant.age-category = '65+' AND
applicant.gross-yearly-income >= 39000 AND
applicant.gross-yearly-income <  56000 AND
```

```
residence.description.rent >= 600
    INDICATES
rent-fits-income.truth-value = true;

applicant.household-type = multi-person AND
applicant.age-category = '65+' AND
applicant.gross-yearly-income >= 56000 AND
applicant.gross-yearly-income <  70000 AND
residence.description.rent >= 810
    INDICATES
rent-fits-income.truth-value = true;

/* decision rules */

correct-residence-category.truth-value = true AND
correct-household-size.truth-value = true AND
rent-fits-income.truth-value = true AND
residence-specific-constraints.truth-value = true
    IMPLIES
residence-decision.value = eligible;

correct-residence-category.truth-value = false
    IMPLIES
residence-decision.value = not-eligible;

correct-household-size.truth-value = false
    IMPLIES
residence-decision.value = not-eligible;

rent-fits-income.truth-value = false
    IMPLIES
residence-decision.value = not-eligible;

residence-specific-constraints.truth-value = false
    IMPLIES
residence-decision.value = not-eligible;
END KNOWLEDGE-BASE measurement-system;

END DOMAIN-KNOWLEDGE

INFERENCE-KNOWLEDGE assessment-inferences;

KNOWLEDGE-ROLE case-description;
    TYPE: DYNAMIC;
    DOMAIN-MAPPING:
        residence-application;
END KNOWLEDGE-ROLE case-description;

KNOWLEDGE-ROLE case-specific-requirements;
    TYPE: DYNAMIC;
    DOMAIN-MAPPING:
```

```
        SET-OF residence-requirement;
END KNOWLEDGE-ROLE case-specific-requirements;

KNOWLEDGE-ROLE decision;
    TYPE: DYNAMIC;
    DOMAIN-MAPPING:
        residence-decision;
END KNOWLEDGE-ROLE decision;

KNOWLEDGE-ROLE abstracted-case;
    TYPE: DYNAMIC;
    DOMAIN-MAPPING:
        residence-application;
END KNOWLEDGE-ROLE abstracted-case;

KNOWLEDGE-ROLE norm;
    TYPE: DYNAMIC;
    DOMAIN-MAPPING:
        residence-criterion;
END KNOWLEDGE-ROLE norm;

KNOWLEDGE-ROLE norm-value;
    TYPE: DYNAMIC;
    DOMAIN-MAPPING:
        residence-criterion;
END KNOWLEDGE-ROLE norm-value;

KNOWLEDGE-ROLE norms;
    TYPE: DYNAMIC;
    DOMAIN-MAPPING:
        SET-OF residence-criterion;
END KNOWLEDGE-ROLE norms;

KNOWLEDGE-ROLE evaluation-results;
    TYPE: DYNAMIC;
    DOMAIN-MAPPING:
        SET-OF residence-criterion;
END KNOWLEDGE-ROLE evaluation-results;

KNOWLEDGE-ROLE abstraction-knowledge;
    TYPE: STATIC;
    DOMAIN-MAPPING:
        residence-abstraction FROM system-description;
END KNOWLEDGE-ROLE abstraction-knowledge;

KNOWLEDGE-ROLE norm-set;
    TYPE: STATIC;
    DOMAIN-MAPPING:
        residence-criterion FROM measurement-system;
END KNOWLEDGE-ROLE norm-set;
```

```
KNOWLEDGE-ROLE requirements;
    TYPE: STATIC;
    DOMAIN-MAPPING:
        residence-requirement FROM measurement-system;
END KNOWLEDGE-ROLE requirements;

KNOWLEDGE-ROLE decision-knowledge;
    TYPE: STATIC;
    DOMAIN-MAPPING:
        residence-decision-rule FROM measurement-system;
END KNOWLEDGE-ROLE decision-knowledge;

INFERENCE abstract;
    ROLES:
      INPUT:
        case-description;
      OUTPUT:
        abstracted-case;
      STATIC:
        abstraction-knowledge;
    SPECIFICATION: "
        Input is a set of case data. Output is the same set of data
        extended with an abstracted feature that can be derived
        from the data using the corpus of abstraction knowledge.";
END INFERENCE abstract;

INFERENCE specify;
    OPERATION-TYPE: lookup;
    ROLES:
      INPUT:
        abstracted-case;
      OUTPUT:
        norms;
      STATIC:
        norm-set;
    SPECIFICATION:
        "This inference is just a simple look-up of the norms";
END INFERENCE specify;

INFERENCE select;
    ROLES:
        INPUT:
            norms;
        OUTPUT:
            norm;
    SPECIFICATION:
        "No domain knowledge is used in norm selection: the
        section is a random one.";
END INFERENCE select;

INFERENCE evaluate;
```

```
    ROLES:
      INPUT:
        norm,
        abstracted-case,
        case-specific-requirements;
      OUTPUT:
        norm-value;
      STATIC:
        requirements;
    SPECIFICATION: "
        Establish the truth value of the input norm for the given
        case description. The underlying domain knowledge is
        formed by both        the requirements in the knowl-
edge base as
        well as additional case-specific requirements, that are
        part of the input.";
END INFERENCE evaluate;

INFERENCE match;
    ROLES:
      INPUT:
        evaluation-results;
      OUTPUT:
        decision;
      STATIC:
        decision-knowledge;
    SPECIFICATION: "
        See whether the available evaluation results enable a
        decision to be taken. The inference fails if this is
        not the case.";
END INFERENCE match;

END INFERENCE-KNOWLEDGE


/* Tasks */

TASK-KNOWLEDGE assessment-tasks;

TASK assess-case;
    DOMAIN-NAME: asses-residence-application;
    GOAL: "
        Assess whether an application for a residence by a certain
        applicant satisfies the criteria.";
    ROLES:
      INPUT:
        case-description: "Data about an applicant and a residence";
        case-specific-requirements: "Residence-specific criteria";
      OUTPUT:
        decision: "eligible or not-eligible for a residence";
END TASK assess-case;
```

```
TASK-METHOD assess-through-abstract-and-match;
    REALIZES:
        assess-case;
    DECOMPOSITION:
        TASKS: abstract-case, match-case;
    ROLES:
      INTERMEDIATE:
        abstracted-case: "Original case plus abstractions";
    CONTROL-STRUCTURE:
        abstract-case(case-description -> abstracted-case);
        match-case(abstracted-case + case-specific-requirements
                -> decision);
END TASK-METHOD assess-through-abstract-and-match;

TASK abstract-case;
    DOMAIN-NAME: abstract-applicant-data;
    GOAL:
        "Add case abstractions to the case description";
    ROLES:
      INPUT:
        case-description: "The 'raw' case data";
      OUTPUT:
        abstracted-case: "The raw data plus the abstractions";
END TASK abstract-case;

TASK-METHOD abstract-method;
    REALIZES:
        abstract-case;
    DECOMPOSITION:
        INFERENCES: abstract;
    CONTROL-STRUCTURE:
        WHILE HAS-SOLUTION abstract(case-description
                -> abstracted-case) DO
            /* use the abstracted case as the input in invocation of
            the next abstraction inference */
            case-description := abstracted-case;
        END WHILE
END TASK-METHOD abstract-method;

TASK match-case;
    DOMAIN-NAME: match-residence-application;
    GOAL: "
        Apply the norms to the case to find out whether it satisfies
        the criteria.";
    ROLES:
      INPUT:
        abstracted-case: "Case description plus the abstractions";
        case-specific-requirements: "Criteria specific for a
                certain residence.";
      OUTPUT:
```

```
            decision: "Eligible or not eligible";
END TASK match-case;

TASK-METHOD match-method;
    REALIZES:
        match-case;
    DECOMPOSITION:
        INFERENCES: specify, select, evaluate, match;
    ROLES:
      INTERMEDIATE:
        norms: "The full set of assessment norms";
        norm: "A single assessment norm";
        norm-value: "Truth value of a norm for this case";
        evaluation-results: "List of norm together with
                        their truth values";
    CONTROL-STRUCTURE:
        specify(abstracted-case -> norms);
        REPEAT
            select(norms -> norm);
            evaluate(abstracted-case + case-specific-requirements
                + norm -> norm-value);
            evaluation-results := norm-value ADD evaluation-results;
        UNTIL
            HAS-SOLUTION match(evaluation-results -> decision);
        END REPEAT
END TASK-METHOD match-method;

END TASK-KNOWLEDGE

END KNOWLEDGE-MODEL housing;
```

Glossary of Graphical Notations

Task Decomposition

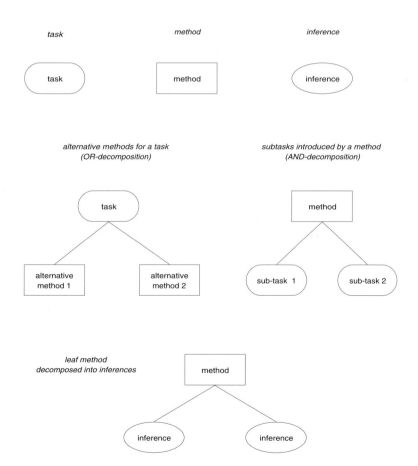

Inference Structure

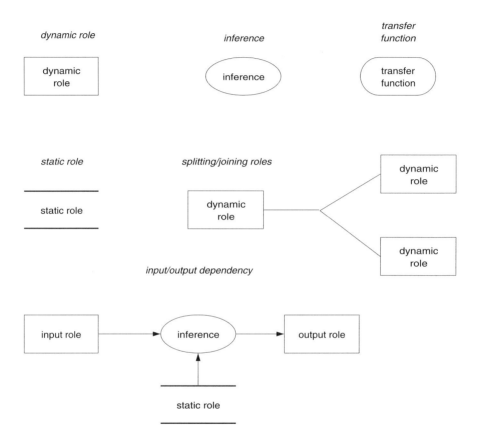

Domain Schema (1)

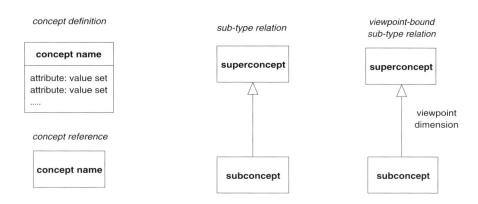

binary relation (use arrowed line if directed)

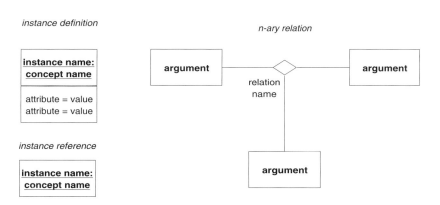

Domain Schema (2)

relation as concept

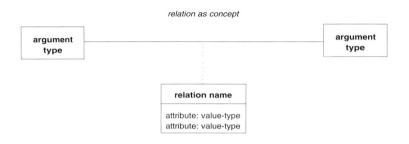

rule type

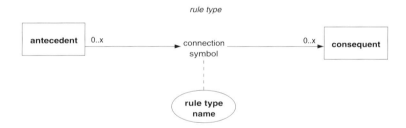

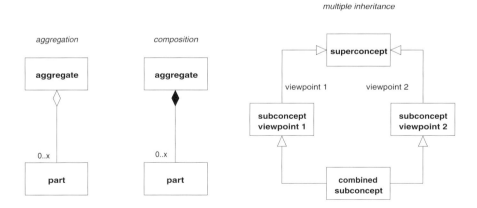

UML Class Diagram

class

class name
attribute: datatype ....
operation(args) -> returndatatype ....

For the rest: see the domin-schema notations
class = concept (without operations)
association = relation

UML Use-Case Diagram

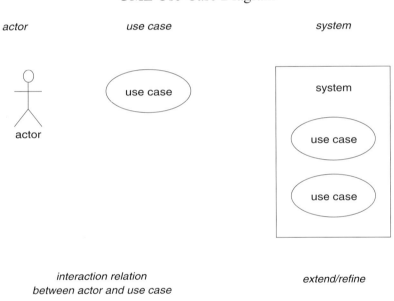

actor   *use case*   *system*

interaction relation
between actor and use case   *extend/refine*

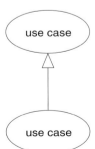

UML Activity Diagram

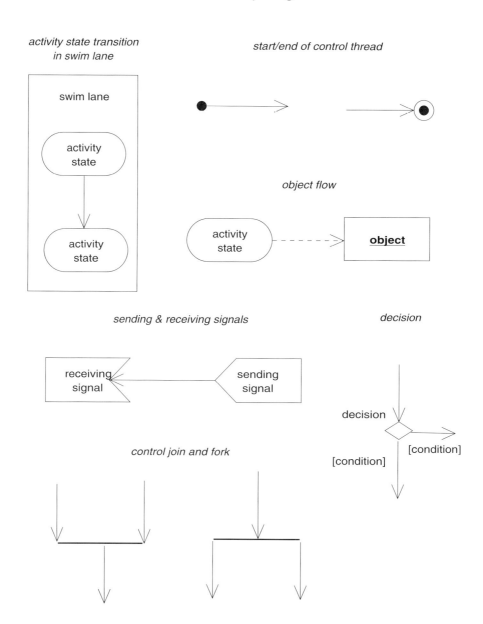

*activity state transition
in swim lane*

start/end of control thread

object flow

sending & receiving signals

decision

control join and fork

UML State Diagram

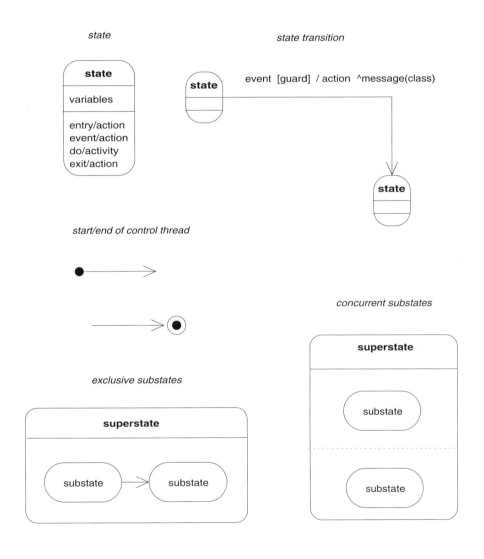

References

Aben, M. (1995). *Formal Methods in Knowledge Engineering*. Ph.D. thesis, University of Amsterdam, Faculty of Psychology.

Akkermans, J. M., Gustavsson, R., and Ygge, F. (1998). An integrated structured analysis approach to intelligent agent communication. In Cuena, J., editor, *Proceedings IFIP 1998 World Computer Congress, IT&KNOWS Conference*, London. Chapman & Hall.

Akkermans, J. M., Ygge, F., and Gustavsson, R. (1996). Homebots: Intelligent decentralized services for energy management. In Schreinemakers, J., editor, *Knowledge Management – Organization, Competence and Methodology*, pp. 128–142. Würzburg, Germany, Ergon Verlag.

Angele, J., Fensel, D., Landes, D., and Studer, R. (1998). Developing knowledge-based systems with MIKE. *Journal of Automated Software Engineering*.

Argyris, C. (1993). *Knowledge for Action*. San Francisco, Jossey-Bass.

Ben-Natan, R. (1995). *CORBA: A Guide to Common Object Request Broker Architecture*. New York, McGraw-Hill.

Benjamins, V. R. (1993). *Problem Solving Methods for Diagnosis*. Ph.D. thesis, University of Amsterdam, Amsterdam.

Benjamins, V. R. and Fensel, D. (1998). Editorial. *International Journal of Human-Computer Studies*, 49(5).

Benus, B. and de Hoog, R. (1994). Knowledge management with CommonKADS models. In Liebowitz, J., editor, *Moving Towards Expert Systems Globally in the 21st Century*, pp. 193–200.

Boehm, B. (1981). *Software Engineering Economics*. Englewood Cliffs, NJ, Prentice-Hall.

Boehm, B. (1988). A spiral model of software development and enhancement. *Computer*, May:61–72.

Booch, G. (1994). *Object-Oriented Analysis and Design with Applications*. Redwood City, CA, Benjamin Cummings.

Booch, G., Rumbaugh, J., and Jacobson, I. (1998). *The Unified Modelling Language User Guide*. Reading, MA, Addison-Wesley.

Bradshaw, J. (1997). *Software Agents*. Cambridge, MA, MIT Press.

Brazier, F., van Lange, P. H., Treur, J., Wijgaards, N. J. E., and Willems, M. (1996). Modelling an elevator design task in DESIRE: the VT example. *International Journal of Human-Computer Studies*, 44(3/4):469–520.

Breuker, J. A. and Van de Velde, W., editors (1994). *The CommonKADS Library for Expertise Modelling*. Amsterdam, IOS Press.

Breuker, J. A., Wielinga, B. J., van Someren, M. W., de Hoog, R., Schreiber, A. Th., de Greef, P., Bredeweg, B., Wielemaker, J., Billault, J. P., Davoodi, M., and Hayward, S. A. (1987). Model Driven Knowledge Acquisition: Interpretation Models. ESPRIT Project P1098 Deliverable D1 (task A1), University of Amsterdam and STL Ltd.

Carbonell, J. G., editor (1989). *Machine Learning: Paradigms and Methods*. Cambridge, MA, MIT Press.

Chandrasekaran, B. (1988). Generic tasks as building blocks for knowledge-based systems: The diagnosis and routine design examples. *The Knowledge Engineering Review*, 3(3):183–210.

Chandrasekaran, B. (1990). Design problem solving: A task analysis. *AI Magazine*, 11:59–71.

Chandrasekaran, B. and Johnson, T. R. (1993). Generic tasks and task structures: History, critique and new directions,. In David, J. M., Krivine, J. P., and Simmons, R., editors, *Second Generation Expert Systems*. Berlin, Springer-Verlag.

Checkland, P. and Scholes, J. (1990). *Soft Systems Methodology in Action*. Chichester, UK, Wiley.

Chi, M. T. H., Feltovich, P., and Glaser, R. (1981). Categorization and representation of physics problems by experts and novices. *Cognitive Science*, 5:121–152.

Chi, M. T. H., Glaser, R., and Farr, M. (1988). *The Nature of Expertise*. Hillsdale, NJ, Erlbaum.

Clancey, W. J. (1985). Heuristic classification. *Artificial Intelligence*, 27:289–350.

Cleaves, D. A. (1987). Cognitive biases and corrective techniques: proposals for improving elicitation procedures for knowledge based systems. *International Journal of Human-Computer Studies*, 27:155–166.

Davenport, T. and Prusak, L. (1998). *Working Knowledge*. Boston, Harvard Business School Press.

de Hoog, R., Benus, B., Vogler, M., and Metselaar, C. (1996). The CommonKADS organization model: content, usage and computer support. *Expert Systems With Applications*, 11(1):29–40.

Drucker, P. (1993). *Post-Capitalist Society*. Oxford, UK, Butterworth-Heinemann.

D'Souza, D. F. and Wills, A. C. (1998). *Objects, Components and Frameworks with UML: The Catalysis Approach*. Reading, MA, Addison-Wesley.

Edvinsson, L. and Malone, M. S. (1997). *Intellectual Capital*. New York, Harper Business.

Ericsson, K. A. and Simon, H. A. (1993). *Protocol Analysis: Verbal Reports as Data, revised edition*. Cambridge, MA, MIT Press.

Eriksson, H.-E. and Penker, M. (1998). *UML Toolkit*. New York, Wiley.

Feltovich, P., Ford, K., and Hoffman, R. (1997). *Expertise in Context – Human and Machine*. Cambridge, MA, MIT Press.

Fensel, D. and van Harmelen, F. (1994). A comparison of languages which operationalise and formalise KADS models of expertise. *The Knowledge Engineering Review*, 9:105–146.

Fletcher, S. (1997). *Analysing Competence – Tools and Techniques for Analyzing Jobs, Roles and Functions*. London, Kogan-Page.

Gaines, B. R. (1997). Using explicit ontologies in KBS development. *International Journal of Human-Computer Studies*, 45(2).

Gamma, E., Helm, R., Johnson, R., and Vlissides, J. (1995). *Design Patterns: Elements of Reusable Object-Oriented Software*. Reading, MA, Addison-Wesley.

Goldberg, A. (1990). Information models, views, and controllers. *Dr. Dobbs Journal*, July:54–61.

Gruber, T. R. (1993). A translation approach to portable ontology specifications. *Knowledge Acquisition*, 5:199–220.

Gruber, T. R. (1994). Towards principles for the design of ontologies used for knowledge sharing. In Guarino, N. and Poli, R., editors, *Formal Ontology in Conceptual Analysis and Knowledge Representation*. Boston, Kluwer.

Guarino, N. (1995). Formal ontology in the information technology. *International Journal of Human-Computer Studies*, 43(5/6).

Haddadi, A. (1995). *Communication and Cooperation in Agent Systems*. Berlin, Springer-Verlag.

Hall, E. (1998). *Managing Risk – Methods for Software Systems Development*. Reading, MA, Addison-Wesley.

Harrison, M. (1994). *Diagnosing Organizations — Methods, Models and Processes*. Thousand Oaks, CA, Sage Publications.

Hayes-Roth, F., Waterman, D. A., and Lenat, D. B. (1983). *Building Expert Systems*. New York, Addison-Wesley.

Hori, M. (1998). Scheduling knowledge model in CommonKADS. Technical Report Research Report RT0233,

Tokyo Research Laboratory, IBM Japan.

Hori, M., Nakamura, Y., Satoh, H., Maruyama, K., Hama, T., Honda, Takenaka, T., and Sekine, F. (1995). Knowledge-level analysis for eliciting composable scheduling knowledge. *Artificial Intelligence in Engineering*, 9(4):253–264.

Hori, M. and Yoshida, T. (1998). Domain-oriented library of scheduling methods: Design principle and real-life application. *International Journal of Human-Computer Studies*, 49(5):601–626.

Jacobson, I., Christerson, M., Jonsson, P., and Overgaard, G. (1992). *Object-Oriented Software Engineering*. Reading, MA, Addison-Wesley.

Johansson, H. J., McHugh, P., Pendlebury, A. J., and III, W. A. W. (1993). *Business Process Reengineering*. New York, Wiley.

Johnson, L. and Johnson, N. (1987). Knowledge elicitation involving teach-back interviewing. In Kidd, A., editor, *Knowledge Elicitation for Expert Systems: A Practical Handbook*. New York, Plenum Press.

Kahneman, D., Slovic, P., and Tversky, A., editors (1982). *Judgement Under Uncertainty: Heuristics and Biases*. New York, Cambridge University Press.

Kelly, G. A. (1955). *The Psychology of Personal Constructs*. New York, Norton.

Kirwan, B. and Ainsworth, L. (1992). *A Guide to Task Analysis*. London, Taylor & Francis.

Klinker, G., Bhola, C., Dallemagne, G., Marques, D., and McDermott, J. (1991). Usable and reusable programming constructs. *Knowledge Acquisition*, 3:117–136.

Linster, M. (1994). Sisyphus'91/92: Models of problem solving. *International Journal of Human Computer Studies*, 40(3).

Marcus, S., editor (1988). *Automatic Knowledge Acquisition for Expert Systems*. Boston, Kluwer.

Martin, B., Subramanian, G., and Yaverbaum, G. (1996). Benefits from expert systems: An exploratory investigation. *Expert Systems With Applications*, 11(1):53–58.

Martin, J. (1990). *Information Engineering*. Englewood Cliffs, NJ, Prentice-Hall. Three volumes. See especially Vol. 2: Planning and Analysis.

McGraw, K. L. and Harrison-Briggs, K. (1989). *Knowledge Acquisition: Principles and Guidelines*. Prentice-Hall International.

Meyer, M. A. and Booker, J. M. (1991). *Eliciting and Analyzing Expert Judgement: A Practical Guide*, Vol. 5 of *Knowledge-Based Systems*. London, Academic Press.

Michalski, R. S., Carbonell, J. G., and Mitchell, T. M., editors (1983). *Machine Learning: An Artificial Intelligence Approach*. Berlin, Springer-Verlag.

Mintzberg, H. and Quinn, J. (1992). *The Strategy Process – Concepts and Contexts*. Englewood Cliffs, NJ, Prentice-Hall.

Motta, E., Stutt, A., Zdrahal, Z., O'Hara, K., and Shadbolt, N. R. (1996). Solving VT in VITAL: a study in model construction and reuse. *International Journal of Human-Computer Studies*, 44(3/4):333–372.

Newell, A. (1982). The knowledge level. *Artificial Intelligence*, 18:87–127.

Nielsen, J. (1998). *Usability Engineering*. San Diego, Academic Press.

Nonaka, I. and Takeuchi, H. (1995). *The Knowledge-Creating Company*. Oxford, UK, Oxford University Press.

Parnas, D. L. and Clements, P. C. (1986). A rational design process: How and why to fake it. *IEEE Transactions on Software Engineering*, 12:251–257.

Peratec (1994). *Total Quality Management*. London, UK, Chapman & Hall.

Porter, M. (1985). *Competitive Advantage*. New York, Free Press.

Post, W., Koster, R. W., Sramek, M., Schreiber, A. Th., Zocca, V., and de Vries, B. (1996). FreeCall: A system for emergency-call handling support. *Methods of Information in Medicine*, 35(3):242–255.

Post, W., Wielinga, B. J., de Hoog, R., and Schreiber, A. Th. (1997). Organizational modeling in CommonKADS: The emergency medical service. *IEEE Intelligent Systems*, 12(6):46–52.

Puppe, F. (1990). *Problemlösungsmethoden in Expertensystemen*. Studienreihe Informatik. Berlin, Springer-Verlag.

Quinn, J. (1992). *Intelligent Enterprise*. New York, Free Press.

Ricketts, I. (1998). *Managing your Software Project*. London, Springer-Verlag.

Rumbaugh, J., Blaha, M., Premerlani, W., Eddy, F., and Lorensen, W. (1991). *Object-Oriented Modelling and Design*. Englewood Cliffs, NJ, Prentice Hall.

Runkel, J. R., Birmingham, W. P., and Balkany, A. (1996). Solving VT by reuse. *International Journal of Human-Computer Studies*, 44(3/4):403–434.

Schein, E. (1992). *Organizational Culture and Leadership*. San Francisco, Jossey-Bass.

Schreiber, A. Th. (1994). Applying KADS to the office assignment domain. *International Journal of Human-Computer Studies*, 40(2):349–377.

Schreiber, A. Th. and Birmingham, W. P. (1996). The Sisyphus-VT initiative. *International Journal of Human-Computer Studies*, 43(3/4).

Schweickert, R., Burton, A. M., Taylor, N. K., Corlett, E. N., Shadbolt, N. R., and Hedgecock, A. P. (1987). Comparing knowledge elicitation techniques: A case study. *Artificial Intelligence Review*, 1:245–253.

Scott-Morgan, P. (1994). *The Unwritten Rules of the Game*. New York, McGraw-Hill.

Shadbolt, N. R. and Burton, A. M. (1989). Empirical studies in knowledge elicitation. *SIGART Special Issue on Knowledge Acquisition, ACM*, 108:15–18.

Shaw, M. L. G. and Gaines, B. R. (1987). An interactive knowledge elicitation technique using personal construct technology. In Kidd, A. L., editor, *Knowledge Acquisition for Expert Systems: A Practical Handbook*, New York. Plenum Press.

Sommerville, I. (1995). *Software Engineering*. Harlow, UK, Addison-Wesley.

Sommerville, I. and Sawyer, P. (1997). *Requirements Engineering – A Good Practice Guide*. Chichester, UK, Wiley.

Spencer, L. M. and Spencer, S. M. (1993). *Competence at Work*. New York, Wiley.

Steels, L. (1990). Components of expertise. *AI Magazine*, Summer.

Steels, L. (1993). The componental framework and its role in reusability. In David, J.-M., Krivine, J.-P., and Simmons, R., editors, *Second Generation Expert Systems*, pp. 273–298. Berlin, Springer-Verlag.

Stefik, M. (1993). *Introduction to Knowledge Systems*. Los Altos, CA. Morgan Kaufmann.

Stewart, T. (1997). *Intellectual Capital – The New Wealth of Organizations*. London, Nicholas Brealey.

Studer, R., Benjamins, V. R., and Fensel, D. (1998). Knowledge engineering: Principles and methods. *Data & Knowledge Engineering*, 25:161–198.

Sveiby, K. E. (1997). *The New Organizational Wealth: Managing and Measuring Knowledge Based Assets*. San Fransisco, Berrett-Koehler.

ten Teije, A., van Harmelen, F., Schreiber, A. Th., and Wielinga, B. J. (1998). Construction of psm as parametric design. *International Journal of Human-Computer Studies*, 49:363–389.

Tissen, R., Andriessen, D., and Deprez, F. (1998). *Value-Based Knowledge Management*. Amsterdam, Addison-Wesley.

Tu, S. W., Eriksson, H., Gennari, J. H., Shahar, Y., and Musen, M. A. (1995). Ontology-based configuration of problem-solving methods and generation of knowledge acquisition tools: The application of PROTÉGÉ-II to protocol-based decision support. *Artificial Intelligence in Medicine*, 7(5).

van der Spek, R. and de Hoog, R. (1994). A framework for a knowledge management methodology. In Wiig, K., editor, *Knowledge Management Methods. Practical Approaches to Managing Knowledge*, pp. 379–393. Arlington, TX, Schema Press.

van der Spek, R. and Spijkervet, A. (1994). Knowledge management. dealing intelligently with knowledge. Technical report, CIBIT, Utrecht, the Netherlands.

van Harmelen, F. (1998). Applying rule-base anomalies to KADS inference structures. *Decision Support Systems*, 21(4):271–280.

van Harmelen, F., Wielinga, B. J., Bredeweg, B., Schreiber, A. Th., Karbach, W., Reinders, M., Voss, A., Akkermans, J. M., Bartsch-Spörl, B., and Vinkhuyzen, E. (1992). Knowledge-level reflection. In Pape, B. L. and Steels, L., editors, *Enhancing the Knowledge Engineering Process – Contributions from ESPRIT*, pp. 175–204. Amsterdam, Elsevier Science.

van Someren, M. W., Barnard, Y., and Sandberg, J. A. C. (1993). *The Think-Aloud Method*. London, Academic Press.

Vanwelkenhuysen, J. and Rademakers, P. (1990). Mapping knowledge-level analysis onto a computational framework. In Aiello, L., editor, *Proceedings ECAI–90*, pp. 681–686, London. Pitman.

Waern, A., Höök, K., Gustavsson, R., and Holm, P. (1993). The CommonKADS Communication Model. Esprit Project P5248 Deliverable KADS-II/M3/SICS/TR/003, Swedish Institute of Computer Science, Stockholm. Available from the CommonKADS Website.

Watson, G. (1994). *Business Systems Engineering*. New York, Wiley.

Weggeman, M. (1996). Knowledge management: The modus operandi for a learning organization. In Schreinemakers, J., editor, *Knowledge Management — Organization, Competence and Methodology*, pp. 175–187. Würzburg, Germany, Ergon Verlag.

Wielemaker, J. (1994). *SWI-Prolog 1.9: Reference Manual*. University of Amsterdam, Social Science Informatics, Amsterdam. For information see: www.swi.psy.uva.nl/usr/jan/SWI-Prolog.html.

Wielinga, B. J., Sandberg, J. A. C., and Schreiber, A. Th. (1997). Methods and techniques for knowledge management: What has knowledge engineering to offer? *Expert Systems With Applications*, 13(1):73–84.

Wielinga, B. J. and Schreiber, A. Th. (1997). Configuration design problem solving. *IEEE Expert*, 12(2).

Wielinga, B. J., Schreiber, A. Th., and Breuker, J. A. (1992). KADS: A modelling approach to knowledge engineering. *Knowledge Acquisition*, 4(1):5–53. Reprinted in: Buchanan, B. and Wilkins, D. editors (1992), *Readings in Knowledge Acquisition and Learning*, San Mateo, CA, Morgan Kaufmann, pp. 92–116.

Wiig, K. (1996). *Knowledge Management Methods: Practical Approaches to Managing Knowledge*. Arlington, TX, Schema Press.

Wiig, K., de Hoog, R., and van der Spek, R. (1997a). Knowledge management (special issue). *Expert Systems With Applications*, 13(1).

Wiig, K., de Hoog, R., and van der Spek, R. (1997b). Supporting knowledge management: selection of methods and techniques. *Expert Systems With Applications*, 13(1):15–27.

Wolf, M. and Reimer, U., editors (1996). *Proceedings of PAKM '9*, Basel.

Wong, B., Chong, J., and Park, J. (1994). Utilization and benefits of expert systems: A study of large American industrial corporations. *International Journal of Operations & Production Management*, 14(1):38–49.

Ygge, F. (1998). *Market-Oriented Programming and its Application to Power Load Management*. Ph.D. thesis, Lund University, Sweden.

Yourdon, E. (1989). *Modern Structured Analysis*. Englewood Cliffs, NJ, Prentice Hall.

Zuboff, S. (1987). *In the Age of the Smart Machine*. New York, Free Press.

Zweben, M., Davis, E., Daun, B., and Deale, M. J. (1993). Scheduling and rescheduling with iterative repair. *IEEE Transactions on Systems, Man, and Cybernetics*, 23(6):1588–1596.

Zweben, M. and Fox, M. S. (1994). *Intelligent Scheduling*. San Mateo, CA, Morgan Kaufmann Publishers.

Index

Entries in sans serif represent references to inferences or transfer functions.